Issigonis

The Official Biography

Gillian Bardsley

ICON BOOKS

Originally published in 2005 by Icon Books Ltd

This edition published in the UK in 2006 by
Icon Books Ltd, The Old Dairy,
Brook Road, Thriplow,
Cambridge SG8 7RG
email: info@iconbooks.co.uk
www.iconbooks.co.uk

Sold in the UK, Europe, South Africa and Asia
by Faber & Faber Ltd, 3 Queen Square,
London WC1N 3AU
or their agents

Distributed in the UK, Europe, South Africa and Asia
by TBS Ltd, Frating Distribution Centre, Colchester Road
Frating Green, Colchester CO7 7DW

This edition published in Australia in 2006
by Allen & Unwin Pty Ltd,
PO Box 8500, 83 Alexander Street,
Crows Nest, NSW 2065

Distributed in Canada by
Penguin Books Canada,
90 Eglinton Avenue East, Suite 700,
Toronto, Ontario M4P 2YE

ISBN-10: 1-840467-78-9
ISBN-13: 978-1840467-78-9

Typesetting by Wayzgoose

Printed and bound in Malta by Gutenberg Press

CONTENTS

Praise for Gillian Bardsley's *Issigonis*

'Gillian Bardsley's first-rate biography should be compulsory reading … the fascinating story of a remarkable engineer … Bardsley's work illuminates the way personal circumstances and characteristics influenced Issigonis's career … as a dominating innovator … and as a technical specialist.'

Times Higher Education Supplement

'The great man's life spanned the high years of the British motor industry … a conclusive account … A clear presentation of the true facts that enhances the Issigonis legend.'

Classic Car Mart

'An amazingly thorough book, with plenty of insight into Issigonis's life and work. Bardsley paints a colourful image of a shy yet stubborn engineer, and has unearthed some amazing design sketches … Even if you're not a Mini nut, this is a must.'

Auto Express

'Gillian Bardsley writes simply and succinctly … to damn some of the myths that have grown up around Issigonis and his work … brilliantly researched.'

Autocar

'Fascinating new information … a very readable account which gives a lot of insight into the whole motor industry of the period.'   *Automobile*

'Absorbingly readable, painstakingly researched, and contributes plenty of valuable insights to the Issigonis story.'

Classic and Sports Car Book of the Month

'An impressively detailed account … difficult to put down … we would not hesitate to recommend it.'

Classic Car Weekly

'If you like Issigonis or even just admire his work, you'll love this book.'

Classics Monthly

'An authoritative account of the life of this British icon … clearly illustrates how his ingenious designs had a lasting influence on modern motoring.'

Oxford Times

List of Illustrations

ACKNOWLEDGEMENTS

I HAVE CHOSEN to avoid using footnotes or giving detailed references to sources in favour of readability. Instead, quotations are explained where they occur in the text. The bibliography lists the full range of sources from which every fact presented and conclusion drawn in the text originated. In addition it includes a general list of books and articles already published about Issigonis and his cars along with useful books about the historical period.

The quotations from Issigonis come from two main sources: first a set of interviews recorded by Tony Dawson, and second the verbatim transcript of an interview which was given to Mike Borrisow in 1964. Please look carefully before blaming the author for any outrageous statements – you may find the views expressed are those of that skilled exponent of the provocative opinion, Sir Alec himself, and are therefore intended to raise hackles.

There are many people who deserve credit for the fact that this book has finally come to be written over a rather prolonged period between 1996 and 2005. I owe everyone mentioned my gratitude for their help but none of them, of course, bear any responsibility for errors or omissions which may have crept into the text. Now for the thank yous, and if the following sounds like one of those endless speeches at a dull awards ceremony nevertheless all these people deserve to be acknowledged.

Thank you is an inadequate phrase to offer Rev. Colin Corke whose help and support has been relentless in the difficult process of shaping raw material into a coherent story. The Archive has proved to be his natural environment and what began as a lot of hard work gradually became great fun.

The Issigonis family too have contributed greatly to this book. Alec's 'cousin' May Ransome was a wonderful lady who sadly died in 1998. Two years earlier she gave me her only interview (apart from the conversations recorded with Tony Dawson) on the subject of her illustrious relative. Her children, Mark Ransome and Sally Elliott, have shown me endless hospitality, patiently answered all my irritating questions and opened up to me a treasure house of photographs and memorabilia which illuminated the extraordinary childhood shared by May and Alec. I received the same generous response from his goddaughter Penny Plath, daughter of his best friend George Dowson. It would not have been possible to attempt an authentic portrait of the private man without their help. This book owes a great deal to their goodwill and that of their partners, Jane Ransome, Ramsay Elliott and Dick Plath. Michael Issigonis, a Canadian descendant of the original Greek family, also shared with me his extensive research into the Issigonis genealogy which revealed the complex history of the paternal family line.

The British Motor Industry Heritage Trust, for whom I have worked as Archivist since 1990, has also been generous in its support. I have received constant encouragement in researching their unique and extensive Issigonis Collection of documents, photographs and sketchbooks, which is the source of many of the beautiful illustrations reproduced in this book. Many sketches are published here for the first time and the Trust can be justly proud of saving these works of art, some of which have been at risk of disappearing into private hands, for the benefit of the nation. Derek Barnes deserves special mention for giving me excellent advice completely free of charge on many occasions.

David Weguelin never let me forget that he was expecting me to finish this book. The great Oliver White bestowed his peerless knowledge about the history of motor racing and made the important identification of Alec's first car project as a Bleriot Whippet. Doug Nye also contributed his expertise about motor racing. John Bacchus gave constant encouragement from the earliest days, imparted his experiences of a lifetime in the motor industry and enthusiastically assisted in the interviewing of colleagues and friends of Issigonis.

All the interviewees who generously agreed to be grilled about their memories helped to provide the human element to the story which mere documentary evidence can never evoke. They are listed in the bibliography but special mention should go to Jack Daniels and John Sheppard who were two colleagues who spent almost their entire working lives in his company and therefore knew more about Alec Issigonis the designer than anyone else.

Finally, I would like to pay tribute to Paddy Dawson who is sadly very ill at the time of writing. It would have been impossible to write a comprehensive biography without the material which was gathered by her husband, Tony Dawson, the friend that Issigonis had chosen to write his life story. His research was passed on to the Trust after his death and in the earliest days of the project she showed me great kindness. In 1996 she told me of her sadness that Tony had never been able to fulfil his promise to write the biography because of his own ill-health and said she was happy that I was going to be the one to carry it forward. I hope that if she had been able to read this she would have felt it was a biography which was true to the memories of both Alec Issigonis and Tony Dawson.

Gillian Bardsley
March 2005

Picture Credits

Issigonis Estate: 1.1–1.7, 1.8 (top), 2.2, 2.4 (top), 4.8 (steam train), in-text sketch of train carriage
Mrs Penny Plath (née Dowson): 1.8 (bottom), 2.4 (bottom), 2.5 (bottom left)
BMIHT: 2.1, 2.3, 2.5 (top and bottom right), 2.6, 2.7, 2.8, 3.1–4.7, 4.8 (all except steam train), sketches in text (all except train carriage)

FOREWORD

FROM THE BRITISH MOTOR INDUSTRY HERITAGE TRUST
CHAIRMAN OF TRUSTEES

THIS IS THE story of a remarkable and competitive man. It sets his crowning achievement – the design of the Mini – into a context which includes the turbulent political and industrial climate of the time and shows, with his successive projects, how his design ideas developed into a holistic philosophy of design management.

Issigonis was innovative in his working methods and relied heavily on his immediate staff and his supplier partners to turn sketched ideas into detailed drawings. He became a self-developed master of what today's vehicle engineers would refer to as package engineering – the art of making the interior spaces in a car as large and as functionally effective as possible while making the outside of the vehicle as compact as was practicable with all that is implied for weight and cost minimisation. In this Issigonis was a pioneer and his ideas have led directly to the packaging 'bucks' – existing as either full-size mock-ups or as digital images held on a screen – that are an integral part of any vehicle design today. As a competitive driver himself in his younger days he understood the importance of what makes driving fun – good ride, handling, stiff structures, light and direct controls.

He was in the right job in the right place and at the right time to deliver a product which would change our perception of car design and motoring for ever.

Robert A Dover
Gaydon, July 2004

INTRODUCTION

WHO IS THIS MAN?

Biographers come in two main categories. One is the archival ferret, who pesters old ladies and deciphers faded pencil notes in the process of mining raw material. The other is the tale-spinner, who takes the material, as a museum takes an archaeologist's finds, and arranges a proportion of it into a narrative web.

Literary Review, 1996

I HAD JUST taken a job as an Archivist for the British Motor Industry Heritage Trust when a request came in from the *Dictionary of National Biography*. They wished to include an entry on Sir Alec Issigonis in their next edition but had been unable to find a contributor to write it. Could we suggest anyone?

I didn't know much about Issigonis. His name was unusual and made him sound interesting. I had a notion he might be Italian. He sketched his designs on tablecloths and napkins. He was 'The Man Behind the Mini', a car which possessed an individuality and character generally lacking among the set of cloned people-movers which currently filled the roads. I came to the Mini late in its life when some of its original features had been excised, but it was still the first car I enjoyed driving though I could not have explained why. I was, however, puzzled to find other road users regularly flashing their lights at me. Was I driving badly? Was there something wrong with the car? After a while I realised it was other Mini owners, welcoming me to their special community which always recognised a fellow traveller on the road.

So I volunteered, thinking the task would be as easy as writing a school essay. It wasn't. There was plenty of coverage in magazine articles and short monographs but he was strangely elusive. First the reader was presented with some sketchy information about his early life in Smyrna, the Issigonis family's flight to London ahead of the invasion of the 'Turkish hordes', his humble education at Battersea Polytechnic, his hatred of maths and his entry into the motor industry. Then came the success of his first significant design, the post-war Morris Minor. After that we sped through the next decade towards the Mini – at which point our protagonist dissolved before our eyes to become one with his most famous creation. Their personalities were fused, as if Alec Issigonis and the Mini were the same thing and to talk about one was to talk about the other.

Completing the article had proved surprisingly unsatisfying so I decided to look further. He surely did not cease to exist when the Mini was launched in 1959? The obvious place to start was the dark brown wooden plan chest which had been brought from his office in Longbridge shortly before his death. It had hardly been touched in the ten years that it had lain in the archive repository but it was in a sorry state, having been dropped several times as it was moved round the Longbridge factory so that its contents were scrambled like a 10,000-piece jigsaw puzzle. As I pulled out each of the large, shallow drawers I found the individual pieces left over from a man's life, a jumble of paperwork, magazines, photographs, medals and awards. To restore some order I started to remove the drawers from their runners and at the very bottom of the chest I found an Arclight notepad which had fallen down the back. It was easy to identify from its characteristic off-white pages and sepia cover which was clearly marked with the date 1952, scrawled in blue ink on the top right-hand corner in Issigonis' own handwriting. As I carefully retrieved the notepad from behind the bar where it was wedged and smoothed out the crumpled top page, I was rewarded with the sight of the most beautifully executed drawing of his 'lost' design, the Alvis, on which he had toiled for three years only for the project to be scrapped with not even a photograph of the prototype to remember it by. The Alvis had long vanished from history yet here it was in all its three-dimensional glory, and I could see that this sketch was only the first of page after page of images lovingly drawn from every angle.

As I began to sort the cabinet it became clear that the discovery was not a fluke. There was a whole series of Arclight notepads, each dated and sometimes with a subject inscribed in the familiar blue ink and spidery scrawl. Inside were thousands of sketches drawn in a style which developed and matured from the very first book marked '1938' to the last one marked '1957, Future Projects'. It was clear that the stories of tablecloths and napkins had grown in the telling. Each of these pads still had most of its pages firmly attached and appeared to represent a comprehensive record of twenty years of creative effort, like a diary of his imagination. The quality of the best of them was breathtaking and I knew then that this was the closest it was possible to get to the extraordinary mind of a very gifted man. He was an engineer and I am not, but the drawings drew the eye at an artistic as well as a technical level, so much so that it felt as if I was seeing exactly what he saw as he drew.

Now I had to find out more about him. It was time to become an archival ferret and unravel the proliferation of notes, letters and memorandums which lay there crying out for order. I discovered original diary entries which told a slightly different history of the Mini project to the common legend. I read about the testing of the Morris Minor and the Alvis. I analysed his correspondence with friends, colleagues and celebrities. I began to pester old ladies, and old gentlemen too, to find out what sort of person he was. I discovered that he loved his mother and was obsessed with work. I heard about 'Arragonis' who had no patience with those who could not keep up with his brilliant mind, about 'Issygonyet' who was the scourge of the drawing office, 'Ginigonis' who was a charming and loyal friend and 'Minigonis' who became the most celebrated British car designer of the 20th century. I visited the surprisingly modest houses he lived in and examined hundreds of photographs which told many stories about his childhood and his youthful friendships and enthusiasms. I visited the National Archives to trace his family's origins in the turbulent region of Turkey where he grew up. I discovered that he had planned his own biography and listened to the audio-tapes he made for a book which never got written, reminiscing about his childhood and youth. Through all of this he emerged as an ordinary person with an extraordinary gift.

Here, then, is the story of this enigmatic man. But, as I was to discover, whatever raw material I mined in the telling of this tale, I never got as close to the real man as in the moment when I smoothed the page of the Arclight notepad to reveal the lines which flowed so easily from his pen, transforming the flat page into a window on his mind.

SMYRNA

CHAPTER 1

My love of design came from my father.

Sir Alec Issigonis

ON 2 OCTOBER 1988, the national news bulletins announced the death of Sir Alec Issigonis, Britain's most celebrated car designer and one of the few of that profession whose name was widely recognised. The Morris Minor and the Mini were two cars still held in general affection and both of them were unusual for their close association with the individual who designed them in an industry where the final product was more often the work of an anonymous team.

A few days later his closest friends and relatives gathered together to bid him a tearful and affectionate farewell in a small Anglican church on the outskirts of Birmingham. They listened quietly to a moving tribute written by the actor Peter Ustinov, lauding the achievement for which Issigonis would always be remembered:

> There is no more fitting memorial to Alec Issigonis than his greatest creation, the Mini. Not only because it places him comfortably among the greatest innovators of automotive history but because it so faithfully reflects his own twinkling personality. His eyes, of surprisingly intense blue, were recreated in the wide-eyed innocence of the Mini's head-lights, an innocence which is at once childish and highly sophisticated.

Producing the Mini was, in retrospect, his finest hour. It is therefore very tempting to identify the charming, sophisticated, intelligent and witty Issigonis with the cheeky, lively Mini, but to do so is to ignore the many contradictions between them. Alec Issigonis created a cultural icon embodying classlessness, rebelliousness and the spirit of competition for an era obsessed with the idea of 'youth'. Yet alongside the charm and wit, his characteristics could be said to include obstinacy, emotional reserve and social conservatism before we even consider that by 1959, when the Mini was launched, Alec Issigonis was already 52 years old, almost two-thirds of the way through his life. He was not a youth but a mature man. His character was already well formed. The Mini was not a catalyst to his life nor was it a finishing point, it was just a step along the way.

For most of his life he did little to promote understanding of his character. When he became popular, with journalists and authors clamouring to take an interest in him, he responded enthusiastically and was always 'good for a quote'. It is not surprising that he was quite happy to be identified with the design that made him famous, to hear it praised and smile when other cars were compared unfavourably with it. Over time the Mini came to be viewed as the high point of his career and he began to play down the significance of anything which had gone before or which came afterwards. He discouraged all personal questioning and developed a repertoire of anecdotes and witticisms which became the Issigonis canon. A trail of interviewers struggled to put what they felt to be incisive and important questions, only to be answered with a familiar story which often had little connection to the question asked. Issigonis had decided on his version of himself and he stuck to it.

By 1980 he had brushed aside several approaches from people hoping to write his biography. It was a subject that began to worry him and he developed an intense fear of misrepresentation as the monographs and biographical articles multiplied. He decided the answer to his problem was to choose his own biographer and he turned for help to his friend Tony Dawson, a longstanding press officer for the British Motor Corporation and later British Leyland. Dawson had dealt with much of the publicity surrounding the famous designer following the success of the Mini and after Issigonis' retirement continued to act as his personal public relations channel. As Issigonis grew increasingly old, reclusive and infirm, so he relied more and more on Dawson, meeting people and giving interviews exclusively through him. To Issigonis, his friend appeared to be the ideal candidate to represent his life story to the rest of the world, but by 1986, when the project got underway in earnest, Dawson was himself in his 70s and his own health was not good. He survived Issigonis by only six years and never got beyond the gathering of source material.

Perhaps the most important thing which Tony Dawson achieved in researching the biography was to persuade Issigonis to record a series of conversations reminiscing about his childhood. It was not a subject which Issigonis was prepared to talk to journalists about in great depth and yet it holds the key to his character. Although he appeared to be the perfect

English gentleman, he had in fact spent his childhood and youth in the unique environment of an expatriate community which lived at the edge of Asia Minor, the heart of some of the early 20th century's most violent political and military conflicts. His father was of Greek origin, his mother of German origin, and both of them had been born and raised in Turkey.

In his anxiety to get everything 'right' Issigonis asked his cousin May Ransome (born May Walker), who had shared the same peculiar childhood, to help him remember. The recording sessions are quite lively affairs and since all three participants are over 70 they often become quite testy. Tony Dawson constantly interrupts and misses the point, Issigonis jumps backwards and forwards through the decades, often more preoccupied with telling amusing stories than providing profound insights into his formative years, and May Ransome struggles to make him 'tell it properly'. After a while, Dawson and Issigonis start to argue about what stories have and haven't already been told and in exasperation May begins to take over the questioning herself. This is a typical exchange:

'Alec, when did you first get interested in machines?' May asks him.

'In our factory my dear. You remember our house, when you went up the stairs. The first room with the balcony was my father's dressing room. He had a drawing board there and I used to go and watch him working. It was also a bedroom, there were three bedrooms on that side, then the dining room and then Tia Angelico's bedroom. Do you remember her?'

'That was your father's cousin was it?'

'No, the chatelaine, she used to run the house. My mother never went in the kitchen or anywhere like that, nor did yours ...

'Yes my mother always went in the kitchen, she used to make the cakes.'

'We used to have a toy where you held onto two sticks and somebody turned the handle to a magneto and gave you terrible shocks.'

'I bet your father made that!'

'May, you must tell us more about Mrs Elliott's wig ...'

'No, come on Alec, let's get down to this thing seriously ...'

Given the scarcity of information about his early life, these conversations, along with the family photographs, take us as close as we can get to the formative years of the man who, for a few decades, was to become the

British motor industry's first and only celebrity. When he does start to 'take it seriously' his words evoke both sadness and respect. Not surprisingly he is vague about dates and specific events but he talks with a moving fluency of his family, of the insulated life they lived in Smyrna as European politics exploded into conflict around them and of the traumatic experience of evacuation from a familiar, comfortable life to a far from predictable future. Throughout his life Issigonis rarely spoke about his childhood even to his closest friends and this makes his account, when he finally does begin to give it, fresh, unrehearsed and remarkably honest. The memories are vivid and compelling and leave no doubt that this unusual childhood was the clay from which the rest of his life was moulded. They also reveal that, though his mother was to dominate his adult life, she was not the only influence on his feelings and ambitions.

We must therefore travel back from the chill interior of the Birmingham church on a gloomy autumn day to the rather more temperate atmosphere of Asia Minor where, almost 82 years earlier, he had been born.

THE OTTOMAN EMPIRE

Alexander Arnold Constantine Issigonis was born on 18 November 1906 to Constantine and Hulda Issigonis, two rather eccentric parents who in turn belonged to a singular expatriate community living in the Aegean port of Smyrna. The personality of this town was governed by its geographical position because while it was physically part of the land mass of Asia Minor, in terms of trade and commerce it belonged to the Mediterranean. Over the centuries, it had become a crucial point of contact between Eastern and Western cultures, a hub of trade exchange and a flashpoint between competing European and Asian empires. For centuries control had passed backwards and forwards between Asia and Europe but by the time Alec was born it was once again part of the decaying Ottoman Empire.

The textbooks tell us what we need to know about the Ottoman Empire. At its core was the province of Anatolia, a large region of southwestern Asia which roughly corresponds to the present-day boundaries of Turkey. The nomadic tribes who lived there had gradually grown into one of the world's dominant cultures until, at the height of their influence in the 15th and 16th centuries, the Ottoman sultans controlled an extensive Muslim empire which included vast areas of Asia, North Africa, the

Middle East and Europe, including Greece and the Balkans. Their seat of government was at Constantinople, which is now Istanbul, still a major Turkish city but no longer a capital.

By the 19th century, the Ottoman Empire was fading in the face of a series of political and military challenges which undermined the control of the ageing hereditary regime. Efforts at reform were half-hearted and one subject area after another began to gain political independence. Greece was the first to break away, setting up a sovereign state with its own monarchy in 1832. The borders of the new state were considerably smaller than today's borders and the next century saw Greece embark on a mission to enlarge its territory, something which would have no small effect on the important coastal port of Smyrna.

The youthful Western European powers sensed the old empire's weakness and exploited every opportunity to challenge its authority, particularly on its outer reaches in the Balkans and the Middle East. Britain, France, Italy and Russia nicknamed the Ottoman Empire 'the sick man of Europe' and embarked on a series of secret agreements to divide the area into 'spheres of influence' which they intended to convert into full political control when the opportunity arose. In the meantime they bent their considerable energies towards establishing their influence in preparation for this day by transforming the infrastructure of the region with new forms of trade and communications. Throughout the 19th century, French and British investors poured capital into the development of rail networks, ports, banks, mines, oil refineries, water treatment plants, electricity generators and gasworks throughout Turkey and its Middle Eastern territories.

This was the background into which Alec Issigonis was born.

SMYRNA

When he spoke about Smyrna, Issigonis would always remark 'Smyrna "brackets" Izmir', referring to the town's modern name. The setting is dramatic, the town being situated round a great bay and ringed with mountains, but though Izmir is still Turkey's third-largest city, the impressive architecture which the Issigonis family would have known has been swept away by the upheavals of the early 20th century. Its buildings are modern and its present-day population is predominantly Turkish. It has even gained a new role as the entry point for British and German tourists heading for the developing resorts of southern Turkey. A further international element was added when it was chosen as the site for the head-quarters of the North Atlantic Treaty Organisation (NATO).

Only a few hundred years earlier, Smyrna had been one of the most important ports along the coast, inheriting that status from Ephesus whose access to the sea had silted up. By 1900 the city was one of the most cosmopolitan in Turkey, with a population which was predominantly Christian and Jewish rather than Muslim.

At the peak of Smyrna's social pyramid were the home-born expatriates who held jobs at the various consulates, or had invested in the railways and other large foreign-owned concessions. There were two major railways: a coastal route sponsored by the French which provided a link to the Ottoman capital of Constantinople in the north; and the British-backed Ottoman-Aydin railway which ran from Smyrna through the interior of the continent towards Baghdad. This had attracted engineers looking to make their fortune such as cousin May's English grandfather, Joseph Walker. There were also a number of British concessions such as the Ottoman Gas Company which in the early 1900s was managed by Mr Charles Gandon, and the Standard Oil Refinery run by Mr Smith, both of whom will feature in our story.

Just below the foreign expatriates were those – like the Issigonises – whose families owned property and businesses in the town and had been there for several generations. The largest such community was Greek, the result of a strong mercantile tradition which had led them to travel and trade widely throughout the region for many centuries. With the wealth that they accrued these merchants sponsored a number of Greek colleges and Greek became the basic language of Balkan and Mediterranean commerce. Smaller Italian, German and Jewish communities ran local businesses such as the brewery which was founded by Alec's maternal great-grandmother, Clara Stengel-Prokopp.

There was a substantial Armenian community of Christians which originated from an area of West Asia divided between the Ottoman and Russian Empires. Persecution had scattered them throughout the region but they were not regarded as equals by the rest of the 'Christian' expatriate community and Issigonis told Tony Dawson that if any member of the 'European' community married an Armenian they were shunned socially. Equally considered outsiders were the local Turkish population, many of whom worked as servants, labourers, bazaar traders or street vendors. Also significant was a large pool of migrant labourers from Malta.

This mix of nationalities meant that numerous languages were in use in the town, including Greek, Italian, German, French, English, Turkish and Arabic. As the region became more volatile, possession of a foreign passport was a very valuable commodity indeed and best of all was a British passport. Yet, despite its diversity, the top levels of this community were united by the social elevation which they felt placed them above and apart from the other citizens of Smyrna. They socialised with and married each other according to social status rather than national origin. Contact between the higher class and those they considered their social inferiors was confined to employing them as nannies and servants or buying basic commodities from them. This social structure is clearly reflected in the family background of the two people who were to become the parents of Alec Issigonis.

The Family Background

So how did it come about that, despite his father being of Greek origin and his mother of German origin, Alec was actually born a British citizen?

Many islands lie scattered in the Aegean sea between Greece and Asia Minor, and their inhabitants were happy to migrate to either mainland according to the opportunities available and regardless of national boundaries. Páros is one of these islands, part of the Cyclades group which stretches out between the mainlands of Greece and Turkey. The island contains plentiful reserves of marble, which was for a long time the basis of its economy. The quarries around Mount Marpissa had provided raw material for such distinguished monuments as the façade of the Temple of Apollo in Athens and the statue of the Venus de Milo. During its history the island had been subject to Egypt, Rome, Venice and the Ottoman Empire before finally becoming part of an independent Greece. This was home to the Tsigonias family whose present-day descendants believe that the family's origins lie with a merchant who emigrated there from Venice in the 17th century.

Antonios Tsigonias was the first to leave for Smyrna in the mid-1830s where he founded a school for girls which became known as the 'Greek Boarding School' and his brother Ioannis joined him as a teacher. The brothers changed their name to 'Issigonis' because they felt it sounded more Greek, using a double 's' to reproduce the 'ts' sound so as to ensure the name was pronounced correctly. A third brother, Georgios, had stayed on Páros, but his son Demosthenis, born in 1828, followed his uncles to

Smyrna when he was still a young man. Demosthenis was a talented engineer who had designed and built a new type of water pump and he decided that Smyrna would be an excellent place from which to manufacture and market his invention as widely as possible. In 1854 he set about building his factory in the Alsancak district on the waterfront and he lived with his wife, Irini Psalti, in a flat above the works where they produced a large family of eight children between 1856 and 1874. The two youngest were Konstantinos, usually referred to as Constantine, born in 1872 and Miltiades, known as Milti, born in 1874.

In his later years, Alec Issigonis often used to repeat the story of how Demosthenis sent Constantine to England to study engineering so he could one day take over the family business. Constantine apparently fell so in love with England that he stayed for fifteen years and acquired British nationality which in due course he passed on to his wife and son. This is a romantic story which fitted well with Issigonis' view of himself as an 'English gentleman'. It was Demosthenis, however, and not his son who was originally granted this extremely valuable asset. The D. Issigonis factory had been a major contributor to the initial construction and subsequent maintenance of the Ottoman-Aydin railway. As relations between Greece and the Ottoman Empire steadily worsened Demosthenis traded his support for British citizenship, which he obtained through the British Consulate in Smyrna in order to protect the factory and his family in the event of a conflict between Turkey and Greece.

Nonetheless Constantine did go to study in England and it is also true that this was the prelude to a life-long love of English culture which he was to pass on to his son. The details of his stay are unclear but he seems to have spent some time working on the railways in the London area and also to have lived in Cheshire which he described as 'a wild country with no leaves'. The earliest likely date for such a journey, given Constantine's date of birth, would be 1886 when he would have been fourteen years old. Again, it is reasonable to suppose that the death of his father in 1898 would be enough to trigger his return home, so it seems unlikely that he was in England for longer than twelve years.

By the time Demosthenis Issigonis died in 1898 his business interests had spread to a second factory in Beirut which was inherited by his elder sons. The two youngest sons took over the Smyrna factory with Constantine providing the engineering expertise and Miltiades looking after the accounts. The living quarters where Demosthenis and his wife

ISSIGONIS FAMILY TREE

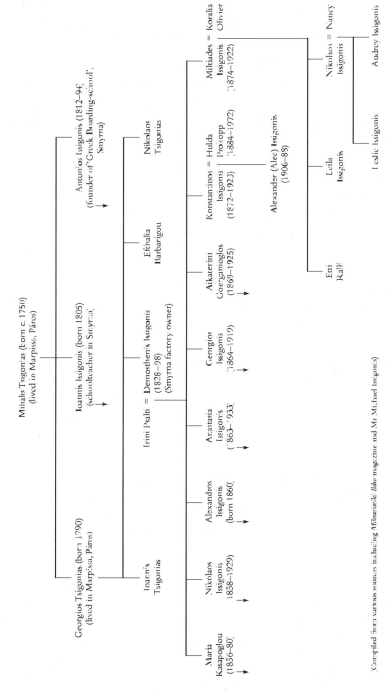

Mihalis Tsigonias (born c. 1750)
(lived in Marpissa, Páros)

Antonios Issigonis (1812–94)
(founder of 'Greek Boarding-school',
Smyrna)

Ioannis Issigonis (born 1805)
(schoolteacher in Smyrna)

Georgios Tsigonias (born 1790)
(lived in Marpissa, Páros)

Irini Psalti = Demosthenis Issigonis
(1828–98)
(Smyrna factory owner)

Efthalia
Barbarigou

Nikolaos
Tsigonias

Ioannis
Tsigonias

Maria
Kasapoglou
(1856–80)

Nikolaos
Issigonis
1858–1929

Alexandros
Issigonis
(born 1860)

Anastasia
Issigonis
(1863–1933)

Georgios
Issigonis
(1864–1919)

Aikaterini
Goergamioglos
(1869–1925)

Konstantinos = Hulda
Issigonis   Prokopp
(1872–1923) (1884–1972)

Miltiades = Koralia
Issigonis   Olivier
(1874–1922)

Alexander (Alec) Issigonis
(1906–88)

Etti
Ralli

Leila
Issigonis

Nikolaos = Nancy
Issigonis

Leslie Issigonis

Audrey Issigonis

(Compiled from various sources including *Mikrasiatiki Ikho* magazine and Mr Michael Issigonis) had raised their large family were now divided into two separate flats where the two brothers could raise their own, rather smaller, families. This arrangement was just as well since it would seem that the brothers did not get on. Part of the reason seems to have been that, even though they shared the privilege of British citizenship, they had rather different views on the subject of their origins. While Constantine was a fanatical anglophile, Milti had decided he preferred to be Greek. Issigonis remarked of them: 'They were always at loggerheads, you could hear them quarrelling the whole time and the families were not on speaking terms.'

The conflict between the brothers had a significant influence on Alec's childhood because it resulted in a closer relationship with his mother's side of the family. Constantine – known to the family as 'Costa' – waited for seven years after his return to Smyrna before he decided to marry. Now 32, his choice fell on Hulda Josephine Henriette Prokopp who was then twenty years old. The Prokopps belonged to the same social stratum as the Issigonis brothers since they too came from a well-established expatriate family which owned a local business, but their genealogical background was more complicated, consisting of a bewildering set of uncles, aunts and first and second cousins. Though their blood relationships were much more complicated than those of the two feuding brothers, ironically, they formed a much more cohesive and close-knit family unit than the Issigonises, dominated by a series of women of strong character.

His mother's side of the family had a 'founding mother' rather than a 'founding father'. This was Clara Stengel who arrived in Smyrna with her husband in the 1840s to set up a successful business brewing German beer. The Stengels came from the small town of Jagsthausen just north of Stuttgart, then state capital of the Kingdom of Württemburg. Jagsthausen was also the birthplace of 'Götz (or Gottfried) mit der eisernen Hand' – 'Götz with the Iron Hand' – a local Robin Hood figure who kidnapped nobles for ransom and attacked merchant convoys, giving the proceeds to the poor. Württemburg, like its larger and more powerful neighbour Bavaria, was at that time an independent principality which did not become part of a unified Germany until 1871. Both then and now its inhabitants were regarded with some contempt by their northern neighbours from the dominant German principality of Prussia who nicknamed them 'Spätzle-Schwaben' or 'Swabian dumplings'. 'Swabian' was a reference to a pagan Germanic tribe which originally lived in southern

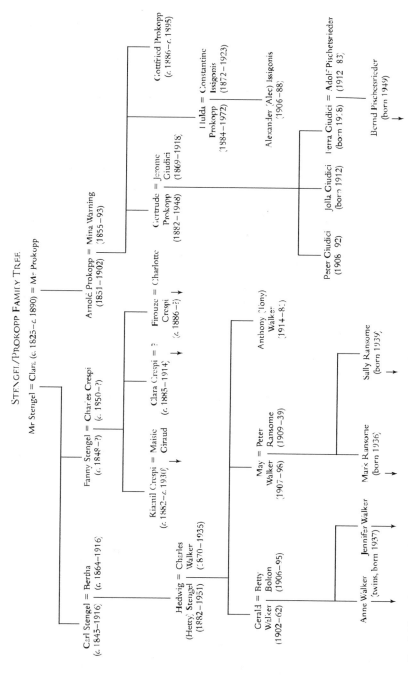

STENGEL/PROKOPP FAMILY TREE

Mr Stengel = Clara (c. 1825–c. 1890) = Mr Prokopp

Carl Stengel = Bertha
(c. 1843–1916)   (c. 1864–1916)

Fanny Stengel = Charles Crespi
(c. 1848–?)   (c. 1850–?)

Arnold Prokopp = Mina Warning
(1851–1902)   (1855–93)

Gottfried Prokopp
(c. 1886–c. 1995)

Hedwig = Charles
(Hetty) Stengel   Walker
(1882–1951)   (1870–1935)

Kiamil Crespi = Maisie
(c. 1882–c. 1936)   Giraud

Clara Crespi (= ?)
(c. 1885–1914)

Firouze = Charlotte
Crespi   Crespi
(c. 1886–?)

Gertrude = Jerome
Prokopp   Giudici
(1882–1948)   (1869–1918)

Hulda = Constantine
Prokopp   Issigonis
(1884–1972)   (1872–1923)

Gerald = Betty
Walker   Bolton
(1902–62)   (1906–95)

May = Peter
Walker   Ransome
(1907–96)   (1909–39)

Anthony 'Tony'
Walker
(1914–8?)

Peter Giudici
(1908–92)

Jolla Giudici
(born 1912)

Terra Giudici = Adolf Pischetsrieder
(born 1918)   (1912–83)

Alexander 'Alec' Issigonis
(1906–88)

Anne Walker   Jennifer Walker
(twins, born 1937)

Marc Ransome
(born 1936)

Sally Ransome
(born 1939)

Bernd Pischetsrieder
(born 1949)

(Compiled from various sources including Mrs May Ransome and Mr Bernd Pischetsrieder)

Germany, while 'Spätzle' was the favourite local dish. The type of German which was spoken in the region was also regarded as inferior to that spoken in Prussia, as was their Catholic religion in contrast to the Protestantism of the north. Though it encompassed the Black Forest, in general the region was lacking in natural resources and a large proportion of its inhabitants were engaged in manufacturing or trade.

This manufacturing tradition would prove to be significant for Württemburg descendant Alec Issigonis for it was in Stuttgart that the motor car first took shape in the workshop of Gottlieb Daimler and Wilhelm Maybach. A number of unsuccessful attempts to build steam-driven vehicles had been made during the early 19th century but the building of a genuine, practical motor car became possible only when the gas engine – which became universally known as the internal combustion engine – was invented by Etienne Lenoir in Paris in 1860. This engine was designed for industrial use and it was with this in mind that Nicholas Otto of Cologne worked to refine the machine, coming up with the four-stroke cycle based on induction, compression, ignition and exhaust which became and remains the basis of modern engine technology. Gottlieb Daimler worked as Otto's chief engineer for ten years until 1882 when he formed a partnership with Wilhelm Maybach and set up his own workshop in Stuttgart. He was one of the first to recognise the potential of Otto's light engine for powering a genuine 'horseless' carriage. After doing considerable work to refine the power unit to make it suitable for their purpose, Daimler and Maybach built a motorcycle in 1885 and in 1886 fitted one of their engines to a three-wheeled carriage, thus creating the first genuine 'horseless' carriage. The same year, in the city of Mannheim, capital of the neighbouring state of Baden, Karl Benz produced a working motor car completely independently. These two vehicles, both built close by the little town from which the Stengel family originated, were to mark the beginning of a technology which resulted in the flowering of a new industry all over Europe within the next ten years. Interestingly, Daimler was 51 years old when he made this breakthrough, while his rival Benz was 41 years old – which implies that maturity and experience count for more than brash youth in the field of innovative engineering, something which will be relevant when considering Issigonis' later career.

To return to Mr and Mrs Stengel; Clara bore two children named Carl and Fanny between 1840 and 1850. When Mr Stengel died she sent back to Württemburg for a new manager. Mr Prokopp, an accountant, duly arrived and soon became husband number two. A third child, Arnold Prokopp, was born in 1851. When Mr Prokopp went the way of Mr Stengel, Clara's beer was given the label 'Veuve Prokopp' (Widow Prokopp) and two stone beer bottles bearing the title were embedded in the wall outside the main entrance of the brewery and are still there today.

By the early 1880s Clara's three children had all married and, though they were locally born, they looked back to Europe for marriage partners. Carl's wife, Bertha, was born in Austria, Fanny's husband, Charles Crespi, came from the Balkans while Arnold Prokopp's wife Mina was from Germany. When Clara died her children, like the Issigonis brothers, divided the running of the brewery between a new family syndicate. Arnold Prokopp inherited the role of accountant from his father, Carl and Bertha Stengel took control of the beer-making process while Charles and Fanny Crespi managed the business. The Prokopps, Stengels and Crespis built three separate houses in the brewery grounds and they appear to have lived together rather more amicably than the two Issigonis brothers.

The children of these three couples — three boys and four girls all born between 1882 and 1886 — represent the third generation of the Stengel/Prokopp family and they grew up together more like brothers and sisters than cousins. This is particularly true of the girls who will be the main characters in this part of the story. There are a number of photographs of the young companions: Hedwig Stengel (known as Hetty), Clara Crespi, and the two Prokopp sisters, Gertrude and Hulda. They seem to have been lively, fun-loving girls with a taste for the exotic. They loved dressing up as Turkish maidens, they entertained themselves with plays and dances, they even rode bareback horses in mock circus performances. The Prokopp sisters were extremely handsome and look out from their portraits with self-confidence and a certainty about their place in the world. Though they got on well enough, it seems there was a division of opinion between them in that Gertrude loved everything German while Hulda loved everything English which echoes Constantine's preference for England over his brother Milti's insistence on being Greek. Issigonis joked that the family nicknamed Gertrude 'the Kaiserina' because of her devotion to Wilhelm II, the Kaiser of a now unified Germany.

Hetty was also extremely pretty but in her photographs she looks more tentative and sad than her cousins. In later life she would say how she regretted being an only child and this perhaps made the sisterly relationship with Gertrude, Hulda and Clara most important to her. The boys are more shadowy figures. Gertrude and Hulda had a younger brother named Gottfried, perhaps after local hero 'Götz with the Iron Hand', but he was very unlike his namesake, a sickly child, born with one lung and poor eyesight, who died as a child. Also a possible influence on the young Alec was Clara's elder brother, Kiamil Crespi, who excelled in draughtsmanship and art. He shared the family's tendency to eccentricity and reputedly would walk on his hands across the marble floor of the entrance hall to the Crespi house if he arrived home to find the servants had just mopped it.

Unlike their parents, the third generation of the Stengel/Prokopp family looked for marriage partners within the Smyrna community. Their partners did not have to be of German origin but it was not acceptable to look beyond the bounds of the 'European' community so the four girls faced a restricted pool of men. 'You didn't have much choice about who you married in Turkey', May bemoaned. Nor were their personal feelings given much consideration since their marriages were considered to be business arrangements rather than love-matches. Hetty, Gertrude, Hulda and Clara all married much older men who brought property or other capital with them.

Clara Crespi, it seems, was the least fortunate of the four. In photographs she looks a jolly, pleasant girl, though not so handsome as her three cousins, but her life was to end early in complications from childbirth. Hulda, as we have seen, linked her fortunes with Constantine Issigonis in 1905. Although he was twelve years older and of Greek origin there is no reason to conclude that she was displeased with the choice. He brought with him – however it was obtained – the advantage of a British passport and a devotion to England which matched her own. Hulda moved to the flat over the Issigonis factory and the two of them set about creating an English environment in which to bring up their only child, Alexander Arnold Constantine, born in 1906. Their marriage seems to have been a happy one and throughout her life she always spoke with admiration of both her husband and her father-in-law, Demosthenis, whom she considered to be a clever man who built a prosperous foundation for her family.

There was a similar age difference between Gertrude and her husband, Jerome Giudici, a merchant banker from an Italian family. They retained the Prokopp house inside the brewery and also set up a home in the comfortable suburb of Bouja where they brought up three children,

Peter, Jolla and Ferra. Alec often played with the Giudici children and, when remembering his childhood, it is clear whenever he mentions his 'aunty Gertrude' that he liked her very much, despite the somewhat prickly relationship between the two sisters.

Hulda seems to have been closer to Hetty than to either of the other girls but Hetty was not so happy with the arrangement made for her. In February 1900 at the age of seventeen she was married to Charles Joseph Simes Walker who was twelve years her senior. Charles had been born in Smyrna in 1870 and was the youngest in a large family being raised with some difficulty by a Mr and Mrs Simes. They were happy to allow Joseph and Regina Walker to informally adopt one of their children when the Walkers found they were unable to have any of their own, a not uncommon type of arrangement at the time. Joseph, born in 1840, had come out to Smyrna from Calke in Derbyshire as an engineer on the Ottoman-Aydin railway and accrued considerable wealth which his adopted son would inherit. At the time of his marriage, Charles was a well-established civil engineer. He built a new house situated opposite the railway station and just round the corner from the factory which was run by his good friend Costa Issigonis. Their friendship reinforced the sisterly relationship between their wives with the result that the Walker children became the main companions of young Alec. There were three of them – Gerald Eric (Gerry) born in 1902, May Mary Regina, only one year younger than Alec, born in 1907, and the baby, Charles Hubert Anthony (Tony), born in 1914. So although Alec was technically an 'only child', he was also part of a large, close and affectionate extended family, in which the aunts played a far more dominant role than the uncles.

It is not clear why, but establishing a type of 'national loyalty' appeared to be extremely important to the generation of the family to which Alec's parents belonged and they all made quite different decisions. Constantine and Hulda Issigonis were firmly intent on being British despite their own origins, while Hetty became British by marrying into a genuine English family. Both women had grown up speaking German and had to learn English after their marriages but their children were brought up with English as their first language. When having the traditional family portraits taken, the Walkers dressed young Gerald in the typical English Victorian child's sailor suit. Gertrude, however, despite marrying an Italian banker, was determined that her children would grow up speaking German and she had little Peter Giudici photographed in the full national dress of southern Germany complete with lederhosen, braces and a Tyrolean hat with a feather. Milti Issigonis on the other hand decided his family's Greek origins were more important than his family's British citizenship and his three children were brought up to speak Greek and follow Greek traditions. These choices of loyalty would shape the relationships between the different parts of the family and would also decide their fate when civil war broke out in Turkey and the families had to make a decision about where their futures lay.

DAILY LIFE

Life for Constantine, Hulda and their young son was comfortable and privileged though not luxurious. The D. Issigonis Works had begun life as a foundry but by the 1900s it had become a substantial marine engineering business covering a total area of approximately 7,000 square metres. The site was made up of open yards, sheds and stores alongside the foundry, a sawmill, a pattern shop and a nail-making department. Steam engines, marine engines for large sea-going tugboats, and complete ship's boilers were manufactured in various machine and erecting shops. The boiler shop was particularly noisy from the constant clank of the boiler plates being riveted together, a sound which Alec declared he hated.

Alec took an interest in the activities of the factory from an early age. He was fascinated by the hissing of the stationary steam engine which kept the machinery running. He would watch the clerks in their offices, writing entries into their copybooks and answering letters from customers in Greek. Constantine and Milti shared an office but, while Milti spent his days there working on the accounts, Constantine would spend most of his time supervising the engineering activity in the works. He had a very distinctive working method. After making rough drawings of his ideas on scraps of paper he would annotate them with copious notes which he then brought to the factory to discuss with the engineers. They were expected to interpret these discussions and turn the drawings into a finished product. Young Alec was watching all this, and there is no doubt that the daily routine of the factory made a deep impression. It confirmed in him his inclination towards engineering and mechanical things and also influenced his ideas about working relationships and methods.

The flats were on the second storey, built in an L shape above the quieter fitting and erecting workshops and the office area; but they must still have been quite noisy since the foundry and one of the main yards were very close by. Some 800 square metres of living space was divided roughly equally between the two families and each had a completely separate entrance. If you climbed the stairs to Constantine's flat, the first room you would approach was his dressing room and balcony. He kept a drawing board here and Alec would sit with him and watch while he sketched. Along the corridor was a series of three bedrooms for the family, a dining room and drawing room and at the end a smaller room allocated to Tia (aunt) Angelico who was Constantine's cousin and acted as the family's 'chatelaine' or housekeeper, a large bunch of keys fixed to her apron declaring her position in the household. At the back of the flat were the kitchen and the servants' quarters. Alec later claimed that throughout his whole childhood he never went into either of these areas.

In the corner of the factory yard was a house for the watchman or 'Kavass'. During the day he stationed himself in the offices below the flat, wearing a Turkish uniform with poms on the end of his shoes, but he was also detailed to keep an eye on young Alec and usually accompanied him on visits outside the factory to the bazaar and other public places. Then there were Alec's haircuts which were administered by a Greek barber in the pantry at the Walkers' house.

Alec spent a lot of time on his own as a child and one of his favourite occupations was to go on long, solitary cycle rides out into the countryside. The streets of Smyrna were cobbled and scored with tramlines so he would cycle along the edge of the quay where the smooth slate stones made for a more pleasant ride. One day, his pedal got caught in the rope attaching a rowing boat to the quay and he fell into the shallow water and had to be dragged out by the fishermen. He retreated back home dragging the bicycle with its punctured tyre, drenched from head to toe and wondering what he was going to tell his mother, whose bicycle he had been riding at the time.

Nevertheless he did not lack for childhood companions because in a very small area round the factory were the houses of many relatives and friends. Just round the corner and opposite the railway station 'uncle Charlie' had built his new house, a rather grander affair than the living quarters at either the Prokopp Brewery or the Issigonis factory. At the top of the house were the family rooms, above which was an attractive roof terrace, at the bottom were the basement, kitchens, cellars and laundry, and linking the two was the 'entre-sol' – literally 'in between floors' – where the servants used to sleep. At the back was a large and private walled garden. Alec was closest to May Walker who was only six months younger and described him as 'like another brother', whereas the age gap of four years up to Gerry Walker and eight years down to Tony Walker was sufficient to make them unsatisfactory playmates. Gerry he remembered as looking down on the younger children – 'he wanted nothing to do with us!' There were also the Crespi and Giudici children who lived in the three brewery houses close by, and the ins and outs of the brewery were a favourite playground for all the cousins.

Alec's other great friend was Donald Alfred Riddle, whose family lived across the road from the factory. May Walker and Donald Riddle were the only two Smyrna friends with whom he would maintain close and constant personal contact throughout his life. Alec and Donald shared a lifelong joke based on the fact that they were born on the same day, Alec at eight in the morning and Donald at eight in the evening. Issigonis commented: 'Later in life, if I was with Donald discussing something, I would say "Donald my dear boy, you're too young to understand what the problem is" and if we were going downstairs he would say "You're very old, you need some help."'

Donald's father, Eddie Riddle, worked as an assistant civil engineer at the railway yard under Charles Walker. The Riddle family was large – four girls and Donald, plus another boy who died. As well as a birthday, therefore, Donald and Alec had in common the fact that they were 'only' boys in a female-dominated environment. Alec was rather chubby-faced well into his teens in contrast to his more gaunt appearance as an adult. He seems to have been a normal child with a sense of mischief, whether it was roller-skating on the marble hallway of the Walker house, teasing Donald's sisters to provoke a stone fight, hunting for aunty Gertrude's pet chameleon or deliberately annoying an unpopular playmate by cracking cherry stones very loudly between his teeth. May recalled that Donald and his sisters used to tell them tales of events at the railway yards and 'make us laugh at the incompetence of our fathers'. The children were self-sufficient in many ways, living in a world removed from their elders who cushioned them from the political chaos developing around them.

The family recognised that Alec was an exceptionally intelligent little boy and although this reinforced his parents' pride in him, it perhaps also distanced him from his peers. His cleverness was directed into practical channels which formed a sharp contrast to his friend Donald Riddle. Donald was clumsy with his hands and when the pair made paper darts to throw out of the upstairs windows, Donald's failed to fly, earning him the nickname 'Zo' or donkey from Alec. On the other hand, Alec did not share Donald's love of books and complained when Constantine tried to make him read Jules Verne though he did enjoy the *Boy's Own* magazine. Alec avoided 'academic' subjects like mathematics or literature and concentrated on playing with his Meccano set, using it to put together imitations of his father's engineering designs.

All in all life was leisurely, pleasant and civilised and the expatriate community enjoyed a high standard of living. Sanitation was good, the water supply was clean and there were several European-trained doctors such as family friend Dr Spatali. Smyrna's doctors were, however, unable to do anything for the eye condition from which Constantine suffered and he used to visit an eye specialist in Vienna once a year. Charles Walker sometimes accompanied him, but Hulda and Hetty stayed behind. These visits provided an opportunity to bring back some exciting items such as a gramophone player, not readily available in Asia Minor. The Issigonis and Walker households were often filled with music, as the children sat round to listen to uncle Costa's gramophone records, or to share in the excitement of uncle Charlie's pianola. Constantine had a good singing voice and liked Victorian English tunes such as 'Daisy, Daisy give me your answer do' while Charles Walker was an accomplished violinist. For a short time Alec took piano lessons and even dancing lessons but though he showed promise he soon grew bored and went back to his bicycle and Meccano set.

Among the adults, balls, parties and card games were favourite pastimes. In the summer Hulda and Hetty also liked to indulge in the 'masquerade', dressing up in colourful local costumes and going from house to house with a small band of musicians. There was much jollity as friends pretended not to recognise each other and Alec clearly remembered these occasions: 'They'd go from one house to another, the grown ups, I used to be allowed to sit on the top of the steps and watch them all go by.'

There was also a theatre in Smyrna, situated on the quay. It was built in a mock-Italian style which greatly appealed to Alec and was approached by a vast sweep of marble steps. Touring companies from Europe visited to stage grand operas such as *La Bohème* but the Issigonises preferred the popular, lively operettas which were coming out of Vienna throughout the 1900s penned by such composers as Franz Lehár and Leopold Fall.

When the touring companies were in town Hulda would take the excited children on an expedition by tram to matinée performances of *The Merry Widow*, *The Count of Luxemburg* or *The Dollar Princess*.

The Smyrna quay also contained a communal sea-water baths where Hulda taught Alec and May to swim. After their lessons they would buy ring doughnuts sprinkled with sesame seeds from the traders who positioned themselves outside the entrance. Dress was strictly European and the photographs show Hulda, Gertrude and Hetty as young mothers dressed in the most exquisite embroidered gowns. These beautiful garments were made to order by a local seamstress who would visit the household to take the necessary measurements, then sew by hand whatever material had been chosen, delivering the finished product several days later.

The bazaars were easily able to supply all the requirements of everyday life, from a wide selection of meat, fruit and vegetables, to material for clothes and household goods. Food could also be purchased from street vendors who toured the streets on donkeys loaded with panniers full of fruit, vegetables and fish so fresh it was sometimes still alive. It was possible for the family's domestic staff to buy whatever the household needed at almost any time of day on any day of the week, including ice if the weather got particularly hot. Smyrna's status as a major trading port meant that the best of everything passed that way. Camel trains regularly came down from the interior carrying spices, grapes, figs, silks and carpets to the docks and the children loved to run in and out between the camels' legs. The British and French railways also transported vast quantities of goods and all along the route local villagers would barter and exchange their goods with the traders travelling to the coast. Coming in the opposite direction through the harbour by boat were European commodities such as wool, tin, steel and enamel, not to mention the wines and spirits of France, Italy and Spain.

As well as giving their parents a living, the railway oiled their social life. Twenty minutes out of town on the train was the fashionable suburb of Bouja where Gertrude had her second house and the young people patronised the numerous tennis clubs which were situated here. Just before Bouja was Paradise Halt, the favourite location for grand picnics which were another major form of entertainment. On these occasions an entourage of ten or twenty neighbours along with their servants would make their way out into the countryside, hiring donkeys to take them from the railway station to a nearby Roman aqueduct laden with baskets full of provisions and boxes filled with crockery, cutlery, glasses and table-cloths. On arrival temporary camp would be set up beneath the trees with the emptied boxes supporting planks to make benches for sitting on and the tables groaning with every kind of food and wine available. The guests would be very careful not to expose themselves too much to the sun on these trips. Tanned skin was the mark of road-diggers and agricul-tural labourers. Nor was there any question of 'casual' dress. The men wore suits with waistcoat, tie and hat; the women dressed in high-necked Victorian frocks; the servants sported full uniform; and the children were dressed in imitation of their elders.

Though the railway was a reasonably modern form of transport for the region, nevertheless in many ways this was a community which was just on the edge of the 20th century. Smyrna was a large town and peo-ple needed to move around it for economic and social reasons but they did not enjoy access to motorised trams, buses or lorries such as those which had steadily taken a hold in Europe throughout the 1900s. The main means of getting around was walking. The better-off members of the community, including the Issigonises, had their own horses and traps. Alec clearly recalled the family's open carriage which had four wheels, the two smaller wheels at the front being steered with the horse. It could carry six people, with two seats across the front, two at the rear facing each other and a step up at the back. Though his mother was an accom-plished horsewoman and he would not see a motor car until after the First World War, the young Alec took a great dislike to horses and never learned to ride. He could not, however, avoid the horse-drawn trams, which were open in summer and closed in winter. One day when looking down onto the street from May's house, Alec's attention was attracted by the screech-ing of brakes as a tram-driver tried to avoid an animal which had run out into the road. The unfortunate horse pulling the tram which was follow-ing close behind hastily jumped sideways as the two vehicles clashed together with a horrible crunch. The carriages swayed perilously before coming to rest in an upright position and the dazed passengers stepped down onto the street, grateful that the only damage sustained was to their nerves.

The use of horse-drawn trams may seem rather backward but there was a good reason for it. Smyrna had no electricity supply because the Ottoman Gas Company, run by Charles Gandon, owned a gas concession which stipulated that no electric substations could be set up. The houses were therefore lit by gaslight and the children would be sent to bed with a candle and a matchbox in case they needed a light during the night. Water for baths, laundry or cooking was heated by a geyser fuelled with firewood. Smyrna's climate fluctuated between intense heat in the summer, and snow-capped mountains in the winter. The vagaries of the seasons prompted a lively debate between Alec and May.

'It was freezing cold in winter,' Alec insisted, 'colder than England ...'

'But not for long Alec. It was never very long ...'

'It doesn't matter how long, it was very cold. We had paraffin stoves and fireplaces, I think you did, you had a fireplace in your dining room.'

'And in the sitting room. And upstairs on the landing we used to have an enclosed anthracite burning stove where they used to burn coal cuttings.'

'In our house we had a "cosy corner" with a tandoori, do you remember it? A lovely woodwork table with a charcoal fire underneath ...'

'Yes, there was a platform underneath the table where they used to put the tandoori which was an open copper stove full of ash, and they used to light a charcoal fire in the middle of it and see that it was burning well before they brought it indoors because of the carbon monoxide it gives off. On the top of the table there was an enormous eiderdown and people used to sit at each corner, sometimes two at each side if it was big enough. The women used to sit around playing bridge on the eiderdown. Your mother did. It was very warm, except for the people who weren't sitting round it.'

The highlight of winter was Christmas which was celebrated by the Walker and Issigonis households in the manner introduced to Victorian England by Prince Albert. Under the subdued lighting of gas lamps and candles, the children would be led blindfold to the Christmas tree to heighten the sense of anticipation before the beautifully decorated tree surrounded by their presents was finally revealed.

In summer things were different. The heavy curtains were replaced by mosquito nets which were attached to an iron rail running round the ceiling over the bed. Alec remembered lying in bed watching the movement of the net and anticipating the start of an earthquake. Small earth tremors were quite common and somehow, to the little boy, it always seemed to happen during the night. Smyrna had been devastated by some serious earthquakes during its history but the family did not consider themselves to be in great danger. The houses were sturdily designed and Constantine used to position himself under a door on the principle that the wooden lintel would be able to sustain a quake without breaking and would therefore protect him from falling debris. Alec clearly remembered how his father would shout 'God save the Queen!' when the factory chimneys began to wobble, even though the old Queen had been replaced some time ago by an old King.

Many of the expatriates were able to escape Smyrna at its most unpleasant in the height of summer. The Issigonis and Walker families had their own very special retreat and one of the most vivid memories recounted by Alec and May was of the holidays they used to share every summer on the out-of-town estate called Azizeah which Charles Walker had inherited from his wealthy father Joseph. It was some 60 miles away, not that far from the site of Ephesus, and had its own halt on the railway line which is nowadays known as Camlik.

Azizeah was a remote and beautiful place situated in the middle of some wild countryside. The political turmoil of the Ottoman Empire at the time brought with it the danger of attack from local brigands so protection bars were fitted to the windows. The house was comfortable rather than grand and the family were able to live a very pleasant existence here, eating food produced by the farm attached to the estate. They would amuse themselves by playing at being farmers, joining in annual events such as grape harvesting while leaving the serious everyday labour to the estate workers. Constantine and Charles often went out on horseback to hunt wild boars whose carcasses added another ingredient to the family diet.

Another item that the two friends had purchased on one of their Vienna trips was a camera, and they used their holidays at Azizeah to hone their photographic skills. This allowed them to express a more artistic side to their natures which was usually hidden in their town life, focussed as they both were on their careers as engineers. Charles Walker was in charge of the camera while Constantine's input was the most creative since his job was to 'arrange' the subjects of the pictures. The result was a series of intimate family snapshots which are unusual for the period.

These included compositions such as 'the sultana harvest' where the family are seen posing with the estate's fruit pickers, or 'the race' where a grinning Alec, a decorous May and a disgruntled Gerry line up on an imaginary starting line for a race through the woodland in front of the house.

A 'BRITISH' UPBRINGING

Because Alec and his mother lived together for almost 66 years and she was undoubtedly a dominant influence in his life during that time, it would be easy to assume that his father, who died when he was only sixteen, was of little significance to him. It would be a great mistake to think so, however. They may not have married for love, but the partnership of Constantine and Hulda does not seem to have been an unhappy one and it was Constantine rather than Hulda that was the driving force behind the obsession to make young Alec an 'Englishman'.

Home-life revolved around his parents' desire to be English above all else in rather perverse contrast to their actual surroundings. This amounted to their interpretation of what 'Englishness' really was, especially in the case of Hulda who had never travelled outside Smyrna. Initially Alec was baptised into the Greek Orthodox Church like his father, while his mother's family were Roman Catholics. But as he grew older his father decided that Protestantism was an important mark of being British and sent Alec to morning Sunday School every week with his best friend Donald Riddle. The family tried to observe the Greek custom of giving children lambs as pets which would then be slaughtered at Easter. In Alec's case, when the time came he began to cry inconsolably and so he was allowed to keep his lamb which, according to his recollection, grew up into a big bad-tempered ram that used to chase the children round the brewery yard. Nevertheless he insisted to the end of his life that he could not bear lamb chops.

When it came to language, Alec had to be quite versatile. At home Constantine would always speak to him in English and so did all his young friends. Hulda, on the other hand, would speak to him in German. Then there was the everyday language known as 'kitchen' Greek which was used for general communication with merchants, traders and servants. It contained not just elements of Greek but, like most pidgin languages, was influenced by the vocabulary and grammar of the many different communities that used it. Alec had to understand and respond in all these languages though later in life he conveniently 'forgot' anything other than

English. Hulda, too, abandoned German and spoke English with an accent she never lost.

Constantine's friendship with a genuine Englishman, Charles Walker, strengthened the anglophilia prevalent in his household and Alec shared a private but exclusively English education with his Walker cousins. May's elder brother, Gerry, attended a school which was a half-hour rail journey away but this was not considered suitable for the younger children so they were taught at home. It is often said that Issigonis missed out on a proper education because of the circumstances of his childhood. This is a misconception because he benefited from personal tuition by a series of good teachers in a wide range of subjects. This was another subject Alec and May discussed:

'Going to school wasn't really feasible. Alec and I shared a Mrs Newton, who was a governess who had been brought out by the Gandons ...'

'I never knew that May ...'

'Yes, Mr Gandon was the man in charge of the gasworks. They were a well set up family, the tip-top of the English community. She was heavily recommended and he brought her out to teach Phoebe Gandon and I think she taught a lot of the Bournabat people as well, but they were all grown up by then so she was passed on to us.'

'Yes, because Phoebe was about Gerry's age or older.'

'She was older than Gerry.'

'Gerry used to absolutely scorn us when we were young, two or three years difference, he used to absolutely ignore us, do you remember May, and tease you ...'

'He used to bully us.'

'I remember the dada [nursemaid] chasing him with a broom, he'd done something to tease May ...'

'This is a very important thing that I'm going to say now, your mother still kept your first writing book. She always said that you could write and read at two years old but I don't really believe that. Could you Alec, can you remember?'

'No my dear, this is news to me!'

'Well, it's interesting because with private tuition children learn that much earlier in life. We all had lessons long before five years old which is when English children start school. She was an excellent teacher and she took us through elementary reading and writing. I can still remember learning with her, I can still see the words in that book we used to have. We treated her with great respect, we always enjoyed our lessons. We used to have them in the middle of the day usually in the garden or on the veranda. Particularly in the summer there were hordes of mosquitoes about and she used to make us sit with our feet in basins of water with carbolic soap rubbed over our legs to keep away the mosquitoes …'

'She had completely white hair and always dressed in black so it gave her the appearance of being old. To us she looked about seventy but I don't suppose she was anything like that. May, I think she used to drink …'

'Well later she did, poor soul. She had a very unhappy life, poor woman, she was in a strange country, she was a widow, the only income she had was from teaching. Life must have been so difficult and she took to the bottle, you can't blame her. You might say where did she find the money, but in those days you only drank wine and it practically came out of the tap it was so cheap. But what I think is completely unforgivable and I think terribly unfair is that despite all the people's children she taught no one did anything to help her as she slid down the social scale. I remember one day, she took us for a walk along the quay. She'd obviously had something to drink because she started rolling down the road and her hat came off. We all gawped at her and laughed but luckily one of the local nursemaids pulled her together and we all got back safely.'

'What was the name of that man who came to teach us after that?'

'Mr Everett. He taught us during the war. The boys, it was their first step in mathematics, he used to take them in geometry and algebra but I was very bad at that and didn't continue for long. I was more on the literary side. He used to teach us the whole school curriculum because there was no school to go to.'

'He was an Irishman and he had a blind eye. He used to make Gerry and I sit at the window so he could look at Thelma Rice as she went by.'

'He was terrible, he used to follow all our housemaids around.'

'And he had a carpentry school where we used to go and make things. Do you remember when we made dolls furniture?'

'Oh yes, and it was exhibited in the sale room of the MacVities shop.'

'Yes, they had a furniture shop in the suburbs …'

May went on to be taught in a convent school where she learnt to speak fluent French. Constantine had ambitious plans for Alec's future and around 1912 booked him into Oundle, a public school near Northampton which had a reputation for engineering. Had it not been for the outbreak of war in 1914, Alec would therefore have reached England sooner and in very different circumstances than was actually to be the case.

It was not only in the type of education provided for his son that Constantine was to have an influence over the formation of his character. In later years, Alec spoke very little about his father, perhaps giving the impression that he was ambivalent about him. But, when he began to describe the details of his childhood to Tony Dawson, it was clear that he not only admired him, he aspired to be like him. He spoke with pride of his father's design skills and of how he had made a seismographic device for measuring earthquakes from a pattern he devised himself. When asked by the Royal Society to name the influences which shaped his life, Issigonis had no hesitation in remembering … 'my father moving round in his dressing room'. He echoed this when he told Tony Dawson 'my love of design came from my father'.

Constantine encouraged his son's inclinations to be an engineer and his annual trips to Vienna provided the opportunity to seek out some unusual toys. When his ship entered the harbour to bring him home from the big wide world outside, a rowing boat would be sent out to bring disembarking passengers back to shore. Hulda often joined the boat to greet him, taking her son with her. On one such occasion he handed over a splendid clockwork model submarine. Since they were already at sea Alec decided to try it out immediately. He wound the mechanism up and leaned carefully over the side of the rowing boat to drop it into the water. The submarine sank slowly beneath the surface exactly as it was supposed to and he waited in anticipation for some moments for it to reappear. Unfortunately it never did, being lost at sea, producing a rather subdued end to the excitement of the homecoming. Aviation was another technology in its infancy and around 1912 Constantine took his son to a racecourse near their favourite picnic spot at Paradise Halt to witness a flying demonstration by the French aviator Adolphe Pegoud. Alec, who as yet had still not seen a motor car, was thrilled by the sight of the Blériot monoplane and although Pegoud performed only the simplest of manoeuvres for the crowd by taking off, circling round the paddock and safely landing again, the whole event seemed wonderful to the mechanically minded boy.

This was, after all, an age and a society which assumed that children would follow in their fathers' footsteps so the push towards a future in engineering was quite natural. Gerald Walker was given the same type of encouragement. One year, his father and his 'uncle Costa' gave the young boy a beautiful 'Prince Henry' steam locomotive. The two men were slightly put out when Gerry showed absolutely no interest, but they soon recovered their temper by playing with it themselves. It was unfortunate for Gerald that he never felt any inclination towards engineering, being 'more of a philosopher' according to his sister May. Whatever his personal feelings were, as he became an adult he did what was expected of him and became a civil engineer, joining his father on the Ottoman-Aydin railway. Alec was luckier because his inclinations matched his family's expectations.

Issigonis kept very few things relating to his early life so the items which survive among his personal belongings are worth commenting on. One is a baby's leather shoe which was clearly a prized possession of Hulda Issigonis who wrote the words 'Alec's first shoe' on the sole. The second is a faded business card bearing his father's name. The third is a contemporary drawing in black and red ink of the layout of the 'D. Issigonis Works' in Smyrna. These three things sum up very neatly the major influences of his early life.

MALTA

CHAPTER 2

That part of the world is dead for us.

May Ransome

THE EFFECTS OF WAR

THE MEMORY OF life in early-20th-century Smyrna could sound idyllic when it was recounted by those who were so brutally cut off from it. In reality, living through those times was an ever-growing nightmare. As the strains they faced increased, the adults tried to protect their children from the daily worries that continued to multiply. The Constantinople government was losing control of more and more territory and decades of swelling nationalist movements in Eastern Europe, encouraged by Russia, culminated in the Balkan Wars of 1912–13. The result was resounding defeat for the Ottoman Empire. In the aftermath the existing Balkan states argued over how to carve up the newly 'liberated' territories while Turkey itself was further destabilised by a *coup d'état* in Constantinople in 1913. The rest of Europe was hardly more tranquil and there was little surprise when the nations of Europe found themselves embroiled in the First World War. Many of them had been eagerly anticipating such a conflict for some time, believing that it would be the best method of lancing the boil of international hostility which had grown to such unmanageable proportions by 1914. Unfortunately the nature and the duration of the war in which the Franco-British alliance and Germany now found themselves engaged proved to be very different from the short victorious campaigns which both sides had planned.

The rapidly deteriorating political situation within the Ottoman Empire had not so far had a direct effect on the rather independent-minded inhabitants of Smyrna, who put their energies into their very successful commercial life and did not trouble themselves too much about what went on in the Middle East, the Balkans or even Constantinople. The outbreak of a major European war, however, would re-define the future of the Issigonis family and all their friends. The Smyrna community was about to find its comfortable way of life crumbling away and its self-confidence would be profoundly shaken by the events of the next ten years.

Their troubles began when the Ottoman Empire decided to throw its interests in with Germany. Many influential people in Constantinople argued that Turkey should stay neutral because of the substantial British and French investments inside the country; but when the old enemy Russia joined the Franco-British alliance it turned the tide towards the militant elements of the government and an alliance was forged with Germany. One outcome of this was that German warships were allowed to use Smyrna as a naval base.

The Issigonis brothers were in a difficult position. Their Greek origins and British nationality would seem to link them firmly to the Allies in opposition to the Turkish government. Ironically, this did not turn out to be their problem; the real issue was the usefulness of their factory to the war effort. Alec Issigonis described what happened and, if we imagine a similarity in temperament between father and son, it is a scene not too difficult to picture:

> A German officer came to our house one day in the factory compound and with my mother being German father received him but he was a bit stand-offish. He said to my father that he would like to keep our factories open so that we could repair the German submarines when they came into the harbour. And my father said 'not on your bloody life, get out of here'. And the German said 'I'm afraid it's the other way round, you must get out of here.' So we had to leave our house ...

The factory was duly confiscated and it was Hulda's sister, Gertrude Giudici, who came to their rescue. She gave over the house inside the brewery compound to her sister's family and moved her own family to Bouja for the remainder of the war years. The Issigonises hurriedly transported what furniture and belongings they could. Their household of servants, housekeepers and cooks had to be dispensed with, except for one Greek servant called Katrina who asked if she could stay without pay so that she would have a roof over her head. Constantine's stubbornness did not just mean he lost the house and the business. All his money was frozen as well.

Their situation was particularly severe because they depended on the factory for their livelihood. Charles Walker could continue to work on the railway and Jerome Giudici had his job at the bank while the family syndicate still had their brewing business. Gertrude and Hulda's father, Arnold Prokopp, had died in 1902, but Hetty's parents Carl and Bertha Stengel along with Charles and Fanny Crespi continued to brew German beer, bringing in the income needed to support all the families living in the brewery compound.

Alec had reached the age of eight in 1914 and the same year Hetty had given birth to a second son, Tony Walker, who became the latest charge of the Walkers' old Greek nurse. Alec was an excellent mimic and he used to amuse the other children by imitating her cry of 'what a time to be born!'. Most of the memories of wartime which he offered to Tony Dawson were similarly light-hearted. For example, he recounted the fate of the abandoned gasworks:

There was no electricity in Smyrna, only the gasworks managed by Mr Gandon. Of course, being English my father and he were very friendly. The Allies had taken an island which was not far from Smyrna and one ancient Farman biplane used to come over every morning at half past six to drop a bomb on the gasworks. Well all it did was to kill a lot of goats and bombs used to fall in the cemetery nearby. I can see it now, flying along, and lots of smoke from the Turks or the Germans who were firing at it, they were always behind it. It was such an ancient thing that the man who held the bomb sat on the wing. And in the morning I used to say to Donald, shall we go swimming before or after the raid? Because it always happened at half past six in the morning.

Even in 1914 this was a rather old-fashioned way of going about things. It had not taken long for the newly invented aeroplane to be pressed into military service and the first experimental shots from an aircraft in flight were reputedly fired in August 1910 by Lieutenant Jake Fickel of the US army using a Springfield rifle while perched bravely, without a harness, on the lower wing of a biplane. Amazingly he managed to hit a 3 x 3-foot target twice using only four shots. By 1915 a great deal of work had been done to develop aircraft with more efficient fixed machine guns which were designed to have a greater chance of hitting their target and less of killing their operator. Like many of the acts associated with this particular war, the bombing raids which provided Alec and Donald with such amusement were an empty gesture. British concessions such as the gasworks and the oil refinery were closed down for the duration of hostilities and their proprietors, Charles Gandon and Mr Smith, took their families home to the safety of England until peace returned. The inhabitants of Smyrna reverted to candlelight, using techniques such as mixing coal dust and quicklime to produce the fuel they needed to cook and keep warm.

GREEK OCCUPATION

For a while the Ottoman government made an effective contribution to the war, tying up Allied troops in Asia Minor and the Middle East, and on several European fronts. By 1916, however, there was growing discontent inside Turkey itself about the negative effect that involvement with Germany was having and substantial desertions from the army began. The Cabinet resigned in October 1916 and a new government signed the Armistice of Mudros which marked Turkey's withdrawal from the war. It was too late to save the Ottoman Empire. As we saw earlier, the Allies had already agreed among themselves how Ottoman territory would be divided up between them once the fighting was over. By the time they were in a position to act on their secret treaties unforeseen political changes such as the Russian Revolution had taken place. They therefore settled down to extensive re-negotiation of their old agreements during the post-war Peace Conference at Versailles.

The victorious European Allies, however, saw no need to wait for a formal peace treaty before moving in on the Ottoman territory they had so long coveted. During 1918 British, French and Italian troops occupied parts of Constantinople, the French marched into Cilicia and the Italians took parts of southern Turkey. Finally, in May 1919 Greek troops landed in Smyrna harbour, accompanied by a British destroyer. Their arrival was not bloodless and a number of people were killed in exchanges between Turkish and Greek troops as well as riots which broke out in parts of the town. The occupation thus began in a spirit of violence and antagonism which would mark its entire course over the next three years.

Despite the warning signs, the Versailles Conference rubber-stamped these occupations by publishing the Treaty of Sèvres on 10 August 1920. The Ottoman Empire was abolished although the sultan was allowed to remain in Constantinople under the financial control of the Allies. Two new independent states of Armenia and Kurdistan were created on the frontier with the Soviet Union and Iraq. Former Ottoman territories in North Africa and the Middle East were divided out between France and Britain and passed out of Turkish control for good. Most important for Smyrna, the Greek occupation was endorsed.

Though this might superficially appear to have been good news for the large Greek population of Smyrna, it was in fact the beginning of the end for them. These events triggered a fierce national resistance movement inside Turkey headed by Mustafa Kemal (who later took the name Ataturk or 'father of the Turks'). Kemal had been a distinguished Ottoman officer during the First World War. Now he decided he would use the troops under his command to repudiate the Treaty of Sèvres and establish an alternative capital in Ankara. He told his followers that the sultan was nothing more than a prisoner of the Allies and he began military operations against both Constantinople and the region occupied by Greece.

So 1919 did not bring a return to normal life, instead it represented even more anxiety for the Smyrna community as world war was replaced by civil war. Constantine and Hulda, Hetty and Charles all tried to put a brave face on things in front of their children but they knew that their town, for so long the pivot in the commerce between southern Europe and Asia Minor, was now the focus of a bitter war of liberation. In later years Hulda would complain angrily to Hetty about 'that awful Lloyd George who gave Asia Minor to the Greeks with no protection'.

There was little that most of them could do in the circumstances, since all their business and property interests lay in Smyrna and they had no way of knowing how the crisis would resolve itself in the long term. Gertrude Giudici was the only one who felt that the best course of action would be to emigrate. Following the death of her husband Jerome in 1918 she returned to Germany with her three children, settling in Munich, the capital of Bavaria, about 120 miles south-east of the family's original home. This was a brave decision. Her grandmother had left a small town in an independent German state. Gertrude was returning to a unified Germany which had just lost a draining and vicious war.

On the more positive side Constantine and his brother Miltiades were able to resume their business at the D. Issigonis factory which brought some welcome financial security back to the family. The Stengel family syndicate had by now dwindled away. Carl and Bertha Stengel died in 1916 and were not survived for very long by the Crespis. Following Gertrude's departure for Germany, Constantine and Hulda remained at the brewery house rather than moving back to their flat over the factory; but although the once prosperous brewery had supported them through the war years, the loss of the older generation plus the worsening political situation sent it into a decline from which it never recovered.

Alec was now thirteen years old and it was decided that it was time he got a taste of work on his own account. A job was found for him in the drawing office at the railway yard where his cousin Gerry was already working as a civil engineer alongside uncle Charlie, and he would work here for the next three years. On his first day, he reported for duty rather apprehensively. His new boss was Mr Elliot, the Chief Mechanical Engineer, and the occasion when he had caught Alec riding on an engine in the shunting yards, and beaten him for his misdemeanour with a large stick, was still fresh in the youngster's mind. He was right to be worried since he was about to encounter an attitude rather different from that of his adoring parents. He recalled with amusement many years later, '... this was a shock because the first job I was given was to make a turntable for trucks. I thought this so degrading because I expected to design a loco-motive straight away!' Thus began the engineering career of the designer of the Mini.

It was around this time that Alec came into contact with his first motor car. By the early 20th century there was a flourishing motor industry throughout Western Europe and much public, commercial and military transport had been motorised. This trend increased throughout the First World War and by 1919 Smyrna's horse-drawn trams were having to share the streets with a variety of heavy motor vehicles. The private motor car, however, was strictly a luxury item and only those people at the top of the social tree could afford to buy one. Turkey had no indige-nous motor industry, but when the expatriates who had fled to their home-lands during hostilities began to return to their posts in 1918, many of them brought with them examples of the motor vehicles which were becoming popular among the wealthy classes of Europe and North America. The first models which Alec remembered seeing were a Model T Ford and a Willys Overland; but the biggest impression was made by the third vehicle he saw. Mr Smith had returned to his post at the Standard Oil Refinery on the other side of the bay. He brought with him a splendid V8 Cadillac, a modern and powerful machine which could do speeds of up to 65 miles per hour and might have cost him anything between $2,000 and $4,000 depending on the body style. When news of this new arrival reached Alec he decided to befriend Smith's sons, Eric and Norman, so he could use the opportunity of his visits to ingratiate himself with the family's Greek chauffeur, Giorgi. Issigonis never forgot his first experience of the motor car:

> I was absolutely enthralled with this car and became great friends with the chauffeur because he would take me for short rides whenever no one was looking. This car ran with no noise at all; he used to drive it with the tyres running on the tramlines which were just the right gauge to avoid the rough cobbles. It was then perfection – not a sound.

A rather more familiar sight than the occasional Ford or Cadillac were the military lorries and tanks which were now lumbering daily over the cobbled streets. The damage that this heavy military traffic was causing to the infrastructure of the town was a matter of great annoyance to another returned expatriate, Charles Gandon, the manager of the Ottoman Gas Company which still held the concession for supplying power to Smyrna. He had been forced to suspend the gas supply to the town because the Greeks had refused to honour previous agreements with his company. In April 1921, Gandon appealed to Sir Harry Lamb, who was Consul General and Representative of the British High Commissioner in Smyrna, for assistance in obtaining the payments which were due. At the same time he complained about the serious amount of gas leakage which was making matters even worse:

> Most of the increase [in leakage] is due to the destruction of the Company's mains as the result of the extraordinary traffic occasioned by heavy military lorries and the excessive speed at which they are driven. I need hardly point out that the streets of Smyrna were designed to carry light horse and cart traffic and are quite unsuitable for heavy motors.

But the British government were powerless to intervene, insisting that there was nothing they could do until the military situation was resolved.

So the inhabitants of Smyrna did not get their gas supply back and this was just one example of the economic stagnation caused by the occupation. Also badly affected were the large number of Maltese citizens who were mostly labourers and could not find any work in the current situation.

This was becoming a problem for the British government because many of them were claiming support from the British Relief Fund. Though Malta was a British colony it had been granted self-government in 1921 and Sir Harry Lamb therefore felt it would be reasonable to appeal to F.M. Plumer, the Governor of Malta, to take over responsibility for the relief of the Maltese section of the population, in order to release funds for other British citizens in need. The reaction of Governor Plumer to the British government's request throws an interesting side-light on some of the attitudes the Smyrna refugees would encounter when they were evacuated to Malta a few months later. The Maltese government refused to assist anyone not born in Malta and further stated that they would not accept the repatriation of such people either. Plumer wrote to Lamb from Valletta on 19 May 1922:

> The Government of Malta owes you a debt of gratitude for the assistance you are good enough to extend to such of the Maltese colony as are in distress; nevertheless, while sympathising with those who have been overcome by misfortune mainly owing to the conditions produced by the War, the Government is not prepared to depart from the general policy hitherto followed and to authorise an indiscriminate grant of financial assistance to persons of Maltese descent or nationality. The Government is at present endeavouring to cope with a serious financial situation and is obliged to practise strict economy in all branches of the expenditure; it will, however, always be prepared to consider on their own merits any cases representing features of a special character.

The political situation was deteriorating as rapidly as the economic one. Though the British were still supporting the sultan in Constantinople and the Greek regime in Smyrna, it was the kind of support which comes from fear of the alternatives rather than endorsement of the status quo. The British High Commission at Constantinople reported back to London on 4 July 1922, '... what renders a considerable change undesirable is not any positive advantage in the retention of the present government, but the possible danger of something worse'.

The something worse, of course, was Mustafa Kemal. Initially the Greeks had been able to move inland towards central Anatolia in an attempt to establish control over the territory they had been given by the Treaty of Sèvres and they had reached the outskirts of rebel Ankara by

July 1921. The nationalists stood their ground and cleverly managed to remove some major players from the equation by making a series of agreements first with the Soviet Union and then with France and Italy. This enabled them to counter-attack and win a decisive victory at the Sakarya River in September 1921. Soon the tide was moving inexorably against the Greeks and in favour of the nationalists. A retreat rapidly turned into a rout and thousands of Greek soldiers were taken prisoner while the remainder fled back to Smyrna.

Most of the European powers, including Britain, decided to let events take their course and declined to offer support to either side. Badly equipped and low in morale, by 1922 the Greek occupying army had little more than a few tanks and a handful of biplanes. They parked them on the seafront and fired them up from time to time in an attempt to convince the locals they were still a force to be reckoned with. Typically, Alec took more interest in the tanks and the planes than the political situation, hanging around the seafront and chatting to the soldiers in the hope that they would let him climb up onto a tank or invite him into the cockpit of one of the planes where he could get a better look at what, to him, were simply fascinating machines.

The Fire of Smyrna

By September 1922 the nationalists were closing in on Smyrna and most expatriates prepared, once again, to depart for home. The Smith family from the oil refinery were among them. On one of his final visits Alec saw his old friend the chauffeur for the last time, wearing a Greek army uniform. He recalled this event clearly:

> There came a point where Mustafa Kemal's army was only 80 miles away from Smyrna and I remember visiting the Smith children at the oil refinery and Mr Smith was telling my hero Giorgi, the Greek chauffeur, that he's got to join the army. The Smiths were leaving before things got bad. Giorgi wasn't sacked, he was allowed to live in the compound of the oil refinery, but he did join the army because I remember seeing him wearing a Greek uniform. The Smiths took the Cadillac away with them.

The decision to leave was much more difficult for those born in Smyrna to make because their wealth was tied up in local property and they risked losing everything if they did not stay. Moreover their emotional attachment to Smyrna was much greater. Despite their 'English' way of life, women like Hulda Issigonis and Hetty Walker had never been abroad let alone visited their 'homeland', nor did they have any friends or relatives to go back to. Most of them therefore stayed on though it was now obvious that events were reaching a very unpleasant climax. As the Greek troops began to withdraw, thousands of refugees flooded into the city from the surrounding countryside ahead of the Turkish advance. Early in September, Britain, France, Italy and the United States all sent warships into the harbour to safeguard the interests of their citizens ashore.

It was at this point that Constantine's British citizenship was to come to the rescue of the family. When the British decided that it was not safe to wait any longer, they sent their marines onshore during the night to bring as many British citizens as possible to the safety of the navy ships. Alec Issigonis gave an account of that night to Tony Dawson and this is the only time during his narrative of the events of his childhood that he betrays the painfulness of some memories:

The Turkish army were very close and the British navy – we had battleships in those days – came to evacuate the small colony of British people because they felt that by the time the Turkish army arrived, Smyrna would be in a state of war. So, at midnight one night, some marines came to the house and they said to my mother and father: 'just take some blankets, don't take anything else, you must come immediately.' The Greek soldiers were lying, dead tired in the streets, I remember this so well, it was a moonlit night. Then they took us on board a little ship called the *Antioch*. May and Donald and all my friends were there. We were given the choice of either going to Malta or going to Cyprus and my father immediately said Malta because it was nearer to England. In fact almost everybody on the ship said Malta. Next morning my father got permission to go back into Smyrna to collect documents and money and I asked if I could go with him though this was rather dangerous because, you know, the Turks were so close by then. I wanted to go because I wanted my Meccano set and to let the ginger cat out of the house. I remember opening the window to let him out.

By the time they returned to the *Antioch* it was crammed so full of people that it was becoming difficult to move around so later that day the Malta-bound refugees were transferred to a larger hospital ship called the *Maine*. From here, the families watched in horror as street fighting broke out and then the town started to burn.

The arrival of Kemal's army sparked a brutal fight whose viciousness reflected the mutual bitterness which had characterised the whole Greek occupation from the day the first shots had been exchanged back in 1919. When fire broke out thousands of inhabitants were trapped. Thick smoke began to engulf the narrow streets and billowed towards the waterfront where desperate people ran for escape towards the sea. Many died in the fire, others drowned after jumping in the water. The glow of the flames could be seen from ships up to 50 miles away and by the time the fire had burned out several days later most of the historic city of Smyrna had been destroyed. The boats full of refugees remained anchored in the harbour for days before sailing for Malta and Cyprus and it is probable that Alec and his family witnessed much of this tragedy. All he said to Tony Dawson in conclusion was: 'I saw the street fighting from a distance and smoke rising. And then there were three days of hell on the boat.'

JOURNEY TO MALTA

Alec had never been on an extended sea voyage and he was seasick from the moment he stepped on board to the moment he disembarked. At the same time Constantine fell seriously ill so for once his mother was too preoccupied to pay her son much attention. By the time they arrived in Malta the refugees had lost not merely their lifestyle and position but also most of their worldly possessions and nothing could have been a greater shock than the reception that greeted them on this Mediterranean island.

The Issigonises, the Walkers, the Riddles and all the other refugees were taken from the boat to an isolated building called 'the Lazaretto' which stood on Manoel Island in Valletta harbour, cut off from the rest of the town. In 1423 Venice had been the first town to build a 'lazaretto' on an island outside the city in an attempt to guard against the spread of disease, particularly the plague, by maritime traders. The word quarantine comes from the *quarantina* or 40 days which the Venetians established as the period of isolation. Other cities followed their example and a series of lazarettos sprang up throughout the Mediterranean. Malta's lazaretto had been built by Grand Master Lascaris of the Order of St John in 1643 following two serious plagues and, as was the practice, was located on an island outside the capital city of Valletta. Through the years many visitors, regardless of rank, had been forced to stay in the building and among its distinguished residents had been Lord Byron returning from Greece in 1811 who called it 'an infernal oven'. He was followed by Disraeli, Coleridge, Thackeray and Sir Walter Scott who commented in 1831, '... it is unpleasant to be thought so uncleverly unclean and capable of poisoning a whole city'. This old quarantine station was chosen as the most suitable place to house the refugees because of an outbreak of the plague which had swept across the Middle East and down the Mediterranean during the early summer of 1922, affecting a series of twelve ports. Each place affected became the subject of a similar announcement in the *Malta Government Gazette*:

> Information having been received that an infectious or contagious disease, dangerous to mankind, to wit plague, exists at Smyrna, it is hereby declared that Smyrna is an infected place within the meaning of article 1 of the Regulations made under the Fourth Sanitary Ordinance, 1908. 24 August 1922, M. Dundon, Minister for Public Health.

The order against traffic from Smyrna was not lifted until 13 July 1923 when the town was officially declared free of infection. For the new inhabitants of the Lazaretto this was an unpleasant situation. On 22 September, shortly after their arrival, a declaration was made that no craft could land on Manoel Island without permission on the grounds of public health. They were luckier than the refugees who went to Cyprus, however, who were charged three shillings each in landing charges.

Statistics compiled by the British Consulate in Malta show that by 2 November 1922 the refugees from Smyrna included 669 British citizens of whom 196 had already left the island, 384 were in quarantine in the Lazaretto and Fort Manoel and 89 were living in hotels and private residences. Two funds had been set up in London to help them, the All British Malta Appeal run by Algernon Maudslay and the British Refugees from Smyrna Relief Fund administered by F.S. McVitie. Both these gentlemen soon began to receive letters complaining that the money being sent was not reaching the British refugees. They passed the complaints on to the British government on 6 November and the civil servant who was asked to review the correspondence made the following comment:

... these papers were handed to Mr Maudslay on the 31st October. Mr McVitie was with him and was extremely sore about the treatment of the refugees at Malta. Making every allowance for the feeling of men suddenly reduced to penury, the writers' complaints seem to shew that at the least the British refugees have been unsympathetically and tactlessly handled. So far £1,000 has been sent to Malta for the All British Appeal and the statement that no funds had been distributed to the British refugees made Mr Maudslay and Mr McVitie wonder what was happening to the money. It seems possible that it is being spent on buying food and owing to the circumstances to which the money was subscribed it has to be administered impartially between British born and Maltese and alien refugees. It appears that the last thing the authorities ever intend to do is to help a British subject. A Greek or a Turk is to them so much more romantic!

For Hulda Issigonis and her son the situation was particularly distressing because Constantine had been taken from the boat straight to a naval hospital near Attard which was some miles away from Valletta. While Alec remained in the Lazaretto with the Walker family, Hulda had to divide her time between her sensitive son and her sick husband. Alec therefore suffered from the added pain of being separated from his adored father and, for much of the time, from his doting mother too. None of the refugees had any money because of the haste of the evacuation. The Issigonises and the Walkers now found themselves crowded together in a single room, living on meagre rations of baked beans and dry bread. Washing and toilet facilities had to be shared with the hundreds of other families inhabiting the barrack-like buildings.

The letters handed over to Maudslay and McVitie describe the miserable living conditions endured by the Issigonises and the Walkers inside the Lazaretto. Initially the refugees were promised a food allowance of five shillings a day per adult and four shillings per child. This promise was later withdrawn and they remained dependent on the food provided by the Maltese authorities. A local resident, Mr Whittall, wrote from Valletta on 25 October:

... the food is getting worse and worse, not fit for a dog, and even bread stinted when it was found that the refugees (I suppose they are taken for convicts) eat too much bread, the quality was changed, or else the bread was kept till it became stale and hard so as to be almost uneatable … If something is not done there will be mortality.

A group of residents formed the Lazaretto Refugee Committee which initially appealed to Governor Plumer but he referred them on to the Minister of Public Health, one of the Legislature's appointed Ministers. At first, the Minister seemed to be more sympathetic and the Legislature agreed to grant the refugees the allowance they had been promised. Each refugee family signed an official form of acceptance which had been drawn up by Dr Bernard, Chief Sanitation Officer, stating that the allowance was granted as a loan to be repaid when possible. On the strength of this several of the refugees found themselves more comfortable lodgings outside the Lazaretto, some even paid three months' rent in advance for furnished houses. Then, two days after the offer had been made and all the acceptances sent in, the Maltese authorities posted up a notice at the Lazaretto warning the refugees not to search for houses and withdrawing the allowance. The Lazaretto Refugee Committee was appalled and its Chairman, Robert Hadkinson, wrote an angry letter to the British government pointing out that refugees who had reached London and Cyprus had been granted a fixed sum of £10 to buy clothes plus an allowance of five shillings per day in compensation for their situation yet the £1,000 sent to Malta by the All British Appeal specifically to be distributed to the British refugees had never been passed on to them by the Maltese government:

We may add that Lord Plumer, Governor of Malta, surrounded by his staff, visited our quarters yesterday and was led by the guides into one or two of the best rooms at the Lazaretto, with the idea no doubt of giving him a favourable impression. His attitude towards us could scarcely be called sympathetic, he never addressed any one of the refugees but merely remarked in an offhand way that we were sufficiently fortunate in having saved our skins. Asked if we would be given the capitation allowance promised, he curtly replied that we would not. Before closing we may mention that we have been authoritatively informed that the Smyrna British refugees will shortly be shifted to other quarters and that the men and women will be lodged separately. This is how we, victims of the British policy, who have lost all that we possessed, are being treated by the Representatives of his Majesty the King.

The British government in London were extremely annoyed when they received these complaints and began to look into the behaviour of Governor Plumer. Almost as soon as the evacuation was over notices had begun to appear among the refugee communities in Cyprus and Malta urging people of certain professions to return to Smyrna. On 19 October 1922 the Governor of Malta sought to endorse this view by posting a notice repeating information received from the British High Commissioner in Constantinople:

> The Angora [i.e. Ankara] Government have been asked for assurances of the safety of British subjects wishing to return to Smyrna. Reply has not been received but the attitude of the Local Authority is sufficiently favourable to justify the return of British subjects having property or urgent business. They must do so at their own risk but we do not consider it a great risk and the Vice Consul considers the presence of persons without families desirable and in their interests.

The inhabitants of the Lazaretto were infuriated by this disregard for their safety. Now that Mustafa Kemal had won a military victory he was involved in negotiations for a political settlement with the former Allies. The refugees were highly suspicious that Kemal was encouraging British citizens to return to Smyrna on the pretext of recovering their property as a ploy to obtain hostages in case the conference negotiations did not go the way he wanted. The British government had similar fears and stated emphatically that no one should go back to Smyrna at this stage, publishing a notice to that effect in the *Malta Government Gazette* on 13 November 1922 which declared:

> ... the British Authorities at Smyrna urge that no one (and particularly no women and children) be encouraged to return until after the Conference, unless he has interests requiring attention. They do not consider that a partially looted house alone constitutes a sufficient reason for anyone to return.

This notice described a situation characterised by military requisitioning, the destruction and looting of property belonging to foreign nationals, the halting of all commercial activity apart from salvage operations and the dismissal of all non-Turkish employees on the Ottoman-Aydin

Railway. The British Consulate pointed out that their representatives were not officially recognised by the nationalist government and were therefore dependent on their activities being tolerated. They could give no guarantees that they would be able to protect any British citizens who returned to Turkey.

Nor did they want to add to the financial burden of looking after subjects who were still trapped in Smyrna. Sorting out the situation in Malta was a much cheaper option so they put pressure on Governor Plumer to improve their treatment. The promised allowances were finally paid and those refugees who could afford to do so left the Lazaretto. Hetty Walker was among those able to gather together the money necessary to move with her children to a more pleasant house in Sliema district on the east side of Valletta harbour. The Walkers stayed here for many months and life took a turn for the better. The young people were able to bathe off the rocks, idle on the beach and resume the pleasant picnics of Smyrna days. While May enjoyed herself flirting with the navy boys, Gerry Walker indulged in high-spirited pranks along with his friends, as Alec recalled:

They were up to every kind of trick, Gerry and his gang. Do you know what they used to do at night? They put a thin string of sewing cotton from one knocker to the other across this street on every house so when a carriage came by all the knockers went! Now if that isn't a joke I don't know what is.

ENGLAND AT LAST

This turn of events unfortunately did little to improve the situation for Hulda Issigonis. Constantine still lay desperately ill in the hospital at Attard and had lost his sight completely soon after his illness began. As the refugees began to move out of the Lazaretto his wife and son moved near the hospital to be with him. Alec entertained himself in the meantime by making use of the Meccano set he had rescued from their abandoned house and he won a prize for his efforts in a competition held in Valletta.

Hulda realised that her husband was not going to get better but she did not share this knowledge with her son. Instead, as the Lazaretto episode drew to a close, she decided she must carry on to England and establish Alec there on his own. The two of them set off on an epic train journey across Europe, something which required considerable courage on the part of Hulda Issigonis as neither she nor her son had ever accompanied Constantine on his travels around Europe. They left Malta for Sicily via the small island of Gozo and travelled north to the town of Messina. On the way Alec got his first sight of a volcano as they passed Mount Etna, an experience which impressed him so greatly that he would return there 50 years later. They travelled the length of Italy to reach Switzerland where they broke their journey for a week, lodging at Lausanne near the Lakes. Though he was used to the snow-capped mountains surrounding Smyrna, this was the first time Alec had seen deep snow close up and he was allowed to spend a day or two tobogganing and riding on the funicular railway. Then they undertook the final part of the journey through France to reach England.

Their destination was a boarding house in Crescent Grove, situated in the Clapham district of London. Hulda was given the address by another one of the refugees, Mrs Elliott, the wife of the railyard's Chief Mechanical Engineer who had until recently been Alec's boss. Crescent Grove was approached from Clapham Common through a set of impressive iron gates. Mrs Elliott's sister lived in one of the big Georgian houses to the left of the square and she was able to recommend a boarding house which formed part of the elegant terrace to the right. It was run by a couple who kept a flat in the basement and rented out the upper floors. Hulda settled her young son into rooms on the first floor, reassured him that she and his father would join him as soon as possible and then made the same arduous journey in reverse back to her husband in Malta.

Not surprisingly the parting between mother and son was a tearful one. Though he was sixteen, Alec was a shy young man who up to this date had lived a sheltered life at the heart of a large extended family. Now he was left alone for the first time in his life, among strangers and in a foreign country. London was a very different proposition from either Smyrna or Malta with its busy streets full of motor cars, buses and lorries and its more restrained, less exuberant way of life. At least it was spring and he did not immediately face a freezing English winter. Hulda left him under the watchful eye of Mrs Elliott's sister across the square. His fellow boarders befriended him and his landlady mothered him. All the same, time hung heavy on his hands while he waited, as he hoped, to be reunited with his parents so they could begin a new life together in their promised land.

He cheered up when May Walker was sent to join him ahead of her family, though he did not enjoy her company for long before she was despatched to a boarding school in Essex. She took this development somewhat badly as she felt she was now too grown-up to settle in such unfamiliar and formal surroundings. Finally the worst happened when, after a nine-month illness, Constantine died in Attard on 1 June 1923. Alec was distraught when his mother returned to Crescent Grove with the news. Throughout his childhood and youth he had modelled himself on his father whom he both loved and admired. His attachment to the country where he was now living and his ambitions for the future had been inspired and nurtured by him. When Tony Dawson asked him what caused his father's death, Alec did not attempt to explain his illness but replied simply and with feeling: 'I think he died of a broken heart.' This mutual loss was deeply felt by both mother and son and would form a very close bond between them which endured to the end of their lives.

Soon after Hulda rejoined her son, Hetty also arrived in England with Gerry and Tony, moving into St Marie's Hotel in Purley which was already home to several other refugee families. Shortly afterwards the political situation in Turkey was resolved by the final agreement to arise out of the First World War. The Treaty of Lausanne was signed on 24 July 1923 after seven months of negotiation and replaced the discredited Treaty of Sèvres. Under its terms, the sultanate was abolished, the modern borders of Turkey were established and the country's financial and political independence was recognised by the former Allies. In return, the new state dropped any claims to former Ottoman territories in North Africa, the Middle East or the Balkans. In October 1923, the new secular Republic of Turkey was established with Mustafa Kemal 'Ataturk' as the first President. Its capital was to be his own power-base in Ankara, not the ancient seat of power at Constantinople which was now renamed Istanbul. Smyrna was also given the new name of Izmir and it was finally possible for some of the refugees to return there in an effort to recover some of their property. Hulda and Hetty were among those who visited their former home to see if anything could be salvaged while the children stayed in England. Gerry, now aged 22, began to assume the role of head of household, taking responsibility for the two families when either of them was away. His main concern, however, was Tony who was still a child of ten, since May and Alec were now young adults and could be expected to look after themselves.

Though Charles Walker had travelled with the rest of his family to

Malta he did not join his family in England. The Treaty marked the end of the turbulence and blood-letting which had followed the nationalist re-occupation of the town. The new Turkish government were sensible enough to realise that sacking skilled railway engineers simply because of their nationality would not help to rebuild the economy, which was in poor shape after four years of civil war. It therefore appealed for them to return and Charles Walker was among those who decided to take up the offer. Hetty saw Charles when she visited Izmir with Tony during 1924. After this she returned to Purley while Charles remained in Turkey, supporting the family through his job on the railway until his death at an Istanbul nursing home in 1935 at the age of 68.

When Hulda and Hetty first returned to Izmir they found that the factory and the brewery had survived the fire but this did not help them to recover their property. Miltiades Issigonis, despite his British citizenship, had stayed in Smyrna with his family and died sometime during 1923, though the exact circumstances are not known. His wife and children eventually settled in Greece. Following Milti's death, all the equipment and machinery from inside the factory had been taken away and sold. Charles Walker's splendid house had been taken over by a local family. As for the brewery, the women discovered that no title-deeds had ever been drawn up so they were completely unable to establish a claim on the business in order to sell what was left. Nor could they convert their shares in the railway into cash. Their efforts continued for many years and in the end it became a kind of family mantra that any relative short of money should 'go and try to sell the brewery'. May commented sadly, almost 70 years later, 'that part of the world is dead for us'.

Early Years in England

CHAPTER 3

*What loads of fun it all was to be sure, and what a lot of fuel has flowed
through the pipes since then.*

Duke of Richmond to Sir Alec Issigonis in 1969

The 'Grand Tour'

As soon as she revisited Izmir it was clear to Hulda that she would never
be able to recover the family wealth. She therefore took the alternative
course of action open to her by claiming compensation from the British
government for her losses as a British citizen and refugee. Though the
exact amount which she received has not been recorded it was probably
in the region of £10,000, a considerable sum in 1920s values. She told
Hetty of her disappointment that she was not awarded the full amount of
her claim but the money she received was enough to live on comfortably
while Alec resumed his education with the intention of equipping himself to get a job which would support both of them.

The next step was to find a proper home. Early in 1925 Hulda and
Alec moved out of the Clapham boarding house into a rented bungalow
at Overhill Road in Purley. This had the rather rustic name of 'Barton'
and even today its setting is pleasantly suburban. Purley had become the
centre of a small community of Smyrna exiles whose members would
stay in close touch for many years to come. Hulda's 'sister' Hetty and family
were already there, now established in a house in nearby Bencombe Road.
Other neighbours included Alec's old boss, Mr Elliott, along with his wife
who had helped Hulda to find her first lodgings in London. Their daughters, Hilda and Maudie, were good friends of May Walker as was another
exile, Ethel Heginbotham. While Alec, his cousin May and their young
friends seem to have been able to put the horror of their recent experiences behind them very quickly, the older generation of Smyrna exiles
did not find it so easy to come to terms with their situation. Sometimes
the Walkers, Riddles, Goüts, MacVities, Petters, Harleys, Heginbothams,
Elliotts and all the rest would get together to reminisce and underlying

53

the chat and laughter of old friends was a lingering sense of melancholy and loss.

Once they were settled, and before the, matter of Alec's continued education was pursued, Hulda felt that the family needed to counter-balance the trauma of the last two years with some well-earned self-indulgence to boost their spirits. During the summer of 1924 she had treated her son to his first motor car, a brand new 10 hp Singer saloon fitted with an optional fabric Weymann body which was designed to be light and rattle-free. This cost the substantial sum of £275. The motor industry was now well established in Britain and, after some initial resistance to the new invention, motorised vehicles had become the predominant form of transport alongside the railway network. The privately owned motor car, however, was still a relatively expensive item. Even those in the better-paid professions would be taking home only around £5 a week so Alec's new Singer represented an entire year's wages. The young man was obviously very proud of this new possession and he photographed it from every angle as it sat in the road outside their lodgings at Crescent Grove, the solitary car even in this well-heeled street. He pasted the pictures into his photograph album and captioned them – 'Salome, one week old'. Hulda decided in the summer of 1925 that they would take 'Salome' on a 'Grand Tour' of Europe. Cousin Gerry was invited along too, perhaps to assist Hulda with the more practical aspects of the trip, but also as a thank-you for the role he had played in supporting the family during the early days in London while Hetty and Hulda were travelling backwards and forwards to Turkey.

The tour lasted several weeks and was quite extensive, beginning with the First World War cemeteries of Belgium and the battlefield of Arras on the Franco-Belgian border, then on to the palaces of Versailles and Fontainebleau just outside Paris. After this they drove across the width of France to the main resorts of the French Riviera. On their first visit to Monte Carlo Alec and his mother fell in love with the atmosphere, marking it down as a place to which they would return many times when their circumstances improved. After the excitement of Monaco they made for the grandeur of the Swiss Alps and then turned back for home. Alec appears to have taken up his father's interest in amateur photography though he displayed considerably less talent. We therefore have a series of snapshots of the tour showing the three travellers *en route* – four if we count 'Salome', who seems to be Alec's favourite subject. As neither

Gerry nor Hulda ever learned to drive a car, young Alec must have done all the driving himself which was quite impressive for a nineteen year old who had only got behind the wheel for the first time a year earlier. While Hulda and Gerry viewed the sights Alec could often be found in the nearest local garage supervising the repair of the car. By the end of their journey the inner tubes had worn away and he later described the trip as 'an uninterrupted series of punctures', claiming that they had to fill the tyres up with grass to get from one village to the next. Motor transport may have become well established by the 1920s but this was an early lesson to one of its biggest fans, Alec Issigonis, that there was plenty of scope for improvement.

BACK TO SCHOOL

Once the 'Grand Tour' was over Alec's return to college was a necessity. At nineteen he was rather old to become a student and more than old enough to take a job straight away but his lack of formal education or qualifications would have made it very difficult for him to obtain a decent apprenticeship. Hulda was an ambitious mother with a high opinion of her son's abilities and she was determined that Alec should achieve the type of position she felt he deserved. He therefore prepared to follow in his father's footsteps by enrolling to study engineering at nearby Battersea Polytechnic. The journey was a straightforward one by train and Hulda gave him a weekly allowance of ten shillings to help him on his way. She must have calculated that the compensation money would see them through the time he would need to complete his education and it seems that the intention was not just to matriculate from the polytechnic but to go on and get a BSc degree at university. This would be a lengthy and expensive project and life at Barton cottage included a great deal of 'counting the pennies'. Their difficulties were greatly reduced, however, when Hetty generously offered to help with Alec's educational expenses. Though she was by no means well off, Hetty was in a slightly more comfortable position than Hulda since her husband was still alive and supporting the family even though he was not living with them. Gerry meanwhile had attended the Crystal Palace School of Engineering and gained an apprenticeship as a civil engineer on the London Underground so he too was contributing to the household expenses.

One of the familiar stories which Issigonis used to tell in later life concerned the debate which took place in the family over his education.

He claimed a suggestion was made that he should study art because of his talent for drawing but that he himself insisted he only wanted to do engineering. Like the story of Constantine's British nationality, the truth seems to have been less romantic. It is absolutely true that he was determined to be an engineer but we have already seen that this would have been a natural outcome of his background. It seems unlikely that someone who belonged to a family with such a strong tradition in engineering would have been encouraged to divert into some academic subject like art – after all what career would it have fitted this particular young man for? Hetty had an interest in this too since she was helping to pay. Her own eldest son had been firmly directed into a career in engineering somewhat against his inclinations because this was considered the most sensible option. Besides, Alec was well aware of where his own talents lay. In 1964, now a famous and successful designer, he freely admitted that '… oddly enough I am a very bad artist apart from design drawing. I can't manage the human form at all for instance. I suppose this is surprising really, but it is probably due to my mechanistic mind.' This is amply borne out by the sketchbooks which, in over 2,000 sketches, contain only one rudimentary drawing of a person rather than a mechanical object.

Issigonis struggled with the academic parts of his course, in particular mathematics which he claimed did not interest him because it was not 'creative'. On the other hand he excelled at mechanical drawing and looked forward to these classes in which he got the highest marks. He gave this account of his college days:

> As a boy I went to Battersea Polytechnic, in London, and I wasn't particularly brilliant academically. I just couldn't bear mathematics. Looking back on this now, I remember all of the end of term exams and the finals when I could only just scrape through. I was not interested at all, because, I think, if you have any kind of creative ability you inherently revolt against mathematics, which are not really creative things at all … The thing that I took easily to at college was drawing. It was a three year course and you did quite a lot of machine design drawing, as it is called, and I could hardly wait for the time that I got into this class with my drawing board. And as you got into the second and third years you were given not just simple exercises, but more creative things to do yourself. You had a choice as to what design study

you were going to make in that term. I found this most fascinating and I always passed with very high marks.

He also recalled his weakness in another compulsory part of the course, languages, which is odd considering that in his youth he had spoken two other languages at least competently – German and 'kitchen' Greek. It is hard to believe he could not have mastered these skills if he had really set his mind to it. We have seen this tendency already in his childhood when he resisted his father's attempts to make him read Jules Verne but would spend hours making things with his Meccano set. It would also be evident throughout his career, in which he was always prepared to work immensely hard at the things that interested him – the design process or testing and proving the vehicles – but had no time for those things he considered mundane and boring – such as post-production problem-solving or day-to-day paperwork and administration. So although he would become famous for his lateral thinking, he was also in some senses extremely inflexible. A wider perspective may have ultimately served him better since single-mindedness can also be narrow-mindedness.

This would prove to be a costly character trait but its full effects would not become evident until later in his life. The more immediate result was that he failed to matriculate for the BSc. After failing his exams three times he finally settled for a first class Diploma in Mechanical Engineering which he was duly awarded by Battersea Polytechnic in 1928. It was a bigger disappointment than he was prepared to admit but he soon put it behind him. There were other routes into the career he had chosen.

MOTHER AND SON

While Alec went about getting an education, Hulda concentrated on providing a settled home life. Construction of 'Barton' and the neighbouring group of houses had been completed only in February 1920 so it was a relatively new property when Hulda and Alec moved there in early 1925. Photographs show it to be right on the edge of the conurbation with a long garden behind backing onto surrounding fields. Though their circumstances were much reduced since leaving Smyrna, Hulda tried to create a similar atmosphere on a less grand scale in their new home. One of the traditions she revived was picnics. She would organise groups of friends, some from the 'exile' community, others their new neighbours, on trips to local beauty spots such as Richmond Park and

Box Hill. In 1969 one of these neighbours wrote to Alec to congratulate him on his knighthood:

> Dear Alec, Glancing through today's Honours List your name stands out – reminding me of the days when we were all very young – and I would like to add my congratulations to the many you will be receiving. It seems wrong to ask someone who has led such a creative and forward looking life to cast their mind back some 40 years or so! But, should you do so, can you recall Marjorie and Gwen Harrison? ... Only recently Marjorie and I were talking of you and your wonderful Mother who was so good to us and the gay parties and picnics she organised at your home in Purley. Is she with you? And if so please remember us very kindly to her.

Hulda Issigonis had been faced with a daunting set of challenges within a very short space of time: forced to leave her birthplace in the worst possible circumstances, deprived of a husband she was deeply attached to, settling in a country she had never visited whose first language was not her own, securing her beloved son's future during a period of great economic depression. The way she coped with all this shows her strength of character but there was more to Hulda than bossiness and will-power. Her nature was optimistic and fun-loving and one of her favourite sayings was 'every age has its pleasures'. By 1925, when their difficulties at last seemed to be behind them, she was only 40 years old and still a very handsome woman, five-and-a-half feet tall with intense grey eyes and a lively, extrovert character. On her slim wrists she wore beautifully crafted Turkish half-bracelets made of twisted gold which had to be slid onto the arm like an amulet. Her adventurous spirit was the driving force behind several motoring tours to the Continent. Issigonis would claim that the Singer had clocked up a magnificent 80,000 miles before it was replaced in 1928. Hulda liked to enjoy herself and to give pleasure to other people. She was vivacious, witty and noisy; she would shout querulously at the whistling kettle 'shut up, shut up, I'm coming' before sweeping into the kitchen to silence it; she would sit and thump away at the piano in the sitting room; she organised lively parties and picnics for the neighbourhood. In these early years it was she and not her son who was the leading personality in the Issigonis household. May Ransome recalled, 'when she was with us she was more outstanding than Alec, she took up people's attention more'.

Hulda never lost her strong 'foreign' accent, which contrasted vividly with the rather aristocratic tones of her gentleman-son. Though she had grown up speaking German, those who remember her describe her accent as more Mediterranean than German, stretching out the vowels in a tone that was high-pitched rather than guttural but nevertheless strident and sing-song, drifting upwards at the end of sentences. She matched her vocal dexterity with her hand movements – and when the moving hand was also holding a cigarette, which it usually was, this could be very exciting indeed. She was similarly uninhibited when it came to people she did not like. It was not anything that she said, but rather the adoption of a hard, cold expression which created an atmosphere that was almost tangible. This was something mother and son shared. They were quick in their judgements and made no attempt to tolerate people they did not find congenial or interesting. May Ransome would often say in despair of their dismissal of some unfortunate acquaintance for no obvious cause: 'The Issigonises – there's no reasoning with them!'

In contrast to his extrovert mother Alec remained a reserved youth who in many ways seems to have been more like the father that he himself would later describe as 'stand-offish'. He could be remote and often moody, yet at other times he would be full of fun. By now he had lost the plump, boyish look evident in the Smyrna photographs and was a lanky young man of almost five feet eleven inches tall. His feet and hands were disproportionately large and, like his mother, he would wave his hands about in a Mediterranean manner when in conversation. His face was thin, gaunt and rough and his expression was commonly one of intense concentration. This was particularly evident when indulging in his daily habit of solving the *Daily Telegraph* crossword puzzle. He took up this habit early in life, but he was not interested in the highbrow version with its cryptic clues; instead he did the 'Quick' crossword which he set himself a target of ten minutes to complete. He also possessed an underlying eccentricity and enjoyed making outrageous statements to provoke a reaction, characteristics which would become more pronounced as he grew older.

In the space of a few years the large family network that had once supported their emotional and social lives had dwindled to just Hulda, Hetty and their four children and of course this deepened their mutual dependence. It has been suggested that Hulda was a possessive mother who hindered her son by putting a brake on his emotional life and discouraging any women who might take an interest in him. This is not entirely borne out by letters such as the one from Gwen Harrison quoted above, or the presence of a number of young women apparently on friendly terms with both mother and son in the photographs of Barton at this period. His personal photograph albums are littered with pictures of girls with nicknames such as 'Baby', 'Noggs', 'Gee-Gee' and 'Podge' larking around with both Alec and his mother.

Nevertheless the attachment between mother and son was extremely strong and it was more than just the past that bound them together. They shared a distinct set of social attitudes and ambitions which they had carried with them from their life in Smyrna. They were also united in their belief in Alec's ability and in their determination that he should fulfil his potential and nothing was to be allowed to stand in the way of that.

MESSING AROUND WITH CARS

It was natural that their social life should be centred around Hulda's friends and family so a great deal of time was spent with the Walkers and other Smyrna exiles. At the same time Alec was beginning to develop interests of his own and his attention was soon attracted by motor sport.

As soon as motor cars were invented, people started using them to race each other. At first the sport was dominated by serious racers who risked their lives on the open roads of Europe, often financed by manufacturers looking for ways to publicise their products. The dangers of road racing were quickly demonstrated as both drivers and spectators were killed with a frequency which was considered unacceptable in England, where the pastime was illegal. English followers of the sport therefore had to find an alternative and as a result a dedicated circuit was set up at Brooklands near Weybridge in Surrey in 1907. Here, alongside straightforward first-to-the-finish motor races, another type of competition began to develop which tested the limits of not just the driver but also the machine. Brooklands became famous for a section of banking which formed part of the racing circuit of 3.75 miles, but it also incorporated a challenging 'test hill'. The annual diary soon included events such as reliability and speed trials, hill-starts, or braking and acceleration tests.

In April 1925, shortly after the move to Overhill Road, Alec joined the Junior Car Club (JCC) London region which would have cost him 25 shillings, presumably funded by his ten shillings a week pocket money since he had only just started his career as a student. The JCC had been

founded in October 1912 by a band of enthusiasts who wanted to promote the development of what they christened the 'light car', a vehicle
which would fit somewhere between the tricar – which was often no
more than a glorified motorcycle – and the large and expensive autocar
which was still out of the financial reach of most people. Thus he became
involved in the movement to promote small, affordable cars at an early
period in his life. His prime motive in joining at this particular time
seems to have been to gain eligibility for the club's first High Speed
Reliability Trial which was held on 2 May at Brooklands. It was called
'high speed' because this was the first reliability trial run in Britain with a
scheduled speed above 20 mph. It took place over a distance of 100 miles
round the Brooklands circuit.

The car which Alec entered for this event was the rather unlikely
Singer saloon, one of eleven starters in Class A which covered cars up to
1100 cc with an average speed of 33 mph. Four scrutineers checked that
cars were standard production models and did not vary from the owner's
handbook, which was the most extensive document available about the
maintenance of the car in the period before workshop manuals. Richard
Twelvetrees, one of the excited participants, described his experience in a
rather breathy boys-own manner to the *JCC Gazette* in 1925:

> I thought I knew something about chassis inspection – but I am sure
> those scrutineers would have discovered if the painters had put the
> paint on the wrong side out. Anyhow they did their long and tiring
> job to the satisfaction of everyone, except those who were unwise
> enough to attempt to get away with anything non-standard.

The event was not supposed to be a race but, as Twelvetrees reported,
thanks to the activities of the course bookmaker 'Long Tom', some of the
competitors got a little carried away:

> Whether it was the businesslike appearance of the Super-Sports Alvis
> or the super-yellow jerseys of its occupants, it is hard to say, but Long
> Tom suddenly dropped our starting price from 'eights' to 'threes'. As
> things turned out eventually, however, it made no difference at all.
> Indeed, it was largely due to the sporting instincts of Long Tom that a
> perfectly respectable lot of Club members were induced to turn a per-
> fectly respectable reliability trial into a sort of race, but we all sincerely

hope the club officials will take no exception to this entirely unpremeditated circumstance.

Perhaps this explains Alec's uncharacteristic behaviour in his first event. After losing eight places straight away when the rather workaday Singer sailed majestically but slowly off the start line, he gripped the wheel, slammed his foot down and valiantly built up as much momentum as the little saloon could muster. He was just getting into his stride on lap eight when he foolishly tried to make up some of the lost places by lunging past a fellow competitor in a no-overtaking area. Without hesitation a marshal thrust his flag into the air and he was out of the competition, ignominiously disqualified. Did mother know that her nineteen-year-old son had sneaked off with the family saloon to thrash it round a racing circuit? What did she say when he got home?

After this little indulgence Alec settled down to being a student, not having the time or the money to actively participate in his new hobby. All the same he continued to join in the JCC's social events which included dinners, dances, treasure hunts and days out at Croydon airport. But though he didn't enter any more trials during his time at college he did begin his first experiment in tinkering with cars. 'Salome', despite her excursion to Brooklands, was definitely family transport and not available for his engineering experiments. So with the financial assistance of Gerald Walker he acquired an old cyclecar which he christened 'Susie'. He spent many hours working on this car in the back garden of the Purley bungalow, where, like 'Salome', she was lavishly photographed from every angle.

Alec's photographs tell us most of what we know about this car. Superficially it looks like a very unusual machine but in fact it can be identified as a perfectly standard Bleriot Whippet, one of a generation of cyclecars which had some popularity in the 1920s. Cyclecars were generally of very lightweight construction, often with two-cylinder air-cooled engines, and were intended to provide a cheap and practical form of transport for those who could not afford a 'proper' car. Eventually they succumbed to the competition of 'real' small cars such as the Austin Seven and original Morris Minor. There is therefore a certain neatness in the idea that Alec should use one for his first experiments in engineering.

The Bleriot Whippet was built by the Air Navigation and Engineering Company at their factory in Addlestone, Surrey, which was quite

close to the Brooklands circuit. The design underwent various modifications between 1920 and 1927. The company optimistically began with
quite a high production run but the vehicle was so difficult to drive that
it did not endear itself to its owners. Alec's car was one of the earliest
models with a 998 cc V-twin Blackburne engine of 8 hp (RAC rating)
which drove through an infinitely variable transmission via a belt drive to
a solid rear axle. Suspension at each end was by quarter elliptical springs
mounted on top of the wooden chassis side members. There are records
of these cars being used in competition at Brooklands in the very early
1920s but with little success. There is no record of Alec ever entering
'Susie' in any competition or event.

By the time Alec and Gerry acquired the car around 1927 this model
was seriously out of date as the later ones had moved to shaft drive. They
were probably able to pick it up very cheaply with the objective of seeing
what Alec could do to improve it. The photographs show he made no
mechanical changes to the chassis and his main effort seems to have gone
into providing it with a sporting body style. What is probably the earliest
surviving Issigonis sketch appears on the back of one of these photographs, a fanciful body design that echoes the sportier cars of the era. The
car was completed and registered with a rather less ambitious body made
of aluminium rather than the original wooden structure and there are
pictures of it with Gerry at the wheel and Hulda in the passenger seat
despite the fact that neither of them could drive. Also helping him was
one of his neighbours, Peggy Willoughby, who appears in some of the
photographs with 'Susie' and many years afterwards wrote to Alec asking
if he remembered his 'first apprentice'.

The exercise taught him some lessons. He later jokingly claimed that
it was 'my first transverse engine', which is true in the sense that the V-
twin was mounted longitudinally in the chassis so that the crankshaft was
parallel to the rear axle for ease of transmission design. It was not, however, Alec's arrangement – it was that of Mr George Herbert James of
Shrewsbury who designed the car. Similarly, it could be said that the
Whippet was his first acquaintance with something else which was to
interest him in his later years, a gearless car.

GETTING A JOB

By the time Alec finished his college career the British motor industry
was well established and there were hundreds of firms in operation in this

field. From its inception, the heart of the industry had always been in the West Midlands and all the biggest manufacturers – names such as Daimler, Humber, Standard, Singer, Austin, Wolseley, Riley and Rover – were concentrated around Birmingham and Coventry. There were nevertheless some significant manufacturers in other regions. Ford, for example, first established themselves in Manchester and then moved to Dagenham in Essex in 1931, Vauxhall was based in Luton and William Morris set himself up at Cowley near Oxford. There were several smaller manufacturers too such as Rolls-Royce who operated from Derby, Bentley based in Cricklewood, London, and Jowett of Bradford. Feeding off the car manufacturers were thousands of other firms. Coachbuilders, repair shops, parts suppliers, service garages, petrol stations, dealers and distributors sprang up all over the country to supply and service the trade. The Automobile Association (AA) and the Royal Automobile Club (RAC) promoted the interests of motorists. The Society of Motor Manufacturers and Traders (SMMT) championed the cause of the industry as a whole. In the space of little over 30 years motor vehicles had driven horses off the road and the motor industry had become one of Britain's crucial areas of economic growth.

Like the key moments in most people's lives, Alec's entry into the motor industry was a result of the opportunities which came his way rather than any deliberate career plan. He had shown a keen interest in all types of mechanical objects throughout his childhood. He grew up watching the engineering of boats, he was fascinated by aeroplanes before he ever saw a motor car and his first job was in the railway yard at Smyrna. During his college career, however, he had begun to gravitate towards motor cars, joining the JCC, spending time at Brooklands and experimenting on 'Susie'. It was clear to Alec from an early stage that this young but flourishing industry could present him with an excellent opportunity. With this in mind, he began to attend evening lectures held by the Institution of Automotive Engineers and when the time came to look for a job it was through their Secretary that he made contact with Edward Gillett.

Gillett ran a small engineering firm from his premises at 66 Victoria Street in London where he was working on the 'freewheel' concept, a mechanism which worked much like the freewheel on a bicycle by disengaging the drive from the driven wheels. The advantages of this were two-fold. First it provided fuel economy. Second, it allowed 'clutchless' gear changing. The conventional gearbox of the time required a great deal of skill and co-ordination to use because of the need to 'double-declutch'. There was naturally a great deal of interest in any device which would make the job easier. The disadvantage was that while a car was 'freewheeling' there was no engine-braking. As yet, the brake linings fitted on cars were unreliable as a method of slowing a car down so the experience of hurtling down a steep hill in a vehicle with its drive disengaged was one which required strong nerve on the part of the driver.

Not only was Alec the only draughtsman on the project, he was also the principal salesman, which must have been character-forming for someone of his rather reserved temperament. He did achieve some successes. He persuaded the American firm of Chrysler to take out a licence to manufacture Gillett's design, while at home the Rover Company incorporated it into the 1933 Rover Ten Special saloon. The car was introduced at the Earls Court Motor Show in October 1932 where the concept was promoted in a special brochure emblazoned with the title 'Freewheeling':

> For 1933 Rover offers the motorist a new experience in luxurious road travel – Freewheeling made optional – an experience that once tried will prove so fascinating that the ordinary type of fixed transmission becomes merely a memory. In its operation it reproduces on a much larger scale the joys you knew with your first freewheeled cycle and just as personal effort is saved on the cycle so is there a saving of engine effort in the car with the resultant elimination of unnecessary wear. The progress of the Rover Car with the freewheel can only be compared to gliding, the driving force being non-apparent. Gear changing with the Rover Special 4-speed Easy-free Gearbox and freewheel is simple, positive and noiseless, whilst the use of the clutch after starting is rendered unnecessary. Gone are the fears of crashing, and no more will it be necessary to master the operation of double de-clutching.

Though Issigonis would later make it sound as if he spent only a brief and insignificant period working for Edward Gillett, in fact this early part of his career lasted for six years. It gave him no opportunity to indulge his ambitions as an engineer but it taught him something about 'selling' a concept to sceptical businessmen. Just as significantly, although his wage would not have been large, the job marked his transition from a young boy dependent on his mother's limited finances to an independent young man making a contribution to the family income.

AUSTIN SEVENS ON THE SCENE

1928 was a pivotal year for Alec, the year he left Battersea Polytechnic and became a working man. Though he kept up his interest in motor competition, 'Susie' had never been a contender for the track and he had not entered any event since 1925. Now he was a wage-earner he could afford to take up his hobby in earnest by equipping himself properly for the first time. In the 1970s he told journalist Courtenay Edwards:

> As a young man I did yearn for a 2.3 Bugatti in near racing trim, that is to say the wheels would only be covered by small mud-guards because it is so nice to see them going round when you are driving.

Needless to say this was well beyond his budget. Instead, he followed the example of many other young men with the same interests by acquiring an Austin Seven. This was far more promising raw material than the Bleriot Whippet. Issigonis later reckoned he had 'lived on bread and cheese lunches' to afford this first Austin Seven but he also got substantial help from his indulgent mother who sold one of her valuable rings to help finance the purchase. This became a joke within the family who nicknamed Alec's new plaything 'the diamond ring car'. It was a standard Austin Seven which was originally registered in Norwich in early 1928 with the number VG 620.

It is very fitting that the inventor of the modern small car should have begun by experimenting with its two predecessors, the cyclecar and the Austin Seven. What was so important about the Austin Seven? Well, in many ways it foreshadowed the Mini itself, being the first really practical small car, built for family use to provide cheap and enjoyable motoring. It had other attributes too which helped it to become a leading competition vehicle, beloved by the amateur motor racing enthusiast throughout the 1920s and 1930s. It was not too expensive, there was a plentiful supply, it was easy to work on, and many of its engineering features – such as its excellent suspension and lightweight engine – meant it was also very competitive.

Just when it became possible to devote more energy to his favourite pastime, Alec acquired a new friend who shared his interest in adapting cars for competition. His name was Peter Ransome and he had recently been introduced to May Walker by Maudie Elliott at the Purley tennis club. Born in 1909, Peter had been adopted as a baby by John and Helen Ransome, who would also have three daughters of their own, one older and two younger than him. The family had moved to Purley in 1920 following the death of John Ransome from blood poisoning and, at the time of his meeting with May, Peter was a civil engineer by profession, working for the Metropolitan Water Board at Teddington. They began a lengthy courtship which continued until their marriage in 1933 but a considerable amount of this time was in fact spent with May's cousin Alec. The two men worked together on their cars for many hours in the spacious back garden at Overhill Road which began to take on the aspect of an outdoor garage.

In March 1929, Alec made his first competition appearance since his adventure in the Singer when he entered the JCC's second Half Day Trial event. The entry fee was seven shillings and sixpence and entrants could look forward to an evening dance as well as a day's sport. This time the result was more creditable and he got a first class award, though the Austin Seven which he drove was not the 'diamond ring' car. Three months later he attended the JCC 'Members' Day' which consisted of an exciting variety of events including the 'To and Fro Race' – described by *Light Car and Cyclecar* as 'just as alarming to the spectators as to the racers'; exercises in accelerating, stopping and starting; a relay race; a driving skills test; a one lap handicap; and the 'Test-hill Sweepstake'. Alec, with Peter Ransome as his riding mechanic, chose to take part in the High Speed Trial and they were rewarded with a gold medal in the 850 cc class for the feat of exceeding the set speed of 32 mph by 20 per cent. Having made such a promising start the two friends entered more Brooklands events during 1930 and continued to win medals, though it has to be said these awards do not seem to have been that difficult to come by. Soon they branched out to different venues, most notably the Shelsley Walsh hill-climb which we will look at shortly.

Hulda seems to have been happy to let her son get on with what would appear to have been his major recreation. She would not have disapproved of either the technical knowledge he was gaining or the social circles his interest in racing brought him into contact with. As well as the chance to test their own engineering and driving skills, places like

Brooklands and Shelsley Walsh offered other opportunities to young men like Alec and Peter. The most obvious benefit was the chance to see the best racing drivers of the day along with their superior machinery. In its earliest days, motor racing was less structured than it would later become and there were a limited number of circuits and courses available on which to compete. It was therefore common practice to stage professional as well as amateur races at the same locations (though on different days) and Issigonis was as eager a spectator at the former as he was a participant in the latter.

The ambience of the paddock also offered social opportunities. The JCC was very much a gentleman's club and it was necessary to have a certain level of connections even to join because new members had to be proposed and seconded by existing members of the club or alternatively provide a reference. This is reflected in its magazine which is both snobby and laddish – '... the Ladies are grumbling because the police limit of 10 minutes for parking in one-way streets does not give sufficient time to purchase a hat or frock' was a typical comment. John Dugdale was a young reporter on *The Autocar* in the 1930s and an enthusiastic participant in the amateur racing scene. He later gave this account of Brooklands in its heyday:

> Brooklands was a whole lot of fun in the thirties. Only about 30 miles south-west of London, the old track provided a wonderful meeting place for car enthusiasts and their girls. Rich and impoverished sports mingled. Glamorous aces like Tim Birkin, Malcolm Campbell, Kaye Don, John Cobb, Oliver Bertram and Whitney Straight all held the outer circuit record from time to time. They attracted a fashionable crowd including the Royal family – especially Prince George – and some of the horse racing set led by George Duller who was both a Bentley team member and a champion hurdle jockey. Actresses from London theatre were there, well dressed and attractive, and social people like the Dunfee brothers – Jack and Clive. The latter, who married Jane Baxter, a popular young West End star, was tragically killed in 1932 when his Bentley went over the banking.

Motor sport venues were by no means a social melting pot. Despite the advent of the Austin Seven, motor cars were still an expensive pastime. Talented racing drivers were always likely to find some motor manufacturer anxious to shine by hiring their services. In the amateur scene, how-ever, it was the moneyed classes who were likely to be able to afford the most impressive machines, along with the time to practise using them. Alec and his mother no longer enjoyed the social position that they had occu-pied in Smyrna but his interest in racing helped to put him back on the fringes of this world and he seems to have possessed some skill as a social climber. Despite his very un-English lineage and background, he was very quickly able to take on the mantle of an English gentleman with enough confidence to gain a high level of acceptance in motor racing circles. He could not yet afford the Bugatti but he began to gather a group of friends which would steadily expand throughout his competition career which stretched from 1928 to 1950, briefly interrupted by the Second World War. Throughout this period he became friends with people like David and Joe Fry, whose family were prosperous chocolate manufacturers in the Bristol area; Rupert Instone whose family had invested in the first British motor factory and owned one of the earliest British commercial airlines; Dennis Poore who became a senior executive with Manganese Bronze; John Cooper who would become a Formula One team owner; and Peter Ustinov the well-known actor whom he met at a race club dinner.

This did not quite gain him acceptance to the true upper classes. This is well illustrated by a letter he received in 1969 from 'Freddy Richmond', otherwise known as the Duke of Richmond, congratulating him on his knighthood. The letter looked back to these days and enclosed a picture of the starting line at Brooklands for the JCC High Speed Trial of 1929, where the two men's cars sat side by side on the start line. Though Freddy Richmond seems happy to associate himself with the famous designer in retrospect, it seems clear from the tone of the letter that this was far from the case at the time:

Dear Alex – I really must add my hoorah's to all those you will be get-ting on this great news of your 'not-a-moment-too-soon' honour. The fact that we have only met on the most rare occasions, if that, fails to convince me that we are not in equal fact very old acquaintances at the very least! I venture to give proof of this by enclosing a photo-graph I have just come across of my first event at Brooklands. I think it was 1929. The JCC High Speed Trial. Your Austin was No 8, next to me and Jackson in the MG. What loads of fun it all was to be sure, and what a lot of fuel has flowed through the pipes since then.

SERIOUS COMPETITION

Though he enjoyed the ambience of the Brooklands paddock, Alec took his chosen hobby extremely seriously, applying himself with considerable dedication. Even at this stage in his life he was capable of an intense focus on what might seem frivolous to an uninformed outside observer and he expended a great deal of energy on the technical performance he could get out of his cars. There was a simple reason for this. As a fairly lowly employee of Edward Gillett, he had very little scope for his engineering ambitions so he channelled them into his private projects and these happened to dovetail neatly with his social life which was centred on motor competition. He told journalist and friend Piero Casucci in later life: 'Don't forget I come from a racing background. You know I love racing cars and sports cars. My idea of a car that handles properly is a car that has wheels on each corner.'

The outings to Brooklands had produced some encouraging results and on this basis Alec decided to add a second car to his collection. In 1930 he bought a new Austin Seven Sports, registered under the number GH 1645 and bright yellow in colour. The sporty model was more expensive than the basic version, costing around £270, but with this car he could set his sights on more ambitious events. He scored his first success almost straight away when he won a silver medal at the 1930 Kent and Sussex Light Car Club Trials at Race Hill, Lewes, which consisted of a 700-yard sprint from a standing start. His performance in the same event in 1931 was even more impressive. Not only did he secure another silver medal, he also managed to come third out of 30 starters with a time of 25.2 seconds. The importance of this achievement is clear only if set against the quality of vehicles and drivers against which he was competing. First place was won by Dick Nash driving a Frazer Nash known as 'the Terror'. *Light Car and Cyclecar* excitedly described how he 'broke the speed trials record into little bits' by reducing it from 20 seconds to 18.8 seconds. Second place was taken by a 1.5-litre Bugatti driven by Lemon Burton.

It was the famous hill-climb at Shelsley Walsh, however, which was to be the main arena for his adventures with Austin Sevens and he competed with various supercharged versions between 1930 and 1935. Shelsley is the oldest hill-climb course in Britain and though the track is fairly short at 1,000 yards, its steep ascent and sharp corners offer a serious motoring challenge. Like Brooklands, a mixture of professional and amateur events were held there and even the most skilful professional drivers regarded the course as a particular challenge, as Raymond Mays explained in his foreword to a history of the event in 1945:

After eighteen years as a racing-driver during which time it has been my good fortune to compete on numerous road and track courses in two continents, I have yet to discover an event demanding a more exacting technique, or imposing a harder physical and mental strain, than Shelsley. But surely, it may be argued, not much can happen in a thousand yards? Can't it! *Everything* can happen in a thousand yards – that particular thousand. A 37.37 secs. Shelsley climb is a little motoring life-time, standing in its own grounds. It is, indeed, the very shortness of the tortuous hill, with its four major bends and other lesser ones, that makes it the acid test of driver and car … You must drive as you read a book – with your mind on the sentence ahead of the one that is coming out of your mouth. Mentally you are grappling with as-yet unborn broadsides at the Crossing before your slide through Kennel Bend has dissipated itself in a stench of scorching tyre tread and burnt alcohol. While the car is airborne, and straddling the road after striking the Concrete Patch, a busy little piece of your mind hustles on ahead, and goes through an unseen dress rehearsal of the geometric slide-correct-and-slide-again routine demanded by the Esses. Finally, as you approach the FINISH line, with your foot on the floor and three hundred horse-power howling in full chorus, a little voice with an eye to the immediate future keeps saying 'Now look Mays, do we ease 'er a bit and perhaps chuck the record away, or do we keep this hoof plastered down and chance pushing a hole through the hedge out beyond yonder greensward?' Echo (Wordsworth's faery friend you remember) uncharacteristically doesn't answer. If he had time he would probably counsel a rapid and craven unplastering of the right foot. As it is, not knowing what is good for it, the foot stays jammed down, the revs. rise in a screaming cadence to sixty-five hundred – that means 110 m.p.h. in top gear – and thanks to the men who designed these modern brakes, we don't prang any holes in the hedgerow after all. But only just.

Raymond Mays' account is that of a driver not an engineer but it reminds us that a considerable amount of driving skill was required to tackle a course like Shelsley Walsh. Alec was and remained throughout his life an enthusiastic driver as well as a designer. Perhaps it was this which helped him to create vehicles like the Morris Minor and the Mini which were, above all else, a pleasure to drive.

The layout of a hill–climb track dictated that once participants had completed the course by reaching the top of the hill, they had to wait until all the other competitors had finished their attempts before they could return to the bottom and try again. Thus a day's sport would usually consist of two practice runs in the morning and two competitive runs against the clock in the afternoon. It is possible to chart the progress made by Alec and Peter at Shelsley Walsh between 1930 and 1935 by examining a number of surviving photographs alongside the records preserved by the Midland Automobile Club. In 1930 they brought the brand new supercharged Austin Seven Sports and did two respectable runs of 60.0 and 60.2 seconds. The first run was the fastest in its class, the second was beaten only by another Austin Seven. This was very encouraging and over the next year Alec carried out some extensive experiments to improve the car. First he lowered the suspension to provide a better centre of gravity which would have taught him the effect of different configurations on the handling of a car. Then he turned his attention to the bodywork in an attempt to improve the car's aerodynamics. The revised car was ready to make its appearance in 1931. Extra modifications were made on competition day. A large part of the exhaust, including the silencer, was removed with the intention of making it noisier and, presumably, marginally faster. He must therefore have been disappointed when he put in a very uncompetitive time, a dismal 76.4 seconds which was by far the slowest time in his class on that run, over 20 seconds behind the fastest time, set by an MG Midget.

This disastrous run seems to have prompted a rethink. Issigonis and Ransome returned in June 1932 with the 'diamond ring' car instead of the Austin Seven Sports. There is a photograph of the two friends working together on this vehicle in the back garden at Overhill Road. The steering wheel has been lowered, a supercharger fitted, and a racing type of 'hoop' bulkhead installed in front of the pedals to provide stiffness. The car was equipped with a standard five-gallon petrol tank which was required for driving to and from meetings as they did not use a trailer. The emphasis of this work was not on reducing drag as with the Austin Seven Sports, but on weight reduction. On the day, Alec ran the car with most of the bodywork removed. This was a well-known ploy which produced maximum lightness and increased the power to weight ratio, since the body provided a disproportionate amount of the weight of the overall car. The result was a rewarding 55 seconds which compared very favourably with the fastest time of 49.2 seconds recorded by an MG Midget and another Austin Seven.

Alec decided to apply the lessons learned from the 'diamond ring' car back to the Austin Seven Sports which reappeared in June 1934. This time the streamlining which had proved so unsuccessful in 1931 had been replaced with a new low suspension combined with considerable efforts at weight reduction. Though he was by no means the fastest on the day, Alec nevertheless put in his best times ever in this car, achieving 51.1 and 52.1 seconds.

Superficially these endeavours illustrate a young man and his best friend enjoying themselves by experimenting with the wonderful raw material of the Austin Seven and driving round various competitive events to try out the results. At a deeper level, Alec Issigonis was beginning to train himself to think like a designer. He had begun his working life with Edward Gillett as a draughtsman and engineer but it was by no means clear at this stage that his future lay in design. It was in his hobby and not his working life that he was developing the skills he would need. He makes alterations to his cars for a specific purpose, asking 'what will happen if I do this or that?' then tests them out in competition and reacts to the results. He begins by concentrating on styling, trying to create an aesthetic shape that will make his car distinct from other people's, but then moves on to the underlying element of suspension, finally abandoning style for performance. At this stage he shows no interest in engine design.

The Shelsley Walsh outings provide us with an interesting snapshot of the way Issigonis and his friend Peter Ransome collaborated, running the two cars available to them in different configurations and apparently applying a different design approach to each car. Though they worked on the cars together, Alec appears to have been the source of the ideas. He was also the only one who competed, and this could be interpreted as being the equivalent of conducting his own test programme on the results. In this way their partnership provides a foretaste of his future working methods, with Alec firmly in charge of the direction in which the cars were developed while Ransome was confined to practical help in putting these ideas into practice.

A PROPER JOB — HUMBER LTD

For six years Alec travelled around promoting Edward Gillett's version of the freewheel concept, though there were a number of other firms also working on the idea. In his capacity as salesman rather than draughtsman he often travelled up to the heart of the British motor industry in Coventry using premises loaned to Gillett by the local engineering firm Coventry Climax to run demonstration cars for potential customers. As we have seen, he persuaded Rover to adopt the concept, but Humber took more interest in the young salesman himself. In 1934 their Chief Engineer, Jock Wishart, offered him a job as a junior draughtsman at the firm's Coventry works. From Alec's point of view the timing could not have been better. Not long afterwards the freewheel concept was overtaken by the synchromesh gearbox, developed by General Motors, and Gillett's firm collapsed. More importantly, Britain's flourishing car industry was by now entrenched in the Midlands and this was the right place to be to further his career.

The 1930s was not generally a happy time for British industry, which was struggling to cope with the worldwide economic depression triggered by the collapse of the American stock market following the Wall Street crash of 1929. The motor industry was one sector which managed to come through the crisis in relatively good shape, mainly because, unlike more well-established heavy engineering industries, it was able to adapt to the changing circumstances. Though many of the smaller firms did indeed go under, the effect was to make the 1930s a period of consolidation through merger, leading to a leaner but more efficient set of companies. Not only were many of the smaller manufacturers absorbed by the bigger ones, but many of the peripheral engineering and coachbuilding firms also disappeared into the mainstream industry. By 1939 the industry was dominated by a much smaller collection of companies which represented a fusion of different marques and activities. The major players were the Nuffield Organisation which was centred on Morris Motors in Oxford and now included the MG, Riley and Wolseley marques; the Austin Motor Company and its subsidiaries based at Longbridge in Birmingham; the British incarnation of the American Ford Motor Company which was based in Dagenham, Essex; and the Rootes Group based in Coventry which was run by the Rootes brothers, William and Reginald. They had begun their careers as dealers and by 1930 had taken control of Humber and Hillman, adding Sunbeam and Talbot to their stable within a few years. Against the trend, these firms saw an increase in their business which was halted only by the outbreak of another world war. As a result the industry's output in 1935 was almost double that of 1926 and Britain had overtaken France as Europe's leading motor manufacturer.

Moving to a job at Humber was to be the end of Alec's apprenticeship – which could be said to have begun at the railway yard in Smyrna – and the beginning of his proper career in the motor industry. He was now part of a serious design team in the drawing office of a mainstream motor manufacturing company and he began to form relationships with people who would be friends and colleagues for the rest of his life. His first task was to draw out suspension systems and already he was showing independence of mind, being critical of the standard designs he was given to work on. Since he spent so much of his spare time messing around with the suspensions of his own racing cars he considered himself enough of an expert to profess himself bored with the beam axles used on Rootes cars. The Hillman Company had brought out the Hillman Minx in 1932 which was challenging the Austin and Morris domination of the medium-sized car market. Alec made friends with another young engineer called Clapham and the two of them managed to persuade their boss to let them build an independent front suspension system for the Minx. Together they designed the necessary parts, had them made in the experimental shop and fitted them onto the car. Unfortunately they assembled it with the steering reversed, an oversight which was spotted by the chief experimental engineer when they attempted to take the car out for a trial run down the works drive. They were ordered back to the workshop to sort the problem out but eventually the car ran very creditably. Issigonis, however, grumbled because he was not allowed to use leaf springs as he wanted. Coil springs were required for the simple reason that the Rootes Group owned a subsidiary which manufactured them but the young engineer did not like his creativity to be confined by practicalities.

The car never progressed beyond prototype stage. It is nevertheless the first example we have of Issigonis' ability to persuade his superiors that he should be allowed to undertake innovative projects which were beyond his apparent rank and experience within the company. His initiative seems to have been noticed because soon afterwards he was assigned to the team of Bill Heynes, head of Humber's small technical department, to work on an independent front suspension for the Humber Hawk. This was a new idea which was being developed in America by General Motors. British manufacturers were notoriously conservative when it came to engineering experimentation and the standard design of the time was the rigid beam axle which Alec had originally been put to work on. The Rootes brothers, however, had begun life as car dealers rather than manufacturers and they were perhaps more attuned to what might sell a car than some of their rivals. The idea of superior suspension, and therefore a more comfortable ride, interested them and they asked their design department to work on it. As a result, Issigonis found himself working on the team which produced the 'Evenkeel' system, which used a transverse leaf spring at the bottom with wishbone links at the top and finally found its way onto a series of 1936 Humber models which were among the earliest mass-produced British cars to incorporate independent front suspension.

Bill Heynes left Humber in 1935 to work for SS Cars, which at the time was designing a model named 'Jaguar', launched in 1936. The company's name was derived from the initials of its parent company 'Swallow Sidecars' but following the Second World War this acronym had taken on rather unfortunate connotations. The firm therefore decided to adopt the Jaguar marque name instead. Bill Heynes would rise to become Jaguar's Chief Engineer and his friendship with Issigonis would be maintained throughout both their careers.

New Friendships and New Projects

The job at Humber signalled the proper start to Alec's career in the motor industry and the move to Coventry was also the final step towards creating a personal life away from the old Smyrna associations which had surrounded the household at Overhill Road in Purley.

It was Hetty who moved on first when, in 1932, she bought a plot of land about ten miles south-west of Purley in a new development at Kingswood, Surrey. Here, she employed a local builder to construct a house which was given the name 'Rustlings'. Meanwhile her children were striking out on their own. Gerry's career on the London Underground was progressing well and in time he rose to a senior post. Following his marriage he moved to nearby Chipstead and became absorbed in his own family life when twins arrived in 1937. Tony had attended prep school at Swanbourne and then gone on to public school at Cranleigh. In September 1933 he became an apprentice at the Riley Works in Coventry where he stayed until December 1934. Though he enjoyed his time at Riley and showed a great deal of aptitude for engineering, Hetty felt that family interests would be better served if he followed a different course in life. During 1935 he left England to become a tea planter in Ceylon, a career he pursued till retirement apart from the period during the Second World War when he served as an officer with the Gurkha Regiment in the Eighth Army in North Africa.

Most significant for Alec, however, was the date of 26 August 1933 when May Walker and Peter Ransome were finally married from the new house in Kingswood. Alec was Peter's best man while Ethel Heginbotham acted as May's chief bridesmaid. On the back of the marriage certificate the wedding guests wrote optimistically 'the undersigned wish GOOD LUCK to the bride and bridegroom' and signed their names underneath. For a brief period the couple stayed with Hetty at Kingswood, but Peter was an ambitious man. In the harsh economic climate of the 1930s he decided there were better prospects in taking a well-paid post as an irrigation engineer for the Crown Colonies. Peter and May sailed for Malaya in 1934 and two of the key companions of Alec's early life in England disappeared from his life for the foreseeable future.

By the time this happened the Issigonises had left Purley so that Alec could take up his job at Humber. Initially he went up to Coventry on his own, staying at a boarding house in Eaton Road just round the corner from the railway station. The landlords were a Mr and Mrs Ayres and the rent was 30 shillings a week, which included breakfast, lunch and high tea. His stay there, away from the watchful eye of his mother, seems to have been an enjoyable interlude. A number of his fellow boarders were also young men working in the motor industry and in the evening they would all go out for a beer or two at the 'Queen and Castle' in the nearby village of Kenilworth. It would appear that these outings could get quite boisterous and on one occasion an incident involving a bottle of tomato ketchup and a piano resulted in a temporary ban for the group of friends.

It was not long before he found a semi-detached house to rent at Rouncil Lane in Kenilworth so Hulda and the Austin Sevens could move north to join him. This house was remarkably similar in size and style to the one in Purley, once again a recently finished property built in 1932. At the front of the house, a stylish red brick arch stood in front of a recessed door which featured a fashionable circular stained glass panel. Alec was more interested in the back of the house which, like Purley, contained a long, spacious garden with a large wooden garage where he could work on his cars. For mother and son this marked a new phase in their relationship. Alec was now supporting his mother financially rather than the other way around. By moving away from Purley the two of them also left behind the Walkers and all the other Smyrna exiles and became more dependent than ever upon each other emotionally. Though they continued to regularly exchange visits with the Walkers, the link inevitably grew weaker than it had been during the years when they were living only a few streets away from each other, especially now that Peter, May and Tony had all gone abroad.

These changes allowed Alec to become more involved with his own circle, which was still dominated by his motor racing acquaintances. Through this route an important new friend slid onto Alec's horizon – George Dowson. They first met during the social outings to the Queen and Castle. Dowson was working as an engineer at English Electric in Rugby where he also had his digs. They were introduced by Rupert Instone who knew Alec through the JCC, had been to the same prep school as George and was also a regular at the Kenilworth pub.

George Dowson was not actually called George – his real name was John Miller Pendlebury Dowson. How did John become George? The answer is that in the mid-1930s someone – and the likelihood is that it was Alec – said to him, 'you're not a John you're a George', and thus he became George to his hill-climbing friends while remaining John to his family. His parents, John and Enid Dowson, ran a farm near Pershore called the Poplars and he was part of a large and affectionate family. There were two sisters, Mary or 'Babs' and Lydia or 'Biddy', and a brother named Harry. Alec quickly became almost one of the family, enjoying a warm relationship with siblings and parents alike. George's education was rather more conventional than that of his new friend and perhaps followed a pattern that Alec would have wished for himself if the opportunity had been given to him. After prep school at Dunchurch, George attended Uppingham followed by an engineering degree at Cambridge before beginning his career with English Electric. His sisters loved horses and country pursuits but George was always more mechanically minded and particularly keen on cars which is why he chose to pursue a career away from the farm.

Initially George Dowson assisted by offering his 3-litre Bentley and trailer to tow one or other of the Austin Sevens to various events. Alec, however, now had something more fundamental in mind and in George

Dowson he had found another willing partner to play a full supporting role on his most ambitious engineering project yet, the building of the innovative and beautiful Lightweight Special competition car. As in his previous partnership with Peter Ransome, Issigonis supplied the design ideas and Dowson provided the practical assistance. When describing this part of his life Alec suggested that he had already started the design when he met Dowson:

> When I moved to Coventry for the new job I entered the Austin Seven for hill climbs like Shelsley Walsh and soon discovered that the venture was not competitive, because the car had to be used for both racing and day to day running about. That made me determined to build a racing car of my own. I set about designing one based on as many parts of the original car as possible, since funds were short. In Coventry I met George Dowson, who was equally mad about racing cars. We lived in Kenilworth at that time and I had already cut wood, in this case, since the chassis of the car was made out of special plywood.

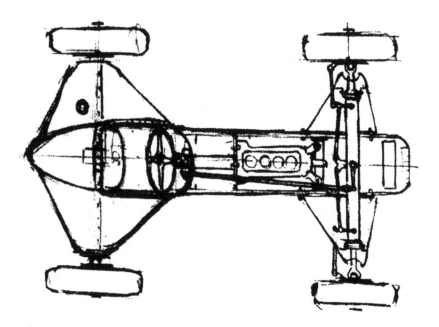

The 'Lightweight Special' was started in 1933, the first car that Issigonis designed from scratch. This 'plan' or overhead view provides an early example of the sketching technique he would later develop to work out his engineering ideas.

Their dedication was remarkable and they approached the task more like a career than a hobby, though there is no doubt that they derived intense pleasure from the enterprise:

> You might call it fun but you need to be very thorough in everything. I think I learned a lot about life in that period because I realised that here was a small project all on its own. I was the master of it; I could either win or lose simply according to what I did with the situation and thoroughness was the most important of all – not to have friends coming up and saying 'what a nice day it is'; you just roughly brushed them on one side because you did not have time for anything like that! On the site George and I had it absolutely off pat; we would not speak to one another – we had a drill.

This is an early example of his focus, his ability to cut himself off from everything and everyone outside the task which was immediately pre-occupying him. When he joined Humber, Alec was 28 years old. Though he was gradually being given more responsible design work to do, he was still just a humble draughtsman and there was no opportunity for him to be involved in the design of a complete vehicle, which was what he longed for. He therefore continued to use his private projects to further the learning experience. He later claimed that he was often reprimanded by his new boss Jock Wishart for working on drawings for the Light-weight Special in the Humber drawing office. One small 'Jackson's Technical Notebook' survives. Other than the fanciful body drawing on the back of the Bleriot Whippet photograph, these pages contain the earliest examples of Issigonis' technical sketching and it is clear he is still developing his style and technique. Mostly, the notebook consists of written notes and geometrical calculations but there is one three-dimensional sketch showing the body structure, suspension and engine compartment of his new car which is the clear precursor of his future drawing style.

In his typical eccentric manner he drew the final engineering design onto the wall of the wooden garage at Rouncil Lane where the two friends began the project in 1934, initially cannibalising parts from the Austin Seven Sports. Alec described their efforts:

> George and I worked away on the car at weekends and when I was short of funds to buy some vital part, we used to spend our time

drilling holes with hand drills into bits of the car that were finished to lighten it as much as possible. In this way both the car and we got lighter at the same time!

They built the car without any power tools or welding equipment. Every part had to be cut and formed manually, every hole to fit the hundreds of rivets had to be drilled by hand. It would eventually take them five years to complete but at its beginning they were still looking for ideas and Alec would turn to mainstream motor racing for his inspiration.

GERMANY 1935

The 1930s saw top-level motor sport become more and more professional with the introduction of a new formula for Grand Prix cars in 1934. Motor sport was by definition a dangerous occupation and sadly it was not unusual for both amateur and professional drivers, and sometimes even spectators, to be killed in high-speed accidents. In 1933, however, motor racing suffered one of its most tragic days when three drivers died in a single afternoon at the same corner on the banking at Monza. The 1934 rules were introduced to try to slow the cars down, specifying a maximum weight without fuel, oil, water or tyres of 750 kg and a minimum width of 850 mm. This accelerated the trend towards the development of cars specifically for racing and the big motor manufacturers from all over Europe began more than ever to concentrate on motor sport as an opportunity to promote the value of their marque. At the same time France, Italy and Germany were beginning to treat success on the racing track as a matter of national prestige. The Nazis had come to power in Germany in 1933 and saw participation in the new formula as an opportunity to promote the idea of German superiority at home and abroad. When manufacturers facing economic difficulty appeared reluctant to co-operate they were encouraged with subsidies. This, combined with the Nazi ability to put on a rabble-rousing show, allowed the Grosser Preis von Deutschland to steal the accolade of premier race of the season from the Grand Prix de France for the first time since Grand Prix racing had begun.

The 750 kg formula was the beginning of a set of rules which finally transformed themselves into the Formula One series which is still considered to be the top professional motor racing category. From this time the amateur and professional sides of the sport began to go their separate ways and the intermingling of the two became a thing of the past. Though it might be assumed that this would put off eager amateurs such as Alec Issigonis and George Dowson this does not seem to have been the case. One of the major side-effects was that the professional machines being constructed were becoming more impressive and sophisticated with every year that passed and motor car fanatics such as Alec and George felt nothing but enthusiasm for these developments and longed to see the results for themselves.

So in 1935, when they were only one year into building their own car, the two friends climbed into Dowson's 3-litre Bentley and set off on a trip to the Continent to enjoy a variety of motor racing events and get ideas for the Lightweight Special. Their first stop was the Grosser Preis von Deutschland, to be held at the Nürburgring in the Eifel Mountains on 28 July. Here they saw in the flesh the Mercedes Benz and Auto Union racing cars which were changing the face of motor sport. These two German manufacturers had, for the second season running, set the pace in every category of motor sport. Ironically, they were not to be the heroes of the hour on this particular day. They were beaten on home ground by a technically much inferior P3 Alfa Romeo piloted by one of the most talented racing drivers of his era, Tazio Nuvolari. The crowd were treated to one of the most exciting races of the year as Nuvolari drove his car to the limit in one of the best performances of his life while von Brauchitsch in the leading Mercedes W25 made an error of judgement by not changing his tyres at the final pit stop. The result was a burst rear tyre while he was leading on the last lap which allowed Nuvolari to surge past him to victory. It was a perfect example of supreme skill, luck and good judgement combining to allow inferior technology to beat a seemingly invincible competitor.

In an era when the only possibility of experiencing such a sports event was to actually be there, the many motor racing fans who could not do so had to rely on the lively reports which appeared in magazines such as *The Autocar* for some impression of what a race had been like. These reports provide a vivid account of the excitement of the event which Alec and George would have witnessed. This particular race report was given the title 'Drama at Nürburg' and it began by describing the atmosphere before the race as the cars – each of which was painted in the national colour, silver for Germany, red for Italy, blue for France and green for England – lined up on the grid:

The Grosser Preis von Deutschland! The great day for which hundreds of thousands of enthusiasts of all nations have been waiting has arrived. Even yesterday morning the roads around the wonderful Nürburg Ring, the finest road-racing circuit in the world, were thick with would-be spectators. To-day has dawned with a slow drizzle, attempting vainly to quell the inimitable grandeur of the scene. Mist cloaks the pine-clad mountains amid which the course lies, but from the stands a full view is possible looking down the valley which the cars will traverse. Patches of light fall on the scene as they float above the pits and grandstands. Opposite the pits, twenty cars are lined up; nine silver-coloured German machines – five Mercedes and four Auto-Unions – three scarlet Ferrari Alfa-Romeos, three scarlet 'official' Maseratis, two other Maseratis, an unofficial Alfa-Romeo, a blue Bugatti, and – a green car at last! England has a champion in the German Grand Prix, and a worthy champion. Raymond Mays with his 2-litre E.R.A. There are many English spectators amongst the crowd and all wish him luck. Nor are they alone, for the sporting Germans too, are enormously pleased to have an English car in their race. Mays has won all hearts by his plucky driving with a car far smaller in capacity than its rivals. The cars are pushed up to the start as files of Nazi troopers parade and impressive anthems blare from the loud speakers.

Though it is unlikely that George and Alec had much on their minds other than enjoying a rare opportunity to be part of a great sporting event, even they could not help but notice the extra significance which was placed on the expected success of the German cars. They commented to their friends on their return that they were shocked to find the crowd was expected to give the Nazi salute before each race. The superiority of German engineering demonstrated by their dominance of motor sport was seen as a boost to the national pride which the Nazis sought to foster and this attitude was to be clear again, this time with athletics, at the Berlin Olympics in 1936. But now it was time for the race to start:

They are arrayed upon the grid, while the usual murmur of excitement from the serried crowds grows louder and louder. But soon, as 11 a.m., the hour of the start, approaches, all other sounds are drowned by the roar of exhausts as engines are started. In a few seconds even these give place to the shrill sound of the Mercedes superchargers, and then an electric signal – similar to the traffic light – releases the champing cars. It is a tremendous sight as white, red and green – yes green – cars fight for the lead before the sweeping hairpin after the stands. Caracciola's Mercedes just shoots clear of the pack and Nuvolari with his Alfa is so close to Fagioli's Mercedes that the scarlet and silver wheels almost touch. Spray is flung high, and car after car hurtles past, while the crowds in the stands leap to their feet amid cries of '*Hinsitzen!*' ('Sit down!').

Even the spectators at the track would have seen only small parts of the action since the German Grand Prix was run over a distance of 14.17 miles. Though the track had been purpose built, large sections of it wound through the wild country of the Eifel Mountains and had no specific accommodation for spectators. Alec and George may not have been able to afford a seat in the stands and they would probably have joined the many spectators that risked their lives by the side of the road. To protect them from the drizzle which fell steadily throughout the day they acquired a big cream-coloured canvas umbrella emblazoned with the Auto Union logo. After the Lightweight Special was finished and started to compete, this prized possession was carted around with them to all their race meetings, even when it began to get faded and dog-eared.

It was not necessary to be in the stands to follow the race, since the crowd was treated to a live commentary from 'announcing stations' situated at various important corners and hairpins. There was also a score board by the grandstands on which the numbers were changed every lap to show the order in which the cars were running about two miles before they came in sight of the stands. *The Autocar's* account of the last laps describes the excitement of the crowd as the race reached its thrilling climax because against all probability, and even though a Mercedes was leading, Nuvolari had managed to get his Alfa Romeo into second place immediately ahead of another Mercedes and two Auto Unions, and he was keeping it there:

Now for the last lap. Von Brauchitsch! A pause. Here is Nuvolari, driving like a demon; but the Mercedes has gone faster still and is now 35 seconds ahead. A minute and a half later Stuck [Auto Union] comes by third, and then Caracciola [Mercedes] as he passes his pit shakes his head and gestures that he can go no faster. The Karussell announcer is on

Hulda Issigonis and baby Alec, Smyrna 1907

Azizeah 'The Sultana Harvest'. Left to right: Hetty Walker, Mr Ritchie, Clara Crespi, May Walker, Constantine Issigonis, Alec Issigonis, Hulda Issigonis, Gerry Walker

Constantine Issigonis as a young man

'An English Education'. On the bench: Alec, Hulda, May, Mrs Newton. Standing behind: Hetty and Gerry

Azizeah 'The Race'. Alec, May and Gerry line up on an imaginary start line

Smyrna 1922. Back row: British Consul Sir Harry Lamb, Hilda Elliott, Mr Elliott, Mrs Elliott, Mr Smith, Alec Issigonis. Middle row: naval officer, David Lorimor, Mr Evans. Front row: Ruth de Jong, Joyce Jolly, May Walker, Maudie Elliott, Ethel Heginbotham

Smyrna burns, 14 September 1922

After the trauma, a 'little well-earned self-indulgence'. Hulda and Alec take their Singer saloon 'Salome' on a 'Grand Tour' of Europe

Purley 1926, Alec the student with May Walker and his mother

Alec took a snapshot of Gerry Walker posing with 'Susie', the Bleriot Whippet, and on the reverse he drew his first sketch

1932, Alec and Peter Ransome work on the 'diamond ring' Austin Seven in the garden at Purley

Modifications complete, Alec rewards Peter Ransome for his help with a ride in practice at the Shelsley Walsh hill-climb

In 1930 Alec bought himself an Austin Seven Sports. Over the next few years he transformed it from standard factory car to 'Issigonis Special'

1934, Alec shows off the Lightweight Special, still in its early stages, in the front garden of the Kenilworth house

1939, Alec gives George Dowson some advice before the finished Lightweight Special makes an attempt on the Prescott hill-climb

the air! 'Von Brauchitsch is followed close by Nuvolari!' 'Von Brauchitsch has burst a tyre!' 'Nuvolari has passed him.' There is silence in the stands. Every man is on his feet. The suspense cannot be borne. 'Von Brauchitsch is trying to catch up on a flat tyre!' 'Caracciola has passed the Karussell driving all out!' Now we turn our eyes to the changing numbers on the indicator board. 'Nuvolari!' Now the little Italian appears, and such a shout goes up as never before was heard. Alfa-Romeo wins the Grosser Preis von Deutschland! A magnificent ending to a race in which thrill has followed thrill; but it is cruel luck for Mercedes, cruel luck for von Brauchitsch. Stuck arrives and is cheered to the echo. Caracciola now! Second place for Auto-Union, third place for Mercedes. What a reversal of fortunes. Rosemeyer [Auto Union] is fourth, after a good race. But one more scene is to be played in this finest of all races. Von Brauchitsch is signalled on the indicator board. All hats go off, every man begins to cheer and clap long before he comes into sight! Von Brauchitsch, leader till five miles from the finish, brings his gallant Mercedes over the line on the rim! Von Brauchitsch climbs from his car. He is crying like a child. So ends a drama.

After all this excitement Alec and George crossed the border into Austria to watch the Grossglockner mountainclimb, a new event on the international calendar which would be every bit as thrilling as the Grand Prix they had just witnessed. The Grossglockner Hochalpen Pass was officially opened on 3 August 1935 by President Miklas of Austria and had been built to connect Austria to Italy. The scenery in the heart of the Alps was spectacular and from the top of the pass where the ceremony took place it was possible to see 37 different mountain peaks. The Grossglockner mountainclimb was scheduled to take place the following day using 12 miles of the road which was so new it was still covered with a thin layer of loose stones. The brave competitors, starting deep in the valley, were required to pick their way as quickly as they could up the terrifying labyrinthine track to a height of nearly 8,000 feet with sheer drops on all sides. In such extreme conditions the mechanical superiority of the Mercedes and Auto Unions was secondary to the skill and experience of the drivers. The event was won by Mario Tadini in an Alfa Romeo run by the Ferrari team but Dick Seaman came in a fine second for Britain in his ERA, a fine performance even though he finished twelve seconds behind the winner.

Alec and George were lucky enough to have witnessed some of the best motor sport events of the year and they were both lost in admiration for the superb driving skills of Nuvolari and Tadini. Alec never forgot watching Nuvolari's feat at the Nürburgring and would mention it to journalists to the end of his life. But he was equally enthralled by the design and engineering on display. At Grossglockner it was possible to get much closer to the cars than at a Grand Prix meeting. The opportunity to get into the paddock and take a really close look at the latest racing machines was not wasted, for there is no doubt that the elegant lines of the Mercedes W25 influenced the final look of the Lightweight Special.

MORRIS

CHAPTER 4

Working under the Chief Engineer was a shy, reserved young man named Alec Issigonis. In spare moments – sometimes during a night's fire-watching session – the three of us would sit and exchange ideas. Alec always used to put his suggestions forward in a most tentative way. He had some very fundamental new ideas about motor car construction ...

Sir Miles Thomas, *Out on a Wing*

JOINING MORRIS MOTORS

ISSIGONIS HAD QUICKLY made his mark at Humber but it was not able to hold on to him for long. After only two years the Chief Engineer of Morris Motors offered him an even better opportunity in the design office of the Cowley factory in Oxford. Since Morris Motors and the Austin Motor Company were the two giants of British motor manufacturing during the 1920s and 1930s, he could hardly have received an offer more favourable to his progress.

The astute businessman who had founded the company which Issigonis was about to join had begun life as William Morris, a humble cycle mechanic working from his home in Oxford. He had prospered sufficiently by 1894 to set up a more ambitious enterprise for the repair, servicing and hire of cars which he called Morris Garages. He founded his first motor manufacturing business in 1913, though the First World War prevented him from making immediate headway. After four years devoted to the war effort, he relaunched the company as Morris Motors in 1919. Britain's first dedicated motor manufacturer, the Daimler Motor Company, had been founded 23 years previously, while Herbert Austin, who would become his main rival, had been running his own company for 14 years. As a relative latecomer Morris chose to remain as independent as possible by not seeking substantial finance from outside his existing business. The only way he could do this was to ignore the example set by his better-established rivals. Instead of building up a massive engineering plant where every part of the car was manufactured on site, he concentrated on assembly, allowing his supplier firms to carry the large overheads

87

incurred in production of the component parts. As the 1920s progressed he began to challenge Austin for market share against the background of the world economic depression. Longbridge had been staring bankruptcy in the face until the success of Alec's favourite car, the Austin Seven, launched in 1922. Morris Motors responded with the Morris Minor in 1927 and this car did well in the small car market though it was never as popular or as versatile as its rival.

Ford too were coming to the fore. In 1914 the American company had simultaneously introduced mass production methods to its facilities in Detroit, Michigan and Trafford Park, Manchester. Most firms copied Ford's moving assembly lines for the manufacture and assembly of mechanical parts but the labour-intensive nature of crafting the bodywork meant these methods could not be fully exploited. Until 1926 bodies for motor cars were made by traditional coachbuilding methods which involved hand-building a wooden frame and beating out metal panels with which to clad it. This dictated a narrow range of body styles which impeded progress towards improved aesthetics or aerodynamics in motor vehicle design. Just as importantly, it sat in the way of the development of full production flow techniques.

Morris was adept in identifying trends which would push the industry forward and at the same time maximise his own profits. On one of his trips to the United States he was introduced to Edward G. Budd, who had devised a new body-making process. At Budd's Philadelphia factory, the whole structure of the body was built up by pressed steel panels which were welded together to make a single body unit. In 1926 Morris joined forces with Budd to establish the Pressed Steel Company of Great Britain. This was one of the most significant moments in the history of the British motor industry because it represented the final piece in the puzzle of mass-production. The new factory was built close by the Morris Motors site in Cowley, a massive building covering some 10 acres and accommodating more than 60 steel presses. It soon became apparent, however, that the involvement of William Morris was proving a hindrance. Pressed Steel needed to reach the whole industry to be profitable but his rivals were hesitant to place orders. By withdrawing his investment he enabled Pressed Steel to stay independent for almost 40 years and it became the major supplier of bodies to the entire range of manufacturers, revolutionising both the appearance of the British motor car, and the numbers which could be produced.

Things continued to move at a stunning pace. When the economic depression began to bite Morris implemented clever price-cutting tactics and became the first manufacturer to offer a car with a price tag of £100 in 1931. This did not mean that motoring had reached the masses yet, but the roads were getting increasingly crowded. Registrations exceeded a million for the first time in 1930, prompting initiatives such as the Highway Code, compulsory third party insurance, pedestrian crossings, speed limits and the introduction of a driving test within the next few years. The industry had to stay ahead of this growing demand and in October 1931 Ford moved the boundaries forward once again when they opened a brand new plant with the most advanced manufacturing methods to be found anywhere in Britain at Dagenham in Essex.

By the mid-1930s William Morris had become a multi-millionaire bearing the title Viscount Nuffield in recognition of his generous charitable donations. He had taken over many of his old suppliers. He had invested in new companies such as MG and bought up a number of his ailing rivals such as Riley and Wolseley. This put him in possession of a business empire stretching from Oxford to Birmingham which came together as the Nuffield Organisation in 1940. He understood, however, that his company would need a serious push to keep up with such strong competition. When he reached the age of 55 in 1932 he announced that he wished to step back from the day-to-day running of the business by taking the post of Chairman and appointing Leonard Percy Lord to the post of Managing Director.

This move signalled the start of a career which would see Leonard Lord become one of the most powerful men in the British motor industry during the crucial decades between 1930 and 1960. He had been born in Coventry in 1896 and attended Bablakes, a local public school, on a scholarship. He was working at Morris Engines when he came to the notice of Lord Nuffield who was so impressed with him that in 1929 he put him in charge of the re-organisation of Wolseley Motors, one of his recent purchases. The flair with which Len Lord carried out this task convinced Nuffield that he was the right man to re-shape Morris Motors and its associated companies, but the affection he came to feel for his protégé was not shared by everyone. He may have been an effective organiser and manager but Lord could also be extremely abrasive and quick-tempered. Miles Thomas was the firm's Publicity Adviser at the time, a cultivated and courteous man who had also been appointed personally by Nuffield, and he summed up the general feeling when he remarked that 'everyone admired Lord's methods if not his manners'.

Leonard Lord did not care what people thought of him. To recapture market position for Morris Motors he initiated a modernisation programme at the Cowley factory and established a new model range. The Austin Seven was ageing by now, and the Morris Minor had never matched its success. This left the way clear for the Morris Eight, launched in 1934, to establish itself as the best-selling small car in Britain, reaching an output of more than 200,000 cars within four years. Unfortunately Nuffield proved unable to detach himself from the business as he had promised and despite the progress the company was making the two men fell out. Lord left at the end of 1936 with a bitterness of spirit which caused him to exclaim that he would 'take Cowley apart brick by bloody brick', a threat it seemed he intended to fulfil when he joined the Austin Motor Company in 1938. Nuffield was hurt by Lord's actions and took the rift extremely personally.

Alec Issigonis joined Morris Motors at this key moment of change but at this stage in his life the problems created by managerial quarrelling did not seem of great significance to him. Indeed, it was one of Lord's reforms which presented him with his latest opportunity. In 1935 the design and engineering operations of the entire group were centralised at Cowley and Issigonis was one of a number of promising recruits brought in to boost the new team. He knew that this post was his best chance yet to get his career as a designer underway. By now he had been experimenting with racing cars for eight years and he believed he knew how a car should be designed:

I soon realised it was no use designing and studying one part of a car. Everything was too tightly integrated for that. The influence of one part on another is far greater than most people think, so before I knew where I was I had become interested in all the other parts outside my specialism and I was soon building complete experimental cars in my spare time.

Professionally he was nowhere near the position he would need to be in to achieve this. He was still only a junior member of the Drawing Office team, just as he had been at Humber. He could only dream of it during his leisure time while building the Lightweight Special, a project which was just past its half-way mark when he joined Morris. But from this point on he devoted himself to convincing those who mattered that this was what he should be allowed to do.

Another recent arrival at the Cowley Drawing Office was William 'Jack' Daniels, who was to become one of the most important links in the new network of working relationships being forged by Issigonis in this formative period of his career. Jack Daniels was born in New Marston, Oxford, in 1912, and began his career as an apprentice at the MG Car Company. MG was established in 1928 as an offshoot of Morris Garages – from which it took its initials – specialising in sports cars. At first the company worked out of small premises in Edmund Road and Jack was one of its first unindentured apprentices. When MG decided to set up its own Drawing Office, the Chief Draughtsman asked Works Manager George Probert to find him an assistant. Probert lined up his six young apprentices and asked for a volunteer. There was a nervous silence until Jack stepped forward, agreeing only on condition that he could go back to his previous role if the Drawing Office did not suit him. This proved unnecessary and he became a trainee draughtsman, learning how to compose drawings and trace them in ink onto blue cloth.

In 1930 MG was formally registered as a limited company with William Morris as the major shareholder but this was a personal investment and the company was not a part of Morris Motors. It was at this time that MG moved to bigger premises at Abingdon and the Drawing Office, along with Jack Daniels, was absorbed by Design and Development, a department which was run by the impressive Hubert Noel Charles. Daniels spent several years working with his new boss on the MG R-type which used independent suspension based on all-round torsion bars. In 1935, Lord Nuffield undertook a general rationalisation of his group of companies and sold a number of his private interests, including MG and Wolseley, to Morris Motors Ltd. As part of the same exercise Leonard Lord implemented the centralisation policy already referred to and the Abingdon Drawing Office was closed down. H.N. Charles, Jack Daniels and colleagues were therefore all sent on their final journey to the Drawing Office at Cowley.

So Jack Daniels and Alec Issigonis came to Cowley within months of each other though they did not begin to work together immediately. They were both, however, an integral part of the office reorganisation which was about to take place. Robert Boyle, the Chief Engineer who had recruited Alec, had just returned from a visit to General Motors in

Detroit. He had observed the practice of splitting the workforce into various teams specialising in particular areas of design, something which of course directly conflicted with the philosophy Issigonis was privately beginning to nurture. Boyle decided to introduce this system at Cowley, creating separate teams to concentrate on bodywork, chassis design, engines, axles and suspensions. Jack Daniels was put onto the chassis design team. As a new recruit Issigonis had to do what he was told despite his personal views on the subject, but he did manage to foil an attempt to assign him to the back axle team by protesting that he would be more use on suspensions, which was certainly the most logical decision given his experience to date at Humber.

This status quo lasted less than a year. In 1937 Robert Boyle left and A.V. (Vic) Oak transferred over from Wolseley Motors to become the new Chief Engineer. As the Drawing Office underwent yet another reorganisation many of Boyle's team leaders departed for other factories within the Nuffield group of companies. Oak studied the remainder of his new team carefully and he was quickly impressed by Alec's attitude to work, his commitment and his flair. At the same time he had an instinct that Alec's greatest asset, his imagination, needed to be channelled firmly but subtly in order for the young engineer to produce of his best. So he asked the practical, down-to-earth Jack Daniels, with his rather more traditional engineering background, to go and work with him and keep his feet on the ground. In his later years, Issigonis remembered Oak as a good friend whose great virtue was that 'he agreed about my view of car design and left me alone in a separate department from the main drawing office, never interfering with my work at all'. In fact, Issigonis was being very intelligently 'managed' without even realising it.

The two of them were as yet only passing acquaintances but Daniels decided to accept Oak's challenge because he was impressed by the odd glimpses he had seen of Issigonis at work. Daniels had noticed that 'he clearly had ideas and he was able to get the people there to let him try them out, which is always the difficult thing, to get management to try something new'. This observation illustrates one of Issigonis' most important skills, his ability to get the right people behind him and to persuade hard-headed businessmen to go against their instincts and let him innovate. After all, Alec was the newest recruit in the department and lacked the experience of some of the men who were displaced when Vic Oak arrived. Despite this, Daniels and Issigonis were given an office together and became the centre of a development unit at Cowley, working with three qualified mechanics whose job was to translate their design work into reality in the experimental workshop. The two men built up an excellent working relationship firmly grounded in mutual professional respect rather than friendship.

It should forever be to the credit of Vic Oak that he not only recognised the spark of genius inside this remarkably focussed young man but he also realised that it needed taming to fulfil its potential. He thereby initiated one of the most successful working partnerships in the history of the British motor industry which would lead to the creation of two of Britain's most enduring icons, the post-war Morris Minor and the Mini.

EARLY PROJECTS

The pattern of the new partnership was set from the very beginning. First Issigonis sketched his basic ideas, then Jack Daniels did the maths and produced the formal drawings. Though Issigonis became the public face of the partnership it was Daniels who had the most experience when it began, having been seriously engaged on major design work with one of the industry's most talented engineers for over six years compared with Issigonis' two years in a junior position in the Humber Drawing Office. Their first project was to be the development of an independent front suspension for the new Series M Ten, due for launch during 1938 and the first Morris car to have a unitary or 'monocoque' construction. The modern method of monocoque construction – made possible by the processes pioneered by Pressed Steel – incorporated the underframe structure into a metal shell welded in one piece as opposed to the traditional method of building a separate chassis and body frame and then bolting them together. The advantage was that rattles were reduced and the integrated structure had more inherent strength. But because the design was more complex it was also more expensive to produce and difficult to alter. The beam axle and leaf-spring suspensions commonly being fitted on cars in the 1930s had not changed very much from those used on horse-drawn carriages. Their task was to design and build a coil spring and wishbone independent front suspension with rack-and-pinion steering which would improve the roadholding and comfort of the chassis.

It was in 1938 that Issigonis first started to keep a series of sketchbooks relating to his professional projects. He used a series of 'Arclight notepads' which were made up of 100 sheets of off-white tracing paper glued together to form a pad between a cardboard back and a sepia cover. He carefully wrote the date on the front of each new book as he started it and the sequence would continue right through to 1957. The notepads which relate to this period of his career were predominantly filled with long reports in neat handwriting describing the experimental work being undertaken. There are only a few sketches, including exploded diagrams showing the parts which made up a conventional front suspension of this era and the reduced number of parts which would be necessary with the new design.

This was the first monocoque prototype that Issigonis had worked on and he found the experience both frustrating and amusing in equal measure. From his earliest days as a project engineer he liked to test-drive the prototypes himself to get a feel for the way a design was working. He would take a car from the experimental workshop which appeared to have been perfectly assembled, only to hear a persistent hammering noise as he got underway or detect a strange smell coming from some undefined quarter. Forced to stop and investigate, he would find some tool which a mechanic had forgotten to remove, or a rotten sandwich carelessly left behind. The workmen were not used to the unitary structure either. In the past the chassis would have been tested with rudimentary bodywork and anything extraneous would simply fall through onto the road; with the monocoque it became trapped in the structure causing intense irritation to its highly strung designer till it was discovered and removed.

Despite the greater simplicity of the Issigonis suspension scheme it proved too expensive to implement on the Morris Ten which went into production with the cheaper beam axle. Independent front suspension was slow to be adopted on mainstream production cars. It was not just the cost, it was also difficult to get the suspension geometry correct, meaning that the end result was not necessarily an improvement on the beam axles which it was supposed to replace. Concurrent with the Morris Ten, MG were trying to develop a small sports saloon with a smoother ride and they earmarked the Issigonis-Daniels suspension for use on the MG Y-type. Though this was intended for launch in 1940, the Second World War intervened and the car was delayed until 1946. From the Y-type, the system made its way onto the MG TD sports car of 1950 and a version of it remained until the end of MGB production in 1980. Thus, the man so closely associated with motoring for the masses also designed a key element of some of the most successful MG sports models.

Though it did not bear immediate fruit, this work absorbed Alec's working life until the outbreak of the Second World War. By 1938 he had achieved the status of Project Engineer for the Morris range of cars but he was still a subordinate member of the Cowley technical department. Nevertheless he was already dreaming about the time when he would be allowed to design a complete car of his own and in the course of his everyday work he began to push the boundaries as far as he could. He started to experiment with the suspensions he was designing, discovering that the Morris Ten prototype would run much straighter and with more directional stability if he placed a couple of sandbags on the front bumper. By such experiments he built up a bank of knowledge to draw on, anticipating the time when he would be allowed the scope to put into practice the ideas he was storing up along the way. He had already decided that his objective was to design a small car in the tradition of the Austin Seven and he would pursue this objective doggedly for the rest of his career.

Finishing the Lightweight Special

1936 was a significant year for both Alec Issigonis and George Dowson, and the changes which were about to occur in their lives would considerably affect the practicalities of their ambitious Lightweight Special project, now two and a half years in progress.

In the case of George, he had left his job in Rugby to take over the running of the family farm in Worcestershire. His change of career was caused by the death of his twenty-year-old sister Biddy, who contracted pneumonia after developing complications from a bout of measles. His parents – particularly his mother Enid – were so distressed that George decided to give up his engineering career and return to the Poplars farm to support them. Despite his inexperience he applied his normal determination to the task and soon became a successful farmer, setting up several new enterprises including glass houses for tomatoes and winter chrysanthemums. Meanwhile, Alec's new job meant he and his mother were on the move once again. They left behind the Kenilworth house and garden for a rather more confined third-floor flat in a block called 'Sollershott' on the outskirts of Oxford. There was no room for the partly built Lightweight Special here so it was moved to the Poplars where work resumed. The engineering drawing on the garage wall in Kenilworth had to be abandoned and its details committed to memory. The next owner of the house must have painted it over never knowing what he had destroyed.

Moving on from adapting Austin Sevens to building a 'special' car of his own for motor racing would have been a natural progression for Alec, something which many of his motor sport acquaintances were also doing. It was so common that one member of his circle, John Bolster, wrote an entire book on the subject in 1949 describing over a hundred such vehicles. The book begins with a definition as follows:

> A 'special' is a car built for a specific purpose by an amateur, either entirely to his own design, or by combining the essential parts of a number of makes. The reason for building it is simply to produce a car with a better performance than anything the constructor could hope to afford to buy ready made.

As well as a lengthy description of the Lightweight Special, Bolster's book includes his own Special – 'Bloody Mary' – and 'The Martyr' built by Rupert Instone. Another notable entry was the splendidly named 'Freikaiserwagen' built by David and Joe Fry who were using the very successful Auto Union Grand Prix cars being built by Porsche as a model, just as Issigonis was drawing inspiration from the Mercedes W25.

This was the first time Issigonis had attempted to design a car from scratch, but many of the ideas, not to mention some of the parts, were garnered from his experiments with the Austin Sevens. The final result was both derivative and advanced. It combined the goal of 'lightweight' with wonderful streamlining and aesthetic appeal. Because the car was intended to compete in the 750 cc class in hill-climbs it was essential to keep weight to a minimum. This was achieved by replacing the conventional chassis with a unitary construction of aluminium-faced plywood, a technique commonly used in aircraft construction of the period. This minimised the weight while still producing a structure that was stiff enough to give good traction and roadholding. It was an early (though by no means the first) example of a monocoque with body and chassis built as a single piece, and every part was as integrated as possible. This of course echoed the construction of the Morris Ten on which he was working at Morris Motors. Rubber suspension was another highly unusual feature adding to the 'lightweight' characteristic in comparison with the standard leaf and coil springs more generally used. Building on his experiments with the front suspension of the Austin Seven Sports and using ideas observed from the Mercedes W25, Alec went further and designed the Lightweight Special with the then unusual combination of independent suspension at both front and rear.

All that remained was to fit an engine and at first it seemed that the only option was to reuse the well-worn unit from the disassembled Austin Seven Sports. Issigonis, however, managed to persuade Murray Jamieson, designer of the Austin Seven racing engine, to let him have a super-charged side-valve racing unit which had been declared obsolete by the Austin Works. The fact that Issigonis worked for a rival firm did not deter Jamieson, who had first met Issigonis while he was still at Humber and had been impressed by the work he had done on the front suspension of his Austin Seven Sports.

Apart from the originality of its engineering, the car was also an aesthetic success. Despite the lack of power tools available to them, the finish of every detail was superb from the carefully upholstered leather seat to the beautifully executed, elegant lines of the body whose aluminium panels were left unpainted to save both money and weight. The steering wheel was cut out of a solid sheet of Vickers spring steel and took six months to make by hand. It was then encased in rubber tubing, bound with bailer twine to make ridges for the hands to grip and finally taken to the local saddler to be finished off in leather, a rather out-of-the-ordinary commission he was happy to undertake. No one has ever summed up the final appearance of the car better than John Bolster:

> The Lightweight is one of the most amazing specials (or should I say *the* most amazing special?) ever constructed. It has that rare thing among specials, a monocoque, stressed-skin construction, and the whole layout was designed on engineering principles, with no compromise whatsoever on account of finance, time or availability of parts. It has the appearance of having been built regardless of cost in the racing department of some great factory, whereas it is the result of sheer hard labour in a little shed, with no proper equipment whatsoever.

Jack Daniels first saw the car when he started to work regularly with Issigonis and it made him realise that his new colleague was an innovator:

I suppose one of the things that made me realise that he had ideas was when he first came to Cowley and brought with him an Austin Seven racing car that he'd built for himself. It had a rubber suspension on it, with elastic bands like an aircraft used to have in the first world war wrapped around a dead piece and a live piece. It was very simple, and it worked, and he was doing pretty well with this car in places like the speed trials on Brighton front.

In later years Issigonis was to scorn the idea that the Lightweight Special taught him anything practical or made any contribution to his development as a designer:

I didn't learn much about design from the Lightweight Special but it was great fun. We do all sorts of things when we're young, that you wouldn't do when grown up. It had no connection at all with the design of the Mini.

This is clearly untrue. Competition experience made Issigonis aware of the importance of good roadholding and handling and undoubtedly contributed to the development of his own distinctive design philosophy. Even more fundamentally he was learning how a designer worked and how to translate abstract ideas into engineering reality.

In 1938, after five years of hard work, the Lightweight Special was finally ready to make its début and it competed regularly for the next two years with Issigonis and Dowson taking it in turns to do the driving. On its very first appearance Dowson crashed the car but they soon put this disappointment behind them at the Prescott hill-climb in late 1938 where the two friends had the satisfaction of beating the Austin factory entry which carried an identical engine. It went on to become the class winner for the 750 cc and 1100 cc events at Shelsley Walsh in 1939, making its first appearance in the Brighton one kilometre sprint the same year. Then, as quickly as it had begun, the Lightweight's brief career appeared to be over as other unpleasant priorities suddenly took precedence.

Designing for the Army

After the political turmoil which had disturbed his childhood and adolescence, Alec had experienced perhaps one of the most happy interludes of his life during the 1930s, making close friendships, exercising his creativity and mechanical curiosity to the full, building firm foundations for his future career and simply having fun doing the things he enjoyed most. But suddenly the Nazi salutes observed at the Nürburgring were no longer a joke when Britain declared war on Germany on 3 September 1939. The following day Alec found this announcement in his *Daily Telegraph*:

> War orders to civilians – Government announcements affecting the life of the civil population were issued yesterday. The instructions include the procedure to be followed during air raids, closing of places of entertainment, prohibition of sports gatherings, and arrangements for schools and unemployed persons … sports gatherings and all gatherings for entertainment and amusement, whether outdoor or indoor, which involve large numbers congregating together are prohibited until further notice.

Though this was the second major international conflict during their short lifetime, at least this time Hulda and Alec were not living at the centre of it and despite his British citizenship Alec found himself in the fortunate position of not having to join the forces. The first call-up papers were sent out as early as August 1939 but it was many months before full conscription was implemented. At the age of 31, Alec was well within the age range for compulsory military service but the engineering industry was one of the occupations classified as 'reserved' so instead of donning a uniform he would be expected to help the war effort by designing vehicles to defeat the enemy. George Dowson tried to volunteer soon after the war broke out but he was initially turned down because farming was also a reserved occupation. He strongly felt that his engineering skills were more vital than his ability to grow tomatoes so he re-applied, describing his occupation as 'private income' instead of 'farmer', and this time he was accepted into the RAF as an engineer. The two friends were separated for the rest of the war period and the Lightweight Special stayed in the garage at the Poplars.

During the war the production of new cars for civilian use was halted and the big motor manufacturing companies turned their attention to armoured cars, ambulances, tanks, aircraft, gun carriers, mines, torpedoes and even jerry cans. At Morris Motors, the company and its engineers were required to set aside their vehicle designs and settled down to producing a rather outlandish range of vehicles intended for the battlefield. At first Issigonis and Daniels carried on working together but around 1942 they were separated when Daniels was deployed on other projects. There was much discussion in the Cowley Drawing Office about what sort of vehicles would be required and it was Issigonis who came up with the idea to design a lightly armoured reconnaissance car which would provide more protection for its operator than the traditional motorcycle. Issigonis used this as a fresh opportunity to experiment with new ideas. He set about designing the 'Nuffield Salamander' which was a small tank with mono-coque construction, torsion bar and wishbone suspension and front wheel drive. These were all ideas that would be used later in his career – unlike the propeller and floats which were also added so the vehicle could negotiate rivers. The Nuffield Film Unit made a publicity film which showed the Salamander scurrying over bumpy terrain and floating gamely across rivers. The commentary proudly proclaimed:

> In designing the Salamander, Nuffield engineers were untrammelled by convention. Sturdy and compact and virile, it is small enough to take advantage of every bit of cover but it is its cross country performance that enables it to make surprise attacks on even a well-concealed enemy.

The military were impressed with the initial prototype and asked for a turret to be added so that it could accommodate two people – the driver, and the officer who would also act as the gunner. This was duly done but then they decided it must fit three people, at which point Issigonis lost interest in the project and handed it on to one of the other engineers.

He transferred his attention to another request from the British army for a vehicle which would give troops the ability to pick up and transport guns and ammunition dropped from an aircraft. This time Issigonis produced a 'motorised wheelbarrow' powered by a simple air-cooled engine of the type used in motorcycles. It was designed to carry a payload of about 300 pounds with a man walking behind using tiller steering. There was an alternative amphibious version which could carry a smaller payload plus one soldier over a river. In order to get the wheelbarrow to the troops in the field it was to be constructed of the lightest available materials and capable of being broken down into its constituent pieces, packed into a long metal cylinder and airdropped by parachute. Theoretically, it

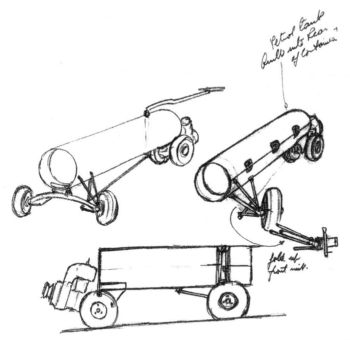

To help the war effort Issigonis devised the 'motorised wheelbarrow' consisting of a tube which could be airdropped to soldiers in the field. The theory was that they would unpack its contents to assemble a compact vehicle for field transport.

would be simple to reassemble, with the cylinder itself forming the body once all the other parts had been unpacked.

The engineers tried to prove this theory by climbing up trees, tying the packed cylinders to the branches and then cutting the rope, but more often than not the containers smashed to pieces on hitting the ground. Glossing over this problem they moved on to testing the capabilities of the wheelbarrow on the ground during extensive trials throughout 1943 and 1944. It is hard not to be amused at the accounts of these tests as recorded by Morris Motors. The official report begins by describing how the land version of the barrow was put through a series of exercises in various configurations and carrying varying payloads. The operators were asked to negotiate a lengthy course controlling the barrow at 'walking pace' which was set at a speed of just under three miles an hour. It is clear that it was a struggle to control the vehicle, especially whenever the ground became bumpy, and the men constantly complained of fatigue. The tests culminated in a rather bizarre 'race' which the deadpan tone of the report only renders even more comical:

Finally as a means of testing the transportational value of the barrow under circumstances approaching actual service conditions, a test was carried out over the main course in which the machine was raced against men carrying weights. The barrow was loaded up to 400 lbs (320 payload) with a CG/track ratio of 8.0 and operated by a crew of two. The same number of men formed the opposing team each carrying 60 lbs. These weights were split into 30 lbs units to be carried by each arm. Comfortable strap handles, as used for carrying mortar bombs, formed the means of support. The barrow crew worked to a pre-arranged plan in which it was decided not to work one man to the limit of his endurance but to make frequent changes. The men took the lead soon after the start at point A where the barrow had to be slowed in order to negotiate tank tracks. This lead gradually increased, and the barrow operator unwisely attempted to reduce the gap by increasing speed on the downhill section of the course between B and D. As a result he reached the latter point in a fair state of exhaustion with the men still well ahead. A rapid change of the barrow crew was executed at this stage.

It is easy to imagine Issigonis relishing the idea of a race of man against machine, but he must have felt considerable chagrin to watch his creation being soundly beaten by two fit men equipped with nothing more than strap handles while the barrow operators collapsed ignominiously in an advanced state of exhaustion.

The amphibious version was taken down the road to be tested on the lake at Blenheim Palace in Oxfordshire and a certain lack of confidence in its potential is suggested by the fact that it was also equipped with oars. It seems to have performed slightly better on water, perhaps because there was no rough terrain to disturb its balance, but the landing manoeuvre sounds rather scary:

The most critical aspect of the machine's performance has been its ability to emerge from the water under its own power ... Unfortunately overturning can be embarrassingly frequent due to the relatively high seating position of the man on top of the load. Tested in this form it was noted that landing operations produced critical situations at the change over period from water to land steer which called for a high degree of skill. If a steep bank is encountered immediately after the vehicle has become entirely land-borne for instance, a rapid change of control points must be affected [sic] otherwise the machine becomes uncontrollable.

Issigonis liked to test his own prototypes. It would have been completely understandable on the strength of these demonstrations if he had suffered a change of heart on this occasion but to his credit he cannot be accused of shrinking from the challenge. He travelled with the amphibious wheelbarrow to the test at Blenheim Palace where he was filmed by the Nuffield Film Unit, controlling the tiller with a confident, self-assured air. He looked rather more nervous during trials on the Devonshire coast where the Royal Navy chose to put the vehicle through its paces by towing it out to sea with its designer on board. Issigonis can be seen hanging on to a rope tied to the back of the boat as the wheelbarrow is dragged along, bobbing up and down alarmingly over a choppy sea.

Although these military projects were useful ground for trying out a few unusual ideas, it is hard to believe that Issigonis took any of them very seriously, and his thoughts were already elsewhere. With his social life severely curtailed, most of his close friends away and the working day frequently interrupted by long hours spent in the bomb shelter during air-raid warnings there was plenty of time to indulge in more interesting reflections about his perfect small car. The senior management too were discreetly considering the post-war future of the company even as they worked away at the war effort. He was therefore encouraged to develop his ideas until the time when it would be possible to put them into practice and we will see how this happened shortly.

KINGSWOOD

Wartime must have been a lonely and frustrating period for Alec, forced to fiddle about with impractical amphibious wheelbarrows, sharing the cramped confines of a small Oxford flat with his mother, cut off from best friend George Dowson and the outlet of his visits to the rather more spacious farm, deprived of the diversion of motor racing and isolated at work by the sudden interruption to his developing working relationship with the sympathetic Jack Daniels. To all this can be added the further blow of the death of his original collaborator Peter Ransome.

At first all had gone well with May and Peter's adventure in Malaya. A son, Mark, had been born in Singapore in 1936 and by 1939, with May expecting her second child, they were ready to return home to Britain. May had not enjoyed the experience of giving birth in Singapore and the international situation was also becoming dangerous so she came on ahead to have her baby at home and also to look for a house for the family to settle in. Tragically, before Peter Ransome could join her he was killed in a road accident aged only 29. May's second child, Sally, was born at Rustlings in 1939 and the young family made their home once again with Hetty.

Hetty and May worked hard to make Kingswood a happy place in which to grow up but life was something of a struggle. Charles Walker had died in Istanbul in 1935 and the two women now had to get by on their rather meagre widow's pensions. Tony Walker, who did not marry, was able to help by sending money back during his time in the Gurkhas and later from the plantation in Ceylon where he returned after the war, and this helped to cover the educational expenses of the two children. Alec also took care to repay his debt to Hetty fully as his career began to take off.

Hetty had become a respected member of the local community and she continued to be a practising Catholic, going to church on the train every Sunday morning. Although she had always been very pro-British, English was not her first language and she never quite lost the feeling of being an outsider. It had been easier for May when she first arrived in Britain because she was both younger and 'more English' but after spending a further five years abroad she now had to adapt to a sudden and unhappy change in her circumstances all over again. Despite their own separate tragedies, however, they both felt that they must put their personal feelings of regret and grief aside to devote themselves to the task of creating a normal and caring environment for the two young children in their care. They became very resourceful, learning to sew and knit so they could make clothes for the family or curtains for the house, doing without the daily help which most of their neighbours engaged and transferring the housekeeping skills they had learnt in Smyrna to their new situation. Hetty became a specialist in the kitchen and was able to conjure up the most complicated dishes from the most meagre ingredients, maintaining her own extensive handwritten cookery book in German. To keep the cupboards stocked she became an expert gardener too, growing vegetables and soft fruit and tending poultry, all of which proved invaluable during wartime rationing. She did not neglect the finer things in life and alongside the vegetables she also produced beautiful flowers and shrubs.

Though there was still a lingering melancholy underlying Hetty's steady determination and stoicism she was above all a calm, stabilising influence which kept the household together through these difficult times.

Hetty and Hulda were no longer living in the same town but the two 'sisters' remained very close. Alec too was extremely fond of his childhood companion May and his aunt Hetty who had stood by him when he needed financial help. Peter Ransome's death was perhaps the biggest shock he had suffered since the loss of his father. It was also the first as the result of a car accident, though unfortunately it would not be the last. During the 1930s their lives had begun to separate as the two families moved in different directions but the circumstances of the war strengthened the contact between them once again and they exchanged frequent visits throughout the 1940s right up until Hetty's death in 1951. The Issigonises always spent Christmas at Rustlings and they would make several more visits during the year. They were there when Sally was born and it was on this day that Alec brought young Mark a special present. He handed over a large brown box, tied up with green string and inscribed with the words 'from Alec to Mark'. Wrapped in the tissue paper inside was a model locomotive, intended to divert the child's attention during the great event.

Over the next few years the arrival of uncle Alec was 'the biggest news in the world' for Mark and Sally who found him to be great fun. With uncle Tony serving in the Gurkhas and uncle Gerry preoccupied with the problems of working on the London Underground during wartime, Alec represented the only strong male figure in the children's lives. Moreover there was the excitement of running out to meet the motor car in which he and his mother always made their grand entrance. Though the costs of owning and running a car had reduced considerably since the very early days of motoring it was still beyond the means of the average working person. In September 1939 petrol rationing was introduced and most private cars were laid up for the foreseeable future. Alec's job meant that he was in the privileged position of having access to a vehicle and the means of obtaining petrol to run it wherever he liked. The children would pester him for rides, though Hetty and May were rather more ambivalent on this subject since his driving style caused considerable alarm in the Kingswood household. He would sweep round the country roads as if at one of his speed-trials, executing daring overtaking manoeuvres on startled locals, with Mark grinning, Sally covering her eyes and May shouting angrily at him to slow down. The only person unruffled by the experience was his loyal mother who had total faith in all her son's abilities. Her first topic of conversation when they arrived would always be how quickly they had done the journey from Oxford to Kingswood.

Just as importantly he always brought with him the most generous presents to be left under the Rustlings Christmas tree. Christmas was a time of year when Hetty and Hulda put in a lot of effort to create a special time for the children. They turned it into a re-enactment of their own memories of magical childhood Christmases in Smyrna. During the afternoon of Christmas Eve the adults would make some excuse to send the children out of the way so they could decorate the tree in secret. It was not much of a secret though since nothing was ever done quietly when Hulda was around and great gales of laughter and raised voices would echo through the house telling the children exactly what was going on. This only served to build up the anticipation. Finally, at six o'clock, Hetty would beat the gong and the children were at last allowed into the room to see the tree lit with candles and the presents piled underneath ready for them.

Over the years Alec added to the model locomotive he had given Mark on the day of his sister's birth. He had a set of beautifully crafted rails made in the factory, far better than anything which could be bought in the shops. There were several clockwork engines, including 'the Flying Scotsman' which he had specially painted for them. There were gaily painted carriages for the engines to pull, tunnels for them to dive through and signals for them to stop at. Alec looked forward to playing with each new object just as much as his young protégés since there was no room for a train set at the Oxford flat. So on Christmas Day after the meal Alec, Mark and Sally took over the house, threading their track around the furniture, in and out of the doors, and behind the Christmas tree, then getting down on their hands and knees to set the trains in motion and watch them go round and round with whoops of delight.

Alec was always thoughtful about the gifts he gave. When Mark was given a Meccano set he brought him a steam engine to go with it and helped him to make a steam-powered crane. May was also thrilled when he bought her a wireless set which was something she could not afford for herself and it kept her company for many hours, allowing her to listen to her favourite music and arts programmes. Sometimes he would use his inventive mind to dream up surprise treats using whatever tools were available, from hacksaws to soldering irons. One year he brought with him the pieces needed to make a doll's house for Sally. While she was in bed, he fitted it all together and filled it with miniature furniture ready to be revealed on Christmas Eve when the family exchanged their presents. Another year he cut down some saplings from the garden and nailed them together to make a crib with a straw roof which he then decorated with small figures.

While Alec amused the children, Hulda and Hetty would retreat into the kitchen and hold long conversations about Smyrna using 'kitchen' Greek to keep what they said private. The two women worked away at preparing the meals, stopping frequently to smoke a cigarette or two, fretting all the time over their losses in Turkey and speculating on fanciful solutions. Eventually, the inconveniences of rationing would be overcome, and a splendid meal fit for five hungry mouths was proudly laid out on the dining room table. The chickens which Hetty kept in the garden usually provided the necessary basic raw material but one year Alec and Hulda got a goose from somewhere and a great deal of fussing and argument followed over how to prepare it. Cookbooks were spread everywhere, Mrs Beeton was consulted and the result was one of the most exciting meals anyone could remember.

Alec was a great raconteur and in the evening after dinner he would entertain them all with stories which he saved up for these occasions. He would embellish tales about their train adventures in the good old days before the war, describing his mother rushing up and down to Smyrna on the Orient Express, or relating a trip on the 'Mistral' where he claimed to have observed from his comfortable seat the terrified French peasantry cowering and crossing themselves as the monster sped through the countryside at hundreds of miles an hour. Many of his stories were told at the expense of his dear old mother. He would make fun of her lack of expertise with the niceties of the English language by repeating some ill-phrased remark that she had innocently made. He would recount how she had opened her window on the car journey down and thrown her cigarette out, not noticing that the back window was open. The cigarette, he declared theatrically, had flown straight back in and set fire to the back shelf. He would imitate her mannerisms and gestures, throwing his hands in the air and exclaiming in a loud voice when asked if he wanted any more food, 'no, no, no, no, *no!*'

A Wartime Summer in Oxford

The visits to Kingswood must have provided a welcome alternative to the suspended visits to the Poplars. Considering the two spacious properties they had lived in previously their new home in Oxford was a somewhat strange choice. 'Sollershott' was a plain block of twelve flats, rather out of character with the surrounding houses which were much grander in their scale and appearance. The flats were built a little way back from the road in a quiet cul-de-sac off a wide, tree-lined road named Five Mile Drive and Alec and his mother lived on the top floor. Port Meadow was less than a mile away offering a large open space where Alec would often go to fly his model aeroplanes.

The flat was approached via a communal stair at the rear of the building and consisted of five rooms altogether. Immediately behind the front door was a narrow corridor off which all the other rooms led. Alec's bedroom was the first door on the left and consisted of a small area partitioned off from a more roomy living area next door. This arrangement gave the flats the flexibility to have either two bedrooms and a living area or one bedroom and a larger-sized living space but in the case of the Issigonises the partition always stayed in place and Alec's wardrobe was wedged up against it. The larger room was the focal point of the household, containing the dining table and the fireplace. It acted as a combined dining and sitting room. A French window led outside onto a narrow balcony which ran back along the wall and fronted onto Alec's bedroom as well. The pleasantness of the immediate environment provided some compensation for the smallness of the living accommodation. From the windows Alec had an uninterrupted view across Linkside Lake towards the distant railway line where steam trains could be observed passing on their way. On the other side of the flat, the first door on the right-hand side was the kitchen, which was fitted with a modern chute device to take rubbish down to the ground floor. Next came a pleasant bathroom and at the end of the corridor Hulda occupied the only decent-sized bedroom.

In 1944, when Germany began to launch its 'doodlebugs' or flying bombs over the south-east of England, May Ransome began to worry about the safety of her children in Surrey. Hulda suggested the family come to stay in Oxford during the summer holidays. They knew the occupants of the other flats well by now so May stayed at a neighbour's flat while Mark and Sally slept on camp beds in Hulda's room as Alec's room was too small for an extra bed. The children found their aunty Hulda a very different proposition from their good-natured, dignified grandmother. Though she was now in her 60s, she still had immense energy and did everything at full volume and top speed. Despite the forcefulness of her personality, the children found her fun to be with and towards them she was always kind and approachable rather than intimidating. She would begin the day by doing physical exercises such as touching her toes in her bedroom and this was just the precursor to an endless routine of housekeeping jobs. When she needed a moment's relaxation from her hectic round of daily chores she would take up her favourite resting place, sitting on the rug in front of the hearth with her legs outstretched or tucked underneath her and usually a cigarette in hand. Very fit and supple, sitting on the floor was a habit she had retained from Smyrna where large cushions were often used in place of chairs.

Hulda rarely felt inhibited or embarrassed about anything but during the war her German origins did make her feel a little uncomfortable. If her accent drew any attention she would insist that she was Bavarian and not German (though her family actually came from the neighbouring state of Württemburg) and point out that this was an independent state and not part of Germany when her family left. During the week while Alec was out at work, the children would sometimes accompany her on shopping expeditions. Hulda never learned to drive so this involved walking down to the end of Five Mile Drive and taking the bus into the small shopping centre a couple of miles away at Summertown. At the end of the day she would have to make this journey in reverse, returning from the bus stop with her heavy bags and carrying them up three flights of stairs, calculating how well the day had gone by weight rather than quantity. These trips were firmly etched on the minds of the two children as a 'real adventure', for Hulda would rush everywhere, full of restless, nervous energy, her arms waving dramatically in all directions, communicating at maximum volume and paying no attention at all to what effect she might be having on those around her. Sometimes they would go into the centre of Oxford and have lunch at the upstairs café in the Elliston and Cavell Department Store. Here she would berate the waitresses for their shortcomings in a loud voice which so embarrassed her nephew that one day he took the threepenny bit he had in his pocket and secretly left it under his plate as a peace-offering. Outside she would cause traffic chaos, grabbing the two nervous children by the hand and dashing into the road without a second glance whenever she felt the need to cross. Once, in her haste, she ran headlong into a cyclist and knocked him off his bicycle, only stopping briefly to give him a puzzled look as if to say 'what's happened to you?'

When Alec returned from Cowley in the late afternoon he might be driving any one of a variety of different vehicles from the pool of works cars. The children would climb the willow trees at the end of the drive and patiently watch to see which car would appear round the corner that day. When they spotted him they ran to the end of the street and made him stop so he could drive them the last few hundred yards. Back at home he looked through the drawings that Mark had done during the day, making suggestions about how they could be improved. Sometimes he stood at the window and impressed the children by identifying the enemy and allied planes from their engine noise, though this was not a difficult feat for an engineer since the German diesel engines sounded quite different from the petrol engines of the British planes.

He usually went into the works on Saturday morning too and sometimes he would take Mark with him. There was much to see at the wartime factory besides military vehicles and munitions. Cowley was involved in the repair of aeroplanes and they would often visit the airfield to see them being flight-tested. Before returning home for Saturday lunch he always went on to the 'Trout' near Godstow on the Thames, a popular local pub which, rather like the Queen and Castle in Kenilworth, was patronised by a variety of people who worked in the motor industry. Many of his hill-climb friends would be there, along with engineers from other firms, and this was an opportunity to mix with a wider circle of people who did not work with him every day but shared his interests. This became an important part of Alec's routine and his visits to the Trout continued until the middle of the 1960s when he moved permanently from Oxford to Birmingham. Though Alec could be nervous when he met people for the first time he was very much at his ease with like-minded people talking about his favourite subject. The group of men would sit out on the pleasant terrace by the river, with the weir as their backdrop, chatting about motor cars over a beer or two. Sometimes the children would go along and be given ginger beer to drink so that Hulda and May could get some peace and quiet while they made lunch. Even when socialising Issigonis had a strongly competitive streak and young

Mark noted that he would somehow always seem to come out of these discussions on top. After an hour or so of pleasant conversation, the little party would make their way home to enjoy the meal that had been carefully prepared for them, and then it was time for a siesta.

At the weekend, the atmosphere could get a little tense around the flat. Hulda channelled much of her boundless energy into her son and the constant attention at times got on Alec's nerves, not least because it made it difficult to find the peace and quiet he needed for creative thinking. Although Hulda could be very domineering, Alec was not easily cowed and when he became frustrated he would tell her off in the most uninhibited fashion if he felt the need. In this way it was a typical Mediterranean relationship in which both parties would vent their anger often but afterwards there would be no apologies or long periods of sulking. Both considered the air cleared, forgot about it and moved on to the next thing. She took her son's teasing with good humour, particularly his rude comments about her cooking, as Alec frequently insisted that she dropped hairpins in the soup or that the food was 'full of ash!'. Though she was careless about where she extinguished her cigarettes this was rather unfair. Hulda was not such an accomplished cook as Hetty but she had a small kitchen to operate in and she worked hard with the restricted range of ingredients at her disposal.

Her cigarettes were a constant source of anxiety to Alec because she never seemed to have an ashtray to hand. As the cigarette slowly burnt down she would get involved in some animated conversation and start to wave it around sending the ash in all directions. She also had a tendency to put down half-smoked cigarettes and then forget about them. Alec would snap in irritation, 'Mother, mind the ash', 'Where did you leave it?' or 'Don't wave it about!' Sometimes he would attempt to track down the missing cigarettes by asking her how many she had smoked that day and she would go through a sketchy list of times and places, counting off the fingers of one hand with the other – 'one, two, five, eight!' The children watched this regular pantomime with delight and would often retreat, bursting with laughter, as Hulda gave them a wink to show she was playing to the gallery.

For all their sparring, Hulda's attitude towards her son was both deferential and admiring. She had absolute faith in his abilities and her life was dedicated to providing whatever support he needed. He was scared of moths, and when they sometimes flew in at his open bedroom window on summer nights she would immediately rush in if he shouted to dispose of them. She also understood his need to concentrate. The dining cum sitting room contained only one table which had to serve as both their dining table and Alec's workspace. Despite the inconvenience, she did her best to keep it clear for the maximum amount of time possible when he was at home so he could sketch, telling Mark and Sally to move around quietly and not disturb him while he was working.

Alec spent a lot of time at the dining room table with his sketchbooks during the wartime period. His collection of Arclight notepads had grown considerably since 1938 but instead of neatly handwritten reports their pages were now being filled with inventive sketches. These represent the first flowering of his creative approach to technical drawing and are unlike anything he had produced previously. They are fluid and artistic, clearly drawn for his own pleasure as much as to inform other people about his ideas. It is remarkable how well formed they are, how accurately they visualise a three-dimensional reality long before a single panel has been beaten. Though a number of the drawings are pure fantasy, including racing cars and aeroplanes, the majority are absolutely serious in their intent. There are nine complete notepads plus a quantity of loose sketches covering the period between 1942 and 1946 and these can be divided roughly equally between two periods, 1942–4 and 1945–6. Morris Motors was naturally looking forward to its post-war strategy by 1945 so it is no surprise to find that the later notepads contain around 170 drawings concerned with ideas for a new small-car project which would be codenamed 'Mosquito'. It is rather more surprising to find that, of the 220 or so drawings from the earlier period, 70 are military designs compared with approximately 150 related to this same Mosquito concept.

THE MOSQUITO PROJECT

Alec was not producing these sketches merely to amuse himself. He was being quietly encouraged to use any time that he might have available to develop his small car ideas by his supervisor, Vic Oak, with the full knowledge and blessing of Lord Nuffield's new Vice-chairman Miles Thomas, who when we last met him was the publicity adviser for Morris Motors.

Miles Thomas was to become a key figure in the chain of events which allowed Issigonis to develop into a celebrated designer because it was he who gave him the scope to produce his first vehicle. He had been born at Cefn Mawr in 1897, the son of a Welsh furniture dealer who had ensured a steady family income by wisely investing in property, which was just as well as he died the year after his son's birth. Thomas attended Bromsgrove Public School and then embarked on a career in engineering. When the First World War broke out he immediately volunteered to join the Forces, though at seventeen he was underage. He progressed from the Motor Machine Gun Corps to the Royal Flying Corps, forerunner of the RAF. After the war he changed career again by becoming a journalist, reporting on motor races all over Europe from the cockpit of an aeroplane; indeed he probably wrote many of the race reports that Alec and George eagerly pored over each week in their motoring magazines. Thus he spent his early career in close association with the two pioneering technologies of his generation – aeroplanes and motor cars.

William Morris was far ahead of his competitors in understanding the importance of promotional techniques and in September 1923 he personally telephoned Miles Thomas to invite him to deploy his journalistic skills in the cause of an intensive publicity programme for Morris Motors. Thomas set to with a will, beginning with the launch of *The Morris Owner* in 1924, the first commercially available in-house magazine to come out of the British motor industry. It was written in popular style, extolling Morris products, giving motoring advice and recounting entertaining holiday tales. Before long other motor manufacturers decided an in-house journal was something they could not afford to be without. Thomas followed this success by creating the Nuffield Film Unit which pioneered the shooting of promotional films to be shown at special shows for groups of Morris dealers. Once again his idea was soon being copied by rivals such as Herbert Austin. So well did he do his task that he was rewarded in 1933 with the post of General Manager of Wolseley in Birmingham followed by that of Managing Director of the same company in 1937. Here he developed his managerial skills and was behind the development of a very successful model range including the Wolseley Wasp, Hornet and Fourteen. In the immediate aftermath of the falling out with Leonard Lord, Nuffield had resumed control of Morris Motors, appointing Oliver Boden as Vice-chairman. When Boden died in 1940 he chose Miles Thomas to replace him and promised that this time he really would step back just as long as he was kept informed about what was going on. Unfortunately he proved no more able to keep this resolution the second time around than he had the first.

Initially things went well. Miles Thomas skilfully orchestrated the Nuffield Organisation's war effort, particularly in the field of aero-engine development, and his achievements were officially recognised by the award of a knighthood in 1942 (though for clarity I will continue to refer to him as Miles Thomas here). He realised, however, that it was also necessary to think about the long-term future and he began to work on plans to seize the initiative as soon as possible after peace came. Since it generally took five or six years to take a new model from conception to production no one could afford to wait until the war was finished before making plans, unpatriotic as this might appear if it was done too openly. He was particularly preoccupied with the development of a small, low-priced four-seater saloon with which Morris might capture the widest possible market and this was how he inadvertently launched the career of one of Cowley's junior engineers. One night during fire-watching duties, Miles Thomas found himself sitting with his Chief Engineer, Vic Oak, and 'a shy, reserved young man named Alec Issigonis'. This was Alec's chance to impress and, with some encouragement, he put aside his reserve and became enthusiastic on his favourite topic, the design of a small car. Miles Thomas described these discussions:

> Alec always used to put his suggestions forward in a most tentative way. He had some very fundamental new ideas about motor car construction and the first thing we decided in the make-up of this small saloon was that we would throw away the conventional chassis, make the body take the reaction stresses from the axles, and employ independent suspension at the front and if possible the rear. We also decided that we must have an engine that attracted low rates of taxation under the RAC horsepower tax and yet would give bonus power for overseas use. Clearly it would have to be unconventional.

This diffident, shy young man is rather in contrast to the legend of the bullying engineer but his attitude at this stage of his life was necessarily coloured by the fact that he was talking to men who were clearly his social and professional superiors. Miles Thomas was impressed by what he heard and Issigonis was planted firmly in his mind. So much so that he began to ask the young engineer for his opinion on other projects. He described one such incident:

... one bright summer's day ... I wanted the opinion of Alec Issigonis, who was particularly expert on suspension systems, on the springing of a prototype RAF reconnaissance armoured vehicle that we were making. I found him in the hush-hush engine test-house, poring paternally over his reluctant two-stroke. I asked him if he would come out with us on the armoured vehicle, and we went to some fairly rough high ground at Shotover – the hill behind the Cowley works. It was hay-making time. I had not known it before, but Alec Issigonis suffered severe hay fever, and as soon as we came anywhere near those sweet-scented pollen-laden fields he began to feel absolutely miserable. He dripped everywhere; nose, eyes; and he sneezed continuously. He was a wretched sight. All the same he rapidly put his finger on the shortcoming of the springing that needed to be traced, and advised what kind of cure should be applied. Back we went to the Works. Alec leapt out of the car and soon had his face over his beloved fuming engine. Immediately he regained his normal composure. The oil fumes overcame his hay fever at once. Factory life does not always consist of enduring dark satanic mills, and country life has its distinct drawbacks for some people.

Despite the Ministry of Transport's ban on the production of cars for civilian use in October 1940, Miles Thomas got the Board to approve a project to develop ideas for a new small car in 1941. Issigonis had already convinced Thomas and his supervisor Vic Oak of his ability to carry out such a task and they gave him the signal to make a start on the serious design work, which explains the proliferation of small-car sketches to be found in the 1942–4 Arclight notepads. His brief was to build an economical four-seat family saloon with an engine which would escape the worst penalties of the RAC horsepower tax and it was Thomas, the ex-RAF man, who gave the project the name of 'Mosquito' after the famous de Havilland fighter bomber.

Because of the need for discretion much work was done during evenings and weekends at the Sollershott flat. The Mosquito began to consume Alec's leisure time as well as his working time and became the main object of his intellectual activity, filling the void left by the completion of the Lightweight Special and the departure of George Dowson to active service. Nevertheless it is important to be clear that this was *not* another one of Alec's personal projects. In later life Issigonis made a comment which has since been much quoted – that he designed the whole car himself, 'even the door handles and the little knob that opens the glove box'. This was true up to a point but it does not reflect the level he had reached within Morris Motors when the project began. Though he had made a positive impression on his superiors he was still very much a subordinate within a reporting structure that went from his immediate boss Vic Oak, through Technical Director Sidney V. Smith, to Vice-chairman Miles Thomas who was in charge of product development and ultimately to Chairman Lord Nuffield who made the final decisions. In this chain of command it was Thomas who provided the direction the project would take and he communicated his decisions through a regular internal correspondence with Oak and Smith. Though some of this correspondence was copied to Issigonis it was never directed to him alone.

In other words, the Mosquito project was the responsibility of a team of which Alec Issigonis was but one part and the notion that the finished product was the result of his vision alone is extremely misleading. The circumstances of the war gave him this unique opportunity because the demands of the military design programme and the need for confidentiality meant the design team had to be small, tight and disciplined. The resulting situation was ideal for everyone. Morris Motors benefited from Issigonis' focus, his vision and his work ethic. Issigonis on the other hand got his first shot at a full car design and the fact that he had to bow to other influences actually enabled him to produce some of his best work.

So from 1942 Alec worked on his sketches whenever he got the opportunity. Alongside Thomas' guidelines he added his own aspirations – a small car which would set new standards in roadholding and the utilisation of passenger space. The earliest three-dimensional manifestation of the vehicle was a scale model produced in 1942 just before Jack Daniels was moved on to other projects. This model, along with the early sketches, shows that he had already fixed on the shape he wanted for the car. During 1943 the experimental body shop were able to prepare the first, hand-built, Mosquito prototype bodyshell and by the end of that year the war was going sufficiently well for the Ministry of Transport to agree that manufacturers should be allowed to work on designs and prototypes for post-war models. Once this decision had been made the project really began to develop in pace. In early 1944 a full version, known by its project number EX/SX/86, was ready for road-testing. A further boost came when Jack Daniels was reunited with Issigonis to assist with the chassis and suspension drawings. Daniels had spent the past couple of years working on the suspension of a series of large-scale armoured vehicles and this had provided him with further valuable experience of suspension design which he was able to put to use on the Mosquito project.

A third member was also added to the team in the form of Reginald Job who specialised in body draughtsmanship. Like Daniels, Reg Job's experience complemented Issigonis' work perfectly since he had formerly worked at the Pressed Steel Company producing bodies for both Austin and Morris monocoque designs. Issigonis and his team were allowed to separate themselves from the main Drawing Office and were allocated a small workshop with a few skilled mechanics to assist them. While Thomas was the impetus behind the overall project, Issigonis was clearly the driving force within the development team and it was his energy which pushed them on, filling them with confidence that they were achieving something unique together. The three of them did everything – body, suspension and engine development. Speaking to Philip Turner in 1978 Issigonis contemptuously compared 'modern' methods of design with their efforts during this period: '... we used to work like stink, we were so dedicated to it. Now, the world is just the other way round. Nobody can make a decision unless you have got 20 people at a meeting because they are afraid to do so.'

The three men all got on together excellently and soon a working technique developed which is reminiscent of the methods Alec had seen his father use in the Smyrna factory. Issigonis would sketch what he wanted and Daniels and Job became experts at interpreting what he had drawn and translating the sketches into fully dimensioned engineering drawings. Many myths have grown up around the Issigonis sketches. It is true that he would use anything to hand if he wanted to illustrate an idea immediately to a colleague. He regularly handed cigarette packets to Jack Daniels, newspaper was another favourite medium and he had a habit of drawing in chalk on the concrete floor of the workshops to illustrate a point. The majority of his drawings can, however, be found within the fixed pages of the Arclight notepads and long sequences of them survive, making it possible to follow the development of his ideas on paper. It was a slightly unusual technique, as he was aware:

This method of mine – making a sketch and then passing it to the draughtsmen – is unorthodox in a sense because I haven't met many designers of my knowledge who have this kind of communication with draughtsmen. It is usually done in a much more verbal sense but I prefer to do it in a pictorial sense because I think it gives better results.

In the case of Daniels and Job the method worked extremely well, with both men testifying that the sketches were so excellent, being both proportionate and in perspective, that they had no difficulties in translating them into formal drawings. Issigonis was always quite happy to explain anything which might not be quite clear in any particular sketch and with Jack Daniels in particular he developed a level of trust which was never quite matched by anyone else. As Jack Daniels remembered of this time, '... he'd got to the point where he knew what I was doing, basically it was all his principle and I was taking his ideas and working them out'. At this stage, Alec was a fledgling design genius and it would seem that his relationship with his colleagues was much more amicable and flexible than would prove to be the case later in his career.

Before any detailed drawings could be made, the 1944 prototype had to be thoroughly tested in order to produce a full specification – all of which had to be done alongside the extensive testing which was being carried out on the motorised wheelbarrow in its various forms. The first Mosquito prototype was a rudimentary machine with a front bench seat, no rear seat and no boot lid. Although the team were also designing a new flat-four engine for the car, it was not yet ready so the prototype was fitted with the Series E side-valve engine used by the Morris Eight. To minimise the number of people involved in the project the task of testing fell to Alec himself but naturally this was something which he relished.

His experience in motor competition had attuned his senses to the nuances of a car's behaviour and he considered driving a prototype to be an essential element of the design process. Jack Daniels confirmed this instant ability to evaluate the qualities of an unfamiliar vehicle. He recalled an incident which happened around this time when they went out together to assess the performance of a Lagonda which had special racing suspension. The car handled so badly that Daniels soon began to feel horribly sick and was incapable of contributing any opinion but Issigonis was able to diagnose the problem very quickly. Jack Daniels spoke of this with admiration:

He knew what he was doing, he could tell what needed doing, certainly far better than I could. I mean, I wouldn't know exactly what was going wrong, to this day. I'd know something was wrong but I wouldn't know what to do about it. He got the answer to it. He was very acute on driving.

In the case of the Mosquito, Issigonis wrote a detailed report entitled *Road Test Impressions of the Car on a Run to North Wales and Back* to summarise his conclusions. In later life he often stated his philosophy that the opinions of ordinary people were not an important consideration when designing a car but his report shows a keen interest in the reactions of passers by:

> The car attracts an almost embarrassing degree of attention, particularly when passing through towns. It was noted that this was not confined to the younger sections of the population. Comment from people who actually had an opportunity of examining the car was 99 per cent favourable. Everybody was impressed with the spacious provision for luggage accommodation considering the size of the vehicle, and it would seem a pity to throw this feature away by making the body into a four-seater. Remarkably few people noted the unusual front-end treatment, while the seat and dashboard layout attracted the greatest praise.

He was so pleased with the vehicle that he took his two colleagues out in it, driving up to an army testing site behind the works. The bench seat was too narrow for three people, so while Daniels got the privilege of the passenger seat the unfortunate Job had to sit on a cushion on top of the steel floorpan at the back and be jolted up and down as Issigonis indulged in a little rally-cross to impress them with his driving skills. His suggestion that the car should be made as a two-seater was never given serious consideration. Following the encouraging test results, Thomas decided they should go ahead with a four-seater saloon which would be slightly larger than the first prototype and asked the experimental workshop to put together a wooden mock-up with various interchangeable panels in order to garner further public opinion before the final specification was decided on. Again this is recorded in a memo sent in February 1945 from Thomas to Oak:

An opportunity has been taken to show both this wood mock-up and the original car to people who have never seen them before and who can be regarded as representative of the cross-section of the public who will buy a car of this type. Their reaction is that the shorter length of bonnet on the actual car accentuates the very remarkable amount of body space that has been provided in such a small vehicle, and the 'snooty' look of the car is, in its unconventionality, an attraction.

Using the information from the public feedback sessions the body design was fixed by April 1945. Six prototypes were then commissioned and Reg Job started to prepare the body drawings.

THE SHAPE OF THE MOSQUITO

So what was the basis of this design, which was already being described as 'unusual' and 'unconventional'?

To start with the chassis and transmission, the Mosquito was based on the monocoque construction which had already been used by the company on the Morris Ten. Issigonis, of course, had worked on this car and he went back to the rack and pinion steering which he had drawn for it. The system had not made it onto the Morris Ten but the Mosquito would be the first British mass-market production car to use this technology. The rack, which was simply a metal bar about an inch and a quarter in diameter and about two feet long with teeth cut in it, was not an easy thing to produce because first it had to be extremely accurate, second it had to be straight and third it had to be very strong. So he took the design to the Wolseley factory and asked them to experiment with it and they successfully devised a new technique of flame hardening with which they were able to produce the parts that he needed.

Suspension was the Issigonis speciality and he had, as we have seen already, done some experimentation with the handling of a vehicle in his sandbag experiments with the Morris Ten, not to mention his work on the Austin Sevens and the Lightweight Special. He credited some of the ideas that he used on the Mosquito to Maurice Olley, a specialist in independent front suspension. Olley had developed special suspensions for General Motors in Detroit before returning to work for their subsidiary, Vauxhall, in Luton in 1937. Issigonis had sought him out on his return to Britain and the two of them spent much time discussing various solutions for improved roadholding. He was happy to concede that it was Olley who convinced him that the answer lay in a softer front than back suspension, an idea which was incorporated into the Mosquito. The engine was also placed unusually far forward in the car to contribute to better balance and stability.

Another major innovation was the torsion bar suspension which cleverly fed loads back into the main hull, avoiding the need for a specially strengthened front end, a development which owed a great deal to the work Jack Daniels had been doing on heavy tanks. Issigonis also experimented with a complicated torsion bar plus torque tube for the rear suspension on the first prototype but this was dropped in favour of a simpler, more conventional leaf-spring rear suspension. This decision was made by Thomas who related, '... we also decided that the split rear axle, although it gave marvellous suspension, was too expensive for a car that was designed to sell at £100'. This is a compromise Issigonis would not have made if he had been in complete control.

The shape and styling of the body were fixed surprisingly early in the project. The first scale model of 1942 already displayed the lines which were to be evident on the final product. From the very beginning Issigonis was preoccupied with the dimensions as well as the engineering of a car, looking to maximise interior space for the occupants. He expressed the opinion that people who drove small cars were the same size as those who drove large cars and they should not be expected to put up with claustrophobic interiors: 'The modern designer has got completely out of touch with the bare space requirements that the average human being needs in which to sit comfortably. Why do the occupants of the modern car have to suffer such discomfort?' The major factor which allowed the engineering principles of the car to complement its space utilisation was the unusual engine position. This allowed for a shortened bonnet which in turn increased the area available for the passenger compartment.

Another innovative feature of the car was its special 14-inch wheels, which were placed at each corner of the vehicle in true sporting style. Issigonis would adopt the 'wheel at each corner' philosophy, begun by the French manufacturer Citroën, as a key feature of his future thinking. These were the smallest wheels designed to that date – the Morris Eight by comparison had 17-inch wheels. The wheels and tyres had to be specially made for the prototype by rubber manufacturers Dunlop and though they certainly contributed to the overall stylishness of the car there were good practical reasons for their use. They helped to lower the car's centre of gravity and reduce unsprung weight, all of which contributed to good roadholding and a comfortable ride. They also helped to create the increased interior space which Issigonis was so determined to provide.

Style was something which was of great importance to Issigonis at this stage of his career. In the light of the views he later expressed on this subject, his opening statement in a report submitted to the Car Development Department in March 1947 following a visit to the Geneva Motor Show is particularly interesting:

Technical presentation was poor due to the very small number of chassis shown on the stands. This shows the outlook of the buying public and manufacturers alike, because the propulsive mechanism of the car is being taken for granted and the emphasis is, at last, on styling, comfort and general accommodation.

A number of the Mosquito sketches are concerned with perfecting the lines of the car to produce a pleasing aesthetic shape. In this he was following the philosophy he had devised for the Lightweight Special. He experimented with several different patterns of radiator grille and finally settled on a configuration which he proudly declared to be the first to feature headlamps integral with the grille (though to his annoyance this feature was one of the first to disappear due to United States safety regulations). The styling was also influenced by contemporary American designs – he always referred to this as his 'American period' – with the wings merging into the doors and the base of the body running as parallel as possible to the ground. Post-war Britain, still deprived of much glamour or excitement, would be all in favour of that. The result was something which looked very modern and fresh compared with the rather boxy pre-war vehicles that still predominated, while Issigonis attained his goal of setting new standards for interior space and roadholding in a small family saloon.

The final element was the engine and Miles Thomas decided that a new horizontally opposed flat-four-cylinder power unit should be designed specially for the Mosquito. His intention was to meet the needs of both home and export markets by taking account of their different road-tax systems. The basic unit should provide good output while evading the domestic 'horsepower tax' which penalised bore size as opposed to engine capacity. Modifications, such as mounting larger cylinders, would provide increased power for overseas markets where the tax system was more lenient. Though the flat-four power unit was not sufficiently advanced to be fitted to the first prototype, it was still a key element of the project in February 1945 when Thomas wrote to Vic Oak: 'I am sure you will agree that, ideally, we want to produce the Mosquito with the flat-four engine at its inception. If we put it over at first with a straight engine and then later introduced the flat-four, it breaks continuity and means that we have got to sell unconventionality twice.'

So although the first tests were done with a Series E engine, the engine compartment was specifically designed to take the flat-four. It was perhaps surprising that Issigonis decided on a side-valve layout for his flat-four when Volkswagen, for instance, had chosen an overhead valve layout on their pre-war flat-four engine arrangement. One reason may have been to minimise the engine package. Overhead valves would have made the engine much more powerful but it would also have made it much wider between the front wheels and could possibly have adversely

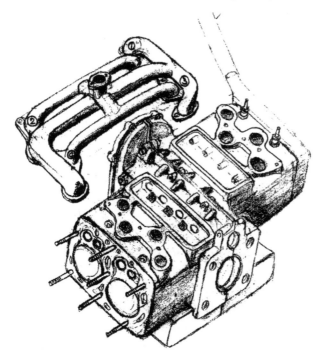

Issigonis designed a new horizontally opposed 'flat-four' engine for the Mosquito though it was later dropped from the project.

affected the suspension design and turning circle. The engine was to be built in two sizes, 800 cc and 1100 cc, and three units were constructed, so of the six new prototypes which had been ordered some would be fitted with the new unit and some with the Series E.

By 1946, thanks to two years of hard work by Issigonis and his team, Morris Motors was well advanced with its plans for the post-war era just as Thomas had hoped they would be. Of course when the project had started no one had any idea how long the war would be or what economic or political conditions would be like when it was over. When peace finally came the British motor industry emerged in a fairly strong position, partly because it had survived the depression in better shape than the older heavy engineering industries and partly because it had been able to make such a vital contribution to the war effort. The same could not be said of the country at large which was financially as well as emotionally drained by the cost of the war. It has been estimated that up to 10 per cent of the national wealth had been destroyed by a combination of physical damage and the running down of capital assets. There was no immediate post-war boom and the next ten years were to be ones of continuing austerity for the British population. Petrol rationing continued until March 1950; food and clothes rationing persisted even longer.

In July 1945 an election was called and the electorate decided to vote for a fresh start, replacing the Conservative administration of wartime hero Winston Churchill with a Labour government headed by Clement Attlee. As A.J.P. Taylor so elegantly phrased it, 'the electors cheered Churchill and voted against him'. The new government needed foreign currency and they expected the car industry to do its part by producing a smaller range of cars for a much wider global market than had been the case before the war. The motor industry, however, could not just switch from military production to motor vehicle production overnight. The only practical solution for the immediate future was to return to their pre-war designs and the cars churned out in 1945 and 1946 looked exactly like those that were being sold in 1938 and 1939. To complicate matters there were widespread materials shortages, particularly of steel, which limited the number of cars which could be produced. As a result, priority in the supply of rationed materials was given to products to be manufactured for export so even if he had been able to get the petrol, the British consumer would have had very little opportunity to purchase a brand new motor vehicle to put it in. This forced the motor industry to shift its focus away from its traditionally insular philosophy and set its sights on overseas markets. The pre-war slogan 'buy British and be proud of it' was replaced with 'export or die' and Britain became the world's leading exporter of cars by 1949.

Under these circumstances Thomas was confident that the Mosquito project would allow Morris Motors to take the initiative very quickly. Like its competitors it put its leading pre-war product, the Morris Eight Series E, back into production, but work on the Mosquito intensified and Thomas decided on a target launch date of January 1947. His intention was that the Mosquito would be quickly followed by a whole family of cars including a Wolseley derivative with a 1-litre in-line four-cylinder engine to be known as the Wolseley Wasp, an intermediate car with a 1250/1500 cc engine to be named the Morris Oxford and a larger car with a 4-litre engine which would be called the Morris Imperial. In September 1945 he tried one of the flat-four-equipped prototypes for himself and opti-mistically assured Oak that there need be no more specification changes and that the tooling could be set up to enable full production to go ahead on schedule for the desired launch date. Reg Job therefore began the com-plex task of preparing accurate drawings to represent the hundreds of parts which went into making up the body shell plus all the other in-ternal and external fittings. Once these were completed they were sent to Nuffield Metal Products in Birmingham where a full-sized mahogany model was made. This provided the basis from which the steel panels would be manufactured in a complicated and lengthy process which involved a great deal of hand-finishing.

Once a project had progressed to this level there was usually no going back, not least because of the amount of expenditure which had already been incurred. Nevertheless Thomas' optimism about the finalisation of the specification proved wide of the mark and last-minute decisions such as the alteration of the windscreen height by three-quarters of an inch in May 1946 frustrated Reg Job because of the advanced stage the body drawings and tooling had reached. Economies also began to creep in so that manufacturing costs could be maintained in order to meet the objec-tive of a cheaper selling price than the Morris Eight. All the same, confi-dence within the team remained high and Vic Oak reported enthusiasti-cally to Miles Thomas: 'I tested out last evening the first prototype "Mosquito" and I am pleased to be able to say that it is, in my opinion, by far the best prototype car I have ever been associated with.'

LORD NUFFIELD VERSUS SIR MILES THOMAS

Throughout 1946 preparations for production rolled inexorably on. Completing the engineering of the project, however, proved to be a great deal easier than getting it accepted into the model range and while Issigonis, Daniels and Job laboured away under the skilled eye of Vic Oak they were largely unaware of the bruising battle which Miles Thomas was waging on behalf of their project with an increasingly obstinate Lord Nuffield. This story is clearly told in the Miles Thomas collection of papers, held in the Archive of the British Motor Industry Heritage Trust, which contains all the correspondence which went downwards to Vic Oak and his team and upwards to the Morris Motors Board in the period between 1940 and 1947.

Thomas had initiated the project and given it his full support in the firm conviction that this was the direction in which Morris Motors must go to secure its post-war future. But he became embroiled in a board-room battle in defence of his plans which was being stoked behind the scenes by Chairman Lord Nuffield who was intent on keeping the Morris Eight at the centre of the product range and ditching the new design. Despite his promise to stand back from the running of the company, Nuffield had proved spectacularly unable to do so and his actions were beginning to cause serious damage. As Thomas rather witheringly put it in his autobiography, 'although W.R. [i.e. Lord Nuffield] had said long before that he was going to leave the running of the business to the Board, he still persisted in exercising what was inappropriately, if undeniably, his right of destructive criticism'. Miles Thomas described his attempt in 1946 to persuade Lord Nuffield that the Mosquito should be put into production as soon as possible:

Lord Nuffield was in no mood for changes. His argument was that we had more orders for the Morris Eight than we could cope with, so what was the point in putting the Mosquito or, as we finally decided to call it, the Morris Minor onto the market? In vain I argued that so great was the demand for cars in these days, in spite of the inflated prices plus purchase tax, that anybody who wanted one put in an order for at least five different makes, and when one of them was delivered the other four orders were not worth the paper they were written on. I pleaded that the Morris Eight was rapidly becoming out of date, the

Morris Minor would give us a commanding lead. He was adamant. The frustration left a sour taste in my mouth.

Lord Nuffield disliked the unconventionality of the car and he drew comfort from the fact that the sales team were also unenthusiastic about the prospect of marketing it while the Board was packed with directors who had served there for 30 years or more and were as conservative as himself in their tastes. He therefore stubbornly adopted the position that Morris Motors should carry on with Morris Eight production for as long as possible and his tactics ensured that no final decision could be made in time for the January 1947 deadline to be met.

In April 1947 Thomas attempted to broker a compromise by conceding that the Morris Eight could continue in production for a further eighteen months with a revised front end, proposing at the same time that the Mosquito should be introduced as an MG 1100 with a conventional engine which would enable it to be priced above the Morris Eight. He argued that MG customers would not object to paying more for a car if they were getting something out of the ordinary. Thomas hoped in this way to circumvent Nuffield's intransigence. His aim was to ensure that the Mosquito in some form stayed in the forward model programme to appear at the autumn 1948 Motor Show where he knew that Austin would be presenting new models and might steal the march on Morris by so doing. The MG survived as the only part of the Mosquito project in the forward plan for quite a while, despite disgruntled opposition from MG's Managing Director, but in the meantime Nuffield was doing everything he could to promote the retention of the Morris Eight beyond its eighteen-month reprieve by suggesting that all that was required was some restyling and the addition of the Mosquito suspension. Vic Oak looked into the practicality of this proposal and even built a prototype to Nuffield's suggested specification. His conclusion was that the tooling costs would be prohibitive and the timescale of a launch in the spring of 1949 unattainable.

Battle was clearly joined. Would Morris Motors base its model programme on a revised Morris Eight as Nuffield wanted or would it take the bolder step of producing the new Mosquito? This was the question Thomas continually put before the Board throughout 1947 but to his dismay the Board's response to a request from the Ministry of Supply to limit the model range due to materials shortages was to drop even the surviving MG 1100 from the forward plan.

While the discussion dragged on and the team waited in vain for the green light to go into final production Issigonis decided to make one last, drastic alteration to the Mosquito. Pondering over the proportions of the final prototype, he went back to the workshop one evening with his mechanics and asked them to cut the bodyshell in half. The following morning they began moving the pieces apart and back together as he watched until he got the balance he was looking for. Alec decided an extra four inches would be just right. This alteration did several things. It improved the look of the car and by widening the frame it provided more stability and helped to avoid roll. It also increased that interior space with which its designer was so obsessed. The widened version was shown to Miles Thomas in late 1947 and when he saw it he was more convinced than ever of the car's importance to the company's future. He therefore wrote perhaps one of the most important documents of the whole saga to Vic Oak, copied to Alec Issigonis, on 14 October 1947 and entitled 'Wide MOSQUITO':

Whether we like it or not, we shall have one day to find something to follow the Morris Eight. At Nuffield Metal Products I was perturbed to see what Mr Tolley graphically called the 'graveyard of the MOS-QUITO' – a pile of tools that have never been used and which clearly represent much locked-up capital.

Mr Tolley tells me that, in so far as the structure back of the dash is concerned, the wide MOSQUITO body can be produced at a cost per body that does not exceed that of the original narrow version. There would, of course, be a tool charge for the change.

Equally, Mr Tom Brown tells me that a side-valve version of the 1100 cc overhead-camshaft engine would cost 30/- or £2 less than the original flat-four 1100 engine. The present 8 hp engine bored out to 950–980 cc would cost even less.

I want two investigations made:

1) to explore the possibility of fitting the present 8 hp engine scant-lings in the wide MOSQUITO, utilizing, if possible, the same wings and the same bonnet top as we have at the moment. If the perform-ance of the car with the bored-out engine is satisfactory, then we have an attractive proposal; if not:

2) let us explore the possibility of altering the front to take an 1100 side-valve engine. This latter proposal does not attract me so much

because it means (a) a new engine which would be more expensive than the current 8 hp, and (b) extra tooling and extra unit cost for the revised front end.

But both angles are worth investigating:

I would like you to fit a wide MOSQUITO with an 8 hp engine bored out.

In making this directive, Thomas had fixed the form in which the Morris Minor would finally emerge. This memo also shows clearly why the flat-four engine was finally dropped. Whether or not the engine would have been successful or practical we will never know but in the end it was just one of too many elements that was blocking the progress of the car. It was an expensive luxury and it had to go. A few weeks later Miles Thomas gave another instruction to Vic Oak which shows that even at this stage of his career Alec was implementing his 'minimalist' view of interior design against the inclinations of his colleagues: 'Mr Issigonis is to continue development work on the job with a view to improving the noise level … I am particularly anxious that the trim scheme of this job should be given careful consideration, so that an attractive well-tailored interior is presented.'

The change of engine required little adjustment to the engineering of the car so Jack Daniels was not particularly concerned about it. Poor Reg Job, however, was faced with fitting Alec's extra four inches into the bodyshell even though much of the body-tooling was already complete. Rather than redraw the whole thing he created a flat area in the centre of the car where the join occurred which avoided any alterations to the rest of the layout. The floor pan had metal strips added in so there would be no need to widen the transmission tunnel. There was one thing which it was too late to alter – the front and rear bumpers had already been manufactured so a piece was inserted in the middle.

Now Miles Thomas had a definitive specification all he had to do was persuade Lord Nuffield to accept it so he could get the Mosquito back into the forward plan. He sent a policy document to Lord Nuffield on 25 October 1947 insisting that dates must be set for the end of Morris Eight production and the launch of the new wide Mosquito. He cited the shortage of steel as an insurmountable reason why there must be the minimum of overlap between the two events. Finally Nuffield gave in. Instead of the Morris Eight with Mosquito suspension that he had wanted, the company went ahead with a Mosquito carrying the Morris Eight power unit. On 10 November 1947 Oak's team were told to get on with the preparation of the 'wide' Mosquito as described to them in his memo eleven days earlier as quickly as possible. The same day, he instructed S.V. Smith to prepare for the production of 50,000 units to begin selling on 1 January 1949, with at least twelve pre-production cars to be available for the all-important 1948 Motor Show.

Having secured the future of the Mosquito and of Morris Motors, Miles Thomas decided to think about his own. The next day, on 11 November, Thomas' resignation was accepted by a full Board meeting presided over by Lord Nuffield. He was thanked for his long service to the firm and awarded a £10,000 settlement by the Board, personally signed by Lord Nuffield. He enjoyed a short retirement for two years before becoming Chairman of BOAC (the British Overseas Airways Corporation, forerunner of British Airways) at a time during which the aviation industry was in a very similar position to that of the motor car industry when he had joined it.

Reginald Hanks replaced him as Managing Director and Vice-chairman. His first action was to completely restructure the Board, sweeping out many of Nuffield's longest-serving allies, a measure he insisted on before accepting the post. He then gave priority to ensuring that there were no further interruptions to the momentum which had built up behind the Mosquito project. In the final version it was decided to stick to the conventional 918 cc capacity power unit and abandon the proposed bored out 980 cc version but otherwise the specification was that laid down by Thomas in his 'Wide Mosquito' memo. One more change was made following Thomas' departure: in December the Board decided to drop the name Mosquito and replace it with the more conventional but nostalgic tag of 'Morris Minor', harking back to one of the most successful small Morris cars of the pre-war era. The car finally went into production and appeared triumphantly at the October Motor Show attracting much attention as one of the most innovative post-war designs on display just as Thomas had always intended. Lord Nuffield declined to accept defeat gracefully and refused to drive the car for press photographs.

At a personal level Issigonis seemed pleased at the change of leadership. He respected Miles Thomas and was grateful for the chance he had given him but he knew Reggie Hanks much more closely both socially and professionally than he was ever likely to know his predecessor. Though in later years Issigonis implied that it was Hanks rather than Thomas who got the Minor into production, the Miles Thomas paperwork clearly shows that he made absolutely sure that the project had reached the point of no return before tendering his resignation. Issigonis, however, would not have known just how much Miles Thomas went through on the car's behalf.

It was not just the engineering of the car which was unconventional; the decision to produce a small car went against the trend since most firms decided to introduce larger cars at the 1948 Motor Show. Issigonis wrote an article on the subject of his new design shortly after its launch which touched on the reasons for this choice:

> Like its long chain of famous predecessors, the new Morris Minor is primarily an economy model. At the end of the last world war we heard a great deal about reforms in car design. Opinion had turned big car minded. With the return of prosperity and abundant supplies of petrol all over the world, why did we want to waste our time building small cars? Victory had brought wealth and plenty to a starved world. The Nuffield Organization framed its design policy on a more cautious view. Above all, whatever the conditions, customer satisfaction comes before wishful thinking. As a result of this policy, the small car development section of the Organization was never dropped when car design was resumed after the cessation of hostilities, and we now find a car available which fits the economic conditions of this rather lean post-war era to perfection.

Thus he claims that the Morris Minor is a triumph of realism over optimism, something which chimed very well with his own personality. The original reason why Miles Thomas had wanted a small car design was the RAC horsepower tax and ironically this disappeared the very year the car was launched. The tax had first been imposed in 1921 and was a major influence throughout the period of its existence on how cars were designed. On 1 January 1948 it was abolished and replaced by a flat rate of car tax at £10 per car. Fortunately, this had no effect whatsoever on the success of the Morris Minor which quickly became the best-selling British small car at home and abroad and earned the proud distinction of being the first British car to reach the million mark in 1960.

Though press reviews in 1949 were written in the polite and self-consciously impartial manner of the time, motoring correspondents found it hard to suppress a glimmer of excitement at 'this attractive newcomer which sets high standards of small-car stability, comfort and economy', as *The Motor* so charmingly put it. The reviewer continued:

> Amongst the record number of visitors to the Earls Court motor exhibition last October there were many who felt that the new Morris Minor 'Stole the Show'. There can be no pretence that it approaches perfection, but it is a car which pleases both driver and passengers and which will almost exactly fulfil the requirement of tens of thousands of motorists in this country and abroad – there has been nothing like it in the economy car class previously.

The review singles out the excellence of the suspension and roadholding by describing two rather idiosyncratic tests conducted to prove these qualities:

> ... perhaps the most sensitive tests of riding qualities are for a passenger to write and sleep in the car. By the former test, the Minor is a fraction too firmly sprung to score the highest marks, but by the latter test it gained a very high rating even while covering an astonishing distance within an hour.

Once the passenger had put his notebook away and was fully awake, he concurred with the driver that the car had a deeper appeal, a 'charm of its own' which made up for its inadequacies in the areas of trim and equipment:

> The Morris Minor is an astonishing car, in that one criticizes freely yet would not dream of condemning – its faults are criticized because, when a small car offers merits normally associated with large and expensive models plus a charm of its own, there is inevitably a 'much would have more' seeking after costly trimmings. The highest tribute to the Minor is that a variety of drivers hitherto enthusing over larger and faster cars suddenly began to feel that this grown-up baby could fulfil all their requirements and double their m.p.g. figures.

When asked about Lord Nuffield's view of the car, Issigonis wryly commented:

> Lord Nuffield hated the Morris Minor as soon as he saw it and so did all the sales people. It was humble pie when we made a million of them, he had the decency to speak to me once after that. He described it as a poached egg. He was furious when he saw it!

Lord Nuffield and Issigonis were well separated in the hierarchy of the Nuffield Organisation and had little to do with each other directly. Nevertheless Issigonis was well aware that Lord Nuffield did not like either him – 'that foreign chap' – or his car – 'the poached egg' – and Nuffield was one of the first to play around with Alec's name in a most unflattering way, referring to him as 'Issi-wassi-what's his bloody name'.

Though this probably hurt his feelings it was a minor consideration in October 1948 when he became the hero of the hour. He may not have had the complete freedom that he would have liked, but Alec had at last done it. He had been given the opportunity to create a new concept in small cars and it was a success. The fact that such a small team, clearly under his direction, had produced every part of this car themselves seemed to infuse a sense of personality into the vehicle which appealed to its enthusiastic owners above and beyond its virtues as basic transport. On 12 April 1948 he received the following memo from the Vice-chairman of the Nuffield Organisation:

> Strictly personal and confidential,
>
> Dear Mr Issigonis, Mr A. V. Oak has informed me of the hard and constructive work you are doing, – which I can happily confirm from my own observations, and I have been very pleased indeed to arrange for your salary to be increased from £960 gross to £1500 gross as a measure of the Company's appreciation of your co-operation,
>
> Yours sincerely, R. F. Hanks.

His reaction to this news was to go out and buy a three-strand string of real pearls with a sapphire clasp which he gave to his mother.

ALVIS

... the 'cigarettes over the partition' era ... they were happy days, the pyjama conferences at MIRA, bonnets flying through the air, plumbing all over the car, shock absorber 'niggles' to mention but a few of the incidents never to be forgotten. I really believe the days spent with you developing 'that other car' were the happiest and most interesting I have experienced during many years in the motor industry.

Harry Barber to Sir Alec Issigonis in 1969

LIFE AFTER THE WAR

WHEN PEACE RETURNED to Europe, the private life of the Issigonises resembled that of millions of other Britons as they tried to get their lives back in order after five years of war followed by continued shortages and deprivations. In 1947 Hetty returned to Britain after one final visit to Izmir and Alec drove Hulda, May and the children to Tilbury docks to meet her off the boat. Hetty had brought a feast of exotic food back to ration-bound England and the family piled into Alec's car and made their way happily back to Kingswood to feast on halva, rolls of dried apricot in wax, fish roe, pistachio and cashews. The following year Alec and Hulda also took a trip to Izmir and Alec spent some time with his old friend Donald Riddle who was now working for British Petroleum (BP) in Istanbul. These were the final attempts by the two women to extract something from their troubled past. Hetty became ill in late 1950 and for the first time the Issigonises did not go to Rustlings for the Christmas celebrations. In October 1951 she died at the age of 68 and Hulda was extremely upset by the loss of the 'sister' to whom she had been so close since early childhood. After Hetty's death the visits to Rustlings became less frequent and Hulda decided that in future she and Alec would celebrate Christmas on their own in the Oxford flat. Sally and Mark, however, continued to visit Sollershott as teenagers and now the lunches at Elliston and Cavell's were supplemented by the luxury of ice-cream in the lounge of the rather grander Randolph Hotel across the road from the Ashmolean Museum.

The end of the Second World War also saw the reappearance of George

Dowson in Alec's life. While he had been away, his parents had taken back the running of the farm with the help of a manager. George's sister Babs Holbrow had moved to Perthshire following her marriage but she too returned to assist when her husband was killed while serving in the RAF. She stayed at the Poplars until the end of the war and then moved to a neighbouring farmhouse which also belonged to the family, sharing it with her brother Harry Dowson and his wife.

After joining the RAF in 1939, George had been stationed at various bases throughout Nottinghamshire and Lincolnshire. His eyesight was not good enough to become a pilot so he took on the job of engineering and servicing Lancaster bombers. In August 1941, while stationed at Syerston near Newark, he met a local girl called Ida Frances Bayliss during a Sunday morning drinks party at the officers' mess. Ida had been born in 1912, the youngest of four children, and at this time she was working at 'Cécile's' dress boutique in Newark. She helped the owner, Mabel Harrison, to run the shop, acting as a buyer for new lines, assisting with sales and serving as the in-house model. The practice of the time was not to sell ready-made off-the-shelf clothes but to allow customers to pick out the clothes they liked, then model the items to them before having them made up in the relevant size. Mabel did not consider 'Ida' to be a good enough name for the duties her new assistant was called on to perform in her rather posh shop so she decided to rename her 'Maxine'. Ida was teased endlessly by her family on account of this and gained the nickname 'Max' by which she would be known for the rest of her life.

George and Max were engaged only three months after meeting and they were married in June 1942 at Newark Parish Church. Alec did not go to the wedding but he did receive a piece of wedding cake in a box, which he found extremely entertaining. 'Cake in a box my dear, what an idea!' he joked to them after the war. During this time there were few opportunities for them to meet. George could take only 48 hours of leave at a time and this was all too easily filled with visits to see his parents in Worcestershire or his sister in Perth plus the occasional trip to London. Alec, by now, was spending every waking hour working on the Mosquito project. It was therefore not until George took Max back to the Poplars in 1945 to resume his life as a farmer that Alec was introduced to the younger Mrs Dowson.

This was a difficult moment because George had left Worcestershire as a free-and-easy bachelor while Max had heard so many stories about

'George's best friend Alec' that she felt considerable apprehension about meeting him. To everyone's relief Alec and Max took to each other immediately. He was already a firm favourite with Mrs Dowson senior so the weekend visits to the Poplars resumed. He was soon one of the family again and he was invited to join George and Max on their first holiday at Polzeath in Cornwall during the summer of 1946, indulging in some fishing and, rather less to Alec's taste, a great deal of walking.

It was now possible to get the Lightweight Special out of the garage. In June 1946 Issigonis and Dowson attended their first post-war event at Elstree aerodrome. They resumed their practice of entering both the 750 cc and 1100 cc classes, each taking the wheel for alternate events. On this occasion Alec won in the 750 cc class. They took ten-year-old Mark Ransome with them and this was the first time he had seen the Lightweight in action, Alec in the cockpit, George push-starting it and flames shooting out of the four exhaust stubs which stuck out of the side of the car making an incredible noise. A few weeks later Alec competed at Gransden Lodge Airfield, again winning the 750 cc class event. They did not attempt to develop the car, but one major change was the replacement of the Austin side-valve power unit. Sometime during 1947 Alec obtained a supercharged experimental Wolseley prototype engine from the Cowley works which, though heavier, gave a better power to weight ratio.

Following these two successful outings they began to compete regularly once again. The Prescott hill-climb became a recurring date in their diary and John Bolster would later comment that the Lightweight Special began to win in the 750 cc category with 'monotonous regularity'. The other event which they favoured was the Brighton Speed Trials which consisted of a one kilometre dash down Madeira Drive on the seafront. They would make their way down to Brighton in George's Lancia Aprilia, towing the Lightweight Special behind in a grey box trailer and often stopping off at Kingswood to break the journey and say hello. The objective was to set a fast time rather than to race, but two cars would be sent out at a time which provided an edge of direct competition. In 1946 Alec took the 750 cc event while George drove the 1100 cc and achieved the faster time of 32.94 seconds. In 1947, however, they swapped categories and this time Alec beat George by two-fifths of a second with a time of 28.54 seconds. George was a little put out by this and told the Kingswood household: 'Well of course Alec's lighter than me!' They were both very competitive and a pattern emerged whereby Alec was usually quicker in track events but George generally beat him in the hill-climbs. They came to a tacit agreement over this as George would state that he preferred hill-climbs because he liked to have the course to himself on the grounds that you never knew what other drivers would do, while Alec for his part claimed that he preferred track events like Brighton because he liked to see his competition:

> I always hated hill climbs like Shelsley or Prescott. You were racing against an invisible factor – the stop watch. I only enjoyed driving when one or more cars were on the track at the same time; then you could visually see how you were doing. George, who was a very good driver, therefore always did the hill climbs, and I raced the car at inter-varsity meetings, the Brighton Speed Trials and events of that type, where you were actually competing against someone you could see in your driving mirror. This gives you the stimulus to drive faster and better.

The trips to Brighton were to lead to another important acquaintance which did not bear fruit immediately but would become of tremendous importance in the future. It was here that Issigonis met John Cooper who had constructed his own 'Special' along with his friend Eric Brandon. Their car was a single seater made out of two Fiat 500 scrap front ends welded back to back to create a chassis with all-independent suspension. It had a 500 cc JAP motorcycle engine fitted behind the driver's seat with chain-drive to the back axle. At the 1946 Brighton Speed Trials, Cooper and Issigonis found their cars matched against each other on the same run, and the result was victory for the 'Cooper 500' over the distance. This was the start of their friendship and they continued to meet at various race meetings.

The winter of 1947 had been extremely harsh and one weekend George and Max, who was now pregnant, got caught in a severe snowstorm on the way back to the Poplars from London and took refuge with Alec and his mother at the Oxford flat till the weather died down. The bad winter was followed by an unusually hot summer so it was a great relief to poor Max when her first child, Penny, was born in August. Alec accepted the invitation to be a godparent and posed for the obligatory picture outside the church with the rest of the christening party, though he declined to be photographed holding the baby as the other godparents were. The guests on this occasion represented the key members of the social circle which was beginning to grow up around the Poplars. It included Flora Baker, who was Max's sister, and Betsy Rusher, who was a childhood friend of George's, as was her brother Tony Whitaker. Betsy was a frequent visitor to the farm, accompanied by her husband John Rusher when he was not away pursuing his career in the navy.

1948 was the last year of the Lightweight Special's brief career in the hands of its creators. Max was expecting the Dowsons' second child while Alec's work responsibilities were increasing following his success with the Morris Minor so the two men decided it was time to call a halt to their racing programme. From then on they restricted themselves to getting the car out at weekends and thrashing round the farm's tracks or roaring up and down the long drive, executing standing starts from the farmhouse door to the farm gate at top speed.

This appeared to have been the right decision when Max went into hospital in 1949 to give birth to a son, Christopher, because this time there were complications. Christopher was born rhesus negative and Max had to stay with him in hospital until he recovered from the necessary medical procedures. Alec came to the rescue as he had done ten years earlier for his cousin May, going down to the Poplars to keep George and Penny company. This time, instead of miniature trains, he spent hours entertaining Penny in the back garden of the house with his latest craze of model aeroplanes. He had recently begun to construct these accomplished pieces of work on the versatile dining room table at the Oxford flat. 'Clara' was the first model to be finished, a small single-engined plane named after the matriarch of the Stengel/Prokopp family which went through several versions. Soon she was joined by a much grander twin-engined plane christened 'Brabazon' or 'The Brab' after an ambitious prototype intercontinental passenger plane designed by the Bristol Aeroplane Company which took its first flight in 1949.

George, his brother Harry and Alec often flew these planes together at the Poplars. They were not radio controlled but designed for 'free-flight' so the flying sessions could be very unpredictable. One day the smaller plane span out of control and headed off over the river, presumed lost. A few days later a neighbour rang the Poplars doorbell and handed a rather battered object back to Max whose exclamation 'Oh, poor Clara!' rather took him by surprise. The damaged plane was quickly whisked away for repair in the farm workshop where Alec and George continued to spend their leisure hours experimenting with model aeroplanes, boats and even a steam engine.

LAST DAYS AT MORRIS

Issigonis had been making some career progress within Morris Motors and in 1950 he was promoted on the back of his growing reputation as the designer of Cowley's most successful current model. The reputation of the Morris Minor tends to obscure the fact that it was just one vehicle in a whole model range. Of the original family of cars which Miles Thomas had envisaged, the Wolseley Wasp and the Morris Imperial were shelved, but after the completion of the Mosquito project the team went on to produce the Morris Oxford MO which was a slightly larger version of the Minor. The model range was completed by the Morris Six, the Wolseley 6/80 and the Wolseley 4/50 which incorporated the key features of torsion bar suspension and rack and pinion steering. None of these cars could be described as exciting or ground-breaking in the way the Morris Minor had been and they were all replaced within six years in contrast to the Minor's life-span of 24 years, but in their day they enjoyed respectable sales and served a useful purpose in the model range.

By now Issigonis had become a minor celebrity, appearing at press dinners and being put forward by the company as a spokesman on design matters. But while he was basking in his triumph, the situation within the top ranks of Morris Motors was rapidly deteriorating. Reggie Hanks did not possess either the political acumen or the determination of Miles Thomas and the changes at board level did little to bring an end to the executive squabbling. Far from breaking the deadlock over the development of the model range, the Morris Minor was beginning to seem like a temporary blip.

Vic Oak was becoming increasingly frustrated that the ideas coming from his department were being continually blocked by Lord Nuffield and though Issigonis tried hard to ignore what was happening the political situation inside the company was not conducive to his creativity. Once he had completed the Minor/Oxford model range he seemed unsure what to do. Since radical new ideas no longer seemed to be wanted he decided to look at what might be done to improve the Morris Minor by making a front wheel drive version. He was inspired by Citroën's pre-war front wheel drive designs because, although the French company had suffered the penalty of initially high unreliability for their innovation, Issigonis had been immensely impressed with the excellent roadholding delivered by such a configuration. He decided to add an idea of his own and fitted the engine transversely across the engine bay of the Morris Minor, with an ordinary gearbox attached to the end in the classic in-line formation which is now the norm for transverse engine, front wheel drive vehicles. The car was taken out and tested but he was not entirely satisfied with the results, despite the fact that the car worked exceptionally well in icy conditions; but the experiment, as ever, was stored up in his mind for future reference.

It was at this time that Issigonis first met the inventor Alex Moulton. The Moultons were proprietors of the firm George Spencer, Moulton & Co. which was based in a former woollen mill known as 'the Hall' at Bradford-on-Avon near Bath in Wiltshire. In North America at the end of the 19th century, Charles Goodyear had invented a process for converting natural India rubber gum into a solid elastic material known as vulcanised rubber. The Moulton family had acquired the rights to exploit this process in Britain and their enterprise was a great success, manufacturing a variety of products such as waterproof capes for the British forces in the Crimea, rubber springs for the railways and dentures. By the early 20th century another product was selling well, the new-fangled pneumatic tyres which were required for early motor vehicles. Alex Moulton was born in 1920 and he was brought up at the Hall by his grandparents, following his father's death at a young age. Like Alec Issigonis, Alex Moulton was influenced by the family business which was part of his living environment and he showed a strong inclination towards engineering in his childhood. He attended Marlborough Public School followed by Kings College at Cambridge University but when he was only one year into his degree the Second World War broke out. He volunteered to join the RAF and was placed at the Bristol Aeroplane Company where he stayed throughout the war working on various engineering projects and this brought him into contact with a number of leading aviation engineers. After the war he joined the family firm and set up his own research department to experiment with rubber suspension and springing. He also decided to go back to Cambridge and finish his education and in 1949 he was finally awarded his degree.

As an innovator himself, Alex Moulton was impressed by the new Morris Minor and was keen to meet its designer, so in 1949 he persuaded Issigonis' racing friend Joe Fry – who also lived in the Bradford-on-Avon district – to introduce them. The two struck up an immediate friendship, having a similar outlook and interests. Moulton hoped to get Issigonis interested in his ideas about the use of rubber springing on cars but Issigonis showed little enthusiasm for his suggestion that they should try putting it onto a Morris Minor. It was not until Issigonis left Morris Motors in 1952, and Jack Daniels took over the research department at Cowley, that Moulton was able to make any real progress with his project. Jack Daniels agreed to assemble a fully rubber sprung Morris Minor which was tested for a thousand miles on the gruelling durability track at the proving ground run by the Motor Industry Research Association (MIRA) without any significant failure. The data which was gathered proved the practicality of rubber as a suspension material and Moulton would later use this test to convince Issigonis that he should consider using this material on his next project. That project, however, was not to be for Morris Motors.

JOINING ALVIS

When Leonard Lord arrived at Longbridge in 1938 he found a situation not unlike the one he had just left behind at Cowley, since Lord Austin was as reluctant as Lord Nuffield to let go of the business he had founded and which carried his name. This obstacle was swiftly removed by Austin's death in 1941, leaving Lord in complete control of Longbridge's fortunes. After the brief interruption of the war, the rivalry between Britain's two biggest motor manufacturers resumed with Nuffield and Len Lord now on opposite sides. But circumstances had changed and their battles were being played out against the backdrop of the weakening position of the British motor industry in world markets. This became fully evident in 1956 when Germany took over from Britain as the leading European motor manufacturer, a position Britain was never able to regain. The only sensible course of action from a business point of view was to effect a merger between the two bitter rivals and this was something that even Lord Nuffield, whatever his personal feelings, came to see the logic of.

A certain amount of progress down this route had already taken place in 1948 when the two companies made a tentative agreement to join forces, but on this occasion the plans were stalled. It was therefore not until February 1952 that they came together as the British Motor Corporation (BMC) with headquarters at Longbridge. Though this was called a merger it was effectively a take-over of the Nuffield Organisation by the Austin Motor Company. It did not take long for it to become evident that Len Lord was determined to make good on the parting threat he had made to Lord Nuffield in 1936. He made the most of every opportunity to belittle the former directors of Morris Motors and ensure that Austin was the senior partner in every way. Issigonis had arrived at Cowley shortly before Lord's departure so he did not know him personally and it was clear to everyone from the beginning that the Austin and not the Morris design office was going to be at the heart of the new corporation. There would be little opportunity for Issigonis to work in the calm and sympathetic atmosphere which his rather delicate temperament required to nurture his creativity. Nor would he be given the level of independence and responsibility which he now felt he was entitled to.

In this unpleasant situation, he asked Reggie Hanks what he should do. His friendly relationship with the Vice-chairman was of little practical help within BMC. Hanks had been a vociferous opponent of the merger and as a result was one of Lord's favourite whipping boys. He advised Issigonis to leave if he had the opportunity. Then Alec heard of a possible opening at Alvis, which manufactured a mixture of aero engines, armoured vehicles and motor cars. It was not in the Alvis tradition to be bold or innovative but as part of their post-war strategy they had decided that they needed a new car to revitalise their model range. After an interview with Managing Director John Joseph Parkes, Alec was offered the chance to design it. Within one month of the merger, he had bailed out to a rather steadier boat.

Alvis was a small company based in premises on Holyhead Road in Coventry and its resources were meagre compared with the might of the new British Motor Corporation. The move would therefore impose the obvious disadvantages of leaving the team with which he had built up such a good working relationship and losing the resources which had enabled him to realise such an ambitious project as the Morris Minor. Alec thought very carefully about what he was doing. After receiving the offer he looked round for someone who might give him some advice. Not many people within the Nuffield Organisation had any experience of working outside the mainstream industry but there was one, and he just happened to occupy the office next door. Gerald Palmer was in charge of design for the MG, Riley and Wolseley model range and he had previously spent six years designing the Jowett Javelin for a modest company named Jowett based in Bradford. At the beginning of 1952 he was surprised to find himself being asked by the celebrated designer of the Morris Minor what it was like to work for a small firm. He considered this an odd question as he had listened to many lectures from Issigonis about his vision for a 'charwoman's car', which had been his favourite theme for a number of years. The vehicle he had in mind would not only make motoring affordable for the average charlady, but would do her the courtesy of delivering the same ease and pleasure of driving as that taken for granted by those who could afford big expensive cars. There would be no chance to work on such a project without the resources of a major manufacturer at his disposal. Nevertheless Palmer tried to be helpful and expressed his opinion that the biggest benefit of such a situation was that 'you were your own boss'. This confirmed the conclusion which Issigonis had already reached. Riding on the back of the success of the Morris Minor, his position at Alvis would be much more personally satisfying than the one he might expect to be given at BMC as a senior engineer in the drawing office of the weaker partner.

There was an interesting postscript to his career at Morris Motors. In 1951 Issigonis had begun to work on ideas to improve the Morris Minor and the strength of his influence inside the design department is starkly demonstrated by the fact that after his departure the design team continued to steer an Alec-esque course as they worked on their first post-merger project and successor to the Oxford MO, the Morris Oxford Series II which was given the project code DO 1033. Though he had been gone for two years by the time it appeared in 1954 the Issigonis trademarks, both good and bad, were all there – excellent space utilisation, a wheel at each corner, spareness of styling, awkward positioning of the steering column. This car would go on to earn the distinction of surviving for many decades in India as the Hindustan Ambassador, ironically making it the 'Issigonis' design with the longest production history of all.

Although his contract with Alvis is dated 5 June 1952 it is clear from his sketchbooks that Alec was active at Alvis from March. His job was to lead an entirely new project code-named TA/350. It is unlikely that Issigonis saw himself spending the rest of his career at the Holyhead Road factory but for the moment it would be a safe bunker to hide in until the missiles had stopped flying between Longbridge and Cowley. This is the likely reason why this time he and Hulda did not move their home but began a routine whereby Alec lived in a hotel in Warwick during the week while Hulda remained in the Oxford flat to which Alec returned at weekends.

John Parkes, Alec's new boss, was only three years older than his new

Chief Designer and they quickly became friends as well as colleagues. Parkes had been born in Barnet though his family came from Coventry and he served his engineering apprenticeship with various local automotive companies. In 1929 he obtained a pilot's licence and spent three years in the Auxiliary Air Force before becoming one of three founder members of a company named Airwork for whom he acted as Technical Manager and Test Pilot. In 1936 he moved to De Havilland Aircraft where he stayed throughout the war until joining Alvis as Managing Director in 1946. Parkes was chosen because of his mix of aeronautical and automotive experience which ideally suited the company's post-war strategy. Like Alec, Parkes was an enthusiast for all new technologies and he held a licence for an amateur radio transmitter.

John Parkes had three children, Michael (or Mike), Annabel and John. Mike Parkes, born in 1931, was just twenty when Alec came on the scene but the two became good friends. He was coming to the end of his engineering apprenticeship at Humber in Coventry and would stay there throughout the 1950s, working on the Hillman Imp project which was an attempt by the Rootes Group to compete in the small car market. This gave him much to talk about with his father's new Chief Designer, as did his personal passion for driving racing cars and flying aeroplanes. Mike's love of motor sport would eventually take him out of engineering and into a career as a professional racing driver during the 1960s, something of which his father strongly disapproved, but it was an immediate point of contact with Issigonis who took him down to the Poplars during 1952 to see the Lightweight Special.

BUILDING A NEW TEAM

Alec's first task at Holyhead Road was to build up a new team and train them to work to his methods. He may have enjoyed this more the second time around because now he was in a position of authority with a growing reputation and could mould his team as he wanted. He did not really have much choice about who to recruit since Alvis was a very small firm in comparison to Morris Motors and there was no large pool of staff to choose from. Alvis' production volume was modest at only 2,000 cars per year and this did not justify maintaining its own body shop so the drawings prepared by its draughtsmen were sent out to a variety of other firms for manufacture.

First to join the new team was Chris Kingham who had been with

Alvis since 1945. He was an established specialist in engine design and was not over-enthusiastic when Chief Engineer Bill Dunn gave him the news that Alec Issigonis was joining the company to design a new car. Dunn asked him to consider being seconded to the project but Kingham, though he did not know Issigonis, was worried that the designer of a successful car like the Morris Minor, coming out of a big firm like Morris Motors with all its resources, would be difficult to work with. Dunn persisted, arguing that it would be a great career opportunity for Kingham, and after some consideration he finally agreed and joined Issigonis in the small office which had been set up for him near the main design office. They had a drawing board each, one large table between them, a plan chest and two ashtrays which were in constant use. Kingham soon found his fears to be unjustified: '... I found Alec autocratic, but very human and I think right from the word go there was a sort of affinity of outlook that made working together with him very easy.' He was not a *prima donna* after all.

When it came to draughtsmen, Issigonis acquired the services of Chief Body Engineer Harry Barber and his two assistants, John Sheppard and Fred Boubier. Like Chris Kingham, Sheppard and Boubier received the news about Alvis' new employee with some surprise. *They* were given no choice about whether or not they wanted to work for *him* and Sheppard was sent, with much apprehension, to introduce himself to the great man. It was therefore a relief when he found Issigonis to be charm itself and he was assigned to work on the chassis drawings while Boubier was to undertake the body drawings. Other team members had to be brought in from elsewhere. Bill Cassels was recruited from the Standard Motor Company to take care of the transmission and with him came Harry Harris to look after the suspension and running gear. Because of the importance put on the project, the TA/350 was given all the back-up that could possibly have been wanted in terms of setting up machines, hand-pressings or jigs. Finally, Issigonis completed his team by bringing in his new friend Alex Moulton as a specialist consultant, despite his scepticism about the practicalities of rubber suspension.

Sheppard and Boubier still reported to Harry Barber, who had his own office, but together with Cassels and Harris they moved into an area underneath the assembly shop which was extremely noisy. The atmosphere in the new workshop was convivial, with Issigonis spending a great deal of time down there looking over what they were doing and pushing the project along. He would stride into the room and wander from one draughtsman to another to see what progress had been made. Then he would get out his packet of 'Wills Goldflake' cigarettes, remarking, 'we can't think without one of these', and call his team together. Sometimes they gathered round the large flat table, leaning on their elbows as they talked or exchanging drawings for comment. At other times they stood round him at one of the drawing boards with pencils in hand, discussing ideas for the development of the car.

A working pattern soon began to emerge within the team. It was different from the relationship with Jack Daniels, which had been one of mutual dependence, the balance of Issigonis' ideas and Daniels' skill in interpreting them. At Alvis he was very much in charge. Kingham kept his distance, determined not to play the role of subordinate. John Sheppard, who was much more inexperienced, had no doubt that Issigonis was his boss and never argued with him about what had to be done. Once Issigonis had communicated the overall concept it was Sheppard's task to work out in formal drawings the dimensions of the floor, suspension and steering which would constitute the chassis portion of the monocoque. It was an immense challenge for a young man still in his mid-20s whose experience to date had been entirely with traditional coachbuilt cars which consisted of wooden frames clad with metal or aluminium castings. This was the first time he had worked on a monocoque construction so he had to learn quickly. The adaptability he displayed in such circumstances helped to cement a warm and friendly relationship with Issigonis, who was intolerant of slow thinkers. Before long they were sharing their coffee breaks and discussing solutions to the *Daily Telegraph* crossword. Not everyone was lucky enough to hit Issigonis' good spot, as John Sheppard recalls: 'We had a wonderful rapport together and I think this probably existed from the first day I met him. I don't know why, other people he used to just dismiss with a wave of his hand and that was the end of them, I was fortunate.'

Sheppard had an early demonstration of this from his colleague Fred Boubier, who was less inclined to do whatever he was told and frequently argued with his instructions which caused Issigonis considerable irritation. Boubier's independence of mind began to cause ructions in the team, even though he was good at his job. Issigonis, certain of what he wanted to achieve, was not really interested in listening to anyone else. At Morris there had been no choice about taking other people's opinions into account. This was no longer the case. After a year of arguments Boubier decided to take a job in the Longbridge styling studio and the harmony of the team was restored. John Sheppard now found himself charged with drawing the whole car by himself but because he had established a better relationship with his boss, Issigonis reacted with surprising sympathy. If he sensed that Sheppard's self-assurance was faltering, he would encourage rather than criticise him, making it clear that he had confidence in him. He reinforced this trust by giving his young assistant difficult tasks in an ironic, challenging way which spurred Sheppard on to show what he could do.

Alec's own dedication, enthusiasm and sheer energy helped to galvanise his colleagues and despite his single-mindedness he was an effective team leader, more of a benevolent dictator than an autocrat. He inspired a loyalty and optimism in his team which made them prepared to work hard and do considerable amounts of overtime to achieve results. This team spirit was fostered during annual visits to the British Motor Show at Earls Court. As the senior men Issigonis and Harry Barber would go down to London in advance, with the rest of the team travelling to join them at the end of the week. During the day, the party would wander round the exhibition hall, commenting on the cars and discussing new ideas over a cup of coffee in the restaurant afterwards. One year Issigonis and Harry Barber invited their junior colleagues to join them for dinner at the Patoria Hotel off Leicester Square. Kingham and Sheppard went to the theatre first so it was eleven at night by the time the meal got underway and Issigonis regaled them excitedly with tales of his day, the highlight of which had been a television interview. 'The lights were shining in my eyes and I couldn't see a thing', he complained. They had finished eating and the party had already started on their after-dinner drinks when Issigonis suddenly decided that what John Sheppard really needed to have was a pineapple dessert such as the one he himself had enjoyed the previous night. Despite the protests of an embarrassed Sheppard he called the waiter over to make his demand only to be informed that the hotel was out of pineapples. He was already an accomplished showman and enjoyed taking centre stage on such occasions. Refusing to take no for an answer, Issigonis retorted, 'don't be stupid, Covent Garden's not very far away, go and get one'. This did the trick and Issigonis got his pineapple dessert which Sheppard duly demolished to the great amusement of the rest of the party, who watched over him with their brandies in hand as he ate.

A Second Family

The move to Coventry had created a hectic routine for Issigonis. During the week he was living in Warwick and spending long hours at the factory before rushing home on Friday to see his mother. His increasing commitments meant there were fewer opportunities for the old visits to see May and her children, who were in any case now growing up fast. Nevertheless Alec made a considerable effort to assist his 'nephew' in establishing his engineering career, just as Mark's grandmother had done for him. He gave him a weekly allowance while he was studying at Battersea Polytechnic during the early 1950s and he used his connections at Cowley to secure the teenage boy a holiday job in the experimental department. Every morning Mark would cycle to work from his digs in Summertown and before returning there in the evening he would visit the flat where aunt Hulda would prepare him a meal. At the weekend Alec would be back from Coventry and Mark joined in their social activities including the continuing visits to the Trout. Alec was also spending a great deal of time at the Poplars, but though Hulda was also on friendly terms with the Dowsons she did not often go with her son on these visits.

When George and Max had returned to the farm in 1946 they were initially subjected to the very strict regime of the senior generation. During the 1930s John and Enid Dowson had employed a substantial workforce of labourers on the farm along with a butler and full staff for the house. George had to run the farm with a much smaller pool of farm workers while Max found herself coping single-handed with an extensive rota of meals, culminating in cocoa and biscuits before bed which she referred to in exasperation as 'the last straw'. The arrival of baby Penny, however, signalled that it was time for George's parents to move from the farm to a house in the nearby village where his father died the following year. The expansion of her family meant that Max was no less busy than before, but at least now she was in charge of her own household, assisted by a nanny and a daily help. Max used to joke that the old kitchen was so far from the dining room that she needed a bicycle to get there, and this problem too was solved by building a new kitchen in a more convenient location. From here she presided over the timely delivery of a slightly less onerous routine of meals which still provided the backbone of the family's day.

Life at the farm suited Alec very well and he fitted in comfortably with the well-rehearsed structure of their days. While Max made sure everything ran smoothly in the house, the two men would play in their workshop and talk about engineering. If it was winter and too cold to go outside, Alec would curl up in a chair in the sitting room reading the paper or enlist George's help to complete the *Daily Telegraph* crossword in the desired ten minutes. When the wind blew in a certain direction it came up from the cellar below the house, howling through the floorboards and making pockets of cold air underneath the carpet, causing Alec to grumble and put the newspaper round his legs to keep out the draught. Sometimes he wandered into Max's domain in the kitchen and asked 'what's cooking?' If it was pork, one of his favourite dishes, he would take a slice of bread and dip it into the pork dripping to eat, earning himself one of his many nicknames, 'Porkigonis'.

He also spent plenty of time playing with the children and answering their questions. As had been the case with cousin May's children, Alec was happy to put as much effort into his relationship with Penny and Christopher as he did with their parents. He had a very practical approach based on the assumption that children could understand anything if it was explained properly. Because he never patronised them he won their trust and appreciation. Better still, he was very entertaining, engaging in constant banter, pulling faces and throwing quizzical looks. He saw it as his duty to provide his goddaughter with exciting presents and it was not difficult for her to persuade him that she must have a charm bracelet like the one her mother possessed. Each year he would bring her an additional charm, often reflecting some current topic of interest. Just before a trip to Switzerland, for example, he gave her a tiny barrel with a St Bernard dog inside.

During the 1950s Alec and the Dowsons went on several skiing trips to Switzerland. Alec and George were competent skiers, Max on the other hand had a tendency to fall over and get left behind. In 1956 they were staying at the Hotel Seehof at Arosa near Davos when George became mysteriously ill with flu-like symptoms and a local doctor had to be called. Max was preoccupied with looking after him until the doctor could make a diagnosis, so once again Alec took on the role of entertainer to the children. Using young Christopher's Meccano set and an electric motor, they constructed a model car and then raced it up and down the hotel corridors. They had so much fun that the crisis over their father was completely driven from the children's minds as intended. George was finally diagnosed as having an irregular heartbeat and he spent several weeks in hospital after their return to England before being put on digitalis which enabled him to regain his full health.

Back at the Poplars, Max was expected to organise lunch and dinner parties for George and Alec's social circle, which she did with great aplomb. These were regularly attended by close family and friends such as Harry Dowson, Babs Holbrow, Betsy Rusher or Tony Whitaker and their spouses. Soon, the guest list expanded to include the fraternity of trials and hill-climbing enthusiasts. There was Dennis Poore who had once driven for the Aston Martin works team and later became an executive with Manganese Bronze which manufactured all kinds of things from London taxi-cabs to kitchen equipment. Alec used to say of Dennis, rather flippantly, 'Oh, he makes pots and pans for a living!' As Poore rose through the ranks he acquired an elegant house in Rutland Gate, Kensington, where Issigonis would visit him whenever he was in London to see the Motor Show at Earls Court or attend the British Racing Drivers' Club Ball at Grosvenor House. Then there were the Fry cousins, two very different characters, Joe being small and dapper, while David was large and rather swarthy with a quick wit which greatly chimed with Alec's own sense of humour. David and Alec remained close friends and Alec became godfather for a second time to David's son Conrad. Joe Fry was killed when their Freikaiserwagen crashed at Blandford in 1950, a sad end for both the driver and the car. Also among the set were fellow engineers like Alex Moulton, who had joined Alec at Alvis as a consultant on suspensions, and John Morris, the Managing Director of SU Carburettors.

Elegant and stylish, Max proved a talented hostess, not interfering in the endless discussions about engineering or motor racing but expertly co-ordinating the evening to avoid any bad-tempered arguing or unpleasantness, something which Alec, who hated conflict, greatly appreciated. Those attending the parties would usually bring a gift for their hostess. On one occasion a guest presented her with a box of chocolates which he proudly announced were hand-made. Alec quickly produced a box of Milk Tray from behind his back with the words 'I'm sorry my dear, I didn't have time to make any.' He was not fond of wine so before and during dinner he would indulge in his favourite drink which was gin and french. Over the dinner table there would be more light-hearted social banter and the guests would then retire to the drawing room while Max cleared everything away. Here they indulged in more talk about motor cars, sipping liqueurs and brandies with their coffee.

On a Saturday evening Alec, George and Max often attended dinner-dances at the Shutonger Manor Country Club which was just outside Tewkesbury and was affectionately known to its enthusiastic patrons as 'Shutters'. This was a private club opened shortly after the war by a group of people which included George's friend Tony Whitaker and it was run by three women – Marjorie, Kate and Phil – who were known as 'The Three Girls'. It originally served as a meeting place for friends throughout Worcestershire and Gloucestershire who had lost contact during the war and it remained a popular haunt throughout the 1950s for those seeking a relaxed night out. It was an excellent location for Alec, George and Max to meet up with many of the same people who attended Max's lunches. They would dance to the piano, trumpet and double bass of the club's own jazz band and at the end of the night Alec and George would jump into their cars to race each other through the country lanes back to the Poplars.

By 1950 annual holidays in Monte Carlo were also a regular part of their social calendar. The Dowsons took their family holidays in Cornwall every September after harvest was over. The Monte Carlo trips, however, were strictly for grown-ups and took place in late spring, timed to coincide with the Monaco Grand Prix. Max's sister Flora would come to the Poplars to look after the children so George, Max and Alec could disappear to the south of France, accompanied by Alec's mother and various other members of their social circle such as John and Betsy Rusher.

They would begin their trip by motoring down to the coast in Max's Morris Minor tourer, which she had nicknamed 'Minnie' after the Disney cartoon character. At Lydd, a few miles south of Dover on the Kent coast, they would put the car onto the cross-channel Silver City air-service which flew to Le Touquet on the north-west coast of France. Then they would drive hundreds of miles across France to the south coast and Monte Carlo. The more people there were in the party the better because the hire of the aeroplane was per car not per passenger and this helped keep down the costs. This was necessary because the trips were complicated by the strict rules applied to British citizens about the amount of sterling that could be taken abroad. Sometimes, in their desire to have a good time, they got perilously close to the limit, which led them into various adventures. Once they had to change to a cheaper hotel in the middle of the night. Another time they fell prey to a con-man who promised to boost their funds by exchanging money for them in a neighbouring country.

But the story which Alec enjoyed the most was of how they got home 'on a handful of washers'. With their funds almost dry 'Minnie' had spluttered to a halt when they ran out of petrol during the long drive back to the plane. After freewheeling to the first garage they could find, the holiday-makers turned out all their pockets to find the small centimes which Alec called 'washers' because they had a hole in the middle. By pooling these objects of contempt they were able to buy just enough petrol to get them safely back to Le Touquet.

They always stayed at a comfortable middle-range establishment called the Beach Hotel, built on the seafront with the cliffs over which the town of Monte Carlo was scattered rising up dramatically behind. Alec would later say that the Monte Carlo of this era was a place full of Edwardian charm before it was scarred by the intrusion of modern buildings. George and Alec liked to lie on lilos in the sea while Hulda preferred to swim in the adjacent pool using an elegant side-stroke. To add to the effect she might wear her bathing cap which was decorated by a large artificial flower or sometimes she swam with a large sun-hat still in place. Just offshore, the hotel had anchored a small raft where its guests could sunbathe. Alec often swam out to it, but not before he had put a pack of cigarettes on his head and pulled on a swimming cap borrowed from Betsy Rusher to keep them dry while he was in the water. Sometimes John Rusher would hire water skis and once Alec tried to join him. The Frenchman in charge of the skis tried hard to oblige, reluctant to lose a customer, but after going through his entire stock he declared in frustration – 'For feet that big? No skis monsieur!'

When they were tired of swimming and sitting by the pool, George and Alec would change into their slacks and open-necked shirts, and Max would put on her summer dress, so they could go out and about to the most expensive hotels in town. After ordering cocktails they would pose on the veranda of grander venues such as the Hôtel de Paris, the Hermitage or the Mirabeau where, of course, they could not afford to stay. Then in the evening, if money allowed, they would go and enjoy themselves in the nightclubs and the casino.

THE THREE MUSKETEERS

Apart from George Dowson, Alec had two constant companions throughout the 1950s. One was Alex Moulton the suspension specialist. The other was John Morris, Chief Engineer of SU Carburettors (a subsidiary of Morris Motors) who had known Alec since he had arrived at Cowley in 1936. Jack Daniels nicknamed them the 'Three Musketeers' because they were always together, discussing engineering and motor vehicle design ideas. During his annual visits to the British Motor Show, Issigonis would meet up with Morris and Moulton in the evenings at a hotel in Half Moon Street just off Piccadilly. Jack Daniels also went down every year and would sometimes be invited to join them, giving him the opportunity to observe the rapport between the three men and the way they used to develop their ideas simply by being together. John Morris, very intelligent but less exuberant than Issigonis, would quietly influence the discussions while Issigonis sat and did sketches as they talked. He was the perfect companion for Issigonis and Moulton since he, like them, found the subject of suspensions endlessly fascinating. Jack Daniels did not join in but simply watched this process with some admiration: 'The three of them, to me, they were a wonderful unit together.' They all had a similar social background, though Moulton was younger than Morris and Issigonis.

John Morris was an engineer by trade and the only one of the three who ever married. During the 1930s he spent some time living in Paris and in the evening would go out smartly dressed, taking a taxi back home. He was very conscious of his appearance and would stop and adjust his cravat or his tie whenever he passed a mirror. With a lively sense of humour which also carried a hint of snobbery that would have chimed with Issigonis, Morris would ask to be dropped off at the Ritz, then walk straight through the hotel and make for his lodgings somewhere on the Left Bank. His daughter Victoria was born in the early 1940s and he brought her up alone after separating from his wife. Shortly after the close of the Second World War he bought an old Victorian house, built in 1880 and situated in the elegant and upmarket Birmingham suburb of Edgbaston. The house had been used as government offices and was in a very dilapidated state. Morris took it on as a personal challenge, attracting the attention of *Ideal Home* magazine which featured a specially commissioned colour illustration on the cover of its March 1950 edition. Correspondent H. Rider-Rider gave an extensive account of the work undertaken by Morris, which provides a strong flavour of his unusual personality. After expunging the dirt and grime, Morris plastered, papered and painted each room with his own hands, creating dreamy clouds on the ceiling and grainy marble effects on the floor. He mastered the art of plumbing so he could engineer his own bathroom and he installed a discarded marble fireplace from a derelict neighbouring property in the wall of his drawing room. He then set about obtaining and refurbishing items of second-hand furniture in equal need of loving care, which were arranged against a backdrop of home-sewn curtains and covers. The finished rooms were brightened with quirky items such as a stuffed owl and a shocking pink flamingo. Finally, Morris indulged his liking for innovation by applying his interest in suspension to the crafting of a hand-made bed. It may well be that the discussions of the Three Musketeers over their dry martinis inspired him in the construction of a steel tubular frame with an inbuilt mattress made out of old inner tubes and connected by rings. The result was a bed with all the characteristics of a trampoline.

Though the rather ascetic Issigonis would probably not have found the fussy, over-ornamented restored house to his own personal taste, nevertheless this illustrates that they were men of the same ilk – vastly individual to the point of eccentricity, exhaustive in whatever project they undertook and gifted with both imagination and vision.

Those who knew John Morris considered him to be a brilliant man though he was never presented with the same personal opportunities as Issigonis. Among his inventions were a carburettor which was wonderful in its simplicity and much easier to maintain than its rivals, and a diesel fuel injection system which was taken up by General Motors in America and used on American tanks during the Second World War. Morris was a keen advocate of the merits of front wheel drive from a very early period and insisted on driving 'Traction Avant' (front wheel drive) Citroëns in preference to anything else. This was undoubtedly an influence on Issigonis who cited this particular car as the inspiration for his Morris Minor experiment. John Morris is now the forgotten member of the trio, but he was a vital influence as they developed their ideas for rubber and Hydrolastic suspensions.

THE BASIS OF THE ALVIS PROJECT

When Issigonis joined Alvis the firm was known for the production of high-quality but traditional cars, so their new project would be a completely new venture for them. The final concept of the TA/350 was very forward thinking in many of its aspects, consisting of a four-door saloon with a unitary steel bodyshell incorporating a 3.5-litre V8 light alloy engine, rear wheel drive, all-independent suspension and automatic transmission. A second version with a 1750 cc engine – the TA/175 – was also planned but no prototype was made. It is difficult now to establish whether the general concept for such a car already existed in any form when Issigonis joined Alvis or if it was entirely his own concept but the car is clearly related to the Oxford Series II design on which Issigonis would have been working at the time he left Morris.

It is possible to follow the process by which Alec created this final specification very closely because a comprehensive set of paperwork exists, including four Arclight notepads all dated 1952 and containing 154 pages of sketches. These pads contain some of his best sketching work – fluent, artistic and full of creativity. In addition there is a further set of written notebooks covering the period 1952 to 1955 which provides a chronology of the project's progress.

This represents the most complete series of material to be preserved among Issigonis' personal papers. It survived in the large wooden plan chest which was transferred from his office in Longbridge to the Archive of the British Motor Industry Heritage Trust shortly before his death. This means that he must have kept it deliberately, even though it relates to an uncompleted project which he later dismissed as an irrelevance. The reason, presumably, was that he continued to develop the ideas he had been working on during this period, telling us that he valued the Alvis experience more than he was prepared to admit in later years. The fact that he subsequently chose to ignore the existence of this work actually helped to protect it. There are frustrating gaps in the paperwork relating to some of his mainstream designs for BMC because his office was constantly raided during the 1970s and 80s for the benefit of journalists or to mount exhibitions of his sketches, and some important pieces have been lost. Few people attached any significance to the Alvis period and an impression was given that no papers survived. They therefore remained intact. Their quality gives us a fascinating insight into his sketching technique and their completeness tells us a great deal about how he worked out his ideas.

THE DESIGN

Serious work on the project got underway in May 1952 with an initial design study, first on the engine, then on the car. Some of Issigonis' notes and sketches indicate that he was considering the use of front wheel drive, which would have been an appropriate move for Alvis as the firm had been early exponents of this layout on their sports cars between 1928 and 1930, but after a while he rejected the idea with the comment that '... it was abandoned on the score of poor steering lock on long wheel-base cars'. One surprise which emerges from his notes at this stage, given his subsequent reputation for 'advanced engineering', was the reluctance with which he accepted the necessity for independent rear suspension, saying: '... we were forced to do it by the nature of the design of the vehi-cle'. Yet, technically, it would be difficult to imagine the unsprung weight implications of the complex transaxle he prescribed for TA/350 if it had not been combined with independent rear suspension.

By mid-1952 the outline specification of the car had been defined and Issigonis had overcome his original scepticism about the use of rubber in suspensions. On his earlier sketches he scribbled the comment 'rubber is always too stiff' but when Alex Moulton was brought in to advise on sus-pension development he took the opportunity to show Alec the results of the experiments he had done with Jack Daniels on the Morris Minor, proving that rubber was a serious contender for springing if utilised properly. Issigonis promptly changed his mind and for the Alvis car they developed a system of back-to-back cone springs. The front and rear were fitted with wishbone links and Moulton rubber suspension units. These were interconnected on each side by rubber hoses filled with water, the first use of a 'Hydrolastic' system. This rudimentary arrangement was arrived at after a series of rather weird and wonderful experiments presided over by Chris Kingham, who remembered it thus:

One of them was a water filled rubber banana, one for each wheel, through a suspension mechanism. We tuned the bananas, which were rubber hoses, with a filling at one end and then connected to the mechanics of the suspension through the other, interconnected by ordinary gas piping and we used to tune the bananas by adding or subtracting the number of hose clips arrayed on the outside of the hose. So crude, but so exciting in a way in exploring avenues that one would never have considered except under the leadership of someone with such a fertile mind as Alec Issigonis.

Yet while these were exciting days for those taking part it is questionable what value some of this work was to Alvis. The experiments were impor-tant to Issigonis in developing his long-term thinking but it was to be another ten years before the ideas found their way into production. It could be said that Alvis was paying for his development as a designer but was not necessarily getting any immediate benefit for itself.

Engine development was also proceeding and by August 1953 the first V8 engine had been put on bench test. This first test cycle demonstrated that the engine would work but there was much development to do. The earliest power readings, taken after sixteen hours' running, were recorded by Issigonis in his notebooks as 'very disappointing'. On 6 October 1953 he noted that they had run the engine again and for the first time got proper power readings of 63 bhp at 2,000 rpm, 100 bhp at 3,000 rpm and 114 bhp at 4,000 rpm, though he commented that roughly 67 bhp at 2,000 rpm was needed. By early December 1953, following various modifications, particularly to the exhaust valves, the power output was up to 124 bhp. A second engine, with a number of modifications including the provision of proper tappets, ran for the first time and showed much-reduced valve gear noise. At this stage the power output was not recorded but was said to be similar to the first engine.

The level of power output which the engine design was managing to achieve was unimpressive for a brand new 3.5-litre V8 and Chris Kingham described the initial engine design as 'a disaster'. Though he had admired Issigonis' innovativeness when it came to the suspension he was less impressed by his skills as an engine designer. Issigonis was insisting that the engine must have a barrel crankcase but he also wished to reduce weight by using a light alloy material and the two things were proving difficult to combine because the expansion of the light alloy block was greater than the expansion of the cast-iron supports for the bearings. The end result was that the engine never stopped rattling. In desperation the engineers drilled a hole right through the crankcase below the crankshaft level to create slots in the bottom of the cylinder block where they could insert tension bolts to try to keep the whole thing together. Eventually Chris Kingham redrew the design in a more conventional form and got the foundry to assist him in producing new aluminium castings. Fortunately the car was light for its size and the combination of high torque, medium power and low weight meant that it was still possible to get reasonable performance from the revised engine, and the transmission was designed to use a centri-fugal clutch at the front with a small foot-operated clutch at the rear of the car operating a two speed gearbox with overdrive on both gears. Two speeds were deemed sufficient, thanks to the high power to weight ratio.

As for the body styling, Alvis could not afford the luxury of a big-

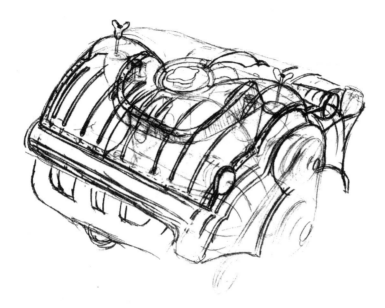

The Alvis TA/350 project, like the Mosquito, included a new engine design. In this case it was to be a 3.5-litre V8 light alloy power unit.

name stylist so once again Issigonis was allowed to indulge his own tastes. Whereas the lines of the Morris Minor had clearly been based on contemporary American styling, this time he took his inspiration from the Lancia Aurelia, the post-war creation of Fabbrica Automobili Lancia of Turin. The TA/350 was not the small car design which Issigonis preferred but he continued to apply his personal philosophy by setting out to create a vehicle which would be as small (14 feet in length) and light (target weight of 23 cwt) as possible within the parameters which had been set for it.

A page of handwritten notes from one of his sketchbooks, dated 4 April 1954, shows how he was beginning to develop a basic approach to body design which would stay with him to the end of his career – features such as 'torsional stiffness', 'a wheel at each corner', 'low waistline for good visibility' and 'simplicity of line without recourse to styling'. This combination of written notes with drawings illustrates how Issigonis used his sketchbooks to work through his ideas. The following extract is typical:

Body shape was dictated entirely by the following considerations:
1. Screen pillars at greatest width for high torsional stiffness.
2. Inside to outside dimension difference not greater than 10 inches?

3. Short front for stiffness.

4. Inter axle passenger seating.

5. Best airflow lines to fit in above considerations.

6. Wheels at widest possible width for stability.

7. Short rear overhang, due to weight distribution created by location of mechanical components.

8. Floors at ground clearance level.

9. Simple panels for production tools.

10. Detachable wings for service replacements.

11. Absence of any leaded joints.

12. Maximum possible engine accessibility.

13. Avoidance of fin areas at rear for good control in cross winds.

14. Low waistline for good vision in reversing.

15. Greatest possible simplicity of line without recourse to styling in order to emphasise the absence of fundamental adequacy of dimensional properties. [*sic*]

16. Much as we dislike the idea of I.R.S. we were forced to it by the nature of the design of the vehicle. We had to set about a scheme which had a reasonable chance of working. There is nothing in this unsprung weight complex, the only advantage is reduced side shake & tramp caused by the beam axle.

No photographs of the Alvis car have survived, but some of the sketches are so detailed that they give a vivid picture of its appearance. Just as the finished Morris Minor looks out at us from the three-dimensional drawings of the 1942 Arclight notepads, so the lost Alvis can be glimpsed in their counterparts of 1952. We get the impression of a slender, low car. Its bonnet is long to accommodate the engine but this is combined with a sleek overall look. The wheels are placed as far into the corners as possible which allows it to have significantly smaller overhangs in every direction than contemporary designs. The headlamps sit at the top of the front wheel arches, ironically in a similar position to the headlamps on the Morris Minor after it had been revised for the American market, even though Issigonis had strongly disapproved of that alteration of his original concept.

He experimented with several ideas for the radiator grille and his first preference was for a distinctive horizontal 'mouth organ' style. This did not find favour with the sales department who declared it to be 'not in the spirit of Alvis'. So he squashed its sides and stretched the top and bottom edges to create a more traditional upright rectangle balanced on the bumper. He injected a pleasing harmony into this arrangement by fixing the distinctive red triangle of the Alvis badge to the top edge of the radiator, echoing in miniature the elegant outline of the bonnet which swept downwards to meet it. The fascia was very basic with a simple set of instruments mounted on a centre binnacle reminiscent of the 1954 Morris Oxford Series II and the passenger space was generous for a car of its dimensions. The overall concept provided a striking demonstration of the philosophy of simplicity and space utilisation which was to become the cornerstone of the Issigonis approach.

The sketchbooks reveal just how closely Issigonis was involved in every aspect of the design of this vehicle. It was not just the chassis layout, suspension details, body-styling or engine design that occupied his thoughts. He drew detailed plans for the layout of the production line and had to think about tooling, product flow round the factory and many other things because Alvis lacked the specialists to devise such elements. He was also required to take a leading role in the testing of the prototype which was now ready.

Issigonis experimented with several ideas for the front end of the Alvis. Finally he created a traditional upright radiator grille carrying the distinctive red triangle of the Alvis badge, echoed by the elegant outline of the bonnet which swept downwards to meet it.

TESTING THE PROTOTYPE

By May 1954 the prototype was ready to undertake its first road tests and the place chosen for this important task was the proving ground owned by the Motor Industry Research Association (MIRA) which was only a few miles from Coventry. As at every stage of this project, he could not call on specialised engineers to take the car away and put it through its paces, so Issigonis and his colleagues had to undertake this crucial operation themselves. This was no great inconvenience to them, however, since they were all motor racing enthusiasts and felt quite at liberty to thoroughly enjoy the task to hand.

MIRA had been established in January 1946, funded by the industry itself. Its purpose was to promote a higher quality of engineering so that the British motor car could become more competitive in the all-important export market of post-war Europe. It was felt this could be achieved in two ways – by providing test facilities to motor manufacturers and by undertaking independent research on behalf of the industry. A search immediately began for a suitable place to set up a proving ground – a need ironically made more acute by the fact that Alec's favourite haunt, Brooklands race track, did not re-open after the war due to concerns over its safety.

In 1948 MIRA took over a former transport command airfield at Lindley near Nuneaton in Warwickshire comprising 650 acres. This site was steadily developed over the years with purpose-built tracks and research laboratories and it became a focus for the development of British motor engineering. In its early days MIRA was required to farm any land not being used for testing purposes under the terms of its lease from the Air Ministry. The track that Issigonis and his colleagues visited would therefore have been surrounded by fields of broad beans and grain. It was also home to a pig rearing unit which supplied the canteen with Alec's favourite dish of pork. The Alvis engineers were more interested in the various roads which had been specially constructed on site using a number of different surfaces. The most exciting development was a high-speed circuit of 2.81 miles completed in 1954. This consisted of a triangular design with three elevated bends built onto shallow banking capable of supporting sustained speeds of over 100 mph and it was available 24 hours a day, seven days a week.

The Alvis crew were among the first to use this high-speed circuit.

One evening a week, after a full day's work at the Coventry factory, a gang of drivers, mechanics and observers would go over to MIRA and take beds in the hostel above the canteen. Issigonis, Kingham and Barber had the privilege of driving. Jimmy Hartshorn, Head of the experimental department, was in charge of looking after the development parts and performing operations such as wheel-changing at the pit stop facility which they set up at the side of the track. Bill Cassels, Harry Harris and John Sheppard got the job of 'riding mechanics' which meant they had to sit in the front passenger seat reading all the gauges and ticking off the times on stop watches. Between 6 p.m. in the evening and 6 a.m. the following morning the three men and their co-drivers would drive for two hours each and then take four hours off to sleep. The aim was to do 1,000 miles during the night, which required a constant speed of about 86 mph. In fact they never achieved the 1,000 mile mark, their best being 895 miles, though they did push the speed as far as 110 mph at one point. They all threw themselves into the task with enthusiasm and Kingham recalled:

I conceded the lap record to Alec Issigonis, but there was one thing at which I always was better and that is the number of miles covered in the hour, because Alec was a very fast driver but he couldn't keep it up!

At the end of the all-night session, the crew would have breakfast together in the MIRA canteen before returning to the works where they would discuss the night's results, particularly any failures on the car. Perhaps the most spectacular of these happened to Harry Barber. While he was lapping at speed, Barber and his co-driver were startled by a sudden bang as an object hit the windscreen and was catapulted over the top of the car, carving a huge dent in the roof above their heads. He stamped his foot on the brake and shouted to his mechanic to jump out as the car screeched to an undignified halt. The culprit was the bonnet which had sprung open and been torn off its hinges. In future the team kept it firmly in place by fastening it down with heavy leather straps. Harry Barber remembered the incident when he wrote to Issigonis in 1969 to congratulate him on his knighthood:

... the 'cigarettes over the partition' era ... they were happy days, the pyjama conferences at MIRA, bonnets flying through the air, plumbing all over the car, shock absorber 'niggles' to mention but a few of the incidents never to be forgotten. I really believe the days spent with you developing 'that other car' were the happiest and most interesting I have experienced during many years in the motor industry.

PROJECT AXED

The final design concept represented by the Alvis prototype was very advanced by the standards of the mid-1950s and those who had the opportunity to drive the car praised its ride and handling. There was one person whose opinion Issigonis valued more than most. Despite the fact that he worked for a rival firm he telephoned Jack Daniels one day and asked him to come over to Coventry and test drive it with him:

Whilst he was at Alvis he actually called me up at Cowley and says, come up and see me Jack, I want you to have a ride in this car. I had a day off and went up there and joined him and had a ride round in the car. As I recall, it was an *excellent* car. I was only being driven around the Alvis area but it seemed to me very good, suspension wise it was unique I thought.

Had it been launched as planned at the 1956 Motor Show it would have created considerable interest, competing directly with the equally distinctive Citroën DS19 which came out in 1955, though with a more expensive price tag. Unfortunately, as the design and testing phase drew near to completion, the finance department was raising concerns about costs. They sounded the alarm bell at quite an early stage in the project. By the spring of 1953 the car had progressed far enough for Mr Howell of Finance to undertake a commercial review of the project. The report which he presented to the Board was largely favourable and he suggested that Alvis would need to fix an annual production volume of 5,000 vehicles to be sold at a price of between £840 and £890. To achieve this the unit cost of producing each car would have to be no higher than £590 plus the one-off costs of tooling and equipment which he estimated would be £675,000. He concluded that profits in the range of £250,000 to £300,000 per annum were feasible but he cautioned that the initial financing of the project could be a problem. He sent a copy of his report to Issigonis along with a covering memo expressing the hope that 'in due course, you will favour me with a copy of yours'. If Mr Howell ever received a response it has not survived. Issigonis, not for the last time in his career, chose to ignore the warning signs.

It is not easy at this distance of time to judge the situation which Alvis faced when the time came to make a decision on whether or not to take their expensive design concept through to production. The Alvis Drawing Office may have been tiny compared with what was available at Longbridge or Cowley but for the Issigonis design they had gathered together their biggest team ever and expended several years of intensive effort. With such meagre resources the final result was astonishingly accomplished. At the price levels and production volume suggested by Mr Howell it might well have been a good investment, as long as the company could raise the funds required and muster the necessary determination to make it work. This was the rub. For one thing some major disagreements were brewing between the designer and the sales department. There had already been clashes over the radiator grille; the next flashpoint was the basic interior, which they wanted to replace with something more in sympathy with the Alvis image and tradition. This is reminiscent of the terse memo Thomas sent to Issigonis about improving the interior of the Mosquito but this time there was no one to give him such an instruction.

Ultimately such arguments were academic because the Alvis Board was beginning to have serious doubts about whether it could find the resources to put this ambitious new project into production. The car was such a departure from anything Alvis had previously produced that it was necessary to look to outside firms such as Pressed Steel for large numbers of components. The tooling would have to be prepared well in advance of the proposed launch date and Pressed Steel required an order larger than the 5,000 per annum which Alvis were planning. The Board looked at the final specification and then looked at their financial situation and came to the conclusion that the firm did not have sufficient capital in its reserves to support the project. When their bankers refused to underwrite a loan for this purpose they had little choice. In June 1955 they made the decision not to progress the project any further.

The prototype suffered an ignominious fate. Chris Kingham was the one who was asked to take it away to the service department. Alex Moulton persuaded Alvis to let him have the suspension systems, and the engine was also extracted, later purloined by Mike Parkes for a racing car that he was building. What remained was pushed into a small windowless room where jigs and body panels were piled onto the car's roof, which, not surprisingly, soon collapsed under the weight. The forgotten experiment sat there for many years before eventually being scrapped.

The fate of the team was equally brutal. Once the decision had been made that the car would not go into production the engineers were asked to resign and leave by the end of the year. Harry Barber was able to obtain a senior post at Pressed Steel through his friends at the Institute of Body Engineers. John Sheppard, Bill Cassels and Harry Harris all began to look around at Coventry's other car firms for new positions. Only Chris Kingham was asked to stay on to continue his engine work. Alec Issigonis had already left, but his erstwhile colleagues were not told where he had gone.

Issigonis later claimed that he was pleased the car never saw production because he was never happy with the final result of his work. Whether or not this is true, it was very convenient for the successful designer of the Mini to say so in retrospect. There are also conspiracy theories which suggest that it was never a serious project but just a plot dreamt up by Leonard Lord and John Parkes to get Issigonis out of the way until things had settled down at BMC. This seems hardly credible. Why would a small firm like Alvis spend so much time and effort (which equal money) on a project they had no intention of profiting from just to humour Leonard Lord? Why would Leonard Lord have been interested in such a plan when he could easily have protected and deployed Issigonis within BMC had he valued his services so highly?

Like so much else in Issigonis' career this period was not just about what type of car he designed and whether or not it deserved to be produced and sold. It was about his development as a designer. This was his first real experience of being allowed a completely free rein. What were the results? On the one hand he developed some brilliant and innovative ideas which he would be able to bring to his future designs, and on the human side he gained valuable experience of building a team and getting the best out of them. On the other hand, unchecked by the subtle management of a Vic Oak or the instinctive understanding of a Jack Daniels, he began to develop some of the obstinacy and intransigence which was not evident in his early career but would become a damaging feature of his later one.

It is clear that while Issigonis got a great deal out of his three years at Alvis, the company did not. For the first time, but not the last, Issigonis worked in a conceptual vacuum, disregarding the connection between his ideas and the profitability of the company were they to reach production. Alvis learnt its lesson and after this brief flirtation with bold experimentation decided to restrict itself to the development of its existing model range, never again attempting to develop an entirely new concept. Alvis published a brief history of the company in 1967 in which they included the following paragraph on the Issigonis Alvis:

> In 1951 Mr. Alec Issigonis joined Alvis to work upon a new car of outstanding technical merit but the project failed to materialise. During the years of design and development the cost of new capital equipment and factory space required nearly doubled when compared with the original estimate and this finally killed the project. Anticipated sales of less than 10,000 cars were insufficient to bear the extra costs and probably the only people who derived pleasure from this failure were those with no wish to see the traditional, individually-built Alvis replaced by a quantity-produced Pressed Steel-bodied car. (An announcement made in December, 1955, stated that Mr. Issigonis would be returning to B.M.C.)

The tone of this summary suggests some residual resentment of this particular episode in the company's history. The same year it was published, Alvis produced its last motor car and from then on restricted its production to military vehicles. A few months later they were swallowed into British Leyland.

THE MINI PROJECT

CHAPTER 6

I did not invent the Mini, I designed it.

Sir Alec Issigonis

LONGBRIDGE

BY THE TIME Leonard Lord received his knighthood in 1954 he had established full control over the British Motor Corporation. Back in 1952 the initial management structure had seemed to display an intention to treat the two parties to the merger equally. Lord Nuffield was named as Chairman, Leonard Lord was Deputy Chairman, while the two Managing Directors of Austin and Morris, George Harriman and Reggie Hanks respectively, were named as Directors. Given the history of the relationship between Nuffield and Lord this was a status quo which could not survive for long. In 1954, at the age of 77, Nuffield attended his last Board meeting and then sadly took himself home to Nuffield Place and into permanent retirement, bearing the purely honorary post of President of the Corporation. For the remaining nine years of his life he would have no further part to play beyond posing for the odd publicity photograph with one or another new model of vehicle.

Leonard Lord therefore became Chairman and Managing Director with George Harriman as his deputy, a true reflection of the situation. Unfortunately in the two years it had taken to get to this point the bad atmosphere in which the merger had taken place had done irrevocable damage to the prospects of the new company. From the Morris old guard, a disillusioned Vic Oak retired in 1953 and Reggie Hanks was sidelined until his retirement in 1961. It would not be true to say that only Austin men prospered under the new corporation. Gerald Palmer, for example, became Chief Chassis and Body Engineer while Sidney Smith, who had been such a key part of the Mosquito project, was made overall Technical Director. There was nevertheless an undercurrent of civil war between the two opposing cultures of Cowley and Longbridge which helped to ensure that the full fruits of the merger never ripened. Instead of creating a new 'BMC' identity, as they should have done, Austin and Morris continued to trade as separate entities with their own factories, suppliers, dealerships and hierarchies. Thus there continued to be a Morris Chief Engineer and an Austin Chief Engineer, though both reported to the BMC Technical Director, and the situation was repeated throughout every part of the organisation. This duplication of effort meant that the corporation achieved little of the rationalisation or economy which should have been the chief benefits of the merger. The finger of blame has to be pointed at Leonard Lord whose own personal vendetta was a major contributing factor.

BMC was also saddled with a vastly overblown model range containing a mish-mash of different badges and design platforms. The new corporation now had six marques in its stable – Austin, Morris, Riley, Wolseley, MG and Vanden Plas, and soon Austin-Healey would be added to the list. Separate pre-merger Austin and Morris designs continued to be produced for the first few years. Some persisted for many years as vans and commercials but two continued in car versions throughout the 1960s. One of these was the Princess, an Austin design first launched in 1947 which continued in various forms until 1968. The other was the Morris Minor which had been given a new lease of life shortly after the merger when fitted with the more modern Austin A-series engine. In spite of its difficult birth, the Morris Minor had gained a vigorous hold on the popular imagination and it celebrated a distinguished landmark when the 1 millionth vehicle was built on 22 December 1960. The continuing success of an original Morris design must have been a considerable irritation to Leonard Lord as he surveyed his model range in 1954 and wondered what direction to take now that he had disposed of Lord Nuffield.

In December 1955, Lord made an agreement with the distinguished Italian design house of Pininfarina. Founded by Giovanni Battista Pininfarina in his home town of Turin, the company was now run by him, his son Sergio and his son-in-law Renzo Carli. This was an ambitious move on Lord's part because Pininfarina had been a major collaborator with Ferrari since the early 1950s and was instrumental in creating some of the legendary beauty which came to surround the Ferrari marque. Pininfarina's first project was to style a replacement for the Austin A35, which was the Austin equivalent of the Morris Minor. The result was the Austin A40 Farina, launched in 1958, a stylish car whose clean straight lines contrasted greatly with the curvaceous A35 whose mechanical components it shared. When styling a body, a car was divided into compartments or 'boxes' and the usual formation was a three-box style of bonnet/passenger compartment/boot. The new Pininfarina design created a two-box car with no overhanging boot at the back. So while the engineering was entirely conventional, the styling was extremely radical. When Issigonis saw the mock-up at Longbridge in 1956 he quickly expressed his admiration, the whole design chiming with his own love of simplicity and compactness.

Lord then decided to embark upon a serious policy of badge-engineering, something which both Morris and Austin had already dabbled in to a limited extent. The idea was to share engineering platforms and bodyshells between different marques, thus reducing the cost of producing the model range while still appealing to the brand-loyalty of customers. From December 1958 onwards, a series of cars was launched, all sharing the same basic body structure but each slightly different in detail to retain a sense of brand identity. The aim was to break away from the disparate styles developed by each marque over the years and create a new marque-independent look. The task was entrusted to BMC's new partner Pininfarina, as a result of which these cars became known as the B-series Farinas. They carried the full range of badges, being launched in Austin, Morris, Riley, Wolseley and MG versions. The finished products were much larger than the A40, and the ample overhangs at front and rear, not to mention the prominent fins, are unlikely to have appealed particularly to Issigonis.

The B-series Farinas presented an opportunity to introduce a level of rationalisation into the model range. Yet, at the same time as taking this adventurous but sensible step, Leonard Lord was still worrying over the idea that the corporation's products were not sufficiently technologically advanced. The honeymoon period which the motor industry had enjoyed with the British press in the immediate post-war period, when patriotism had restrained the desire to criticise, was drawing to a close. British cars were now being compared unfavourably with their continental counterparts and the Volkswagen Beetle in particular was enjoying considerable success. The British motoring press began to hint that a little more vision was required to keep Britain ahead. So even while he was engaging Pininfarina to transform the old range of cars Lord decided to embark on a development programme which would add yet another layer to BMC's complicated product policy.

It is unlikely that Lord had been particularly concerned when Cowley lost its star designer in 1952 since it was his intention to make the Long-bridge Drawing Office the focus of the new corporation. But in 1954, when he cast his eyes over his current design department for someone who might inject the company's products with a little imagination, he surveyed a barren landscape. Alec Issigonis was not the first solution which sprang into his mind, even though Lord had the daily reminder of the best-selling Morris Minor before his eyes. Issigonis, however, had begun to sound out his many influential contacts in the industry as soon as it became clear that the Alvis project was on the point of collapse. John Morris, whose position as Managing Director of SU Carburettors gave him access to the top echelons of BMC, brought it to the attention of Leonard Lord that the services of Alec Issigonis were once more available. On reflection Lord agreed that it would make a great deal of sense to bring back an original thinker like Issigonis to establish a more visible 'BMC' image. He sent John Morris back with a message indicating that he would like the exile to return and spearhead the development of his proposed new model range.

In order to make way for him Gerald Palmer was, in typical Leonard Lord fashion, coldly disposed of on the basis of some bad press reports about the Wolseley 6/90. Palmer's own account from his autobiography makes it clear that he resigned in preference to accepting demotion, even though he had no idea of what his future might hold, and he was never to occupy such a senior position again. He was remarkably sanguine about this turn of events and did not let it estrange him from Issigonis who remained a friend. Palmer did allow himself the restrained but perceptive comment: 'Issigonis may have been a better man for the job but he was not the best of managers. There was too much of what he wanted rather than his listening to other ideas and suggestions.' This was to become a key factor in the years to come. For his part, Issigonis turned a blind eye to the circumstances of his return as he was never eager to face up to unpleasant realities.

Though the initial turmoil within BMC had calmed down consider-ably by the time Issigonis returned the underlying tensions had not disap-peared. They never would. Issigonis hated conflict and when he declared 'I'm not interested in politics' it was not the world's trouble spots that he had in mind, it was internal wrangling of the type which had prompted his departure from BMC in 1952. Yet however much he liked to pretend it was possible to ignore 'politics', in reality they defined his career. No one who rises as high in the corporate structure as he did could fail to fall foul of them at some point. Thus he flourished when management appreciated him and facilitated what he wanted to do and he suffered when he was out of favour. At the point we have reached in his story he had been fortunate that, as yet, he had never fallen on the wrong side of the divide. The Alvis interlude worked perfectly for him, giving him three years of complete freedom to develop his ideas and innovate to his heart's content. At the same time he was removed from the arena of savage post-merger politics and could return triumphant in the autumn of 1955 without being tagged as a 'Morris' or 'Austin' man. He had the full support of the Chairman, who had recruited him personally, and he also formed a close and more informal relationship with Deputy Chairman George Harriman which would be important in the future.

Issigonis returned not to Cowley, but to Longbridge, with its superior technical facilities entirely at his disposal. His employment contract was with the Austin Motor Company rather than BMC and his position was Deputy Engineering Director under the management of Sidney Smith who was now Technical Director of BMC. This line of reporting may have helped to reassure him because Smith was also ex-Cowley and had been deeply involved in the Mosquito project with Issigonis ten years earlier. Austin's Chief Designer, Jim Stanfield, was completely bypassed, even though theoretically he was senior to Issigonis in the management structure. This gave Issigonis a great deal more freedom of action than he had enjoyed at Morris Motors.

THE BRINE BATHS

In 1952 when Issigonis had taken the job at Alvis, he made the decision not to move back to the Coventry area, possibly because he knew the job was only for the short term. Besides, Hulda was very attached to the flat where they had now lived for sixteen years and all her friends were in Oxford. She had already readjusted her life three times, and at the age of 68 she was reluctant to start all over again. So she stayed on at Sollershott while Alec spent the week at a hotel near Warwick and travelled home every weekend. When he moved to Longbridge three years later he knew that this would probably be where he would spend the rest of his career. The British Motor Corporation was one of the biggest motor manufacturers left in Britain – the others being Standard Triumph, Vauxhall and Ford – and all his contacts were there. Hulda, however, stubbornly refused to move from their Oxford flat, summing up her feelings to him with the phrase 'Birmingham, that awful place!' Alec therefore moved his base from Warwick to the Worcestershire Hotel in Droitwich. Each Monday morning he drove up to Longbridge, staying in Droitwich from Monday to Wednesday, then driving back on Thursday evening to spend the following day working at Cowley.

The Worcestershire Hotel was also known as the 'Brine Baths' because the hotel incorporated a natural water spa where guests could bathe for their health. George Dowson sometimes went there to soothe his bad back. The guests would bob around in the water, gathering an encrustation of salt round their necks, while drinks were served to them on floating trays. When they emerged from the pool a friendly member of staff would approach to wrap them in a hot towel. The hotel was fairly well known in the area and was simply a convenient out-of-town location from which Issigonis could get to work but it is hard to avoid the feeling that he would have loved the absurdity of the Brine Baths. It did not offer a home from home in the shape of a comfortable self-contained suite but he was happy enough with a simple hotel room and dinner in the hotel restaurant where he could invite friends to join him as his guests. Frequent visitors were the Dowson family, Mark Ransome who had begun an apprenticeship at Longbridge and Mike Parkes who was working as an engineer for Rootes in Coventry. It also proved a convenient location for entertaining the constant flow of journalists and VIPs who began to seek him out. He would regularly book rooms for acquaintances such as racing driver Paul Frère, photographer Bernard Cahier or journalist Laurence Pomeroy whose visits he hosted as a mixture of public relations work on behalf of BMC and personal pleasure out of hours with congenial companions.

ASSEMBLING THE TEAM

The firm Issigonis joined, the facilities which were available to him and the position which he now held were different from anything he had so far experienced. In the case of both the Mosquito and Alvis projects he had been working within strict boundaries and with an unusually small group of people due to a war in one case and the small size of the company in the other. This meant he had extremely limited technical back-up and a restricted budget. It is this background which made him the sort of designer he became. All of these circumstances tended to exaggerate his desire to be in control of his team, his dislike of delegation and the necessity for him to be involved in every part of the car's design. If he had always operated in the milieu of a large technical department such as the one which existed at Longbridge, he would have been obliged to work in a different way. Whether or not he could have subjected himself to the discipline of collaborative teamwork and still have become a leading designer would not become evident until later in his career. At this stage he would have dismissed such an idea as ridiculous.

He was in no way fazed by the resources which were suddenly at his disposal, but by now he had evolved a working method which suited him and he set about re-creating it at Longbridge. Management had given him their full confidence and their only concern was that he should deliver the brief he had been given. They applied no constraints about what shape his department should take. He therefore set about building up a compact team or 'cell' around him for the third time in his career, with one difference: for the first time he was free to choose who would be part of it.

He wisely decided to surround himself with the best of the working relationships he had already established, first at Morris and then at Alvis. His priority was to retrieve Jack Daniels from the backwater of the Cowley development department. Daniels was now in charge but he had little scope to initiate interesting projects within the BMC structure. When he received Issigonis' offer he decided that number two status in the top division at Longbridge would be preferable to number one status in the second division at Cowley. As Jack Daniels put it, 'I'd had an interesting time and things got done when he was around so I accepted, I went and joined him.' For his part, Issigonis used to describe Jack Daniels as the best all-round draughtsman in the country and he was delighted to have him back.

Longbridge's main administration block was known within the factory as 'The Kremlin' after the Russian seat of government, and it housed the corporation's chief executives. Issigonis and Daniels were allocated a corner office on the first floor of this building, with Harriman's door facing them from the opposite corner, while Sir Leonard's distant suite of offices lay at the far end of a lengthy corridor. Harriman's window faced the front of the building while Alec and Jack were on the 'working' side overlooking the styling studio. Nevertheless the location of their office gave a clear signal about the status of the Issigonis/Daniels team.

175

He began to sound out some of the discarded Alvis team before officially leaving the Holyhead Road factory. He approached Harry Barber first but Barber had already secured a senior position which matched his qualifications and experience with the Pressed Steel Company. He also spoke to John Sheppard who considered the conversation to be rather puzzling since he had no idea what position Issigonis had secured or where. By December Sheppard had managed to get interviews at Humber, Armstrong Siddeley and Standard, all of which were based in the Coventry area where he lived, and he felt optimistic about his prospects. Then Issigonis phoned and asked him to visit Longbridge, which was the first time that Sheppard knew where he had gone. 'Why didn't you contact me?' Issigonis asked unreasonably. 'You knew I wanted you to come with me.' Sheppard decided to take up the invitation and spent a pleasant day with his old boss who gave him a warm welcome and told him, 'my job today is to bribe you to join me'. The young engineer was flattered until he found that he was being offered only the same rate of pay as he had received from Alvis. He was understandably disappointed by this and pointed out that accepting the post would mean he faced a choice between a 30-mile journey each way, or moving house with a very young family. Issigonis was unimpressed and raised the offer only marginally because he knew that the real choice facing Sheppard was not his travelling arrangements but whether or not he wanted the chance to be part of an exciting new project in the well-equipped workshops of the country's biggest motor manufacturer. Naturally, he accepted. Issigonis made a similar approach to Chris Kingham, though probably on more favourable terms as Kingham had a stronger bargaining position. Daniels, Sheppard and Kingham became the core of the new Issigonis team which was ready to commence work by the beginning of January 1956.

The team soon established its own workshop next to one of the experimental shops nearby and this became the focus of the project rather than the plush corner office. Gathered round a large flat drawing board, they would discuss the Arclight sketches, make calculations, and piece ideas together under Issigonis' direction. The specifications produced in the workshop were passed over as a fully operational job first to the Experimental Department and later to the Production Department. The main Drawing Office, to its great annoyance, was excluded from the initial design process. The 'Issigonis cell', as it became known, was like an independent enclave operating in the middle of the grand principality of

Longbridge under the protection of its overlord, Chairman Leonard Lord.

In 1952, just before leaving Morris Motors for Alvis, Issigonis had said about his design philosophy: 'The success of the final product finally rests on the acquisition of the highest possible team spirit between the many engineers engaged in the creation of a new car.' This is a startling statement from a man renowned for his autocracy and individuality who also said 'I hate being helped in my creative work'. Issigonis did not find it easy to accommodate himself to the needs of other people but he realised that the human relationships he forged were as important as the lines that he drew on his pieces of paper. He spoke about 'the human side of the thing':

> I think that what keeps my interest in doing this sort of work is not only the technical side of it, which is probably the easiest side of it, but the human side of the thing which is equally if not more difficult yet so much more interesting. Of course, I suffered agonies of impatience when the Mini was being developed and built. I'm a very impatient man. It's a complex. I feel that people around me are taking longer to do some job than is necessary. Now this takes a lot out of you, because, being human beings, they like to achieve results perhaps not in the direct, obvious way but to deviate a little bit and explore the ground around. And of course, this makes for a great deal of wear and tear on me. Far more, in fact, than doing all the detailed design oneself, for which one hasn't the time. This is what I meant when I said that the technical side of it is the easiest and the human side by far the more difficult. The problems are, one of communication with the human being you are dealing with and two, making him realise that there are short, direct ways of getting results.

John Sheppard gave a precise description of the way the Issigonis cell functioned:

> It was all a one-man job where Issigonis was the conductor and we were members of the orchestra playing to his tune. Provided the tune came out with no discord, we were all right.

This is why the phrase which reverberates down the years through the memories of his colleagues is 'just go away and do it'. He was not interested in arguing about solutions with his colleagues; their job was to take his ideas and make them work. He would get what he wanted whether it was right or wrong. Issigonis would bully them along like a schoolmaster, indulging in scenarios such as visiting Sheppard at his workbench and producing a 2-ounce weight from his pocket with the words 'have you saved that today?' If anyone stepped out of line and spoke up too force-fully, they would quickly be reminded who was in charge. Why were they prepared to tolerate so much? Chris Kingham could speak for all of them on this point:

> His personality was warm, and also because of the breadth of his mind, and the quickness of his mind, he was an exciting person to work with and for, so one would put up with an awful lot because one got such a lot of deep satisfaction from working with such a positive personality.

The self-contained nature of the Issigonis cell should not be overplayed, however, because the co-operation and involvement of many people working in close association with it was essential to its success. This was evident from the very beginning. In December 1955, before the new team was even in place, he took out his Arclight notepad and drew up a schedule under the heading 'Work Administration', identifying and allocat-ing the jobs which would be required:

1. General arrangement drawings style details, Daniels and Johnson – Longbridge
2. Suspension unit design and development, Spencer Moulton – Bradford on Avon
3. Front and rear suspension layouts
4. Test rig work on linkage, Daniels – Longbridge
5. Body engineering, own shop
6. Engine design, Mr Appleby – Longbridge
7. Gearbox design, Mr Appleby – Longbridge
8. Differential layout, Mr La Salle – Tractors & Transmissions
9. Test rig work on engine (crankshaft and oil pump), Daniels
10. Windscreen wiper work, Mr Hall – Cowley
11. Steering Unit, Mr Leese [sic] Cam Gears – Luton
12. Possible development of simple Gogo transmission, outside suppliers

By drawing up this schedule Issigonis was recognising from the very earliest design stage that it would require a wide range of resources, drawn from both inside and outside BMC, to realise the kind of advanced technology Leonard Lord was looking for. His list identifies some of the personnel who would have to be involved and their number grew as the project became established.

Thus Jack Daniels, in charge of development and testing, would be joined by some of the most experienced men that Austin and the Nuffield Organisation could offer. They included William 'Bill' Appleby, BMC's Chief Designer of Power Units; Charles Griffin, Cowley's Chief Experimental Engineer; Gil Jones, Griffin's Longbridge counterpart; and Dick Burzi, Austin's stylist. Similarly, new recruits Kingham and Sheppard gained the assistance of an accomplished set of people drawn from the existing pool of BMC engineers, draughtsmen, mechanics and craftsmen. These included men such as Stan Johnson, Vic Everton, Ron Dovey, Bernard Johnson, Dick Gallimore, Doug Adams, Basil MacKenzie and John Wagstaffe, though this is by no means an exhaustive list. Looking outside BMC, the schedule quoted above already identifies Alex Moulton's firm to work on suspensions and Cam Gears for the steering unit. They would be joined by Dunlop to assist with tyre development and Pininfarina which would become involved with styling. This gives some idea of the massive effort which was to be put behind the Issigonis project. No one has ever expressed this better than his right-hand man Jack Daniels who had one succinct phrase to describe the whole enterprise – 'his was the inspiration and mine was the perspiration'.

First Projects – The XC Prototypes

The common legend, propagated by Issigonis himself, is that he swept back to Longbridge at the personal behest of Leonard Lord and in a whirlwind produced the marvel of the Mini. In reality, the immediate brief of Issigonis and his team was much wider and more long-term than this. Their first priority was not a small car at all. The objective was a proposed three car model range with a variety of engine sizes and each with a different purpose. The project names given to them by the Experimental Shop were XC/9001 (the largest car for long distances), XC/9002 (the medium-sized car for family use) and XC/9003 (the small car for pottering around town). The first of these concepts to be pieced together on the workshop table in January 1956 was the largest, XC/9001.

As in the case of the Morris Minor and the Alvis, an excellent series of notes and sketches covering the XC designs has survived. There are ten Arclight notepads dated between 1955 and 1957. The first eight cover the period December 1955 to February 1957, containing over 300 sketches which are predominantly concerned with XC/9001 and its scaled-down relation XC/9002. These provide a good overall view of the progress of the project, though they depart from the very visual style of the earlier notepads, following a more analytical approach with a great deal of text. Many of the sketches are executed in a less attractive style with a thick black felt tip pen which does not allow for the subtlety or feel of the earlier pencil drawings. Whoever gave Issigonis this pen did not have the soul of an artist. As we will see shortly, however, the Issigonis cell changed its focus from a large to a small car at the end of 1956. The remaining two Arclight notepads, dated between January and May 1957 and containing around 100 sketches, are devoted predominantly to the smaller car, XC/9003, which would develop into the Mini. Once again the XC/9003 drawings are not like the freehand sketches of earlier years, but more rudimentary and diagrammatical.

In the single month of December 1955 – before he had gathered his team around him – Issigonis produced almost 100 sketches. It is clear that his imagination was fired by his new circumstances and he could hardly wait to begin. He was equally prolific during the first half of 1956, concerning himself with every element that would go into the XC/9001 and XC/9002 designs. The sketches range widely over suspension, transmission, body structure, styling and engine design and they reveal that he was constantly comparing his ideas with other contemporary developments, musing on present trends in America and Europe. He made a strict division between what he called the 'American philosophy' of car design which he characterised as the production of 'transatlantic dinosaurs' which in his view were too big, too heavy and too ostentatious, and the 'European philosophy' of compact, graceful and energy-efficient cars. He particularly favoured Citroën, whose suspension development he admired and whose front wheel drive he had already copied on his experimental Morris Minor. The Volkswagen Beetle, on the other hand, may have won great favour with some sections of the British press but it did not meet with his approval. He stated tartly, 'if the public were all very intelligent people you wouldn't sell one Volkswagen Beetle', which neatly combined his contempt for the Beetle and for the general public. His friend the photog-

When Issigonis joined Morris Motors in 1936 he was just a junior draughtsman in the vastness of the Cowley Drawing Office

Key men in the Nuffield Organisation. Left to right: 1946 – Vice-chairman Sir Miles Thomas; 1949 – Sales Director Donald Harrison, Vice-chairman Reggie Hanks, Technical Director S.V. Smith, Chief Engineer Vic Oak

Kingswood in wartime: Hetty Walker, Mark Ransome, Hulda Issigonis

Meanwhile, as part of the war effort, Alec is towed out to sea off the Devonshire coast to test the sea-worthiness of the amphibious wheelbarrow and the nerve of its designer

December 1950 and the year's production of Nuffield vehicles for export has reached 100,000. The landmark vehicle turns out to be Lord Nuffield's hated 'poached egg', the Morris Minor, designed by 'that foreign chap', and the press crowd round to see him drive it off the Cowley assembly line

September 1958, BMC launches the Austin A40 Farina at its Longbridge headquarters. Left to right: Chairman Leonard Lord, Italian stylist Battista Pininfarina, Deputy Chairman George Harriman, Sergio Pininfarina and – top right – Alec Issigonis

A picture of domesticity, Christmas at the Oxford flat. Alec and Hulda Issigonis in the late 1950s

And the high life. After watching the 1959 Grand Prix de Monaco, Alec and his party enjoy a sumptuous dinner at the Hôtel de Paris. Left to right round the foreground table: Alex Moulton, Max Dowson, Dick Burzi, Alec Issigonis, Charles Griffin and George Dowson

1959, Jack Daniels (left) makes some notes about ADO 15 in the Longbridge Styling Studio. The Morris Minor and Austin A35 feature on the display boards behind

Left: 1959, outside the Oxford flat, Issigonis takes his mother for a spin in a works Morris Mini-Minor; Max Dowson is in the background. Right: now a sought-after celebrity, Issigonis exercises his talent for debate on the BBC Home Service in 1962

Issigonis (left) and Alex Moulton (right) share a joke with Robert Braunschweig (middle), one of a group of Swiss journalists invited by BMC to the Garve Hotel in Scotland to test drive the 1800 as part of its launch in 1964

Issigonis was happy to pose with a pristine 1800, which he often said was his favourite design. The journalists, unfamiliar with the limitations of driving in the Scottish Highlands, obligingly used the same car to demonstrate its solidity and strength, much to the annoyance of the locals

1969, British Leyland finally launches the Austin Maxi in Portugal. Chief Engineer Harry Webster deals with the press on location while, back home, Issigonis strikes up the same pose

1970, Lord Stokes, Sir Alec Issigonis and Lord Snowdon chat at the opening of an exhibition of Alec's sketches at the Institute of Contemporary Arts in London

November 1971, retirement party at Longbridge. George Turnbull, Managing Director of the Austin Morris Division, hands over 'the biggest Meccano set you can buy' to retiree Issigonis

January 1972, officially retired, but with no intention of giving up work, Alec returns to his basement office in the 'Kremlin' at Longbridge. A selection of engineering drawings, ashtrays, paperweights, bolts, sketching instruments and a copy of the latest CAR magazine litter the desk

rapher Tony Armstrong Jones, who later became Lord Snowdon, recalled his bad temper on the subject of German engineering during one of their skiing holidays in Davos in the BBC radio programme *The Ironmonger.*

> We used to go tobogganing, which was highly illegal, from Davos down to Klosters down the main road, quite late at night or early in the morning but he was livid because we had to be towed up by some renowned German motor car which he didn't like at all. He was screaming abuse the whole way down about that German motor car.

By March 1956 Issigonis was ready to present his ideas to Len Lord, George Harriman and the rest of the Board in order to get approval to go ahead. He therefore set his team to the preparation of a mock brochure, neatly hand-drawn and hand-written onto tracing paper which was then stuck onto thin card. It was quite extensive at eighteen pages and numerous pencil corrections in Issigonis' own handwriting show that, as usual, he was not prepared to relinquish control of this important document to other people.

He gave the brochure the title 'A New Concept in Light Car Design' and began with a critical analysis of the conventional British design compared with the advantages of XC/9001. As a flourish at the end he gave his frank opinion of the hated 'German Volkswagen'.

1. Incorrect weight distribution with heavy loading at rear, causing oversteer.
2. Poor seating accommodation for length of vehicle.
3. Gear shift requires elaborate linkage to operate rear mounted gear box.
4. Two separate compartments for luggage space, minimises size of luggage and adds to the inconvenience of stowing.
5. Poor ramp angle at rear due to over hang of engine.
6. Petrol tank mounted in vulnerable position if vehicle was involved in a crash.
7. Extra material required for heating and ventilation to be sure of car defrosting.

The brochure went on to describe five different potential design layouts which were a mixture of front engines, rear engines, front wheel drive and rear wheel drive, illustrating the effects of these various schemes on seating space and ending with a discussion of suspension, identifying two basic motions, bounce and pitch. It compared the effectiveness of four different systems and their effect on 'yaw' – in other words the forward path of a car when swerved from a straight course. It then introduced an idea described as the 'hydraulic equivalent of interconnected suspension'.

The Board were pleased with the concept as presented to them and it became the basis of the specification to which the first prototypes for XC/9001 and XC/9002 were built and tested extensively during 1956.

THE DETAILS OF THE DESIGN

The engineering of the XC range of cars was to be a progression of the ideas used on both the Morris Minor and the Alvis. The first prototype which emerged consisted of a conventional front-engined, rear wheel drive car with all-independent suspension. As the wording of the brochure suggests, Issigonis was continuing to develop the Hydrolastic suspension system which he had first experimented with on the Alvis. To this end he lost no time in getting BMC to bring Alex Moulton onto the new project. In 1956 the family firm – George Spencer, Moulton and Co. – had been sold to Avon Rubber. This enabled Alex to set up a new enterprise – Moulton Developments – in the stables at the Hall where he continued with his experiments. It was therefore an opportune moment for Leonard Lord and George Harriman to offer him a three party agreement with BMC and the Dunlop Rubber Company. Moulton Developments would undertake development work at Bradford-on-Avon on rigs which would be for the exclusive use of BMC, while Dunlop would be sole suppliers of the rubber, making the parts at their Foleshill factory in Coventry. Thus Moulton became an official consultant and part of the team, liaising between Longbridge and Coventry.

Issigonis and Moulton were to find that rubber suspension did not work so well on XC/9001 as it had on the Alvis. This time the experimentation was put into the skilled and experienced hands of Jack Daniels and he describes their efforts:

> ... we started off with just the rubber units direct, Hydrolastic units, with a single cheese in the middle of the car underneath the floor which you could couple the rear and front suspensions right into. Why did we kill that? Knock. We couldn't get rid of hydraulic knock. We also tried what they called a python. Now that was a piece of rubber

specially designed with a sort of castellated external side which you moulded in a long length and you then put a non-stretchable cord around the outside of it and fed it into the suspension at both ends and that rubber was the spring. It worked as a spring alright but the trouble was it took on all the moves of the python, swinging about all over the place! We tried to put it down through the sill, we had a big sill in the car and we slid it down the sill, but it still came out like that, it was impossible, you just couldn't control it.

When it came to body style Issigonis, as ever, had firm ideas about how he wanted the car to look. In an Arclight notepad dated 1956 he made a general note which echoes the sentiments he would continue to repeat for the next 30 years:

> Styling – simple shapes if well balanced last longer – examples, Citroën, Ford, Morris Minor, Renault, Volkswagen, Lancia Apprilia [sic]. In Europe we cannot afford 2 years model changes. British cars of today do not take this factor seriously. Basic envelope is governed by engineering. If this is not right no amount of additional styling will put things right.

One person who might have expected to have some influence in this area was Austin's resident stylist. Ricardo 'Dick' Burzi was an Italian who began his career working for Lancia but then found himself in trouble for drawing topical cartoons about Mussolini which were published in the newspapers. In the late 1920s Vincenzo Lancia advised him to leave the country 'for the sake of his health', sending him to his old friend Herbert Austin with a personal recommendation. Burzi became Austin's chief stylist, and one of his quirkier characteristics, considering his profession, was the fact that he was colour-blind. He became a popular team member but, because he retained his Italian citizenship, he found himself interned on the Isle of Man for a short time during the Second World War. Len Lord finally got permission to reinstall him at Longbridge on condition that he was not allowed into the design office for the remainder of the war. Though Burzi was never given an official post or job title he was still resident in the styling studio when the BMC merger took place. The fact that he was a stylist would normally not have recommended him to Issigonis but he had an easy-going Italian charm which ensured that the two became good friends. Issigonis therefore accepted Burzi's help, though he seems to have exercised no influence in determining the basic lines of the prototype.

It was John Sheppard's task to take the shape that Issigonis had sketched out and prepare quarter-scale drawings of XC/9001 from a front, back, side and overhead or 'plan' view. When these were ready, he took them over to the pattern shop and personally supervised the construction of a fully trimmed hardwood model which formed the basis for more discussions in the styling studio about the car's development. The final work on the bodyshells fitted to the XC/9001 and XC/9002 prototypes was undertaken by BMC's new design consultants, Pininfarina, based on models supplied by Issigonis himself. As with Burzi, Issigonis made no objection to their involvement. On the contrary, it was the beginning of a lifelong friendship between the British designer and the two Pininfarinas, father and son.

With regard to the power unit, it is notable that through his career so far Issigonis had started every fresh project with the intention of designing a new engine along with the rest of the car. As yet not a single one had reached production. Chris Kingham was the last member of the team to arrive at Longbridge and he found that there was already one XC/9001 prototype running using an engine that looked very familiar. His task during 1956 was to scale down the Alvis V8 3.5-litre into a V6 light alloy engine intended for XC/9001 and a V4 1.5-litre engine intended for XC/9002. Though this 'transfer of ideas' was not strictly unethical, it was certainly a liberty in the sense that Issigonis was using development work which Alvis had paid for.

The Arclight notepads of this period are much concerned with the use of light alloys in the engine and the relative merits of air and water cooling. This was linked to Issigonis' desire to keep the engine as small as possible because of the effect this had on the overall size of the car:

Air versus water cooling – no in-line engine has yet been effectively air cooled due to greater distances required between cylinders making engines very long – cost of ducting and fan noise – power loss due to cooling and engine noise due to absence of deadening sound of water – rapid cooling due to absence of mass.

He also commented on the location of the engine:

Fore and rear tried – we believe this is best all round compromise – better stability – even on ice – less noise – luggage room.

Transmission was another element to which he gave much thought and he was extremely critical of 1950s American automatic transmission technology:

Transmission – bad for European conditions cannot anticipate kick-down deficiencies – at their best when not working – reverse of American types trend for small cars manumatic etc – power weight ratio – the best automatic transmission should never do any work – not economical to build 4 cylinder engines below $1\frac{1}{2}$ litres – what happens above this size – 6 cyl in line is out as being too long – we find it necessary to break new ground – hydraulic transmissions – American types are always offered with high powered engines to compensate for loss of efficiency – putting a unit into a car will not work – gives impression of less performance – flywheel mass is increased – car must be specially developed for this type of transmission.

In the early stages of the project he pondered over the practicality of the front wheel drive format. The Arclight notepads include a rough layout for a transverse narrow angle V4 front wheel drive unit with end-on transmission, followed a few months later by two similar sketches, more carefully drawn. He rejected this idea, however, because he had not as yet developed the transverse engine concept. In-line front wheel drive layouts created too many difficulties with packaging and gearchange mechanisms which would get in the way of his other objectives. In his notebooks he commented:

The long wheelbase calls for very large front wheel steering angles for turning circles in the order of 28' to 30' – this puts F.W.D. in an impossible position. Front wheel drive absorbs too much body space with the in line type of 4 cyl. engine, whereas the scheme above utilises reasonable space for engine and transmission with a conventional type of engine.

In one of his Arclight notepads, Issigonis wrote what might be regarded as a public relations statement about the new design:

Enjoy the safety of a wheel at each corner

1. Enjoy the luxury and silence of the water cooled engine and secondly – no cooling loss.
2. Enjoy the safety of equal weight distribution.
3. Enjoy the spaciousness and luggage accommodation afforded by the front mounted engine and conventional drive.
4. Enjoy the stability and handling afforded by uncompromising design and independent rear wheel suspension without twisting wheels.
5. Enjoy new comfort with fluid suspension with added stability and cornering power.
6. Enjoy the convenience of four doors giving comfortable access to all seats.
7. Enjoy the thrill of positive gearshifts – position of gearbox avoids long flabby control mechanism.
8. Enjoy the lasting endurance and economy of the large slow speed engine.
9. Enjoy the spaciousness and economy afforded by the correctly streamlined body.
10. Enjoy the absence of toeboard wheel arches and restricted foot room.
11. Enjoy the reliability of fluidless type of fluid suspension which cannot wear or leak.
12. Enjoy the silence of engine mountings not subjected to driving forces.
13. Enjoy the endurance and silence of directly operated valves – OHV camshaft.
14. Interconnected suspension.

The very fact that Issigonis bothered to write this down illustrates one of the greatest strengths of his unique approach – that is his ability to see the car as a whole package. He is interested in the engineering solutions but his starting point is always what can be delivered for the driver, not how clever those solutions are in themselves. This is what motivates his constant concern with interior space, good handling and roadholding, primary safety and fuel economy. So although he would repeat many times that he never asked the public what they thought because he did not think they had the expertise to give the correct answers, this did not mean they were not important to him. He would do the thinking for them:

There is no point in asking the man-in-the-street what sort of car he wants because not being an expert he can't really foresee what can be done. I think it is up to the car designer to look ahead and visualise what would be better for the man-in-the-street, then design it, give it to the man who will then appreciate the advantages of the design.

This was what enabled him to deliver up cars like the Morris Minor and the Mini.

A CHANGE OF DIRECTION — SMALL CARS ARE BETTER

Alec Issigonis showed little interest in the ebb and flow of global affairs yet world conflicts were to have a recurring influence on the course of his life. So it was that the team's steady direction throughout 1956 was suddenly interrupted by the Suez crisis.

The political mayhem which had dominated Alec's childhood had included the annexing of Turkey's interests in North Africa by Britain and France. In 1936 Britain gave up the formal Protectorate it had held over Egypt since the late 19th century but retained control over a zone around the Suez canal. Britain and France were still the major shareholders and, along with Israel, the main users of the canal. They therefore wanted to ensure the security of their oil tankers *en route* from the Middle East to Europe. In July 1956 President Nasser of Egypt nationalised the Suez canal. Confident of widespread international support, the British Prime Minister Sir Anthony Eden joined forces with France and Israel and during October and November troops were sent in to reoccupy the zone. This proved to be a massive miscalculation. The campaign quickly collapsed under the weight of unprecedented condemnation by an unlikely combination of the USA, the USSR, China and the United Nations.

The economic effect at home was six months of oil shortages and the temporary reintroduction of petrol rationing. By the mid-1950s the British economy was finally beginning to recover from the economic effects of the Second World War and the last rationing book had been discarded with great relief in 1954. The Suez crisis and subsequent oil shortage came as an unpleasant reminder that international conflicts were still an ever-present danger. The implications for the motor industry were especially severe and BMC axed 6,000 people from the workforce overnight. The management took this action without any consultation with its employees and it would prove to be a bad mistake for the future. The economic situation quickly got back to normal when petrol rationing was lifted early in 1957 and most of the 6,000 were back at work again within the year but a deep resentment caused by the unnecessary sackings festered on.

It is difficult at the moment in which a major international event occurs to assess either its real importance or its lasting impact. Suez occurred barely ten years after the end of a bitter and draining world conflict and naturally people assumed the worst. In retrospect, the crisis was a minor one and its effects would prove short-lived. Its main consequence was to bring home to the British public the realisation that their country was no longer a world power. Nevertheless, although Britain's failure to assert its authority over Egypt had a far-reaching effect on its international prestige, the economic consequences were negligible.

Suez did, however, have an unexpected impact on BMC's new model programme. Late in 1956, in the midst of the fuel crisis, Issigonis was summoned to Leonard Lord's office. In later years this meeting was the subject of one of his favourite stories and he related many times how the Chairman told him that he wanted him to 'design a proper small car to knock all these bloody bubble cars off the road'. 'Bubble' cars were rather insubstantial and quirky miniature vehicles with small, fuel-efficient engines whose major advantage was that only a motorcycle licence was required to drive one in the UK. Most of them were imported from Germany, and some of the brand names, Heinkel and Messerschmitt for example, carried unpleasant overtones of warplanes from still recent memory. There was a brief explosion in their popularity due to the re-introduction of petrol rationing but Leonard Lord was far too astute to imagine that they posed any genuine threat to BMC.

By emphasising Lord's comments about bubble cars, Issigonis created yet another one of those charming myths which would attach themselves to the story of the Mini. The real issue was the fuel shortages which BMC believed would be the long-term effect of the Suez debacle. Lord had made a snap decision on this basis and Issigonis saw his opportunity to finally make a start on the 'charwoman's car' he had described to Gerald Palmer a decade earlier. He quickly outlined the ten different points which he believed constituted the ideal specification for a small car and Lord instructed him to proceed, as quickly as possible, and produce some evidence of the practicality of his ideas. Only one restriction was put on the new project: to ensure the car reached production in the shortest possible time it must use an engine already in production. Building and testing an entirely new power unit would cost too much money.

Issigonis stepped lightly down the long corridor back to the office he shared with Jack Daniels, with a sense of anticipation which must have rivalled that of his hero Nuvolari on the starting grid at the Nürburgring. The image of his face 'grinning from ear to ear' as he threw open the door was seared into the memory of his right-hand man. Jack knew his elation came from the knowledge that he was now under orders to do exactly what he had always wanted. The perfect small car design had been his favourite subject for most of his career. Just as the Second World War had handed him his opportunity to design the Morris Minor, now Suez had thrown the green light for its successor, the Mini. He was also quite happy with the instruction to produce the car within a two to three year period, which was an ambitious target for the complex cycle from design to production required by a completely original design. The sketchbooks testify to the fact that whatever project he was actually engaged on he was always working over a multiplicity of other thoughts and ideas, so he already had a vision of how he would proceed in his mind.

Jack Daniels and John Sheppard were both caught up by his enthusiasm. Though work on the XC/9001 and XC/9002 prototypes had been going well, this new directive, working against the clock, somehow infused the team with a new sense of purpose. The larger cars were put to one side and they turned their attention to XC/9003. Their aim was to create a fuel-efficient small car in the grand tradition of the pre-war Austin Seven and post-war Morris Minor.

Chris Kingham's reaction was more reserved since Lord's instruction meant that there would be no new engine design for him. Once again Alec's car would go into production with an existing engine but at least this time the decision had been made early enough to incorporate that factor into the basic design. The only thing remaining was to decide which was the most suitable of the power units in BMC's existing range. The answer lay with the A-series, which had made its début in the Austin A30 in 1951 and was now being used in the Morris Minor.

THE INSPIRATION BEHIND THE PERSPIRATION

Morris Motors and the Austin Motor Company had been producing 'solid' products for decades but only the Austin Seven and Alec's own Morris Minor were really inspirational cars helping to move the boundaries of

British car design forward before the Mini came on the scene. It has been said many times that the Mini was the last car destined for the mainstream market to be designed by an individual rather than a committee. BMC provided a unique opportunity for a creative, lateral thinker to apply original ideas in a field whose parameters, for sound economic reasons, were usually prescribed by its market. What Issigonis achieved as a designer does not stand in isolation from the work of his predecessors or his own previous experience; but at the moment he created the Mini he dared to step outside the boundaries of this combined experience and take a chance on a novel solution. Astonishingly, a plodding manufacturing concern which was not renowned for its flair or imagination allowed him to do it.

Though there are many similarities between the methods used to create the Mosquito and XC/9003, the two projects had different starting points. The Morris Minor was based on traditional thinking, scaling down a normal car to a smaller size. Issigonis later told Tony Dawson: 'I designed it that way because at that time of my life I didn't know how to do it better.' He now had a great deal more experience and decided to go back to basic principles, starting from the inside and working outwards. The very first reference to XC/9003 – made before the conversation with Leonard Lord – is in the latter pages of one of the 1956 notebooks predominantly concerned with the large and mid-range concepts which at this stage were all intended to have in-line engines and rear wheel drive. It reads:

1) Send scheme of baby car for design study (give all important dimensions)
2) Design and make floor assembly for above
3) Send floor assembly to Italy for fitting of prototype body
4) Return to Longbridge and make into runner
5) Repeat for bigger car

There is no evidence that the instruction to involve the Italians was ever carried through and in January 1957 he opened the first Arclight notepad devoted to the revised XC/9003 brief. It begins with a series of calculations relating to the material weight of a body which is identified as being 116 inches in length, illustrating that contrary to his protestations Issigonis was perfectly competent at maths. This led him to set himself a target of 120 inches in overall length, a space which had to comfortably hold up to five people and their luggage. The engineering solutions would all be based on realising this principle. He described how he did it:

> You know, many people assume, quite incorrectly, that the first thing a
> car designer does when thinking of a new car is to sit down and doodle
> on a pad of paper until he has arrived at a pretty shape, and only then
> to start thinking about it seriously. This, of course, is totally wrong.
> What you do first is to lay out or sketch out how the people in the car
> are going to sit down. You must do this before you can start – only then
> do you sketch out and try to estimate how much room the mechanical
> parts are going to take. When you've done all this, which takes quite a
> long time, then you begin to think of the appearance. If you doodle a
> shape you may not be able to do these other things that I've just spo-
> ken about. In fact you build the car around the people and the engine.

One of his first decisions was to use a two-box rather than a three-box
design, just as Pininfarina had done on the A40.

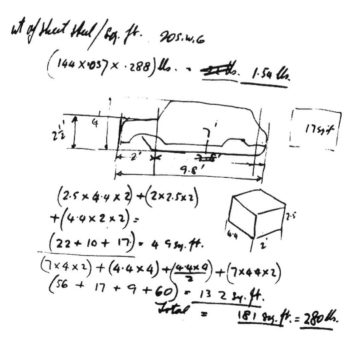

*Issigonis opened his notebook on XC/9003 – which would become the Mini – in January
1957 with a series of calculations relating to the dimensions and material weight of the
body which is identified as being 116 inches in length. The finished car would be 120
inches but his last design for a Mini replacement would return to the 116 inch target.*

Placing the wheels at the extremities of the vehicle produces quite an unacceptable balance of the car as a whole, since the rear section, which has fashionably extended over the years, now becomes an insignificant structural appendix. Judged by any standards the effect is not aesthetic. The difficulty of locating the wheels at the extremities of the vehicle can only be resolved if we revert back to old concepts of car design, and eliminate the rear box altogether. This restores the visible balance of the vehicle and grace and elegance in just the same way that old cars had. The longer wheelbase enables us to attain much needed higher standards of controllability, but the resulting shape of the whole vehicle also achieves a far greater practical aspect because the seating space and the luggage accommodation are now located within one envelope.

By allocating 102 inches to a combined passenger and luggage compartment, Issigonis left only 18 inches for the engine compartment. In his view the engine was an unavoidable but inconvenient necessity which must somehow be hidden as effectively as possible. The challenge was to find the best way of fitting the parts of the car together to achieve this ambitious goal. Now he had put aside the preconceptions on which XC/9001 was based, the answers began to flow. A few pages on from the body-weight calculations he sketched the front wheel drive, transverse engine concept which was to be the trademark of the Mini. By putting the engine in the same alignment as the wheels – that is transversely – and locating the gearbox underneath the engine he was able to achieve the packaging and space utilisation he required. The idea was stunningly simple and effective.

What were the influences on Issigonis as he came to this conclusion? How original was his idea? Neither front wheel drive nor transverse engines were new concepts in 1956 though they had never been much used commercially nor did they necessarily go together. The earliest practical example appeared on what might be described as the world's first true automobile, a huge, heavy steam-powered tricycle intended for hauling artillery designed by the French military engineer Nicolas-Joseph Cugnot. He built two examples of this vehicle during 1769–70 and though he did not solve all the engineering problems associated with such a use of the steam engine he proved the feasibility of steam-powered traction for road vehicles and was copied by many subsequent inventors. Apart from its use of steam power, the other notable feature of the vehicle was its 'fore-carriage' system, with a single front wheel performing both steering and driving functions. As a steam engine enthusiast Issigonis was naturally aware of this piece of history and during one of their annual visits to the Paris Motor Show, he press-ganged Chris Kingham and Dick Burzi into a pilgrimage to the National Conservatory of Arts and Crafts. They must see Cugnot's steam-carriage, he insisted, because it was the forerunner of the front wheel drive vehicle.

His first personal experience of a transverse engine had been the layout of the Bleriot Whippet cyclecar on which he had experimented during the 1920s. He had always been an avid reader of motoring magazines and his involvement in motor competition also gave him many opportunities to study different engineering ideas. He would therefore have observed and read about various European designers during the 1930s who were

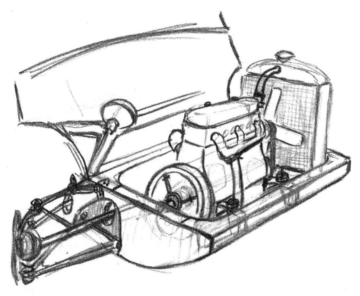

The great breakthrough which made the Mini possible was the transverse arrangement of the engine. This early sketch shows the engine as it was positioned in the first two proto-types, before it was turned the other way round.

experimenting with the front wheel drive concept (though not mounted transversely). He tried front wheel drive for himself with the Nuffield Salamander during the war and with the Morris Minor after it. Likewise he would have been aware of examples of transverse engine layouts such as the DKW, which was a product of the German Auto Union company whose racing cars he so admired.

Perhaps one of the most intriguing possible influences originated much closer to home. Laurence Pomeroy 'Senior' had been a distinguished designer during the earliest years of the British motor industry. His son, Laurence Pomeroy 'Junior', who was the same age as Issigonis, also had mechanical inclinations and a particular interest in motor sport. His career was divided between technical research and journalism and in 1938 he became the editor of *The Motor*. On 7 February 1939 this magazine published an article entitled 'Is the Unconventional Car Justified? Some further thoughts about the Mini-Motor by Laurence Pomeroy Junior'. This is worthy of note not just because of its prophetic engineering suggestions, but also because of the use of the name 'Mini-Motor'. The article sets out some basic ideas for a practical small car and among his criteria Pomeroy lists the following:

> The layout of the Mini-car shown in this article has been based fundamentally on the desire to combine a short wheelbase with comfortable seating and a small engine with a capacity for cruising at reasonable speeds for long distances in comfort. Dealing first with the matter of comfort, this can best be provided by making the front seats sufficiently wide to seat three people ... Putting three in the front demands a flat floor and an absence of gear and brake levers. The latter can be easily arranged by placing these under the fascia panel, but the former, in conjunction with the short wheelbase, gives one very strong reasons for using front-wheel-drive. There are other reasons, of course, for this construction: it gives good stability on snow and ice, fits in well with a simple form of independent front springing and gives good weight distribution ...
>
> ... Having got as far as front-wheel-drive it seems to me that one might as well take advantage of having a small engine by placing it athwart the frame instead of in line with it as normal. The purpose of this is not, I might point out, to save space ... First our friend, weight distribution, is improved once more ... The main point, however, in so disposing of the power unit is to place it as far as possible from the driver ... [in order to] substantially reduce the noise level in the car and make it much less tiring to drive on long journeys.

In December 1974 Swiss journalist Robert Braunschweig sent Issigonis a copy of this article by Pomeroy (who had died in 1966) accompanied by the following letter:

... I came across an article by poor Pom where he suggested a Mini-Motor with transverse engine layout. I should not be surprised if you were behind the scheme at the time. Can you tell me when this engine arrangement was thought up by yourself? And do you remember the Dechaux which was shown at the Paris Salon of 1947? It was a kind of metal board, independently sprung wheels, and an engine mounted across at the front, the whole thing being meant as a platform for a van. It never materialised. Then Dr Luraghi, ex-president of Alfa, published an article in which he said that they had wanted to build a 600 cc mini with a transverse engine in 1954. Among all the ifs and whens, yours seems to be the only one which came to life. It occurred to me that one should publish, some day at least, your various extrapolations of the Mini theme (remember what you let me see years ago?). Do you think the time has come already?

Issigonis wrote back to his friend indulgently but rather disingenuously:

Very many thanks for your charming letter. I was deeply moved to learn that my world-wide reputation as the creator of the transverse 4-cylinder engine turns out to be an illusion.

As an ardent reader of the Motoring Press since my young days, it is strange that dear Pom's article should have escaped me. At that time I may have been too heavily preoccupied designing the Morris Minor. Since the introduction of the present Mini, I have had many arguments with friends that transverse engined cars were not novel, but I have always been quick to point out that these were two cylinder engines (mostly from behind the Iron Curtain), with the exception of some unknown American monster conceived in the early part of the century, which apparently drove the front wheels from both ends of the crankshaft, with no gearbox. I never discovered how it went backwards.

Going back to dear old Pom, to the best of my recollection I met him for the first time after the war. It seems strange that when he wrote the book called the Mini Story he never once mentioned, during the arduous discussions we had while he was writing the book, that he had proposed the 4 cylinder transverse layout.

In the course of the latter stage of development of the Morris Minor, my old friend and colleague Jack Daniels reminds me that we did build a transverse engine front wheel drive version of that car, but when I left to go to Alvis it was immediately put under a dust sheet. When I was recalled to BMC by Lord Lambury, from Alvis around 1955–56, I got my old Morris Minor team together and started to work on the project, with the front drive transverse 4 cylinder engine concept in mind. As you know, it was rather hurriedly introduced into production in 1959.

This letter is the only evidence we have from Issigonis himself about his knowledge of previous experiments and it has many interesting features. It shows that he knew about a wide range of alternative front wheel drive and transverse engine concepts though he denies that he was actually influenced by any of them. He takes a slightly supercilious tone towards the other attempts he describes and is particularly dismissive of 'some unknown American monster conceived in the early part of the century', which presumably is a reference to an experimental car built by Walter Christie in 1904 which used both front wheel drive and a transverse engine. In 1936 Christie was briefly engaged by Morris Motors as a consultant on the design of tanks. Though this coincided with the arrival of Alec Issigonis at Cowley, there is no evidence that they had anything to do with one another. At the time, Issigonis was just a fresh-faced junior in the Drawing Office and the manner in which he refers to Christie certainly gives no hint of any acquaintance, but there is no way of knowing for sure.

In general Issigonis did not like to share any credit for his designs yet he was capable of admitting to influences upon him. He spoke of seeking out Maurice Olley, for example, to discuss his work on independent front suspension and he pointed to Citroën as one inspiration for his work with Moulton on the Hydrolastic system. Nevertheless, though he was sometimes prepared to admit that he admired the work of certain designers he was determined not to be perceived as following other people's ideas. When asked whether or not he examined the cars of rival manufacturers he replied: 'Don't be stupid, if I had a Peugeot or whatever else I should be even more confused than I am now. We *must* be able to resolve our own problems.' Italian journalist and friend Piero Casucci would later comment:

He is an individualist. He admires other people's work, but he tries in every way not to be influenced by it. I happened to visit together with him a London Motor Show and I was suddenly left in the lurch. He did not want to continue the visit because he was afraid to get confused.

Issigonis' amnesia about Pomeroy's article is not very convincing because, as he admits, he always spent a great deal of time reading motoring magazines and 1939 is too early for him to be 'preoccupied' with the Morris Minor as he suggests. Also, while it is doubtful if he ever met Christie, there is no doubt at all that Laurence Pomeroy Junior was one of his circle of friends. As his letter acknowledges, he and Pomeroy collaborated in writing *The Mini Story*, which came to be accepted as the 'official' version of how the Mini was designed. This does not clarify the situation much. In his letter Issigonis insists that they did not meet until after the war, a considerable time after the 'Mini-Motor' article was written. Pomeroy states in his book that by 1956 they had known each other for 25 years, which would mean they met sometime around 1931. But the point Issigonis makes about *The Mini Story* is valid. The book contains a lengthy description of how he arrived at his front wheel drive, transverse engine specification without any suggestion that the author, Pomeroy, had anything to do with it.

PUTTING THE DESIGN TOGETHER

As Issigonis explained to Braunschweig, he had already conducted one practical experiment with a transverse engine allied to front wheel drive and this was the Morris Minor he had been building with Jack Daniels before his departure to Alvis. This vehicle had a transverse engine with the gearbox on the end of the engine, the final drive at the back of the engine and a jackshaft between the drive shafts. When Daniels took over the development department he sent the car to the test track at Chalgrove and was impressed with its roadholding qualities during tests on ice and snow. It therefore seemed an obvious choice of car for his daily journey from Oxford to Longbridge when he joined Issigonis during the winter of 1955–6. He regularly parked it outside the Kremlin in a spot behind the 'executive' car park which was convenient for the elevated office he shared with Issigonis. The appearance of a Morris prototype on the hallowed ground of Longbridge quickly caught the attention of BMC's two top dogs who stumbled over it every morning on their way into the building. One day Harriman and Lord lay in wait for Daniels as he parked the car, so by way of explanation he lifted the bonnet to show them the engine bay's unusual arrangement and they were suitably impressed. They were therefore not too surprised when Issigonis proposed front wheel drive in connection with the new project. The results were immediate for, as Issigonis commented, 'the effect of front wheel drive is much more dramatic in a small car than a big one'.

XC/9003, however, was much smaller than the Morris Minor so it was not mounting the engine transversely which caused the difficulty, it was the location of the gearbox. Using a 2-cylinder engine would solve the space problem but would not provide sufficient performance. Installing a 4-cylinder engine meant there would be no room for the end-on arrangement of the Morris Minor. Issigonis therefore decided on a completely new configuration, placing the gearbox underneath the engine.

All these modifications meant that, despite the use of an existing engine design, Chris Kingham would have his challenge after all. Turning the engine round necessitated a lot of modifications to the transmission. Then there was the problem of the gearbox running on engine oil rather than the engine, gearbox and rear axle each having their own supply of oil. It was a matter of guesswork at this stage what effect this would have on the life of the gears.

Chris Kingham's specially designed engine was not the only casualty to occur as XC/9003 progressed. The team were not able to make sufficient progress with the interconnected 'Hydrolastic' suspension in the timescale available. Discussion about this continued for a long time and it was not until 19 May 1958 that Issigonis recorded the final decision 'no hydrolastic on 9003'. Issigonis and Moulton therefore returned to the system they had installed on the Alvis prototype using compressed rubber cone springs to provide independent front and rear suspension. At the rear the links were run horizontally under the car which not only created further space efficiency, but also contributed to the excellent roadholding which was such a great part of the Mini's success.

As well as superior roadholding, the transversely mounted engine and front wheel drive layout created the extra space Issigonis required inside the car by reducing the transmission tunnel and minimising the intrusion of the mechanical parts into the passenger area. In order to continue his space-saving theme as far as he could, Issigonis reprised another theme from the Mosquito project by targeting the size of the wheels. The Morris Minor's 14-inch wheels were no longer unusually small. The Austin A35, for example, was fitted with 13-inch wheels as standard. So this time he called in his friend Tommy French of Dunlop and asked for 10-inch wheels. French told him this was impossible. 'You can't, you couldn't accommodate the brakes', he protested. Issigonis was never prepared to accept a thing was impossible until he had tried it and satisfied himself that this was really true. 'Look, measure my hands,' he insisted, 'I want to have a wheel this big', and Dunlop duly delivered what had been asked.

Inside the car, Issigonis set about optimising the space he had freed up for the passengers. There was a surprising amount of leg room and ample space under the rear seats for stowing items away, while the dashboard incorporated a generous parcel shelf. There was no such thing as empty space in the original design concept of the Mini. He continually worked on this theme as the car was refined, and the version which went on sale would feature a boot-lid which could be rested open if extra luggage space was needed, complete with a hinged number plate which remained vertical in such circumstances. The final flourish was the sliding windows. By eliminating the thickness required in the door to hide the mechanism for wind-up windows he created extra storage room in the shape of deep pockets front and rear. These, he joked, were the ideal size to hold the ingredients of his favourite cocktail, the dry martini, namely 27 bottles of gin and one of Vermouth. This was a clever idea. Sliding windows were not a common feature on mainstream cars and were usually included only as an economy feature on very cheap and basic models such as the original Standard Eight of 1953. This would therefore serve the useful function of keeping manufacturing costs down, but in choosing them he was thinking primarily of his pursuit of 'minimalism'. It seems the team anticipated some resistance to this element of the design and in July 1958 Jack Daniels wrote to Leslie Ford, Chief Production Planning Engineer at Cowley: 'In order to be ready for possible complaining of the use of sliding glasses we have prepared in scheme form a further arrangement of the doors to incorporate drop glasses.' Issigonis had other ideas. The father of the Mini would show a dogged determination to prevent such barbarous surgery from being performed on his baby.

THE EXPERIMENTAL SHOP

The location of the design project at the Longbridge factory was extremely important because it contained the widest range of experimental shops and engineering expertise to be found within BMC. Cowley had been built round a business ethos which focussed on the end product – the careful assembly of parts provided by other factories allied to clever pricing and promotional techniques. Longbridge by contrast was built on seat-of-the-pants engineering and its development engineers were used to producing something out of nothing on incredibly short timescales and with the minimum of instruction. The key to delivering the project within three years was the priority access which the Issigonis cell was granted to every single facility that Longbridge had to offer. Leonard Lord gave the team a piece of paper which allowed them to go anywhere in the factory and demand immediate attention.

The Experimental Shop was one of the best in the country, manned by an impressive array of highly skilled craftsmen. You wanted something in metal, wood or plastic? The Longbridge Experimental Shop could make it for you. You wanted it by tomorrow? No problem. By early 1957 Sheppard had been able to translate the Issigonis sketches into quarter-scale drawings of the car at various angles. This enabled the carpenters to produce an initial wooden mock-up within a couple of days. The body consisted of laths pulled across the width of the model so that Issigonis could sit inside and check the seating capacity which he had identified as the starting point of the design. After recording the measurements it was possible to add the engine compartment and get some idea of the overall shape and dimensions which would be required. Then the clay modellers took over, turning the wooden mock-ups into full-size clay models for the use of Dick Burzi. The shape of the car flowed naturally from the engineering solutions which had been decided upon, forming a skin round the mechanical components of the car. Once the clay models had been manipulated to fine-tune the details, they became the basis of a sheet steel mock-up made out of hand-crafted metal panels welded together which was painted and given dummy wheels. This went back to the styling studio to be examined from every angle. The metal mock-up phase was not applied to all cars but it helped to provide a more refined final product because it more nearly reproduced the factory process than a plasticine, wood or clay model.

Once the details had been finalised it was time to put together a working prototype by hand in order to prove the basic concepts being proposed. This required intensive work since the only mechanical element which existed at this stage was the engine. The chassis and body had to be put together from scratch. The body parts were all hand-formed around wooden jigs provided by the model shop, created by skilled 'tin-bashers', as they were known to the Issigonis cell. The spare parts machine shop operated 24 hours a day and it could produce absolutely any part specified as well as the machinery needed for manufacturing the part itself. The team made constant use of it throughout 1957. They would sketch and draw what they wanted, pass their designs to the machine shop and go to collect what had been made the next day. The new part would be fitted onto the prototype and tested straight away. If a component was rejected, the process would be repeated day after day until they had all the parts they needed.

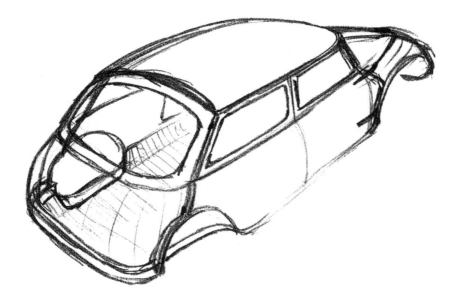

Issigonis was concerned with every aspect of XC/9003 including the shape of the body which he styled himself.

The men in the machine shop were used to responding to tight deadlines but they had never seen anything quite like this. Though Daniels, Sheppard and Kingham were attuned to Issigonis' eccentricity and curt manner, some of those outside his immediate team were grossly irritated by his dictatorial manner and offended by his off-handedness. Many of them had been at Longbridge since long before his arrival and resented the way he would appear with Jack Daniels at half past five when they were ready to go home, sit down on the bench and start demanding alterations. Nor could everyone understand his working methods, particularly the way he used sketches rather than giving verbal instructions. Some of the engineers complained that they just did not understand what he wanted them to do. There were others who enjoyed the challenge and their occasional annoyance was overridden by their admiration for his engineering ability, his intelligence, and the results he seemed to produce from absolutely nowhere. One of these was Doug Adams, who remembers the puzzlement which followed some of the visits which Issigonis made personally to explain what he wanted: 'It was quite strange to us, building doors with pockets and no up and down glass. It seemed odd to make an engine bay with the engine the wrong way round as far as we were concerned.' Whatever their doubts, they always did as they were asked. This flexibility is one of the many things which has completely disappeared from the modern manufacturing process and this is why the design of a car like the Mini would be impossible today.

The efforts of the draughtsmen and experimental engineers together meant that the first rough prototype was ready to try out early in 1957 and Issigonis undertook the all-important first tests himself. He had been obliged to do this during the Mosquito and Alvis projects but he could have delegated the task for XC/9003 by virtue of the seniority of his position. He made no effort to do so because he wished to get a feel for the car as early as possible so he could assure himself that the project was heading in the right direction. He explained:

> One always becomes very much involved with any car one designs, and when a prototype is built like this I always insist on being the first person to drive it because I can get an impression of what a car is going to be like in the first mile and I come back and I think either we go on or we don't go on. I was agreeably surprised with the Mini when I first drove it, but most cars are faulty when they first come out.

It seems that Issigonis was rather too anxious to get his hands on the car. According to Jack Daniels he could not be dissuaded from trying out a test buck put together to work out the suspension system: 'Our very first effort collapsed after AI insisted on trying it and travelling around 100 yards!' The team had to put the rudimentary vehicle back together, this time using stronger suspension materials. The series of test runs which Issigonis undertook in the proper XC/9003 prototype are all recorded in the Arclight notepads. On 9 February 1957 he wrote that the first prototype was within five to six days of its first outing, which proved close to the mark as the first test run actually took place two weeks later:

1st Test Run 22 Feb 1957

Friday 6 p.m. on works circuit, observations: —
1) rear canister housing fouling frame lead to great deal of noise, harshness and general rattle
2) 300 lbs. load needed in boot to trim car
3) pitch frequency 90. This appears too high (ride impression good)
4) low evidence of torsional shake in structure. Side members not boxed up for this test
5) suspension pressure 130 lbs unladen
6) evidence of oversteering on fast corners — possibly due to excessive rear end load.

Issigonis took a second, longer, run on 25 February and made further comments about suspension, vibration and engine roughness. This was followed by three more runs on 27 February, 28 February and 1 March. At this point modifications were ordered in the areas of suspension lever-age, tappet clearance, gear lever and steering column position and pitch frequency. He then took the car out on a further two runs on 18 and 19 March before giving instructions for additional modifications. On 21 March he took the revised car on an 80-mile road test following which, on 15 April, he wrote some general notes about his conclusions:

Fairly extensive testing has shown that harshness can be reduced by various methods now that the problem is understood. Parts are being made to tackle the problem in two ways.
1) larger interconnecting pipe with smaller displacer.
2) airsprung unit at each wheel.
In the meantime tests on oversteer are being tried out.
1) reduction of roll of vehicle with stiffer bounce springs
2) modified rear luggage to reduce rate rise at rear
3) check deflection of rear drums under high cornering forces (Cowley)
Note, 2) is not practical with interconnection and no levelling.

This was followed by a longer set of notes on the problems of harshness and the car's tendency to oversteer. A further note on 17 July 1957 concluded: 'Performance falls between A40 and Morris Minor. Consumption figures not yet substantiated. We are now working on the final production timing.'

As well as trying out the prototype for himself Issigonis liked to test it on people whose driving skills he did not rate very highly. He quite reasonably considered that, since his objective was to design a car for ordinary people, he would not learn what he needed to know by using the best drivers available. He once told Tony Dawson that his ideal tester would be 'my old mother who could break anything'. The traditional testing ground for Longbridge prototypes was the Lickey Hills which formed a picturesque backdrop to the factory. So he picked out two engineers and sent them off into the hills in the rudimentary version of XC/9003. They promptly proved his point by rolling the car, much to the astonishment of Jack Daniels who was in charge of the official test programme.

THE ROLE OF LEONARD LORD

Issigonis was now ready to demonstrate the car to Lord and Harriman. He recorded the results of his own tests in his Arclight notepads. In addition, throughout 1957 and 1958, he kept daily notes about the progress of his engineering projects in two small ringbinders. In the first of these on 19 July 1957 he wrote:

> 1st run by Sir Leonard in 9003 with 4 cyl engine – also Mr Harriman. Good general impression, major defect noisy primary gears – showed production wood mock alongside prototype for final acceptance – in the open – approved for production. Proceed with body design details. Pass over to main D.O. for tooling drawings after discussion of detail.

This appears to be the point at which Lord gave his instruction to Issigonis to begin the preparations for getting the car into production, though the note written two days earlier in his Arclight notepad that 'we are now working on the final production timing' seems to have already anticipated this approval. The project was as yet only six months old. In later interviews Issigonis would give a much more colourful description of Leonard Lord's first ride in the Mini than the clinical account which appears in his notebook. He talked of driving Lord at breakneck speed for several laps of the inner roads at Longbridge before screeching to a halt outside the main door to the Kremlin where a slightly dazed chairman climbed from the car and uttered the now legendary injunction 'Build it!'

This was a momentous occasion and Issigonis realised its significance. He had taken the first step towards realising his ambition of a 'charwoman's car' and BMC's Chairman, of whom he was in some awe, had been impressed. Mark Ransome, now a young Austin apprentice, was waiting in his uncle's outer office late that afternoon when he heard the sound of a car engine pulling away and returning about fifteen minutes later. Alec returned to the office in a state of excitement, exclaiming that he had just taken Sir Leonard round the block and now he was taking Mark back to his hotel for a celebration. He was on fine form during dinner, playing to a receptive audience which included his friend Mike Parkes and his adoring mother, who sometimes stayed with him at the hotel during the week. After dinner Parkes offered to drive Mark Ransome to his lodgings in West Heath on the other side of the Lickey Hills, a ride which complemented the drama of the evening, as they made their way through a fierce summer rainstorm, with Parkes dramatically sliding his specially converted Ford Anglia to the backdrop of lightning flashes and rolling thunder.

This exuberance reminds us of Peter Ustinov's description of Issigonis as possessing 'an innocence which is at once childish and highly sophisticated'. This was not just another day at work to him, it was a step nearer to the attainment of his personal dreams. Nor was he insensitive to the implications of what he was doing. Recounting this time, Issigonis revealed a surprising apprehension and humility about this key moment in his career:

I used to lie awake at nights with fear. Not the fear that what we were doing was not right, but the fear that other people might not see it was right. The responsibility of that enormous amount of money, the numbers of people whose jobs were at stake, the reputation of the men who had to make the decisions, this was something I could not have borne. When Len Lord told me to go ahead and build it I was horrified. I even told him he was mad to build a car on what we had been able to demonstrate at that stage.

The support given by Leonard Lord was absolutely crucial. He was the only person who could mobilise the factory 100 per cent behind the project, which meant not just opening the doors of the experimental department but also allocating vast amounts of money to build the necessary facilities for manufacture. It was Lord not Issigonis who had set the target and timescale of the project but in doing so he showed tremendous faith in Issigonis' ability to deliver. Now, it can be called foresight. At the time some of his contemporaries considered it to be the highest folly.

A telling encounter occurred while Alec and Chris Kingham were testing one of the prototypes inside the Longbridge complex. As they put the little car through its paces they found themselves in the shadow of Leonard Lord's large executive saloon which had suddenly appeared from the opposite direction. When the Chairman saw them he stopped and wound the window down, gesturing to Issigonis to do the same. Issigonis, peering up at the limousine, nervously slid back his window, perhaps anticipating a word of praise, but to his chagrin Lord snapped at him 'get that damned thing out of my sight' and drove off. He turned the car round and drove Kingham back to Burzi's styling studio where he asked his two colleagues in a deeply wounded manner, 'What did he mean? Doesn't he like it?' He brooded over the comment for several days, unconvinced by Kingham and Burzi's explanation that Lord was simply complaining about the car being shown around too much. Apart from Alec's sensitivity, this incident illustrates the extent to which he deferred to Lord as his superior.

The manifestation of this was that by no means all the key decisions about the new project's specification belonged to Issigonis. He ended his account of the 19 July 1957 test run with the words: 'Sir Leonard feels we should use 950 cc engine.' On 24 July he continued, 'S.V. tells me that 800 cc is to be used!', then on 31 July, 'now 950 cc engine approved by Sir L. Lord and Mr S.V. Smith 30 July 1957', and finally a few pages later on 1 August 1957, 'Sir Leonard Lord decides on 850 cc.' The indecision over the size of the engine seems to have stemmed from a fear of providing too much performance in what was intended to be a family car but the decision, when it finally came, was made by Lord in consultation with Technical Director Sidney Smith and not by Issigonis.

Yet even while he was opening every door of the factory to Issigonis in the pursuit of advanced engineering solutions, Leonard Lord was also paying the firm of ERA at Dunstable to come up with an alternative design based on the ideas of none other than Laurence Pomeroy Junior. 'English Racing Automobiles' had originally been set up in 1934 by

Raymond Mays to build racing cars but by the early 1950s it had changed its role, offering specialist research on a consultancy basis to large motor companies. In 1958 it finally changed its name to reflect this and became 'Engineering Research Applications'. Pomeroy worked with ERA's David Hodkin on the project which is briefly referred to at the start of *The Mini Story*. Lord, he states, insisted that he and Issigonis should not discuss their work to ensure that two separate approaches were arrived at. The results of 'Project Maximin' were presented to George Harriman and S. V. Smith in a folder which is preserved in the Archive of the British Motor Industry Heritage Trust. This is dated 25 June 1959 when the Issigonis design had already gone into production and the launch was only two months away. It identifies the start of ERA's study as January 1956 when 'initial terms of reference were agreed' and these show that Pomeroy's project was intended to provide an alternative 'advanced engineering' approach in its widest sense since Issigonis was not at this stage focussed on a small car concept. It would also seem that when Lord changed his brief to Issigonis, he did not bother to tell Pomeroy. Nevertheless the Maximin timetable eerily echoes that of XC/9003, with the first prototype completed in March 1957 and extensive road testing taking place throughout 1958.

The ERA project could not have been cheap because it involved construction of a completely new engine and by the time of the report there were two complete prototypes in existence, with a third under construction, each undergoing a substantial test programme. The design was ambitious with the engine unusually positioned in transverse formation just in front of the rear wheels. The car had a wheelbase of 102 inches and an overall length of 165.5 inches, making it a similar size to XC/9001, but it shared the Issigonis theme of maximum space utilisation combined with an attempt to be innovative in its engineering. Compared with the clean lines of the Mini, however, the body shell is distinctly unaesthetic with a clumsy overhanging rear and bonnet plus lots of the fins and angles so popular on late 50s cars. Ironically, Dick Burzi is identified in the report as being responsible for this design, making Issigonis' decision to do his own styling a sound one. It is unlikely that the Mini would have lasted for 40 years if it had looked like the 'Maximin'. It is remarkable that Leonard Lord spent so much money on a rival project while he was simultaneously allowing Longbridge to be turned upside down to support the pioneering technology of the Issigonis XC programme and signing, with apparent abandon, whatever cheques were necessary for building the tooling and facilities required to produce it. Given the resources available to the Issigonis cell and the fact that the ERA project ended up working to terms of reference which they were not told had been changed, there was little chance of it superseding the official programme.

THE TEST PROGRAMME

Issigonis was right to say that the design had as yet hardly been tested when Lord gave the go-ahead to prepare for production in late July 1957. In the normal course of events there was a long period of transition between experimental and production work. In this case Issigonis admitted that in order to meet the deadline 'we took a slight risk by beginning to tool some of the items which took longest to do, mainly on the body'. It was now time to start transposing the design drawings coming out of the Issigonis cell into full-scale production drawings, detailing all the parts so that instructions could be given for their manufacture. The task of generating drawings for up to 2,500 separate components was beyond the capability of the small development team so, finally, the main Drawing Office became involved. A new unit was set up dedicated to this work and XC/9003 received its official designation of ADO 15. This meant that John Sheppard was on the one hand passing drawings to the Experimental Shop for the development work which had to be done on the prototypes while at the same time transferring information from the Experimental Shop to the Drawing Office.

This created many frustrations and difficulties which were not helped by the fact that Issigonis was reluctant to talk to the draughtsmen directly. He disliked engaging with people outside his immediate circle, especially if he sensed any criticism of himself, so if he found it necessary to go down to the Drawing Office he would take Jack Daniels with him and speak exclusively to him thus giving the impression that he considered them too insignificant to talk to personally. Opinion about him in the Experimental Shop could be described as ambivalent but in the main Drawing Office his autocratic behaviour was almost universally considered offensive and arrogant. They did not take well to his lecturing and they were irritated when he came to the office in the evening after they had gone home to write on somebody's drawing 'I'll see you about this in the morning'. His peculiar surname had always attracted descriptive variations both inside and outside the factory, from 'Issy' which his personal team had always called him to 'Issygonyet' down in the workshops. The one in widest use, however, was 'Arragonis'.

While the production engineers grappled with producing the formal range of drawings required, the Issigonis cell were preoccupied with the urgent task of proving the car and by the time Lord was given his ride they had built a second running prototype. Jack Daniels formed a small test team from engineers already associated with the project in order to minimise the number of people involved, though if secrecy was considered important it was just as well that most of the testing was done at night. The first prototype was, for reasons now forgotten, brilliant orange and the second bright red, both with a black roof and a cream waistband. Their distinctive shape and garish colour earned them the nickname of 'orange-box' among the engineers and the addition of a dummy A35 grille did not contribute very much by way of disguise.

Initially the testing was done at a quiet aerodrome between Stadhampton and Chalgrove just outside Oxford where the prototypes could be driven round the perimeter circuit in secrecy. Daniels personally set a benchmark of 72 miles per hour for the testers to work against and then chose an engineer named Basil MacKenzie from the Experimental Shop to oversee the programme. Thousands of miles were clocked up and particular attention was paid in these early tests to the provisional interconnected suspension. The surface of the Chalgrove circuit was so rough that it quickly showed up several inadequacies which were rectified by the installation of separate sub-frames to diffuse the load. The endurance of the small tyres also had to be checked, excessive oil consumption was noted, fuel consumption was carefully monitored and a tendency towards water leaks also became a recurring theme. Other tests were carried out to examine the car's stability in cornering.

The first two prototypes had the engine carburettor facing forward and the battery mounted in the engine compartment but as a result of all this testing two modifications were made to the third prototype. First the battery was moved to the boot in order to provide a better weight distribution. Then the engine was turned round so the carburettor faced the rear for reasons which Jack Daniels explains:

For the third prototype we turned the engine round, partly because of an icing problem. When working with the engine west to east, the carburettor was at the front. The first two prototypes only were built that way and one of them we took to France right in the middle of the first winter and we had trouble with icing of the carburettor. But that was not the only problem. Although the gearcase was new, the works of the gearbox were fundamentally standard. So when the engine was west to east, the drive to the gearbox was via the pinion to a large and heavy reduction gear mounted on the main shaft of the gearbox. The inertia of that particular gear caused us trouble with the synchromesh elements which tended to wear out prematurely. Synchromeshes were poor in those days anyway, and we had to do something about that. One thing we could do was turn the engine round, put three gears down there instead of two and all of them were a lot smaller. It also made the exhaust so much easier to pass from front to rear … Now I should add that much later I had the opportunity to check what difference the direction of the engine would have made to the temperature of the carburettor and there was only about 1 degree in temperature difference at any time between the two configurations. So the icing problem was not a valid cause for changing the engine round.

As more prototypes were built there were inevitably some minor adjustments to details of the structure and materials used but the installation of the subframes and the turning of the engine were the only major modifications made to the original specification. The initial test programme appeared to have demonstrated that the basic concept was sound and on this basis eleven more prototypes were constructed.

With their expanded fleet, the experimental team began to venture further afield. They would wait for the activity in the Longbridge Works to die down and then take the cars out of the shop in the early evening, returning early next morning before the majority of the workforce had started the day. Initially they used a 100-mile circuit around the Cotswolds, later they headed off through the Lickey Hills and on to the Welsh mountains. After several months of continuous work Daniels was ready to test the ever-improving car on the rough roads in the north of France. He was busy developing the alternative rubber cone spring suspension without dampers because of the problems which had been encountered with the Hydrolastic concept and he felt this would be an excellent opportunity to check out the revised system. Charles Griffin, who was then Chief Development Engineer for Cowley, and Gil Jones,

Griffin's counterpart at Longbridge, were to accompany him. Charles Griffin persuaded Bill Heynes (who was still in the Jaguar Cars design office) to let them take his personal Jaguar as a second car for this trip. Jack Daniels, believing he had done more than enough to earn such a perk after all the miles of testing he had put in, requisitioned the Jaguar for the outward journey, leaving the Mini with its rudimentary suspension to his colleagues.

Inside the Issigonis cell there was a tremendous spirit and excitement carrying them forward, a feeling that their team was involved in something special. In October 1957 Issigonis, Jack Daniels, John Sheppard and Dick Burzi took a break from their efforts to attend the Paris Motor Show together. One evening, enjoying a drink at a café on the Champs Elysées, they noticed that the people around them were constantly looking up into the sky. Burzi was the only multi-lingual member of the party, so he was despatched to find a newspaper. He discovered that the Russians had just sent up the first satellite or 'sputnik' and this inspired them to copy their neighbours and stand up to study the sky. There was nothing to be seen so after a while they sat down again and fell to pondering whether their little car would go round the world as the newspaper said the sputnik was going to do. In their minds these two great events seemed to be linked and they decided to adopt the name. From then on the car was known inside the team as the sputnik.

By March 1958 the specification was sufficiently proved to construct five pre-production cars. Though these were individually built by the workshop, they were produced with standard parts in similar conditions to those which would form part of the final production process. Each was a different colour – light blue, dark blue, red, green and grey – and each underwent a specific programme to check different aspects of the performance. First tests were carried out at MIRA, but by October 1958 they were ready for a trip to Spain as part of a convoy of development vehicles led by Chris Kingham. The participants were deliberately chosen from a group of engineers who had never driven the car or had any previous association with it. At the end of the first day the test-drivers held a 'round table conference' to discuss first impressions and immediately afterwards Kingham wrote down their conclusions in a long letter to Issigonis. The news must have pleased him. Although there were inevitably some problems Kingham was able to report that they were 'concerned with minor details rather than fundamentals'. There were complaints about the position of the seats and the pedals, weak brakes, poor ventilation, severe water leaks encountered in very heavy rain conditions, poor rear vision and excessive body noise. Despite this, Kingham was at pains to point out the general lack of mechanical problems encountered and the positive reaction of the convoy. 'The car has patently won the respect of every member of the team for its performance and handling qualities', he wrote. 'Both the complaints against and the troubles experienced with ADO 15 leave it as the vehicle most generally liked by the team.'

SETTING UP A PRODUCTION LINE

According to *The Mini Story*, Issigonis took Leonard Lord for a decisive ride in ADO 15 in July 1958. Since Pomeroy's description of the event was written in collaboration with Issigonis and has been much quoted, it is worth repeating:

> It was this 'Orange Box' in which Sir Leonard made his first and, as it turned out, his decisive run in July 1958 some fifteen months after he had asked for a car of this kind, twelve months after the design had been completed and nine months after it had gone on the road, during which time it had covered some 30,000 miles ... After a five minute drive around the Works he made perhaps the greatest decision of his life. Turning to Issigonis he said: 'Alec, this is it, I want it in production within twelve months' to which a somewhat startled Alec replied 'Sir Leonard, this will cost many millions of pounds'. Characteristically Sir Leonard came back like a flash and said: 'Don't worry about that; I shall sign the cheques, you get on with getting the thing to work.'

This account is rather puzzling since the documentary evidence tells us that Leonard Lord had been out in the Orange Box a year earlier in July 1957. It could be that Pomeroy is describing a second test-ride, but in this case it seems strange that Issigonis would use the primitive Orange Box prototype when by now there were eleven other prototypes and five pre-production cars available. The dates recorded by Issigonis in his notes show that the timescales given by Pomeroy are also incorrect.

This leads us to the conclusion that the gestation of the Mini was rather more complicated and lengthy than the popular myth would have us believe. Lord gives Issigonis instructions to change to a small car project using an engine from the existing model range in November 1956. By February 1957 a rough prototype has been built and is tested personally by Issigonis during February and March. Modifications are made and by July the prototype is ready to be demonstrated to Lord and Harriman who give approval to tool up for production, specifying an engine size of 850 cc. A year later Lord sets a final production date of August 1959. The whole enterprise has therefore taken two years and nine months. But though this adds four months to the usual account it makes very little difference. It still represents a remarkably short period for the development of a completely new design and this would have its consequences during the first year of production.

The man who had to get ADO 15 into production was Geoffrey Rose, who had first met Issigonis in 1946 while working at the Wolseley factory, which was part of the Nuffield Organisation. Following the BMC merger Rose made the awkward transition to the 'other side' of the company by becoming Works Manager of the car division at Longbridge in 1954. It therefore fell within his area of responsibility to set up the new assembly lines. He was alarmed by Lord's target launch date of August 1959 and equally dubious about the instruction to plan for 3,000 units a week which was at the time an extremely ambitious figure for a completely new model, especially when nobody knew how the market was going to receive it.

An Austin subsidiary called Fisher and Ludlow was chosen to do the body tooling and the original intention was to use their existing plant in Castle Bromwich which was conveniently close to Birmingham. It proved impossible, however, to achieve this within the bounds of the existing plant. Among the reforms introduced by Clement Attlee's Labour government in 1947 was the requirement for manufacturers to obtain an Industrial Development Certificate (IDC) if they wished to expand their facilities. Though there was now a Conservative administration under Harold Macmillan, the IDC system was still in force. Since the intention was to promote increased industrial capacity in depressed areas of Britain, there was little chance of BMC getting approval to expand in the prosperous Midlands. So it was decided to set up a completely new factory at Llanelli in Wales for the production of ADO 15 body panels. In order to install the most up-to-date techniques in their new factory, BMC hired the retired press shop superintendent of the Ford pressing factory at Chicago Heights which was one of the most modern in the world.

Final assembly would take place at BMC's main facilities. Because the car was to be produced in an Austin and a Morris version it was felt necessary to establish two assembly lines but since the Cowley facility did not have the capacity of Longbridge it was clear from the beginning that this would not be a 50-50 split. It was never the case that the Austin version was built at Longbridge and the Morris version at Cowley. The marques were mixed together in both factories until 1969 when the Cowley line was discontinued and all UK production switched to Longbridge.

All the cars currently in the model range were of conventional design requiring equally conventional production methods. Geoffrey Rose therefore had much work to do to ensure that the new assembly lines would be able to accommodate revised techniques which would have to be as advanced as the design itself. Assembling the transverse power unit with a gearbox underneath, for example, demanded completely new machinery while the structure of the bodyshell would require the workforce to learn new welding skills. The car was to set a new pattern in automobile design which would later become standard but it was an expensive, complicated and risky undertaking to pioneer such a route. It required massive investment in new facilities and considerable reorganisation of existing assembly lines. This made the prospect of getting ADO 15 into production within such a short timescale all the more daunting.

Apart from Rose, the other men on the front line were the two Heads of Facilities, Harold Cross at Longbridge and Leslie Ford at Cowley. One eyewitness to their roller-coaster ride was Peter Tothill, a young engineer who had joined the process engineering section at Cowley in 1955 reporting to Leslie Ford. He became involved in much of the day-to-day work which had to be done to set up the Cowley line and had some interesting experiences along the way.

A suitable site for Cowley assembly had already been identified in a vacated paint shop, but Tothill's first problem was to obtain a design layout from the Issigonis cell so he could ascertain what tooling would be required. The technical drawings were taking too long to filter back from the Drawing Office to the production engineers, so a full-size layout of ADO 15 was commissioned to be drawn on a horizontal sheet of aluminium ten feet long. This task was entrusted to George Cooper of the Cowley Drawing Office, assisted by draughtsman Ron Unsworth who had worked on the Mosquito project as a young man. They both insisted on smoking their pipes throughout, blackening the layout with tobacco ash, but this was a small price to pay to gain access to a proper full-scale drawing. Tothill also persuaded Jack Daniels to lend him one of the prototypes for a week and he organised a small team to strip it down and rebuild it. In this way he was able to work out the order in which operations needed to be carried out and identify the relevant stages. The team exhaustively wrote up their conclusions including whether men would be working at the side, at the front, or underneath the car, which was crucial to understanding how many workstations would be needed.

As the year progressed the prototypes underwent significant development, and in December 1958 Daniels sent an ADO 15 saloon to Leslie Ford for evaluation, with a memo saying, 'this vehicle is as up to date as we can make it at the present time'. The car was handed over to Tothill who decided to simulate the style of track on which the car would be built by constructing some static sections out of wood and attempting to carry out the production process *in situ*. To his horror he discovered that the engine had been turned round which had major implications for the scheme he had already devised for dropping the body onto the subframe. Leslie Ford and Harold Cross puzzled over the problem for some time before requesting a meeting with Issigonis and Jack Daniels. They all agreed to meet on a Friday afternoon, the day he regularly worked at Cowley. The production engineers demonstrated to Issigonis and Daniels how the operation of dropping the body onto the moving line had become too complex to be safe and they waited expectantly for a helpful response.

'I've designed the car, it's your problem how you put it together. We can't alter anything' was the one that they got.

This caused an awkward silence until Harold Cross intervened:

'Look, I'm sorry you're taking this attitude, you leave Leslie Ford and myself with no alternative but to report to our respective Directors on Monday that this car can't be built at Cowley *or* at Longbridge.'

Another silence was broken momentarily by Jack Daniels nonchalantly fishing his pipe out of his pocket, for he knew already how this was going to end. Sure enough, Issigonis turned to him and muttered angrily, 'You'd better do what they want.' Without speaking to anyone else he then turned on his heel and stalked off leaving Leslie Ford and Harold Cross asking Jack Daniels, 'What did he say?' Jack Daniels undertook to sort the problem out and created some modifications to facilitate a straight body drop and everybody, except Issigonis, was happy.

Tothill's account of this incident apparently shows Issigonis at his worst, refusing to accommodate the compromise necessary between development and production. Part of the problem was his need to control everything. He did not want to give the production engineers the opportunity to demand fundamental changes to his design. He and they stood at two ends of the spectrum, Issigonis determined to preserve the purity of his design and the production engineers concerned only with how easy it was to manufacture. Neither party was really interested in the other's point of view and the end result was that Issigonis kept them out of the process for as long as possible, leaving them to fire-fight on the assembly line, a situation which brought no advantage to either party. Nevertheless he was not unaware of the issues. He had gone to considerable lengths to design the car so that its assembly would be cheap, easy and practical. One example of this was the way that some of the welding seams had been placed on the outside of the car. He explained it thus:

It takes a long time for a new concept like the Mini to get onto the market because it is so unusual. Not that the technical problems take long in themselves to overcome. What takes the time is, first to convey your ideas to your colleagues who have to help you with the design and last, but not least, to move over to the far bigger problem of actual production when the number of people who have to become involved in the project suddenly becomes a thousand-fold bigger. You have your suppliers to cope with, you've got to make them realise the kind of thing you want done, and impress on them that it must be done this way and not that. When you've gone through all this you've got to cope with the production developments. I can't physically cope with each individual worker but I am very closely associated with the executives in charge of production. Now you see this is only the beginning it is much more difficult than that. The more and more that you get involved in it in the end the more the process slows down.

Nor was Daniels always so accommodating as he had been over the engine bay. During the first three months of 1959 he clashed a number of times with Cross and Ford over proposed modifications to facilitate assembly. Though Daniels is usually presented as the genial foil to the bad-tempered and uncooperative Issigonis the tone of some of his correspondence suggests otherwise. A typical example was this frosty note sent in February 1959 as a result of suggestions that the wiring should be altered:

We very much doubt that an estimated saving of <u>26 pence</u> per <u>body primer labour</u> could be achieved. It appears to be unlikely that the whole operation of laying the harness on the line could cost that amount in the first place. Even if you could verify that figure, its benefit would be substantially minimised by the cost of incidental changes to suit. We therefore ask for re-examination of your proposals.

There were in any case other problems which had nothing to do with what Cross and Ford perceived to be the obstructive attitude of Issigonis. The split between two factories resulted in expensive complications. Longbridge, for example, applied the base coat of paint to the body panels using a 'slipper dip', whereas Cowley used a 'rotodip', which had implications for the structure of the panels.

This was just one of a host of problems caused by the different methods and materials in use in both factories and it raises the question of just what drove BMC to believe that it made any sense to split production over two sites in this way. It was yet another example of their failure to realise the fundamental cost to them of their stubborn insistence on clinging to old company and marque identities.

BABY HAS TEETHING PROBLEMS

Setting up the facilities was only the first step. When manufacture actually began the engineering and production departments were both faced with a whole new set of obstacles to overcome.

The Longbridge track was the first to spring into action and the earliest Austin version of ADO 15 came off the line on 3 April 1959. It was immediately subjected to a thorough test by Gil Jones who produced a five-page report listing an extensive set of defects. Many items had simply not been fitted properly – the doors and rear number plate rattled, the sun visor was 'loose on its hinges and falling down', the position of the petrol pump was incorrect, the radiator was too high, the accelerator pedal was too short, and the self-cancelling trafficator did not self-cancel because it was not adjusted properly. Other items were not built to specification – these included the sliding windows and the shelf trim. These faults might be considered matters of detail. More serious were the mechanical shortcomings. The clutch was impossible to disengage, the steering column was in the wrong place, there was a grating noise in the gears, the water pump squealed because it was so badly fitted, and the handbrake was only capable of locking the offside wheel. It may seem surprising that this report caused little consternation but there was nothing unusual to the BMC workforce in finding so many faults on an initial production vehicle. A similar check at Cowley on the first Morris version produced similar results. Both cars were sent back for rectification.

It would take all summer to diagnose the many problems which arose and prescribe suitable solutions as BMC attempted to get their new product ready for sale. Issigonis received copies of the numerous memos and minutes which were generated but it was Jack Daniels and Charles Griffin who took the lead in sorting things out. The explanations they received were not always helpful, as engineers complained of things such as 'twitter in the bonnet' and 'a noise which we refer to as "bonk" which occurs in the drive shafts'. The solutions too were at times lacking in finesse. Problems with lubrication, for example, led Daniels to issue the instruction that the offending points should be 'liberally covered with grease just prior to assembly, and in the final greasing operation pivots should be charged until grease is seen to exude'.

In other cases the blame was shifted to shoddy workmanship. John Sheppard reported that dents to the body panels were being caused 'by workers at body build and at paint stages, who violently throw open doors until the available travel between hinge leaves is exceeded with consequent reaction on the panels'. On a number of occasions Daniels suggested that problems could be solved by 'a little know-how' on the part of the fitters. Far more faults were being reported by Cowley than Longbridge and Daniels told Leslie Ford: 'It seems reasonably certain that the majority of difficulties experienced by Cowley result from incorrect assembly due to lack of appreciation of the requirements.'

To make matters worse, despite the fact that manufacture had begun, the test programme had yet to be concluded. Jack Daniels and Gil Jones set off on a final exhaustive Continental trip during June to July 1959. This provided a dual opportunity to finish proving the car while showing it to dealers in potential export markets. Their route was extensive, involving journeys of up to 400 miles a day through Scandinavia, across the Arctic Circle and then back through all the major countries of the European mainland.

The faults found during initial assembly combined with the final test results meant that details of the specification were being altered from week to week, continually pushing up the costs of manufacture. One suggested change to the construction of the flywheel would have cost £25,000 in additional capital equipment and even though an alternative solution was found, this nevertheless resulted in the use of more expensive materials. The launch of ADO 15 was not scheduled until the end of August but the vehicles being produced throughout the summer would be vital to fulfil the orders which it was hoped would come flooding in once the new model was in the showrooms. Looking at the paperwork it is clear that the purchaser of a vehicle manufactured in May would find himself in possession of something substantially different from one manufactured in July. Many of the early vehicles were earmarked for export and were already sitting at the docks. Where the faults were sufficiently serious, instructions had to be sent to carry out modifications before vehicles were loaded onto the boat. As the launch approached the engineers battled on to sort the problems out, but their efforts would continue well into 1960.

SELLING THE MINI

Despite all these frustrations and difficulties, the production programme was finally in progress and the cars were rolling off the line. Now BMC had to turn its attention to selling them.

Issigonis had been as co-operative with the Sales Department as with the production engineers, doing everything he could to make sure they did not compromise his design concept. In later years he would rant about them: 'Market research is bunk! It is the designer of the car who knows best what is good for the prospective car owner. I never consulted sales people about what cars they were going to get.' He excluded them from any say in how the car would look and when they finally saw it their worst fears seemed to have been realised in its startling appearance. James Bramley was the overall Director of Sales, an old associate of Herbert Austin who had been at Longbridge since 1932. His Deputy was Thomas Sangster who had joined Riley (which subsequently became part of the Nuffield Organisation) in 1930. Austin's Home Sales Manager was James Penrose who had joined Austin as an apprentice in 1925. Though these men were of similar age to Issigonis they were also traditionalists who disliked the car immediately for its unconventionality, echoing Lord Nuffield's reaction to the Mosquito ten years earlier. Harriman had also been uneasy when he first saw the simplicity of the shape and the starkness of the interior. Issigonis had been urged to do something to liven it up, so full wheel discs were added along with a bright strip along the wing.

In the days leading up to the launch there was a feeling of nervousness and apprehension rather than anticipation in the air at Longbridge. It must have been some comfort to Harriman that one person who did seem to approve was BMC's distinguished design consultant Battista Pininfarina. They were joined by Len Lord and Alec Issigonis for a private viewing in Dick Burzi's styling studio and the Italian was asked, 'Well, what do you think?'

Pininfarina turned to Issigonis with the words, 'Are you a stylist or an engineer?'

'Sir, I find your question most offensive', replied Issigonis with mock indignation. 'I am an engineer *not* a stylist.'

Pininfarina took the joke in good part and laughed, saying with sincerity, 'Keep it absolutely the same, it's unique', which naturally pleased Issigonis immensely.

Whatever their feelings, the sales chiefs had no choice other than to get on with the job of marketing it. The first step was to devise an official model name but the title chosen was not 'Mini', a name which did not as yet exist. The two versions of the car would go back to the roots of their respective marques in order to capitalise on old reputations. They were to be marketed as the 'Austin Seven' (originally spelt 'Se7en' to ram the point home) and the 'Morris Mini-Minor'. The reason that the word 'Mini' was sneaked into the Morris version was simple enough – there was already a Morris Minor on the market, so the 'Mini' would denote that this was a car in the same tradition but even smaller.

Although the only differences between the two versions apart from the name were the grille and badges, the publicity department went to great lengths to produce completely separate press releases, sales literature and marketing slogans. The Morris Mini-Minor was labelled 'Wizardry on Wheels' and the 'World's Most Exciting Car', the Austin version was tagged 'the Incredible Austin Se7en'. Despite these bold slogans, the ambivalence of the Press Office found its way into the promotional material and the Longbridge and Cowley publicity departments did not even seem able to agree on a common approach.

The Austin Press Office issued a set of press releases which seemed to have no particular theme. They talked about the new Austin Seven's technology and the advanced manufacturing techniques behind it. Female buyers were invited to admire its usefulness for shopping because of its interior space and parkability: 'Women of the world rejoice, in a man's world a car has been designed with women in mind.' The designer him-self offered his own version of 'The ADO 15 Story' which ended with this eulogy to BMC: 'The British Motor Industry has sometimes been criticised because of its conservative outlook … We feel that the ADO.15 is an example of what a British design team can accomplish under the leadership of men like Sir Leonard Lord and Mr. G. W. Harriman when innovation is dictated by changing world conditions.' And far from stress-ing the short design to production cycle which would become so much part of the Mini legend, they were at pains to stress that ADO 15 had gone 'from initial design to full production in eight years'. This claim stretched the truth considerably by tracing the car's origins directly back to the front wheel drive Morris Minor, though since this was an Austin press release it was referred to as 'an existing B.M.C. model'. It would seem they were anxious to avoid the impression that the car had been rushed into production.

The Nuffield Press Pack struck a completely different note and was a lot more fun. Dry technical specifications were interspersed with whim-sical musings on the 'design philosophy of the new Morris Mini-Minor'. Technical drawings alternated with cartoons penned by leading satirist Brockbank. Quotations from Admiral Lord Nelson, Roger Bacon, Samuel Johnson and Leonardo da Vinci all led the reader onwards to the final paragraph which proclaimed:

It is hoped that this exposé of the principles which have animated the design of Morris Mini-Minor models will justify the application of Lord Nelson's dictum [regarding his tactical plan for Trafalgar] 'it was new; it was singular; it was simple', and also show that they meet the requirements set down by Leonardo da Vinci 'when you wish to pro-duce a result by means of an instrument do not allow yourself to com-plicate it by introducing many subsidiary parts but follow the briefest way possible'.

Given the unfamiliarity of the product they were unleashing on the pub-lic, this lack of focus and clarity between the two press offices was not helpful in getting a coherent message across to the public. Eventually they agreed on two selling points: its suitability as a family vehicle and its rev-olutionary technology. All the early promotional literature featured the car surrounded by a 'typical' family who appeared to carry round with them an amazing amount of luggage. The themes of fuel efficiency and spaciousness were trumpeted and much was made of the overall size as early film adverts showed them driving round 'crowded' central London in traffic conditions which the 21st-century Londoner would die for. The price was also aimed to hit Mr Average right in the pocket. As the early adverts boasted, 'ten feet long, but roomier inside than many an £800 saloon – yet the Austin Se7en is less than £500 tax paid'.

The car's first official public appearance was to be at an exclusive press launch scheduled for 18 and 19 August and aimed specifically at motoring correspondents. It was wisely thought that the feature which would most appeal to this particular set of journalists was the car's superior road-holding and handling. The Fighting Vehicle Research and Development Establishment (FVRDE) at Chobham in Surrey was therefore an ideal location for them to fully experience the car's performance without venturing onto the public roads. BMC even went to the trouble of providing the press with some comparative data for the cars they considered to be the main opposition. This included the Fiat 600, the Renault Dauphine and the Volkswagen which Alec hated so much.

The event went extremely well. Issigonis attended in person, proving something of a star. Throughout the day he genially posed for pictures, leaning on his shooting stick, jumping in and out of the cars as requested, and charming the journalists with his wit and eccentricity. The technical superiority and originality of the car struck a chord in this appreciative audience who went away to write up the results with a considerable amount of enthusiasm. The sales team would not have felt reassured, however, by the words with which Issigonis chose to address the gathering, saying with no hint of apology: 'Some of you may be appalled by the unconventional features which you see in this new model. We just had to think of something new but which had at the same time to surpass the best of continental baby car designs.'

A week after the Chobham demonstration, the 'Austin Seven' was launched to the wider press at the Exhibition Hall in Longbridge. This event was organised by Tony Ball, one of BMC's younger sales executives who reported to James Penrose. He was rather more upbeat about the new car than his seniors and although flashy car launches were not the norm in 1959 he persuaded his bosses to give him a substantial budget of over £500 for the day. His instincts told him that such an original design should have an equally original unveiling. Instead of dull speeches and a stage full of static exhibits he devised a show with the theme of 'magic' to convey the excitement he wanted the car to generate. Once the journalists had filed into the hall and taken their seats, the lights were dimmed and the tune of 'That Old Black Magic' began to play. A spotlight was shone onto a huge mock top hat in the middle of the stage and Tony Ball emerged from the gloom dressed as a magician and himself wearing a top hat with white tie and tails and carrying a magic wand. He was followed by two showgirls in similar attire who decorously positioned themselves on either side of the stage. When Ball waved his wand, they swung the top hat open to reveal an Austin Seven. The audience then watched in awe as a stream of people emerged from the car one by one. First came three of the largest men Tony Ball had been able to find. His wife Ruth stepped out next, cradling their five-month-old son Kevin, followed by one of her friends and two huge dogs. Once everyone was on the stage they began to unload large quantities of luggage which had been packed into every area available, depositing each piece in front of the audience like a conjuring trick.

The journalists were suitably impressed by the show but they were not so keen as their colleagues from the motoring press to jump in and sample the new Austin Seven. Jack Daniels and Chris Kingham were waiting by the line of vehicles set up outside for their use. They were surprised to see the guests were just looking at them and then walking away so they decided to get into the cars and demonstrate what they could do. The ploy worked and many journalists felt encouraged to overcome their nervousness. It therefore seems rather unjust that Daniels and Kingham were reprimanded rather than praised for their initiative.

A similar launch for the Morris Mini-Minor followed at Cowley and once these formalities were out of the way it was time for the dealers to get the car into their showrooms and onto the roads. BMC had been promising them something 'revolutionary' for some time but when they actually saw what they were being expected to sell they were far from happy. Their discontent was even more serious than that of the Sales Department for they were the people who knew what the buying public might do. A Belgian distributor wrote scathingly to BMC in July 1961, not about the many mechanical problems the early production cars had suffered but about their appearance: 'The general squat four cornered shape is extremely against today's fashion and cannot be called beauty ... Mr Issigonis has had applause in the British auto press for his work on the chassis and engine but if he is also responsible for the body then it is impossible to see how one designer can succeed in one direction and be so lamentable in another.'

Sure enough, although the favourable press reaction brought people into the showrooms in some numbers out of curiosity, they resolutely resisted the temptation to buy. Mr Average was put off by the very basic level of trim and equipment which Issigonis had insisted on fitting, reflecting his own taste but not that of the ordinary motorist. What's more, when compared to all the other vehicles on the road the new car looked, well, distinctly odd and Mr Average just could not picture himself driving it. Look at those tiny tyres, he would say to his friend, how many miles are they going to last? Yes and what about the size of it, his friend would respond, I wouldn't fancy that in a shunt. Perhaps most decisively, its advanced engineering meant that he could not imagine tinkering with it on his front drive. It was not what he was used to.

THE PRESS VERSUS THE PUBLIC

This contrast between press and public reaction is well illustrated in the pages of Britain's leading car journals. In its launch report on 26 August 1959, *The Autocar* introduced the car in this way:

No car introduced by a big British manufacturer for many years has contained so much that is entirely new as the Austin Seven and Morris Mini-Minor models which make their public debut today. Even the original Austin Seven, which startled the world when it was first introduced in 1922, probably borrowed more from previous accepted practice in automobile engineering than the twin cars which have now emerged from the British Motor Corporation. Whereas most new cars represent variations on a theme, it is the theme itself which is different in the new BMC cars.

The article goes on to describe the designer by name, which was the beginning of the very personal association made between designer and car in the minds of the public. This was as unusual then as it is unheard of now. *The Motor* concluded its launch report on the same day with the words:

Publishing an early test report upon a brand new model, it is some-times necessary to make reservations about curable detail faults. Our first intensive trials of the new Austin Seven have shown singularly few such imperfections, and make it obvious that this compact car priced at only £537 6s 8d offers a remarkable combination of speed with economy, roominess with compactness and controllability with comfort.

The praise was not unreserved, however. In January 1960, one of *The Motor*'s correspondents wrote a report which lavishly praised the safety, roadworthiness, utility and spaciousness of the car but added:

The evident effort which has been made to please the public in these practical ways makes it all the more extraordinary that with three interior lights, actuated by three separate switches, it remains impossible for either the driver or front-seat passenger to read at night, and with the front seats fully back the ash tray is so far away as to be inaccessible to all but apes, few of whom normally travel in motorcars and a great majority of whom are, I am instructed, non-smokers.

It is fair to say that the press were bowled over by the car's technical ingenuity and its use of space with some reservations about its presentation. On the letters page of *The Autocar* in November 1959, however, a member of the public, G. Davies, vented his own, rather less complimentary, view:

I really cannot understand why B.M.C. have produced a glorified bubble car which costs nearly £500. Surely it would have been better to have spent the enormous amount of capital wasted on this in reducing the price of the A.35, which was a real motor car. In my opinion this overpowered vehicle with scooter-like wheels and its most unnecessarily complicated front-wheel drive cannot hope to compete with orthodox cars which can be purchased with very little more money. The purchaser of a cheap car is not primarily interested in a maximum speed of 70 m.p.h. – he is quite content with a cruising speed of 45–50 m.p.h., and petrol consumption is of more importance than high performance. If the car had been fitted with a simple, air-cooled twin engine, three-speed gear box, decent sized wheels, and priced below £400, it would have had a much better reception.

J. L. Otway, though appreciative of the handling of the car, was critical not so much of the concept as of its execution:

There are several points of criticism and modification which are urgently required ... I hope that the manufacturers will incorporate them in future production and that any which are adopted will be passed on to early owners at not too great a cost ... On both rapid and slow changes from second to third it is almost impossible to avoid going over too far, overriding the reverse stop spring and then finding that one has lost third altogether, and again on the change down from third to second. I have found difficulty in getting a smooth change because of the extreme stiffness and roughness of the swing across the gate. After heavy rain I discovered that both door wells were afloat with water; feeling somewhat annoyed I got out my drill and prepared to drain some holes in the door bottoms and clear it. On looking at the door bottoms I found two rubber plugs which I at once extracted, and out flowed large volumes of water. I would advise all owners to look at their own cars and do the same thing.

The Autocar's annoyed correspondent had put his finger on an embarrassing design flaw relating to excessive water leakage. It would be untrue to say that this fault had not shown up during the testing programme. Indeed it was a constant theme, from Chris Kingham's test in Spain late in 1958, when he described serious leaking during torrential rain, to the experiences of Gil Jones during the final test in July 1959, when he reported from Lisbon that 'a large quantity of water entered the car during the early stages of the test and a thorough water sealing investigation is necessary'. The Issigonis team seemed reluctant to address this particular problem and throughout the summer of 1959 correspondence from Jack Daniels contained phrases such as 'our information is that whilst not perhaps cured, leaks at this point are very much improved today' and 'it is reported on the Longbridge track that leaks through the screen rubber joint are so occasional that the expression "once in a blue moon" is now employed'. Their complacency was encouraged by an uncharacteristic heatwave which affected England during the summer of 1959.

Sealing in general would prove to be a major problem on ADO 15, but the area worst affected was the floor. It eventually became apparent that the flanges of the floor assembly had been designed the wrong way round, which allowed water to seep in whenever it was wet. This was to be an expensive error. Not only did it damage the car's reputation, thus jeopardising important early sales, it resulted in expensive recalls which wiped out whatever small profit margin did exist. Only four months after the launch Bill Boddy, the acerbic editor of *Motor Sport*, was quipping: 'When driving the "World's Most Exciting Car" I found it to live up to its reputation – part of the excitement being to see which foot got wet first!' It became a standard joke that a free set of wellington boots was on offer with every vehicle and Tony Dawson, then a Longbridge press officer, recalled the black humour of one journalist who arrived at his office one day and invited him to come outside to have a look inside his car where he had installed some goldfish swimming around in the door pockets.

Issigonis felt moved to start a new notebook, writing on the cover 'ADO 15 Water Leaks'. Between July and November 1960 he found himself sitting in a series of meetings with a wide array of senior production and development engineers from BMC, Austin, Morris, and Fisher and Ludlow. Some of them, like Leslie Ford, felt this was just one more example of their advice being disregarded in the months when production was being set up. Solving the problem required considerable effort: a number of new prototypes had to be built and tested; the frame was modified; new sealant materials were purchased; basic engineering drawings had to be revised and the tooling altered. Nevertheless, when questioned about the problem in later years, although Issigonis was ready to admit the mistake, he treated it lightly and even shifted the blame onto the production engineers:

Cars are tested in a very different way when they're in the development stage to when the cars are tested by the public and there's many a slip between the experimental car that you build and the car as it's produced on the production line. It isn't one slip it's thousands of them. It's a matter of communication. If the communication is bad between the design department and the production department certain things can go wrong. But they're quickly put right, believe me!

Other serious problems continued, including the clutch and gear-change, and Issigonis kept a second notebook covering every aspect of the car which detailed 51 items which needed looking into along with notes and sketches about the corrective actions required. By the end of 1960 the majority of defects had been solved but at considerable time and cost and also at the expense of early customers like Mr Otway who found themselves being drafted in as involuntary members of an extended testing programme. Meeting Lord's deadline had been quite a feat but it proved to be one with a huge price tag attached.

Birth of a Design Icon

As sales failed to take off Issigonis was warned by his friend Laurence Pomeroy that many potential buyers were more concerned with how the car would look outside their house than with how easy it was to park, how economical it was to run or how well it cornered. Alec's characteristic reply was 'Yes my dear Pom, I know there are tens of thousands of such people, but I will not design cars for them!' It was nevertheless a worrying time for him and his supporters.

The marketing people did their best to improve the struggling car's image and one ploy was to loan the car for months at a time to journalists in order to keep up its profile and get it talked about. They were also pleased to accommodate Britain's number one racing driver, Stirling Moss, when he expressed an interest in trying out the car and it was agreed that he could take one for a spin round the quiet lanes of the Lickey Hills. As Moss settled himself behind the steering wheel he remarked that the seats were rather uncomfortable to which he got the usual reply that this was deliberate so that people would not go to sleep while driving. He then complained that the pockets were badly positioned and he couldn't get his hands into them, at which, according to Moss, 'Issigonis waved a camp hand at the end of an extraordinarily long arm onto which were attached exceptionally long fingers which swooped down and reached easily into the pocket.'

Moss gave up on the artistic criticism and headed off to the Lickeys with relish, returning some time later with a crumpled engine compartment sustained in a head-on crash. Far from losing his temper, Issigonis congratulated the racing driver on giving ADO 15 the sort of test a car never normally has to face. The crash, he told him, showed that the transverse location of the engine had acted as a safety mechanism. With a longitudinal mounting, he explained, the engine tended to come through the bulkhead, and the steering column crushed the driver. With the transverse engine, the shock of the impact was absorbed on a large enough block to reduce the crumpling of the car.

In September 1960 Issigonis himself suggested that he might host an informal dinner party in London so that around 30 of the 100 or so journalists who had borrowed Austin Sevens and Morris Mini-Minors under the so-called 'extended test scheme' could get together to discuss their experiences. This was held at Manetta's Restaurant next to the Hyde Park Hotel and the importance attached to it is shown by the presence of Technical Director Sidney Smith, Senior Engineer Charles Griffin and Tony Dawson from the Press Office. Despite all these efforts, by the time the car's major faults had been eradicated it looked as if it might already be too late. Throughout 1960 dealers struggled to shift the cars and it looked as if BMC might be about to make a huge loss on its very expensive gamble. Then, to everyone's relief but no one's expectation, it suddenly began to take off as a 'cult' car among the rich and famous with a little help from Alec's circle of influential friends.

One of these friends was the society photographer Anthony Armstrong-Jones who in 1960 became engaged to Queen Elizabeth's glamorous sister Princess Margaret. He and Issigonis had been introduced during the 1950s by Jeremy Fry. In preparation for joining the royal family he now became Lord Snowdon, or Tony Snowdon to his friends. Issigonis told Dawson how he had heard of his friend's engagement:

> I came back to the flat in the evening and my mother said 'that nice friend of yours is engaged to Princess Margaret, it said on the news'. I said, 'which friend?' She said 'I can't remember his name.' I had to wait till the 9 o'clock news to find out it was Tony Armstrong Jones! I had known him for years, we always used to go skiing together with the Frys at Davos!

Princess Margaret was perhaps the most popular member of the royal family. Not only was she an extremely attractive young woman, her busy social life made her seem less remote than some of the other royals. She had been much in the public eye in recent years, gaining widespread sympathy for her decision not to marry Group Captain Peter Townsend. This was widely perceived to have been the result of unreasonable pressure from the Establishment who disapproved of the fact that he was divorced. The royal wedding of this handsome and fashionable couple on 6 May 1960 was therefore considered to be a happy turn of events which was widely celebrated. Issigonis was among the guests and he kept the invitation issued by the Queen Mother from Clarence House along with the admission ticket to Westminster Abbey, writing on the latter, 'I sat next to Noel Coward and Tony's landlady off the Fulham Road when he was a poor up and coming photographer.'

Snowdon wrote to Alec during his honeymoon on the Royal Yacht *Britannia*, thanking him for his wedding present which was – rather oddly considering Snowdon's new circumstances – an electric drill. Though neither of them probably realised it, his comments about a second present were more significant because he also thanked Alec for getting him a 'sputnik'. He went on to ask him to take charge of having the engine bored out for him in order to make it 'go quicker than anyone else's'. Snowdon was a genuine fan of the car and this proved to be a lucky turn of fate for Issigonis because a large number of people took notice when the royal couple were among the first 'celebrities' to be seen driving it. Lord Snowdon and Princess Margaret were as much at the centre of the 60s as John Lennon or Mick Jagger. They epitomised a modern era when a commoner could marry into royalty and the value of their patronage to the car's success cannot be overestimated. Before long Issigonis was being asked to give the Queen a drive round Windsor Park and as the decade progressed a whole host of people who were famous for very different reasons were being seen with the car: Peter Sellers, the Beatles, Twiggy, Marianne Faithful, Christine Keeler – suddenly, it was the thing to have.

The car took on a life of its own and even generated its own name as its new clientele abandoned the clumsy and deliberately old-fashioned labels 'Austin Seven' and 'Morris Mini-Minor' and simply called it the 'Mini'. On 19 January 1962 the Press Office issued the following statement to the press on an Austin letterhead:

To the British Press. Gentlemen: You may like to have the following information for reference. In view of the popular usage of the word 'mini' when referring to the current Austin Seven model, it has now been decided officially to rename this model and its derivatives the Austin Mini.

The 'Morris Mini-Minor' lingered for longer but was finally replaced by the 'Morris Mini' when the Mark II version was introduced in September 1967. 'Mini' went on to become one of the bywords of the

60s and every time it was used for some new craze it called up the original in people's minds.

The most straightforward reason for this transformation was that it was an easy car to navigate and park in what then passed for congestion in London – a fact which had been pointed out in the original sales literature. A more relevant explanation is that its uniqueness and modernity appealed to a generation who yearned to show their individuality by being different from their parents. In the 50s, life was still very formal. Men always wore suits and women hats and gloves on social occasions, the teenager had not been invented, drugs and sexual experimentation were mostly confined to the aristocracy. In the 60s, everyone was allowed to be outrageous and suddenly 'youth' and 'modernity' were the buzzwords. 'Young People' suddenly found they had become a social category and they followed the lead of their heroes and took the car to their hearts for the same reasons that their parents, at whom it had been targeted, rejected it. Nor was it an insignificant factor that for the first time the younger generation had their own disposable income. In an era when it was still not routine to own a car, it was one of the few cheap cars which it was 'cool' to own. In this context the Mini seemed strikingly modern and in tune with the times, an emblem of a free and unrestricted lifestyle and a classless icon which could be afforded by practically anyone. A healthy second-hand market also grew up which put the car in easy reach of many new drivers. This would be the great irony of the Mini. Born in an age of austerity and shortage, created to make motoring accessible to the common man, it actually succeeded only because it caught the imagination of an increasingly affluent and self-indulgent sector of the population in a Britain which had finally left post-war penny-pinching behind. Rather than a charwoman's transport the Mini had become a market phenomenon which was not what Issigonis had intended at all.

Whatever the reasons, the virtues of the car had finally been recognised. Another one of Issigonis' old friends gave the car its final push to iconic status. John Cooper, the fellow motor sport enthusiast who had beaten the Lightweight Special on the seafront at Brighton, was now a successful Formula One team owner. When the Mini was launched he was among the sceptics and said to himself 'this man's a bit of a comedian'. Once he had driven it, however, he realised it was no joke at all. In making the car handle so well, Issigonis quite accidentally laid the foundations for the Mini Cooper version which first appeared in 1961 and would become one of the most successful rallying and racing cars of the 60s. This important story will be more fully told in a later chapter but the success of the sporty Cooper reflected back onto the ordinary Mini and did a tremendous amount to boost its popularity. Just in time, Alec's 'Wizardry on Wheels' had been rescued from a monumental failure which could have ended the career of its single-minded designer and crippled the company which put its faith in him.

Despite this turn-around in its fortunes, not everyone believed in the miracle of the Mini. The way BMC went about pricing its cars was extremely haphazard and engineers from rival companies scratched their heads, insisting that such an advanced design could not possibly be making a profit at the amount which was being charged. The prices of different vehicles can only be compared realistically by looking at the list price before purchase tax has been added, even though this does not represent what the motorist would pay, because it is the difference between the list price on one side and the cost of manufacture, warranty costs and the dealer discount on the other which represents the profit per car. *The Autocar* section 'New Car Prices' for 1959 shows how BMC's new baby car compared with the opposition. The most basic model of the Morris Mini-Minor and Austin Seven was listed at £350 and this can be directly compared with BMC's own alternative products which consisted of the cheapest version of the Austin A35 at £379 and likewise the Morris Minor at £416. Thus two established models with no expensive development or tooling costs attached to them were between £29 and £66 more expensive to buy. British competition came in the form of the Triumph Herald at £495 and the Ford Anglia at £380. These were new designs and therefore more comparable to ADO 15 but again they were both more expensive. Ford's technical department were rather more scientific in their pricing methods than BMC and they decided it would be prudent to investigate in case they were missing something. They obtained a Mini and tore it down to its constituent parts to cost it and were astonished to reach the conclusion that it would have cost them £5 more to build a Mini than it did to build the Ford Anglia, yet it was being sold at a price tag £30 less than their model. Though this does not necessarily mean there was no profit margin, whatever that margin may have been, it was clearly considerably below that of their competitors. BMC did not see what the problem was. They were sure from the very beginning that keen pricing would be a key factor in selling the Austin Seven and Morris Mini-Minor.

Was this a sensible point of view? Leonard Lord may have calculated that by using a new configuration of an existing engine he could have the best of both worlds, revolutionary technology without the cost of building a new power unit. This was a mistake, since despite the use of the tried and tested A-series there were still too many new features in the ADO 15 design to allow its development costs to be minimised. Issigonis had made considerable effort in his design to keep manufacturing costs to a minimum and the materials to be used were revised on several occasions in deference to this. But as we have seen, the rush into production led to the constant need to make changes to the specification even while vehicles were emerging from the track, which meant that costs were continually being pushed back up again. It seems clear that BMC did not factor in the immense expense of pioneering such a revolutionary design. They did not even take enough care to price it realistically in relation to what it cost to build, not to mention the huge warranty and re-engineering costs they incurred because of its initial design faults. They were just too intent on under-pricing their competitors. Other mainstream firms would take their time before adopting the principles on which the Mini was based, waiting until the design had been proved and the cost of the parts and tooling had come down. Unfortunately for BMC this only meant that it was cheaper for their rivals than for themselves to benefit from the technology they had pioneered. It can therefore be argued with some justification that far from being a business triumph for the shaky British Motor Corporation, the Mini was the first nail in their coffin. Leonard Lord's cry of 'Build it!' could be considered as more akin to Cardigan's order of 'Charge!' to the Light Brigade than to Nelson's call to victory at Trafalgar.

Yet it is hard to blame Issigonis himself for any of this, because he did exactly what he was asked to do. The mistakes that were made must be placed primarily at the door of BMC's management for initiating and sponsoring such a project with no concept of what they really wanted it to achieve. Issigonis lived in a different sphere from Lord and Harriman, that of a 'pure' designer who could operate on the level of ideas alone. This is why he could say without a trace of irony:

A designer has only to make a good car that satisfies him and if he is a practical man it will satisfy the world. I have never had any ambition in my life except to satisfy myself and never think of a new car in terms of the people who are going to buy it.

To use his imagination and create something unique is what Lord had asked of him and this is exactly what he did. As a result, the Mini became the car of its time and the man behind it became a celebrity.

TECHNICAL DIRECTOR

The only way I can explain it is that the Engineering Division, of which I am in charge, is very heavily organised in the most disorganised way known to man!

Sir Alec Issigonis

PROMOTION

IN 1961 SIR Leonard Lord stepped down as Chairman of BMC and took the honorary post of Vice-President. Lord Nuffield, though no longer active in the company, continued to hold the post of President until his death in 1963. It was time for George Harriman to step out of Lord's shadow to succeed him as Chief Executive.

Harriman had been born in Coventry in 1903, beginning his engineering apprenticeship in 1923 with the local firm of Hotchkiss which later became Morris Engines. This is where he met Leonard Lord, whose protégé he became. He followed him to Cowley in 1932 and then once again to Longbridge in 1940; by 1944 he had become the Austin Motor Company's Production Manager and in 1945 he gained a seat on the Board. The position he reached in the industry would finally earn him a knighthood in 1965. He was not a complex man and his character was much more charming and easy going than that of his mentor. This was one of the things which made him so useful to BMC's rough-edged Chairman. For his part Harriman knew to whom he owed his position. Lord was not everyone's favourite person, but Harriman was devoted to him. His way of expressing his admiration was to give instructions for Lord's office to be preserved as he left it the day he retired, and this is the way it remained until his death six years later.

For Issigonis these events resembled those of 1947 when the supportive but superior Miles Thomas had been replaced by the more approachable Reggie Hanks. This time his edgy relationship with hard-as-nails Lord gave way to a more relaxed association with the genial George Harriman. By now the Mini and its image had finally taken off and BMC found that it had a celebrity on its hands. The only reward the company knew for success was promotion and this was the unhappy fate which

235

befell Issigonis in November 1961. He was appointed Technical Director of the British Motor Corporation and given a seat on the Board of the Austin Motor Company, which would be followed two years later by a seat on the BMC Board.

Becoming a Board member produced a somewhat unexpected side-effect almost immediately. Sir Leonard Lord was elevated to the peerage in 1962 and chose the title Lord Lambury ('Lord Lord would sound bloody stupid' he is reported to have said). Harriman decided that this would be the perfect opportunity for the Board members of BMC and its subsidiaries to demonstrate to him that they appreciated their former Chairman as much as he did. He wrote a letter informing them all that they were going to host a celebratory dinner at their own expense:

I think that this would be a fitting occasion on which to make a Presentation to Lord Lambury as a mark of our respect and esteem and I am sure you will wish to be associated with this. Also, I feel the Dinner should be given by us all personally and I know this will be agreeable to you.

The full dinner jacket and bow tie affair took place at the Welcombe Hotel in Stratford-on-Avon on 6 June and for the privilege of being a 'joint host' Issigonis paid the sum of £11 10/-.

The post of Technical Director had become vacant due to the retirement of Alec's old protector Sidney Smith. To mark his departure, Issigonis hosted a rather more enjoyable and informal dinner party on behalf of the Engineering Division. Smith's pleasure in the evening and the affection in which he was held are well illustrated by the note he sent to Issigonis afterwards:

I would like to tell you and all my various friends in the Engineering Division how very much I appreciate the gift which you presented to me on their behalf at our little dinner party on Monday night and the good wishes which accompanied it. You will remember that I did not open the envelope which you so surreptitiously slipped under the little parcel, and on doing so after arriving home I realised even more what a wonderful gesture it was from the whole of the boys of the Engineering Division. In the circumstances I feel rather sorry that it was not a formal presentation as in view of the magnitude of the gift

I certainly would have liked to thank everyone personally. However, I hope you will tell all those members of the Division whom I was not able to see how appreciative I am and how touched by their magnificent gift, and I wish you and them every happiness, and success in all your future undertakings.

Alec's promotion prompted plenty of letters of congratulation from colleagues and friends. Perhaps the most prescient was that sent by Joseph Lowry, Technical Editor of *The Motor*, which expressed the sentiment: 'Congratulations upon the exalted new position, and I hope that it will still leave you time to design motor cars in your spare moments from "admin".'

This was indeed the dilemma which faced Alec Issigonis throughout the next decade. The 60s were to mean two contrasting things for him. On the one hand, his fame brought him into the social circles to which he had always aspired. He had many distinguished new friends and was sought out by the rich and famous as well as his peers in the motor industry at home and abroad. On the other hand his working life became more and more difficult as he got further out of his depth, burdened with a management role to which temperamentally he was totally unsuited and grappling with problems that had no interest for him. When John Sheppard had started work at Longbridge almost six years earlier he made the mistake of asking Issigonis where he might get something to eat at lunchtime and received the unhelpful reply 'that's nothing to do with me, make your own arrangements'. A year later Sheppard asked him what the procedure was for reviewing salaries and got a similar response. 'It has nothing to do with me,' Issigonis told him, 'I'm here to design motor cars. I think there might be some kind of annual review in operation but you must sort it out for yourself.' Issigonis had grown no more interested in such details over the years, but now, as well as salaries, allowances, holiday leave, travel arrangements and all the other tedious tasks he was expected to administer on behalf of his staff, his time was increasingly taken up by Board meetings, management meetings, product planning meetings, sales meetings and so on and so on. He had to set his mind to problems with the whole model range not just his own designs. Hundreds of letters of complaint had to be dealt with, dozens of suggestions were sent in by amateur inventors every year. There was the lady who wrote to him in June 1967 on what was, to her, the extremely serious issue of the absence of a bonnet-lock on the 1100:

Dear sirs, I have had a variety of Austin cars over the years and recently acquired a new Austin 1100 last September. I have been on holiday and the car was parked in a public garage and on wishing to start for home I found that my battery had been stolen. This is the first time that the bonnet has not had a locking device and I consider it a very serious defect apart from the general inconvenience caused to me and the loss of my no claims bonus. When I change my car I shall think twice about an Austin.

The Technical Director replied personally:

We are truly sorry to learn of the theft of the battery from your car, and regret that you disapprove of the absence of a bonnet lock. However, we do find it necessary to change the specification from time to time in order to improve our models and to eliminate any item for which we feel there is no general demand; this latter action is doubly important in view of our constant efforts to prevent our prices from having to be raised as a consequence of steadily rising costs. We appreciate your having written to express your views on the subject.

Then there was the Meals on Wheels service which complained that none of the current range of BMC cars had a boot suitable to accommodate the 'Hotlocks' which they used to keep food warm. Issigonis suggested rather unhelpfully that they should choose a larger car and use the back seat instead. Some correspondents merely wanted to show their appreciation, like this well-wisher from New Zealand:

Perhaps you will realise how much you have achieved by your Mini as my late father was killed by a large car … Last Christmas as I was crossing on a 'pedestrian crossing' I was hit in the middle of it but I was able to jump clear only because it was a small car so perhaps you will see how grateful we are. After all in this life it is the little things that count …

Once he had cleared his correspondence he had to undertake the numerous official engagements which plague the life of a celebrity. There were awards ceremonies to attend, frequent interviews and luncheons with the press and even assignments at the request of the British government – a total anathema to the apolitical Issigonis. Sometimes he was sent abroad to represent the company and between 1962 and 1969 he undertook trips to Canada, Yugoslavia and the Soviet Union. In August 1967 he was despatched to Istanbul to open BMC's new plant in Turkey, no doubt considered supremely suitable for this task because of his origins. He received hundreds of invitations every year to give lectures, sit on competition panels, hand out prizes or have them named after him, open town shows and country fêtes. It was hard to anticipate what engagements he would and would not undertake. He was notoriously hostile towards politicians yet in 1965 he happily accepted an invitation to dinner in the House of Commons from left wing Labour MP Tam Dalyell. Following an appearance on *Midlands Today* in 1966 he was offered a chance to take his mother to a recording of the radio serial *The Archers*. The same year he agreed to a request from Laurence Pomeroy to lend his name to an Issigonis Trophy which would be awarded to the winner of a race featuring small cars but 'only on the understanding that it does not involve me personally in speech-making, presentations, etc.' In 1967 he was persuaded by journalist Raymond Baxter to present a different 'Issigonis Trophy' at a Mini Festival organised by the Mini Seven Club at Brands Hatch, even acting as a judge alongside Dick Burzi for a 'Pop Art' painting competition. Just as often he would simply refuse, pleading pressure of work or, if it looked like something which could not be avoided, sending the unlucky Jack Daniels in his place.

He could not, however, deputise the obligation to entertain a constant stream of VIP visitors to the factory such as government ministers, racing drivers, foreign princes or the representatives of suppliers and other manufacturers. In February 1964 he was one of four engineers chosen to accompany George Harriman on a visit to the Bathgate factory in Scotland. This was a relatively new facility, built in 1961 to manufacture and assemble commercial vehicles and agricultural tractors, which would obviously have provided gripping entertainment for the father of the modern small car. While Harriman flew up to Glasgow and stayed in a comfortable hotel, the supporting party had to spend two consecutive nights on the sleeper-train from Birmingham to Glasgow and back in order to occupy the intervening day by padding round behind their leader as he toured the factory.

Fame can clog the mind and make an individual lose focus. This would seem to have happened to Issigonis. As a result, his creativity was stifled and the true asset which he had brought to BMC was crushed under a barrage of administration, policy meetings and public engagements. Stuart Turner, Manager of the BMC Competitions Department throughout the 1960s, made this observation about his attitude to administrative tasks:

He could not have cared less! There is an argument for people like Alec Issigonis for a very luxurious padded cell where you lock them in and put divine food and wine through the letterbox and you say, you're in here for three days, at the end of it we want your thoughts on so and so. But involve them in day to day decisions on whether someone's getting a different grade salary to someone else, that is a total waste of that genius and if you're not careful you can mar the genius by forcing it to think on other things.

This can be graphically illustrated by examining his creative output after his promotion. The familiar Arclight notepads have now disappeared to be replaced by larger, uglier pads with garish orange jackets. The boldness of line and freedom of expression evident in the Mosquito and Alvis drawings has disappeared. There is, to be brutal about it, scarcely a note-worthy sketch from 1960 onwards. The later work seems to reflect a mind that is bogged down in unwelcome detail and losing its confidence and range. These notebooks are filled with page after page of scribbled notes relating to problem solving for a wide range of production models, many of which held no interest to him, reports on policy meetings, and musings on the future BMC product range. A typical note reads as follows:

Policy Meeting 12/12/61
- 1½ Diesel for ADO 38
- Estimate Price for production car
- Specification to be completed as soon as possible as from vehicle tested
- Urgent
- Service to be given samples of 2 priming pumps
- ADO 16 no car to go abroad before 500 cars

Between 1938 and 1958, Issigonis produced 39 sketchbooks containing 1,500 drawings of the highest quality, an average of 73 a year. Between 1959 when the Mini was launched and the start of 1962, the first year of his promotion, he produced a further seven sketchbooks containing 260 drawings of significantly less quality but still equating to 60 drawings a year. Yet between 1962 and 1971 when he retired only a further three sketchbooks exist containing barely 50 drawings, an average of five per year.

Issigonis was aware of what was happening to him – he knew he had more responsibility and less time for design. He spoke of the new demands on his time in 1964:

> I find that one of the disadvantages of being a Technical Director is that I have much administrative work to do and I don't find enough time to do my design studies. But one can't have it both ways. I should really prefer to be on the shop floor or at least working on prototype cars or designing, but I can't, and this is one of the consequences of success.

Yet he was at pains to point out that he deserved his new position, even if it made demands on him which were not necessarily congenial. His assertion that he had worked extremely hard to achieve it cannot be denied:

> Have I been lucky in reaching the position I am in now? Well I don't think so. I was always very interested and on the whole, I think, I have worked very hard. If you do these two things, I don't think it's luck. What I mean is that if some other person is interested and works hard and he doesn't achieve success, it is invariably his fault in some way.

When he describes his method of running the Technical Department, however, he does not seem to be aware that the 'organised chaos' which he is describing is entirely inappropriate:

> We don't have lots of formal meetings here. I have an early morning meeting with my three Chief Engineers to settle the day's programme. This meeting is interesting because we do it over a cup of tea and we might even discuss the weather for quite a long time, but it gets us all on a smooth keel, to start the day's battle. From then on my day is not necessarily organised in any particular way because it depends on what we're interested in at that time. I try to be as free as possible but then one does have formal board meetings with one's co-directors and so on, which one obviously has to accept. But they are rare – once a month. The day-to-day work is never organised to the nearest hour

and I much prefer it this way. The only way I can explain it is that the Engineering Division, of which I am in charge, is very heavily organised in the most disorganised way known to man!

BMC had propelled him into a position which played almost exclusively towards his weaknesses. During the ADO 15 project he had already shown that he worked best when surrounded by a sympathetic team with whom he could communicate one to one. He became moody and irritable when he had to extend communication outside that team, as a result of which the job of dealing with the production engineers and the marketing department fell almost entirely to Jack Daniels, John Sheppard and Charles Griffin. This meant that when he himself was asked to become a member of a wider team – the BMC Board of Management – he did not have the skills to do so successfully. He branded committee meetings as a waste of time, producing 'the lowest common denominator'. Though this was valid from the point of view of pure design he failed to understand that consensus was essential for the efficient running of such a complex organisation as a car manufacturing plant.

Worse still, the departure of Leonard Lord and Sidney Smith had removed any constraints on his autocratic behaviour. Though in his private life Issigonis was a reserved and shy man, in his professional life he exuded belief in his own overwhelming talent. He could not see anyone on the horizon who was likely to supplant him on the pedestal he had come to occupy as 'Britain's great designer'. He was now reporting directly to George Harriman who was influenced by an uncritical admiration for the talents of his Chief Designer whose artistic temperament was so unlike his own. Though Harriman sometimes became exasperated with Issigonis and made half-hearted attempts to rein him in, he never did so very effectively. The adulation that Issigonis received from inside and outside the company meant there was little opposition to anything he wished to do. This was the great problem for BMC. It was very proud of its 'design genius', but how to give his abilities the freedom required while at the same time keeping him under control? How to give him proper recognition for his achievements without stifling his creativity? They failed to find the answers.

Issigonis coped with the situation by relying more and more on the loyal team around him. His young secretary, Suzanne Hankey, took over one of the duties he hated so much, writing all his letters by constructing tactful replies from the spare comments scrawled over the original correspondence. As to deciding people's salaries, signing off holidays, or whatever other tasks he was expected to perform on behalf of his staff, he relied on Charles Griffin to sort things out for him.

Charles Griffin was to be an important support to Issigonis in the 60s, the period which marked the height of his influence at Longbridge. He was twelve years younger than Issigonis and had begun his career as an apprentice at BSA in Birmingham before joining Wolseley in 1940 and rising to the position of Chief Experimental Engineer. In 1949 he transferred to Morris Motors at Cowley as Deputy Chief Experimental Engineer with responsibility for vehicle proving. This was the time when Issigonis was being given his first significant promotion following the success of the Morris Minor and both of them reported to Vic Oak. After the 1952 merger, while Issigonis escaped for his sabbatical at Alvis, Griffin became Chief Experimental Engineer for the Morris Motors Division of BMC and shortly after Issigonis' return he became Chief Engineer for Morris Motors so that once again they were reporting to the same boss, this time Sidney Smith. In this role, he came to be associated with the ADO 15 project and re-established his working relationship with Alec.

After Issigonis was promoted to Technical Director in 1961, Charles Griffin became BMC's Director of Engineering. In March 1962 the corporation made a further attempt at rationalisation when it merged all its design and development activities into a brand new Vehicle Design Building at Longbridge with the exception of sports cars which stayed at Abingdon. It was hoped that this would create a more efficient and more productive department. The new building was directly adjacent to the 'Kremlin' and Issigonis moved the short distance from his corner office on the corridor of power to a modern office on the ground floor of the new design block. Griffin came from Cowley to take up residence in an adjoining office, making him effectively deputy to Issigonis. In between them was a connecting room which housed their secretaries and an assistant by the name of Frank Lester whom, theoretically, they shared though in effect he took most of his instructions from Griffin.

Griffin was very different in personality from the visionary, flamboyant but often difficult Issigonis. By contrast he was ever-cheerful, easygoing, practical and straight-forward. This enabled him to establish a strong and balanced partnership at an equal professional level and there appears to have been no jealousy or competition between them despite the fact that Griffin – like Jack Daniels – was given little public credit for the major technical contribution which he made to the successful execution of the Issigonis designs. If Griffin resented this, he certainly did not show it to his colleagues. To the end of his career, he would pursue the Issigonis philosophy of elevating the 'packaging' of a car over its aesthetics. The two men maintained a close friendship which would continue after Issigonis' fall from grace in the days of British Leyland and which extended beyond work to their families.

Issigonis greatly enjoyed gathering together small numbers of his colleagues to host lively discussions about design and engineering. These events often took place in his own garden or Charles Griffin's, over a lunch washed down by plenty of dry martinis. Dick Burzi was a regular participant, and Sergio Pininfarina or Renzo Carli would join them if they happened to be on one of their visits from Turin. These occasions unfolded like a choreographed drama. Issigonis would take centre stage, making provocative statements to stir up the discussion. This would arouse varying reactions from his audience, some slavishly admiring his performance, others indulgent but irritated. Charles Griffin was the bravest and usually ventured to pose some common sense against the Issigonis posturing only to be told theatrically, 'Charles, leave the room!' On such occasions Issigonis was in his element.

After his move from Cowley, Griffin began to take over direction of the day-to-day work of the Technical Department and fulfil those tasks which were so uncongenial to Issigonis. As if to emphasise the point, Jack Duckham of Duckhams Oil, one of BMC's suppliers, wrote to congratulate Issigonis on his promotion in November 1961 and commented by the way: '... of recent time for purposes of technical developments I have not had to worry you as we enjoy the fullest co-operation, as you may well know, with Mr Charles Griffin and his staffs.'

ISSIGONIS THE CELEBRITY

Next to promotion at work, the most concrete reward which Issigonis received for his success was the honours and awards which came thick and fast during the 1960s. He embraced this new status with satisfaction because, like his new job, he felt he had worked hard for it and deserved it. It also laid to rest any residual criticism of his path to success, in particular his educational background. He often insisted that his lack of formal education was an advantage but there is a strong possibility that he felt intimidated by the kind of education that so many of his friends and acquaintances had received at public school and university, something which he had been marked out for and then deprived of due to the circumstances of his youth. His subsequent failure to matriculate for a BSc had been a severe personal blow and he over-rationalised the supposed irrelevance of such a qualification:

People say that a man couldn't reach my position without this kind of academic proof of ability but I don't know. I don't think it necessarily follows that you must have good educational qualifications to achieve a position like this. In fact, if you look round the industry as a whole I think you will find that this is not so. People in high positions in industry, I think, reach them not because of their academic ability. I don't think you learn about these things very much at the ordinary engineering college. You may do at university but I don't think so. I think the time required to learn about human relationships and administrative matters is so long that it takes a life-time to do it properly. In other words, you do it through age and experience. I am not too keen on young engineers fresh from the college or university with clean hands, as it were. One might think that this type of person is essential, but I don't think this is so. It is very much overplayed. In car design and car work in general the necessity for high education and degrees are very much over emphasised, because the car in the end is a very mechanical, simple sort of thing. It looks complicated but it isn't really.

The variety of the awards he was offered illustrates the many different fields of endeavour which now wished to claim him, elevating his status above that of a mere car designer. He gained no less than seven degrees and fellowships from various colleges and universities, but the academic honour which pleased him most was an Honorary Fellowship from Battersea College of Technology on 6 March 1963, a consolation for his failure to obtain a degree 35 years earlier. He told Piero Casucci, 'I am so honoured that tears come to my eyes.' In 1962 his artistic achievement was recognised with the award of Designer of the Royal College of Arts (*honoris causa*), generally referred to as Des RCA; in 1964 the Establishment welcomed him to their ranks by awarding him a CBE which would be followed by a knighthood in 1969; and in 1966 the Royal Society, celebrating its 300th anniversary, chose him to receive a Leverhulme Tercentenary Gold Medal for his 'contribution to science and its application'.

Perhaps the most prestigious award of all came in 1967 when he was made a Fellow of the Royal Society which put him in the same category as some of Britain's greatest thinkers. Issigonis told his friends how thrilled he felt to sign his name in the same book as King Charles the Second and Sir Isaac Newton. This was perhaps one of the most unexpected awards because Issigonis was no scientific boffin. He had great difficulty in completing the rather pompous questionnaire which the Society distributed to new members because the questions assumed a certain type of social and educational background which clearly did not match his circumstances. The distinguished nominee was invited to catalogue the achievements of ancestors, relatives and colleagues who had paved the way for his pursuit of science. He was asked to describe his own extensive academic achievements, from prep school through to postgraduate research. He was questioned about any pioneering expeditions of discovery and expected to list a full programme of scientific papers and editorships. The answer Alec gave to the question about his publications is typical:

Q: Full list of scientific publications, alone or in collaboration, to date.
A: I failed all my examinations at Battersea.

This is not to say he did not deserve his Fellowship. By choosing him, the Royal Society were displaying a wish to widen their parameters in the face of a changing social climate and it was their questionnaire, not the candidates, that lagged behind.

His employers were delighted as his profile grew ever higher. They had already enjoyed the benefits of his friendship with Lord Snowdon and Princess Margaret which had helped to promote the image of the Mini. He met the royal couple for lunch when he was in London, went on holiday with them, and exchanged Christmas presents and notes. BMC were very happy to find them regularly visiting their stand at the Earls Court Motor Show, so much so that rival firms began to grumble. In September 1963 Snowdon wrote to Alec telling him that this time they couldn't accept his invitation to the Motor Show because 'arrangements had already been made', implying that the choice had been taken out of his hands.

As his popularity increased BMC therefore had every expectation that he would represent the company in a good light to the national press which had so much power when forming the opinion of the average motorist. In some ways his attitude to public relations was a little contradictory. He undoubtedly found formal interviews difficult and avoided appearing in front of an audience which he did not know. He was a very private man who did not wish to reveal too much of himself in public. He made this analysis in 1964:

> I am often told that I ought to be glad to be known as the man who made the Mini. Well, let me tell you that I don't really enjoy it. I am proud of the Mini, yes, but the whole business of becoming well known because of a car is much more harrowing than the man-in-the-street – or the car – would imagine … I have never cared much for personal publicity – as I have said it is something of an embarrassment to me. But I am fascinated by my work. I am very fortunate in that respect I think.

On the other hand he relished putting on a performance in front of people he felt comfortable with or who showed a sympathetic attitude. Stuart Turner described him as 'an extremely theatrical individual, one could almost say camp at times'. John Sheppard also remembers catching sight of him at the Hôtel de Ville in Paris, where they were attending an official motoring function on behalf of BMC along with Jack Daniels:

> We noticed him, dressed in sports jacket and bow tie, sitting, cross-legged on a low circular coffee table holding court and expounding his thoughts on car design to the crowd around him.

He had nurtured warm relationships with a number of leading motoring writers since the days of the Morris Minor. The level of press attention mushroomed after the Mini became fashionable and went far beyond anything which had until then been accorded to a British car designer. Issigonis himself remarked that 'after the success of the Mini all the journalists wanted to be friends which I encouraged and enjoyed rather than the opposite'. To keep things within manageable proportions he turned to another one of his friends, Tony Dawson, who by 1959 was a leading figure in BMC's Press Department.

Tony Dawson had been born into a rather genteel background in 1913. His father edited the *Encyclopaedia Britannica* and also compiled the *Times* crossword, and little Antony's upbringing had been both very formal and heavily academic. He had been destined for a career in the law but was diverted by the Second World War into the army, serving at the siege of Malta during which time he met his wife Paddy. After the war he joined the War Graves Commission, reaching the rank of Major. In 1956 he decided it was time to return to civilian life and since he had always loved writing he sent an article in to the MG Car Company for their consideration. As a result he was offered his first post as Public Liaison Officer just at the time that Issigonis was rejoining BMC after the Alvis adventure. Within a year he had risen to Assistant Press Officer for the Nuffield Organisation and by 1964 he was Executive Press Officer for the whole British Motor Corporation. These jobs saw him at the centre of arrangements for motor shows, new car launches and public events for over two decades.

He carried over the organisational skills he had learnt in the army and added an imaginative flair which made BMC's car launches a favourite among the journalists who attended such events. The press of the 50s and 60s was still a very traditional body of people and it was common for a columnist to stay with one newspaper for his whole career. This was why Dawson, with his network of excellent relationships, was so invaluable to the company. His contribution went far beyond the meticulous organisation which he applied before the event. On the day he worked relentlessly to create a relaxed atmosphere, anticipating the needs and quirks of his guests, cultivating personal contacts, engaging in light-hearted chit-chat and playing the attentive host. The gin and tonics which he handed round, combined with his own nervous energy, often had to serve as his main fuel on such occasions since there was little time for distractions like meals.

Many of the launches he had organised since 1959 had been for Issigonis designs so it was quite easy for Dawson to fall into the associated role of publicity manager for the corporation's most famous employee. They were drawn together by a number of things. A lively sense of humour was important, as was an addiction to smoking. They both liked to dine out at places like the Savoy or the Dorchester and enjoyed the kind of social life epitomised by the Hyde Park Hotel in London. Issigonis christened the last 'my London home' and he taught the barman how to make a 'proper' dry martini by putting the vermouth in a glass, swilling it around and then emptying it out before filling the glass with gin. Though the drink was traditionally garnished with an olive Issigonis was very particular that this was never added to his glass. This was a kind of affectation which he loved.

They shared an almost blind loyalty to the British motor industry, determinedly closing their eyes to its very obvious shortcomings. Despite this, they were both to some extent misfits in a rather philistine world which was full of bluff, plain-speaking engineers who were proud to have pushed their way up from the factory floor and were determined to enjoy every perk available now that they had got to the top. It cannot be denied that it was common practice for those at the higher levels of a large corporation such as BMC to maximise their opportunities, within the law of course, for extracting the greatest reward possible from their position over and above their regular salary. This could range from enjoying expensive overseas jaunts to using the craftsmen of the company to work on their cars or houses. Within the British motor industry it was tacitly accepted that, after spending long years in junior management with what can only be called modest remuneration, this was one of the rewards of finally making it to the highest level.

Dawson and Issigonis shared a rather more artistic nature and also a set of social and moral values which made them feel in sympathy with each other more than with some of the people around them. Though they enjoyed the fine things in life, they were both rather naïve when it came to squeezing the maximum material gain out of their position. Sometimes Alec took the opportunity of a business trip to the Pininfarina Studio in Turin to tack on a personal holiday in Monte Carlo and obtain some rest from his busy schedule. Nowadays he was able to stay at those fancy hotels where he had once posed with Max for drinks on the veranda, instead of at the modest Beach Hotel. He was always careful, however, to pay his own expenses, which included upgrading his ticket from second to first class and purchasing an additional ticket for his mother who still regularly joined him. There were some arguments with the Finance Office about Alec's business expenses, especially after the creation of the British Leyland Motor Corporation in 1968, yet in reality his claims were extremely modest, in the region of £5 for day trips and around £30–£40 for the longer overseas visits, and this is remarkably consistent throughout the decade between 1960 and 1970. He can be accused of little more than using some business trips to cut the overall travel costs of a personal holiday; claiming small amounts of money for dinner parties with business colleagues; and keeping by his fireside a bucket of off-cuts from the styling bucks produced in the Experimental Shop which he used as firewood. There is no evidence whatsoever of any attempt to benefit financially from his position within the company.

Despite his aristocratic affectations and the apparent flamboyance of his social life, the private character of Issigonis was characterised by simplicity and a degree of personal asceticism. Even when he became famous he seemed to have little feeling for the possible value of his personal material in either historical or financial terms. He never sought to profit by selling any of his sketches but on the contrary he referred to them disparagingly as 'doodles' and gave many away quite casually to his friends or allowed journalists to 'borrow' them without ever asking for them back. Nor was he inclined to go out and waste money on new objects when he felt he already had something which was perfectly serviceable. He went to some trouble to get a twenty-year-old watch repaired, sending it back to the manufacturers when a local shop advised him it would be as cheap to buy a new one with the words 'it has been a very faithful servant over the years'. Greed is one vice from which he can easily be absolved for throughout his life he displayed a minimal interest in material wealth. His soul was without any kind of Machiavellian guile, which was one of the things that made him so unsuited to the higher echelons of management. This was a part of Issigonis' moral code and it would not have occurred to him to act differently but he would pay a severe price for it when he finally retired.

Tony Dawson genuinely admired his friend's talents and was therefore quite happy to marshal his own towards arranging his public life for him. He became a two-way conduit between the great man and his audience, an arrangement which benefited them both. Issigonis was relieved to have a barrier between himself and the press while Tony Dawson gained the kudos of being the only man who could deliver the 'Great Designer' whenever required. Dawson also helped him make new contacts among the overseas motoring press. Most important were the Swiss journalist Robert Braunschweig, Italian Piero Casucci and Frenchman Bernard Cahier who was also a racing driver and a talented photographer, taking many pictures of Issigonis and his new set of friends during this period. They would stand by him when things began to get difficult during the 70s and their correspondence shows a warm and familiar relationship. As they became part of the Issigonis social circle they were drawn into the habit of nicknaming. Bernard Cahier, for example, was called 'problem child' while his wife Joan was affectionately referred to as 'the old bag'. Piero Casucci was likewise christened 'Caruso'. In 1967 Casucci wrote a profile of Issigonis entitled 'Minigonis' which appeared in Pininfarina's in-house magazine. The piece was written in Italian but Casucci translated it into English so that he could provide Issigonis with a copy. At the beginning of the article, which showed great insight into the character of Issigonis, he commented:

> Knowing him, and being considered a friend of his, is one of the wishes of those who are often in touch with him, as journalists are. But, be careful, our hero is an unpredictable man and authentically peculiar. Even I thought myself to be among his close friends for the very reason that I had met him dozens of times, interviewed him on many occasions for radio and television, had been with him in solemn circumstances and had the honour of being welcomed in his home in Birmingham. And yet, each time I meet him again I notice a clear effort to remember my name and I am always afraid that he will mistake me for someone else or even that he may not remember at all where he met me before. I have not yet understood whether he does it on purpose or he really hates foreign names. Anyhow, I have given up making him understand what is my real name. He finally decided to call me Caruso.

In November 1979, Issigonis provided the answer to Casucci's question when he wrote on a typed letter from Casucci the comment 'I always called him Caruso in the old days! I don't think he liked it but I did like to tease him.'

As the demands for interviews and public appearances grew, Issigonis devised a strategy for dealing with this possible intrusion into his life. He began to protect his privacy by creating a public persona for himself, developing a repertoire of stories and anecdotes which he would constantly repeat. This was taken one step further with the publication of Laurence Pomeroy Junior's *The Mini Story* in 1964. This book has long been considered the most authoritative document on its subject, yet, as we saw in the last chapter, some details differ in important ways from those revealed by contemporary documentary evidence. It contains many of the stories which would become an accepted part of the Issigonis legend, including the attempt to send him to art school, the 'Grand Tour' and Leonard Lord's whirlwind test-drive. Issigonis wrote an introduction to the book which he ended with the words 'I am very relieved to find that the task

ISSIGONIS

fell upon Pomeroy to write this book instead of myself as I find writing a disagreeable occupation'. In this way he was able to put his own account of events into the public domain while distancing himself from it.

Alongside the carefully chosen stories, he played up to his growing public image. He accepted the 'Arragonis' tag that had been given to him, believing that his talent and his achievements gave him the right to be opinionated. At the same time he began to exaggerate his eccentricity as a defence mechanism. He was clever enough to know that by projecting a certain personality he could say things which would cause outrage if said in another context and he took pleasure in expressing extreme opinions, knowing that his remarks were very 'quotable'. He often talked about the plainness of his vehicles and explained how the purpose was to promote 'primary' safety – that is the safety inherent in the car – rather than 'secondary safety' – that is features designed to minimise the impact of an accident. Too much comfort and luxury would serve only to distract the driver. Therefore it was a positive benefit if the driving position was uncomfortable; the correct driving position was seat back, arms straight, because this helped to keep the driver alert. When asked why the Mini did not have reclining seats he retorted, 'It's a very dangerous practice to drive lying down.' Radios were unacceptable since it was impossible to concentrate properly with 'noise going into your ears'. He complained about the distraction of being talked to while driving and in the mid-1980s would castigate the new danger of mobile phones – though considering the safety concerns since raised on this subject he could be congratulated for his foresight on this point. He told Courtenay Edwards in 1971: 'The modern car is much too sophisticated for my liking because I still enjoy driving without being surrounded by an environment of domestic and household appliances.' He even questioned the principle of seat belts. In his view, if the car was designed for maximum safety the rest was up to the sense of the driver and safety mechanisms such as seat belts could only encourage recklessness. So when his friend Tony Snowdon showed him the safety belts he had fitted to his Mini, Alec merely looked sceptically over the top of his glasses and told him, 'My dear, you can't sell safety, never.'

Such comments were duly printed and though these were in fact his genuine opinions he put them across in a way which made the journalist wonder whether or not he was simply having a joke at his expense. Casucci described the way he did this: 'Differently from his country-men

252

when he talks, he stares at his interlocutor, but his eyes are always ironic: it almost seems that he enjoys making fun of you or that he does not believe what he is saying.'

The press of the 60s and 70s was a different animal from the combative, dirt-digging circus of the 21st century. This was an altogether more deferential era and many journalists were in awe of the 'genius' of the British motor industry. To them the eccentric Englishman with an exotic foreign background was an absolute gift. Once the journalist had got past the scrutiny of Tony Dawson he would be allowed to meet with Issigonis during a press launch, in his office or at a restaurant. Usually, he served up just the dish they wanted – a neatly constructed story, lavishly garnished with his jottings and accompanied by a bottle-full of charm laced with a soupçon of flattery. The first question would invariably be something like 'Well Alec, how did you get the idea for the Mini?' The performance would then begin. 'Dear boy, dear boy', he would exclaim in his carefully cultivated, rather aristocratic manner. The journalist would be treated to one of his canon of stories, perhaps how he failed his exams, the bubble-car edict, or Sir Leonard's exclamation of 'Build it!' Then he would snatch something to hand like a menu, a napkin, or the day's newspaper, produce his fountain pen from his pocket and sketch the front wheel drive, transverse engine configuration for the hundredth time. The journalist, duly impressed that he was about to receive a unique offering from the master himself, would ask for the work to be autographed and go away with his exclusive story, very ready to give this wonderful man, his exciting car and his laudable employer a piece of excellent publicity.

He found recording interviews rather more intimidating than talking to newspaper journalists and he expressed his anxiety about his first broadcast on the subject of the Mini in November 1959 to Enid Dowson: 'The BBC broadcast was a great ordeal but like you most of my friends thought I did not appear unduly nervous.' As his confidence grew he became a regular contributor between 1959 and 1972 to the popular format of the radio discussion programme in which he excelled. Whether it was an intense business discussion, a radio debate or a speculative conversation, he could remember both his own arguments and those of other people without writing anything down or needing to refer to notes. His excellent memory and logical mind made him a great conversationalist and a formidable opponent in a debate. His contribution was fairly wide-ranging. For the African World Service he discussed 'Cars, Cities and the

Future' while for the Home Service and later Radio Four he spoke about subjects such as 'Are cars designed with women in mind?', speed limits, and the future of steam propulsion.

He also began to make TV appearances and, with the assistance of Tony Dawson, was able to form some good relationships with broadcasters as he had done with the press. He felt particularly at ease being interviewed by the BBC's motoring corespondent, Raymond Baxter, because they were already acquainted through Baxter's involvement with BMC. Baxter had been a junior member of the works rally team where for three years in succession he drove a Mini Cooper on the Monte Carlo Rally alongside lead drivers Hopkirk, Makinen and Aaltonen. He also briefly served as Director of Motoring Publicity. He put his knowledge of motor sport to use as the BBC's commentator for Formula One races during the late 60s and early 70s. Issigonis still visited Monte Carlo every spring and he would often meet up with Baxter who was there to commentate on the Monaco Grand Prix. He co-operated with at least two TV programmes about the Mini and was usually happy to make himself available for interviews at the Earls Court Motor Show. The television interviews reveal an excellent performer, engaging with his interviewer and using his mischievous sense of humour to offset the dry technicality of the subjects he was being asked to discuss.

In later times both Issigonis and BMC would have been given a much rougher ride and a significant sidelight on this aspect of his career is provided by a letter from Mark Boxer, editor of the *Sunday Times Magazine*, in response to a complaint from George Harriman about the tone of an article published on the fourth birthday of the Mini. Boxer apologised if the article seemed 'ungenerous' but added:

We are all great admirers of B.M.C. and Issigonis, as I hope our lead story on the 1100 last year demonstrated. We are, however, trying to stop sycophantic motor reporting. In the long run we believe this is in the interest of the motoring industry.

This was a sign that times were beginning to change. The Issigonis archive contains a transcript of an interesting interview broadcast on 6 May 1966 with a Mr Stekhoven of the BBC which gives a hint of the difficulties Issigonis might have faced had he been famous 30 years later. Road safety was a popular topic around this time and Issigonis gave a number of interviews on the subject, deflecting the largely unchallenging questions with rather lofty remarks such as 'When you ask why we don't design safer cars, do you mean cars that it would be safe to have accidents in?' Mr Stekhoven, who seems to have somehow slipped past Tony Dawson's keen eye, unfortunately appeared to be immune to the Issigonis charm and refused to be fobbed off with irony. The resulting interview provides an intriguing glimpse of what a more combative 21st-century news presenter might have made of him.

Issigonis was thrown off balance by Stekhoven's very first question, clearly not expecting his interviewer to be more sardonic than himself. The initial exchange went as follows:

> S: Mr Issigonis, I just read in the papers this morning that some police chiefs were praying for safety yesterday in London. Do you think that this is necessary?
>
> AI: I don't really understand what you mean by praying for safety.
>
> S: Road safety.
>
> AI: How can one pray for it?
>
> S: I'm not honestly sure but obviously they are very worried about it. They seem to think it's about the only thing they can do. Do you agree?
>
> AI: Well, as it's a very topical subject these days, perhaps one has to resort to prayer.
>
> S: But don't you think there is anything one can do apart from praying – from the design point of view?

Issigonis had fallen into the trap of the leading question straight away and for the rest of the interview he would struggle to extract himself. The more he talked about how much primary safety he had designed into his cars, the more Stekhoven implied that this meant he had no interest in secondary safety features such as seat belts and impact tests. As Issigonis came to the end of a long explanation about the inherent safety of front wheel drive and the wheel at each corner principle because they provided superior roadholding he was once again lured into an incautious remark:

> AI: ... we have achieved the highest possible degree of primary safety –
>
> S: Is this really so – the highest – you can go no further?
>
> AI: Oh, you can indeed, but I was just going to say we have reached

the highest possible degree of primary safety within the commercial envelope we are working with. The design of a car after all is a great compromise between what you are trying to do and how much it costs to do it. Because if you design a car which is too expensive, nobody will buy it.

Stekhoven had now got Issigonis to say something which could be interpreted as meaning that commercial imperatives were more important than the prevention of injury in accidents. Annoyed by this, Issigonis countered by suggesting that it did not cost any more to design a car that handled well than one that handled badly and he appealed to Charles Griffin who was sitting in on the interview to support his argument that BMC had gone to great lengths to make its cars inherently safe; but he continued to insist that people did not look for safety features when buying a car. Stekhoven patiently listened to this but then came back to his point that now people *had* become interested in safety they *would* be prepared to pay for it and designers would have no choice but to give it to them. He then turned to his notes and – using a journalistic technique which is now common but was unusual in the 60s – read out to Issigonis his own, well-known caustic remarks about secondary safety:

You've been quoted or misquoted for some rather outspoken remarks about safety. I've heard you say that people should not get into accidents. Now, assuming they do, what about protecting the person in an accident? The protection of his person, his life, his family, his future, when somebody hits him or when he makes a damned idiot of himself?

Issigonis replied sharply:

What to do? Beyond turning the interior of the car into a sort of padded cell I don't see what one can do.

Charles Griffin, as he had done several times throughout the interview, quickly jumped in to soften the impact of the remark:

I think Mr Issigonis made the point that whatever we do, we've got to rely on people to make use of what we've done …

Stekhoven, however, would not be deflected. Finally, he bluntly asked Issigonis what he considered to be his moral obligation to the buyer of his designs. This led to a rather heated exchange:

S: Do you consider it the manufacturer's moral obligation to do as much as he can in every field to protect the buyer of his motor car?

AI: I thought we did this as well as we can within the limitations that are set around us.

S: But there is still the moral obligation. When you are designing a car are you taking into account the buyer? Do you say 'I'm designing a car for this person; I must, therefore, protect him as much as possible?'

AI: We said at the beginning that as far as primary safety is concerned, I think we have done as much as anybody.

S: As a moral responsibility or for other reasons?

AI: The reason is irrelevant. The fact is *we have done it.*

S: So you are not willing to answer on moral or ethical obligations?

AI: I think it doesn't come into the issue at all. I happen to be an engineer.

S: So you are not prepared to talk of morals?

AI: I think it is irrelevant to the argument.

S: Mr Issigonis, thank you very much indeed.

Thus Stekhoven finishes with a flourish having succeeded in making Issigonis misrepresent his own opinions and appear in a bad light. There is a telling note at the bottom of this transcript: 'In subsequent discussion and recording the latter part concerning moral responsibility was clarified with references to the professional integrity of Mr Issigonis as an engineer.' It is unlikely that this was a performance which Issigonis would remember with any fondness.

But this encounter was quite out of the ordinary. In general Alec's skill and flair in handling the media helped to avert bad publicity from the less impressive aspects of his own designs and the increasingly disturbing signs of BMC's deterioration. This stood in sharp contrast to the ineptitude which the company itself displayed when exploiting its key assets. In 1965, for example, they received a personal request by telegram from Enzo Ferrari as follows:

AM MUCH INTERESTED IN PURCHASING BMC MINI
AUTOMATIC TRANSMISSION FOR POSSIBLE IMMEDIATE
DELIVERY STOP THANKING FOR WHAT WILL BE ABLE TO
ARRANGE

Ferrari's profile was high at the time, having won both the Formula One
Drivers' and Constructors' Championships in 1964 and the World Sports
Car Championship in 1965. The gruff response that came back was that
BMC could not help due to 'production problems' and it would take
another year of persistence before Ferrari got his car. An even more startling example is their attitude to the producers of the film *The Italian Job*,
released in 1969. Apparently unaware of the massive public relations
opportunity offered by a production heavily featuring their star car alongside such big box-office names as Michael Caine and Noel Coward, they
argued endlessly about the terms on which they were prepared to supply
cars to the film-makers. Though only three cars in red, white and blue
would appear on screen, dozens of cars were required to complete the
spectacular stunts. According to producer Michael Deeley, BMC sold the
production company six Minis at trade price and then demanded retail
price for the remaining 30. The film-makers were further annoyed to find
that the paint codes of the later deliveries did not match previous batches,
causing them major problems with the continuity of shots. The chase
sequences of the film were set in Turin and some scenes were filmed on the
distinctive roof of the factory of their rival, Fiat. The Italian firm was apparently more attuned to the commercial benefits of such collaboration than
its British counterpart. Fiat chairman Gianni Agnelli provided complimentary Fiat Dinos as studio cars and used his influence with the local police to
get the traffic in Turin stopped while the chase sequences were filmed. He
also lobbied the film-makers to replace the Minis with Fiats, promising a
limitless supply free of charge, and, for a while, the cost-conscious directors of the film were warm to the idea. Luckily for BMC, scriptwriter
Troy Kennedy Martin insisted that this would make nonsense of the plot:

> The idea behind the script was a gentle send-up of British chauvinism
> and the Common Market, with all these criminals coming together
> and the solid British set against the cunning Europeans. The Minis
> came through in the film as a powerful symbol of what we can do in
> Britain; they were the most remarkable elements of the story.

Fiat did receive a small reward when the traffic jam scenes featured masses of Fiat 500s. BMC, rather more undeservingly, got the greater reward of massive publicity for their baby car, but since they had been swallowed into British Leyland by the time the film was released it proved to be more of a swansong than a triumphal march.

Issigonis at least was proud of the achievement. In 1969 he hired a cinema at a cost of £10 10/- (paid by British Leyland) for a private showing of the film which had made such a hero of his design. It was a sign that his own awareness of what constituted good press relations was at times better honed than that of his supposedly more commercially minded colleagues. Issigonis was right when he said to Tony Dawson, 'The Technical Press is very important. They do not want to interview sales directors or managers but the designer of the car. I made many good friends this way including TV. We therefore never got bad reports.' For that, at least, BMC had reason to be grateful and Harriman was more than happy to let him take the limelight.

DESIGNS OF THE 60S

BMC did not see many warning signs of impending trouble during the 1960s. It continued to pursue complicated product policies and the Works also expanded to accommodate ambitious and over-expensive production programmes. Indicative of the mood at Longbridge was the construction of a multi-storey car park during 1960 and 1961 which at the time was both ultra-modern and highly unusual. Nine storeys high, it was intended to house up to 3,300 vehicles straight from the assembly line. This, it was argued, would solve the problem of the vast amounts of space required to store cars awaiting transport to export markets.

As for Issigonis, he had never considered his task to be finished with the Mini. Far from it, his philosophy was one of forward progress. For him, the theme of the 60s was to build on the ADO 15 project by producing a family of cars based on the principles of transverse engine, front wheel drive, but in doing so he wished to continue pushing forward the technological boundaries as far as he could. Once the Austin Seven and Morris Mini-Minor had been launched, the intense pressure which had been on the team to produce the car in record time was removed and they were able to take a more measured approach to their subsequent work. Between 1959 when the Mini was launched and 1962 when he started his first full year as Technical Director Issigonis set several forward projects into motion, splitting his team into three cells to pursue them.

Cell A was headed by Jack Daniels assisted by John Sheppard, and their task was to work on ADO 15 and a series of derivatives from the principles on which it was based. Cell B was headed by Chris Kingham and was given over to the largest car in the model range, what had been XC/9001 and would now be developed into ADO 17, to be launched as the 1800. Cell C was the only unit to be based at Cowley, and was under the leadership of Charles Griffin, working on the medium-sized car which began life as XC/9002 and was now transformed into ADO 16, to be launched as the 1100. In time a fourth cell was set up to work on ADO 14 which would become the Maxi but that story belongs to a later chapter.

This structure was to prove over-complicated and Jack Daniels in particular felt that it became self-defeating in the end. His comment was: 'Basically we had relatively little to do, we were never free of doing anything but there was relatively little to do. Two cells would have been enough in my opinion.' Daniels was right, for the cell structure would prove to be counter-productive. It impeded the flow of expertise across the range of cars and resulted in three models which were sufficiently distinct to each require their own tooling and spare parts. This ultimately put BMC at a disadvantage when compared with Ford, for example, whose model range was based on interchangeable parts which promoted cheapness of assembly for the manufacturer and simplicity of maintenance for the customer.

EXPERIMENTS WITH THE MINI PHILOSOPHY

At the head of Cell A, Jack Daniels along with John Sheppard continued to work on refinements to ADO 15, and several derivatives appeared over the next few years. There was an estate version known as the 'Austin Countryman' or 'Morris Traveller', a van and a pickup and all of these variants enjoyed considerable success. They had a longer wheelbase offering an extra four inches and more rear overhang producing an overall body-length of 130 inches as opposed to the 120 inches of the Mini. The van was particularly popular and would often be fitted with windows in place of the rear panels and treated to a rear seat conversion. This turned it into a practical everyday vehicle at an eminently affordable price, especially when obtained second-hand. A typical 60s street would be littered with Mini vans. Daniels and Sheppard were also allowed to produce more luxurious versions of the saloon for those customers who did not share

Issigonis' asceticism. The Mini Super De Luxe provided a more elaborate standard of trim than the original. The Wolseley Hornet and Riley Elf went even further. Dick Burzi was allowed to work on their exterior shape and the result was a fussy style which, like the Maximin, may have suited the era but would quickly date.

In his attitude to the Mini itself, however, Issigonis began to display the intransigence which became a feature of his reign as Technical Director. Making any kind of adaptation to the basic ADO 15 philosophy would prove to be difficult ground for as long as Issigonis was in charge of the corporation's engineering policy. Much of his own personality had gone into the Mini and this included his love of simplicity. He had fought hard to prevent production engineers and salesmen from interfering with the purity of his design and this was not about to change. He treated Lord Snowdon to a demonstration of his seriousness on this point. Snowdon undertook various alterations to make his Mini more comfortable, including the fitting of headrests and the enlargement of the accelerator pedal. But the item which caused most annoyance to his friend was the replacement of the sliding windows with wind-up windows. This was a cardinal sin against the Issigonis creed of space-maximisation. Snowdon sent the car to Longbridge to have the engine tuned but on getting it back he found that it had regained its sliding window on the passenger side. When he was challenged about the matter Issigonis claimed he had done it in deference to Princess Margaret – 'to protect your girlfriend's hair dear boy'. Of course Snowdon knew this was just a charming put-down. As he explained:

> What he meant to say was, look, don't muck about. He was adamant that he had designed a basic motor car as cheaply as possible and its pur-pose was to get anyone who wanted from A to B efficiently. He couldn't bear what he called 'tarted-up' Minis. He just loathed gimmicks.

Issigonis did not believe the Mini was perfect and he did work to develop it over the years. The changes he allowed, however, were mainly to the mechanical elements so that performance and reliability could be improved. Those things which he considered basic to the philosophy of the car were sacrosanct. On the subject of sliding windows he was unmoveable and the more critics argued against them the more stubborn he became in defending them. The issue became a particular bone of contention in

261

those export markets which enjoyed a tropical climate because they provided such poor ventilation in hot weather. From the West Indies to
Africa, from Asia to the Far East, distributors complained and argued that
sales would surely boom if only they could have winding windows. One
West Indian dealer was bold enough to protest in October 1961:

> No-one I have spoken to is the least impressed by the argument that
> this would lead to a reduction in inside space and higher costs. They
> are convinced that the sacrifice in space (and slightly increased cost)
> would be more than compensated for by improved ventilation. There
> is little doubt that the present Austin Seven window design is a very
> serious sales handicap in the whole Caribbean area and has con-
> tributed to the initial success of the Ford Anglia.

This was mild compared with an opinion offered from Israel in September 1962:

> It is really hard to understand how could you – an organization of
> tremendous experience and repute – market a car in the Middle-East,
> where under the prevailing climate and subtropical conditions driving
> such a car is a torture. The way the door-windows are constructed,
> allowing less than minimum ventilation, are a clear proof that your
> designers never studied this matter, or you do not happen to care. We
> believe that you are guilty on both counts and the designer should be
> sentenced to driving such a car for one summer under the existing
> climatic conditions. We would very much like to see how he felt …

Winding windows were not the only 'improvement' that he resisted. In
July 1961 the Service Department was irked when refused permission to
offer a veneered fascia as an option. The simple dashboard, with its understated central instrumentation and spacious parcel shelf, was another
feature he was particularly proud of. They too ventured to question his
judgement:

> I have the opinion that if we give my Sales people their heads they
> may easily introduce accessories and fitments contrary to the dignity
> of this Corporation! Accordingly, we invariably seek permission from
> your chaps before we commit ourselves to a new line. I gather that

you don't want us to go ahead with this facia panel – and we cheer-fully accept this ruling. On the other hand I can't resist the temptation to point out that, commercially, it is a shame to lose the opportunity! There might, of course, be some very good reason why this accessory cannot be approved. If there is, I should dearly like to know it, so that I can keep my enthusiastic staff at bay.

Issigonis replied rather rudely:

I know how much you adore your veneered facia on the ADO.15 but the reason we must put an embargo on it – as far as B.M.C. service is concerned – is that we are bringing out many new de-luxe facia lay-outs in the near future and we do not want any competition.

The Wolseley and Riley variants did feature a veneer fascia, but this did not become an option on the more luxurious versions of the Mini itself. Another more serious complaint was the quality of the synchromesh on the gearbox. There was no synchromesh at all on first gear until it was gradually introduced during 1967–8. R.D. Niven of Service wrote to Issigonis in September 1961 supplying him with figures which showed that over three months this had resulted in a total of 977 claims at a total cost of £17,000 to the company:

The attached document indicated the cost to B.M.C. Service of claims made against the lack of synchronisation on the ADO 15 power unit. You will, no doubt, be staggered by the amount of these complaints. The purpose of this note is to draw your attention to the fact because I feel very often the action taken by Designs would possibly be a little more positive and with a greater sense of urgency if they were aware of the expenditure which is involved in satisfying customers.

Issigonis resisted the invitation to be shocked, though he might have been expected to show more concern as someone who prided himself on designing vehicles which were easy to drive.

Jack Daniels kept out of these arguments and concentrated instead on less contentious projects. There were several attempts to adapt the Mini chassis for other purposes and one version which made it into production was the Mini Moke. A provisional specification for 'ADO 15 (Military

Version) Pseudonym "Moke'" was produced in February 1959 with its own experimental number, XC/9008. It was described as being bodied in an 'open JEEP style' and by May 1959 a prototype had undertaken a test of 1,748 miles at Chobham, including 360 miles of rough terrain. The Moke had an interesting connection with the quirky amphibious wheelbarrow because it was originally developed in the hope that it could be sold to the military as an easily transportable lightweight vehicle. It was to prove no more attractive to the army than the ill-fated wheelbarrow because its wheels were too small and its ground clearance insufficient for military purposes. It does not seem to have taken long to discover this since the May test reported, among other things, that 'damage is apparent to the front skid plate, the underside of the sump, and the rear sub-frame is badly distorted with resulting misalignment of the rear wheels'. This was partly Harriman's fault since he had vetoed the plan to use larger wheels on the Moke for what he referred to as 'commercial reasons'. He was possibly worried that the change would imply that the wheels on the Mini itself were unsuitable. Even so the team carried on with the design and in April 1962 BMC's South African distributors made enquiries about it as a possible alternative to the Land Rover. Issigonis was alarmed by the implication and wrote to James Bramley stressing:

It is important to all those who will be concerned in assessing the market possibilities of this vehicle to realise that it is in no sense a cross-country type of machine and cannot be expected to give the same sort of performance as a four-wheel drive vehicle. In fact it is really only suitable for road use.

As this statement implies, BMC was never really sure what market it was aiming for with the Moke though the vehicle would eventually enjoy a lengthy, if complicated, career. Its manufacture began in Britain during 1964 but production was subsequently moved to Australia in 1968 and then Portugal in 1981, finally ending in 1996. There were several attempts to develop the Moke into something more serious, including a twin engine version and, in the late 70s, an Australian experiment with four wheel drive. Nevertheless the Moke never really found a role in the model range and its fate was to become a 'fun vehicle', built and sold in limited numbers.

Issigonis quickly moved on from the Moke and turned his attention to a larger low-cost, lightweight off-road vehicle with four wheel drive. This project began in 1964 as ADO 19, code-named the Austin 'Ant' which some of his team rather unkindly suggested stood for 'Alec's New Toy'. Long travel torsion bar suspension and 12-inch wheels made this a more sensible cross-country design with greater inherent strength than the Moke. This vehicle too was tested by the military, but Issigonis was also thinking of people with smallholdings rather than farms who wanted something economical and easy to manoeuvre around the restricted space of their plots. The project advanced far enough for a provisional hand-book and workshop manual to be prepared in 1968. A product report in July 1968 noted that six prototypes had been built, two of which were despatched to North America. It also stated that a further fourteen pre-production vehicles had been produced and sent all over the world for testing, with ten more in preparation. But then circumstances changed with the British Leyland merger. BMC's vehicles became part of a much larger model range and in the overall review of product priorities the Ant was excluded from forward plans in March 1969. It had, nevertheless, in true Issigonis fashion been a vehicle showing foresight as well as sound engineering principles because at this period no one was predicting the emergence of a market for a small vehicle suitable for recreational use. The Ant could be said to have foreshadowed the lightweight Japanese 4x4 vehicles which are now so popular.

There were other, more off-the-wall experiments. Daniels and Sheppard worked on a sports version of the Mini chassis code-named ADO 34 which was intended to accommodate two adults and two children. The only prototype made was fitted with an upgraded Mini Cooper engine and was treated to sporty body-styling. BMC pondered over the idea of badging it MG but this could have provided internal competition with the MG Midget. This is a possible reason why it was dropped at an early stage. There was also a beach-car project which again came to nothing though at least fifteen prototypes were prepared.

ADO 34, the Moke, the Ant and the beach car illustrate the major weakness of both Issigonis and BMC. A great deal of time, effort and expense was put into projects without first considering their market or their competition. Innovation was the Issigonis *forte*, but now he was in charge of the Technical Department there was no one to rein in that originality and give it proper direction.

ADO 16 – THE 1100

By chance, Issigonis had produced the smallest of his range of cars first. Once the Mini was successfully launched BMC urgently needed the middle-sized car which the team had originally been working on. Fortunately, they would not have to wait too long because although the Longbridge team had diverted all their efforts towards turning XC/9003 into ADO 15, the XC/9002 project had continued under the direction of Charles Griffin and in time became ADO 16. Though Issigonis remained in charge of technical development, the day to day engineering work was carried out at Cowley where Issigonis spent only one day per week as opposed to the four he allocated to Longbridge. The opportunity for him to interfere directly was therefore reduced. Griffin enjoyed a status which was relatively equal to that of Issigonis as opposed to the heads of Cells A and B, Jack Daniels and Chris Kingham, who clearly worked for him. It was therefore easier for him to assert his independence when he felt this to be necessary. So although there is no question that the basic design of the vehicle and the ideas it contained were down to Issigonis, Griffin was able to exert a high level of influence over its engineering. This would be critical to its eventual success.

In the interval between the building of the first XC prototypes and the realisation of the Mini, Issigonis' ideas had radically changed. In 1956 he had asserted that 'front wheel drive absorbs too much body space with the in-line type of 4-cylinder engine' and rejected the idea. Following the successful adoption of the transverse engine concept on ADO 15 he did several sketches for ADO 16 reflecting the trend of his ideas towards a larger, stretched version of the Mini which could provide more spacious family accommodation. These included a variety of ideas in different combinations – an in-line B-series engine with rear wheel drive, a transverse A-series engine with front wheel drive, and the possibility of either Hydrolastic or conventional suspension. Some of these concepts were experimented with in prototype vehicles and in the end it was the A-series front wheel drive configuration with Hydrolastic suspension which was chosen.

Issigonis was not content to merely turn ADO 16 into a bigger Mini and he continued to work on new ideas which would make the car significantly different from his last design. There was a downside to this because, although it kept BMC on the technological cutting edge, the

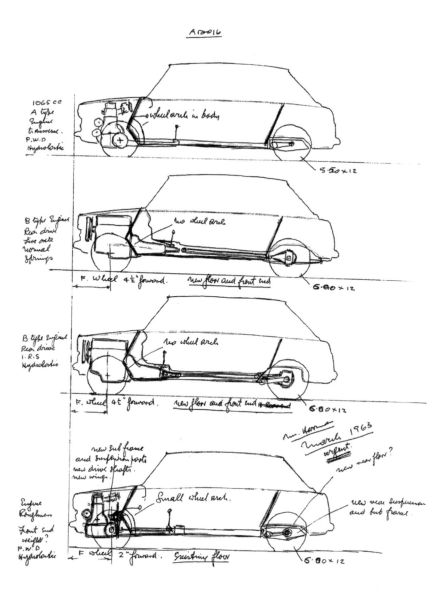

Issigonis sketched a variety of ideas in different combinations for ADO 16 – these included a transverse A-series engine with front wheel drive, an in-line B-series engine with rear wheel drive, and the possibility of either Hydrolastic or conventional suspension. More than one of these ideas was experimented with before the final specification was fixed.

lack of continuity between designs made tooling more expensive to assemble. This was reinforced by the cell system which tended to steer each project down a route which was more individual than was necessary. The major innovation for ADO 16 was to be its advanced suspension. Though it had proved impossible to refine the Hydrolastic system in time for the Mini, Moulton and Issigonis had continued to work on it with early versions being tested on modified Morris Minors. Issigonis had now been working on this system for almost ten years and yet he seemed strangely reluctant to install it on a production car. There is a hint of this in the interview which Issigonis and Griffin gave to *The Motor* to promote the car following its official launch.

Issigonis: We have worked for six years on this Hydrolastic suspension, and as we were approaching some degree of finality we put a spurt on to finish it for the ADO 16.
Griffin: The handling of this long wheelbase car could not have been combined with such a good ride in any other way.
Issigonis: You can only use this interconnected system with all-independent springing. We built about half-a-dozen Morris 1000s with independent suspension all round for testing Hydrolastic. They looked normal enough; no one who saw one would know there was something new on the car. We even went to Monte Carlo in one. Six years ago, at the same time Alex Moulton and I were developing the rubber springs for the Minis, we talked of practically nothing else but this coupled system which derives from it.

This interview contains an undertone of reluctance in the words 'we were approaching some degree of finality' and it is Griffin who interjects with the comment that it had been essential to incorporate Hydrolastic suspension into ADO 16. It seems that Issigonis had suggested retaining the cone-type suspension that had been fitted onto the Mini. Griffin, however, believed the Hydrolastic system was crucial to the sales prospects of the car and he urged George Harriman to put pressure on Issigonis to change his mind.

The frames for the prototype were built by Pressed Steel, supervised by Issigonis' former Alvis colleague Harry Barber. The vehicles were then assembled at Cowley where another of his old associates, Reg Job, was put in charge of bodywork. He continued to display his preoccupation with maximum interior space – this was, after all, still a relatively small car – and the wheelbase was altered to minimise intrusion from the wheel arches. This change also contributed to the car's excellent handling by reducing the tendency to pitch on rough surfaces.

When it came to styling, all Battista Pininfarina had been allowed to do for ADO 15 was comment on the finished product. This time Harriman insisted that Battista's son, Sergio, must be brought in to do a great deal more than give his opinion. He had been concerned by the starkness of the Mini and he was determined that ADO 16 would be more refined. Alec did not raise any objections since he had by now become a friend of the Pininfarinas, having quickly come to the conclusion that Sergio's design philosophy was in harmony with his own:

Farina is not a stylist. I consider him a car body designer with a high standard of engineering background. People like him are far more concerned with the architecture of the thing, the general shape, rather than making it look outrageous in some way. There is a great trend for simplicity nowadays, even in America where the whole of this styling trade thrives. This simplicity influence is European, mainly Italian. In Italy they produce simple straightforward designs because they don't like ornate things, and that's why we employ them here at B.M.C. Why did the British Motor Corporation have to go to Italy – Farina – for the design of some of their products? I personally think it is very understandable. Being an island country we developed a kind of old-fashioned outlook before the war towards the sort of shape a car should be, and it is very difficult to break this down when we are isolated from the rest of the world. In the 'fifties B.M.C. felt they wanted more skill, and the management took on the services of Farina – an arrangement which has turned out to be highly successful. There was a good reason for it and in fact other manufacturers are doing it more and more, copying us. There is a great deal of talent being built up in the British motor industry through this infiltration of European thinking.

During the 60s Issigonis met up with the Pininfarinas at least once a month. Often they would come to Longbridge, at other times he would visit Turin. Their discussions ranged beyond his own designs to the whole model range for which he was now responsible. Their relationship was based on a mutual admiration which was quite genuine and it worked not least because they enjoyed each other's company and this is reflected in the best of their work together. Issigonis would describe the period of their collaboration as 'wonderful times'.

Even so, the brief that Sergio Pininfarina received for ADO 16 was surprisingly detailed. A set of measurements including items such as the wheelbase, engine geography, scuttle height, bulkhead, front and rear overhang and profile was sent to Turin where Sergio analysed the information and translated it into the architecture of the bodyshell. He would then send several options back to Longbridge for Issigonis to choose from. For his part, Pininfarina found that this interplay of ideas stimulated his own creativity and he put as much effort into creating elegance in the humble family-orientated 1100 as he did when working on his more prestigious Ferrari assignments. The result was an attractive design which was calculated to appeal far more to Mr Average than the boxy simplicity of the Mini. Issigonis was even prepared to privately admit the superiority of the Pininfarina design, writing to his friend in 1979: 'The 1100 was completed to your design after I failed to produce an elegant car. It looked bad until you designed the body.'

Though far from lavish, Pininfarina exercised his influence on the interior too, resulting in a higher level of trim than was usual in an Issigonis design. In their interview with *The Motor*, Issigonis and Griffin addressed the question of the greater refinement of the car and put it down to having more time and money to develop it:

Issigonis: This one took us longer than the ADO 15 to develop. It wasn't so urgently needed from a commercial point of view and we were faced with problems of getting much greater refinement. In many ways, it was harder to do, in some ways also it was easier.
Interviewer: such as …?
Griffin: We had more money to play with! Not to spend on development, but to spend on building each car, so we didn't have to simplify things quite as much.
Issigonis: The bigger scale of everything makes problems easier, and there were not such fanatical requirements of space saving as in the little car … ADO 16 is a refined car, not a cut-price one, whereas every inch of the Mini's 10 ft. length was needed for seating accommodation; you cannot make a shorter four-seater.

The only element of the project to be engineered at Longbridge was the 1100 cc A-series engine and transmission. It was this which provided the rather uninspired model designation, though a mock-up brochure prepared by Issigonis suggests that he had toyed with the idea of calling it the 'Morris Minor 1100'. This would have been logical, as the vehicle served the same market as the Morris Minor and should have replaced it. But the original Morris Minor stayed in production and now there was a Morris Mini-Minor too. It was probably considered that this would amount to too much use of a good name.

By the time Griffin moved from Cowley to Longbridge in May 1962, ADO 16 had already begun to roll off the production line. Perhaps in deference to its Cowley origin, the 1100 was launched first in its Morris version in August 1962 with an MG close behind. The Austin 1100 did not appear until almost a year later in September 1963 and it was 1965 before two further derivatives, the Riley Kestrel and Wolseley 1100, joined the family. At the time of its launch, the 1100 constituted the most advanced small saloon in the world and competitors such as Ford were taken by surprise. The end product combined sophisticated styling with superior roadholding and the trademark space efficiency of the Issigonis philosophy. Its major weakness was a propensity for rust. In its heyday it proved to be the most successful of the Issigonis designs and many felt it to be superior to its baby brother, albeit in an entirely different market. It came to represent nearly one-third of BMC's home sales where it consistently outsold the Mini by a factor of at least two to one, regularly achieving over 12 per cent of market share and the number one sales position in the UK market. Between 1962 and 1974 when production ended over 2 million vehicles were made and sold.

It was partly because the project was more than a solo effort from the genius designer that it was a success. By combining the best of Alec's ideas with contributions from Moulton and Pininfarina and superimposing the careful guidance of Charles Griffin, a much more rounded final product emerged which proved more palatable to its target audience. The result was a beautifully engineered car which people found practical, attractive, spacious and stylish – a sophisticated 'grown-up' Mini. The original Mini would have a much longer life but though the larger 1100 could never achieve the status of a 'design icon', in some ways it was the forerunner of the 'supermini' phenomenon which would begin in the early 70s.

The car received a warm welcome from the press, who this time were prepared for something fresh coming out of BMC. *The Motor* introduced its launch report on 15 August 1962 in this way:

Another really new one from BMC – the new Morris 1100 is not just an overgrown Mini. That would be true to a point – but only to a point which would do the new model a major injustice. This car not only falls in a different class but also represents a cross-pollination of ideas from some of the most brilliant engineering brains in Europe. The Mini conception of transverse engine and front-wheel drive to save space is unmistakably the work of Mr. Alec Issigonis, the technical director of B.M.C. Likewise, its all-independent suspension inherits the rubber-cone type of spring developed for the Mini by Mr. Issigonis and Mr. Alex Moulton, but with a most significant difference – the inclusion of hydraulic interconnection between front and rear; and both men would doubtless admit readily that the use of this principle (though not the application) owes something to the work done in this field by Citroën. Equally, a leaf had been taken from the Renault book by designing a cooling system which requires no topping-up, thereby cutting out yet one more routine maintenance task.

The reception from foreign journalists was similarly enthusiastic. Jacques Ickx, the former racing driver, now a Belgian journalist, told *Autocar* on 24 August:

I think that the Morris 1100 will achieve in Belgium the immediate success which was denied to the Mini. Between the models are changes which could well have been dictated by the wishes of Continental owners, from the appearance and dimensions (inside and out) to the handling and general comfort. Unhappily the high price of the British product and the duties which must be paid on it in the Common Market countries will limit a success which could have been a veritable triumph.

His one-time mentor Sir Miles Thomas also wrote to congratulate him in August 1962 'not only on the design, but on the splendid way in which you helped in what we used to know as "putting it over"'. This was yet another sign of the central role Issigonis was beginning to play not just as designer but as a spokesman and ambassador for BMC. Thomas also commented on the innovative suspension, clearly remembering some of their discussions from the days of the Mosquito project: 'You certainly now seem to have come properly to grips with our old friend k^2AB ratio if that is the right way of describing it.' The formula Thomas referred to was to do with the underlying principles of suspension design. Issigonis was pleased and surprised by the fact that Thomas still remembered their discussions and he replied: 'Very many thanks for your letter of congratulation regarding my latest problem child! I am amazed that you remember our old friend k^2AB, as you rightly say, we have at last made his influence not so domineering in the design of this car.'

ADO 17 – THE 1800

Now the small and medium-sized cars were on the market all that remained was to produce the largest car in the family represented by the first experimental project, XC/9001. Because the changes to the original design were significant, including the replacement of Kingham's new engine with the existing B-series, a second experimental car known as XC/9005 was built before the project received its Drawing Office designation of ADO 17. Once again its model name, the 1800, would be derived from the engine size although there is a photograph of a pre-production car which carries an elaborate 'Austin Cambridge' badge. This implies that, as with the 1100, Issigonis had intended to replace the ageing equivalent in the existing model range. The Cambridge, like the Morris Minor, stayed in production and once again the name was not used. More significantly, though ADO 16 was to be a resounding success, ADO 17 would typify all the faults of Issigonis' reign over BMC's Technical Department.

Chris Kingham was put in charge of ADO 17 in early 1960, the first time he had overseen a complete car project. His cell was firmly located at Longbridge and this time Issigonis was far less willing to relinquish control and defer to other people's opinions. This time there were also personnel problems. Ron Unsworth, who had once blackened the ADO 15 layout with his pipe, was in charge of chassis engineering while Reg Korner looked after the body. Unsworth got on well with Issigonis but unfortunately the Technical Director took a dislike to Korner, and Chris Kingham describes the results:

Alec and Reg Korner – you could get the two of them together and the temperature gradually rose until you longed for the session to come to an end and get back to normal. Alec of course was very quick in his mind and his ability to express himself. Reg Korner was one of those slow thinking people who found it very difficult to express himself. The result was that I had to spend a lot of my time pouring cold water on the heated situation which existed between Alec and Reg Korner whenever we were working on the body side of the 1800.

What had now become the trademark features of the Issigonis concept were once again to be applied – the wheel at each corner approach with minimum overhang at front and rear, maximum interior space, transverse engine combined with front wheel drive and Hydrolastic suspension. For both the 1100 and 1800 Issigonis and Kingham considered the possibility of designing a new engine but BMC decided to continue with their policy of using an existing engine. In the case of the 1800 this was the 4-cylinder B-series. For the first time, however, the gearbox was to have the concession of synchromesh on all gears. Once again Issigonis recorded the results of his own personal tests in his notebooks and he noted in particular one feature which would become a source of irritation to future owners in the finished version – the handbrake. On 2 October 1962 he made the startling comment 'hand brake efficiency, check for legal requirement (only just)' and, further down the same page, 'new location for handbrake required'. If it was given one, it is hard to imagine where the handbrake had originally been located since its inaccessibility was to arouse a great deal of comment from frustrated journalists and drivers alike when the car appeared on the market.

Pininfarina was called in once again to do the exterior and interior styling but this time all did not go smoothly because Issigonis refused to give him a free hand. He insisted on styling the middle section of the car himself and then complained that Sergio had modelled the front wings on Fiat headlamps which he thought were very ugly. Though Issigonis had concurred with the upgrading of the styling and trim on ADO 16, now he seemed determined to demonstrate that he was in control of ADO 17 by returning to the minimalism he was so proud of on ADO 15. Inside the car looked stark and bare – the idea according to Issigonis was to emphasise the space inside the car. Outside, the application of the principles which had made the Mini body style look 'chic' on a larger car simply looked ungainly.

The result was that the 1800 lacked both the personality of the Mini and the style of the 1100. For sure, the roadholding and space utilisation were second to none, and Issigonis told journalists 'as you apply this formula to larger cars its space-saving properties become more and more spectacular', but in a car of this size interior space was hardly an issue and the public was not attracted to its idiosyncratic driving position or its plain lack of style. The publicity literature repeatedly trumpeted that it was the stiffest structure ever built but it is not clear why this was considered an overriding virtue. It compromised the performance of the car, as did the front wheel drive formation which put a great deal of weight onto the front wheels making the steering unpleasantly heavy even though it was low-geared. Once again BMC seemed unsure as to what market to aim for but the size and specification of the car put it into clear competition with the big Ford and Vauxhall saloons which boasted easier handling and superior engine performance.

Issigonis even involved himself in designing the sales brochure and he decided to play his trump card by including some of his sketches as illustrations. The overall result, rather like the car itself, was less attractive than the sum of its parts indicated it should be. Despite his interference with the styling, the car was hailed on the cover of the brochure as 'the Issigonis concept with the Pininfarina line'. Inside was a message from the designer himself, rounded off by his signature, lauding BMC as 'pioneers of bold projects' and ending with the telling statement:

> Planned obsolescence is foreign to Austin thinking where engineering for economic long life is, and always has been, a first principle. Many of Lord Austin's cars are still giving useful service with thirty years' life behind them. Ten years from now the Austin 1800 will still have an up-to-date engineering specification.

A Publicity Department release made the even more startling claim that 'the Austin 1800 is a car which has basic longevity factors which will ensure that many of these cars will be running in the next century'. BMC had always stressed that their policy of advanced engineering would result in a longer-lived vehicle than the conventional car which traditionally underwent regular facelifts. From the company's point of view this was essential to recoup the investment. But this point was vastly overstated with the 1800 in a way that made it appear ridiculous. Durability may have been part of the Issigonis philosophy but his employers did not need customers who were so satisfied with their car they would never want a new one.

BMC had grown in confidence with the success of the Mini and the 1100 and decided on an ambitious extended launch for their latest advanced design, taking over the Garve Hotel in the Scottish Highlands for two and a half months. Tony Dawson argued that the press would be expecting the usual type of launch on the shores of the Mediterranean with buckets of champagne and that to do the whole thing in Scotland would provide an element of surprise which it was increasingly difficult to find for this type of event. Issigonis loved the idea. The press were to be brought over to Birmingham in groups of different nationalities for an initial visit to the showroom at Longbridge followed by a factory tour. They were then flown on to Inverness where they spent the next two days trying out the cars. The journalists drove in their usual uninhibited fashion around the narrow roads of the Scottish Highlands and undoubtedly enjoyed the event more than the locals who had to be placated by Tony Dawson on a number of occasions.

At the end of each trip Issigonis, Griffin, Burzi and Kingham received a summary of comments prepared by engine man Bill Appleby. Those of the French journalists were fairly typical. The suspension and brakes received the highest praise. They requested a higher maximum speed, complained about the noise of the engine and bluntly stated that 'the handbrake position was not satisfactory, would prefer one between front seats, also inefficient requiring sharp pull-up for even small gradients'. They were critical about the lack of equipment and suggested a number of improvements. Issigonis approved some of these, including a clock and an armrest for the front passenger. His handwritten comments, however, make clear his opposition to any attempt to make the seats more comfortable. He put a firm cross against suggestions that the backrests should be given more curvature 'to prevent sideways movement' or that the seats required 'more inclination or a stiffer front edge to prevent passengers sliding off when braking'. Most damning of all was the statement that 'at the same price they would prefer the Citroën DS'.

The first reports which came out in the British press were not heavily critical of the car, though they lacked the undertone of excitement which had greeted both the Mini and the 1100. *Motor*'s correspondent on 17 October 1965 remarked, 'at first glance one wonders where the fascia is …', and indicated that the new car was a reworking of a now familiar formula, with the result constituting something of a mixed bag. The cor-

Flat-four engine

Styling model

Interior space

Fascia and bench seat

MG 1100

Morris Imperial

DO 1033

TA/350

XC/9001

XC/9002

XC/9001

ADO 15

ADO 16 'sports'

XC/9001

XC/9002
lines added by Issigonis

Top row: early 50s, a curvaceous line
Middle row: mid-50s, the 'two-box' rectangular shape
Bottom row: late 50s, the Pininfarina influence adds sharp edges

ssigonis with a running prototype of XC/9001

Left: XC/9003, one of the original 'Orange Box' prototypes. Right: Charles Griffin (right) with a prototype of the 'Countryman' or estate version of XC/9003, on test in Switzerland

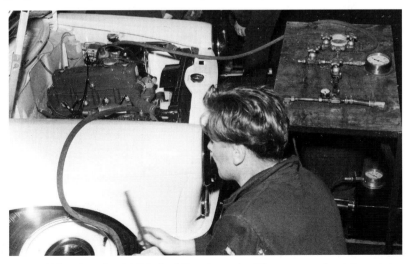

XC/9002 with in-line MG-badged B-series engine. The young mechanic is pumping up the Hydrolastic suspension

Left: an early wood styling buck shows that the pure lines of the production version were not accepted without question. Right: a metal mock-up carries an unattractive wrap-around grille

Left: attempts to add sparkle were defeated by resistance from Issigonis and cost implications. Right: sliding windows, door pockets and central speedo made it to production, but the door bar did not

Despite the experimentation with the shape and trim of XC/9003, it underwent few changes in appearance once it reached the production line. Issigonis is pictured at Longbridge in 1964

Morris

MG

Austin

Vanden Plas

Riley

Wolseley

The front end of ADO 16 undergoes a series of transformations in the styling studio; only the Vanden Plas escapes the photographic sequence

In 1960 Issigonis compared the conventional Austin Cambridge, re-styled by Pininfarina, with the Italian's early thoughts about XC/9001 (later ADO 17)

Issigonis meddled with Pininfarina's efforts as well as imposing his own taste in stark interiors. In early 1964 the badges read 'Austin Cambridge' but this was dropped before the September launch

Three years later, Pininfarina had another go and produced the 'Berlina Aerodynamica' concept

This ADO 14 of 1966 was built with a shorter overall length than the final version, but the requirement to re-use the doors from ADO 17 caused styling and packaging difficulties

By 1968 ADO 14 had grown in size but not in sex appeal. Despite its impressive technical attributes, British Leyland's new bosses were horrified at their first sight of the 'hen coop'

The plain door of the 1968 prototype (left) gains some extra features including added glamour for the 1969 launch (middle) before the introduction of final improvements on the 1970 facelift (right)

Radical attempts were made to improve the styling of ADO 14 in 1968 before launch

All to no avail. When the time came girls appeared to be the only answer

A preliminary idea from the early 60s for a replacement Mini

XC/8368, the 'Mini Mini' – Pininfarina's styling buck at Longbridge, June 1968

Concept for a replacement 9X Mini ...   *and its big brother the 9X ADO 16*

The Issigonis fleet of 9X cars in 1987: two gearless Minis, one geared Mini and an MG Metro   *His last prototype, a 6-cylind 9X engine installed in the Met*

respondent for *Motoring Which?* was more forthright, unconsciously echoing the French journalists:

> The position of the Austin 1800 handbrake was appalling. It was com-
> pletely out of reach of a driver wearing a safety belt. It was difficult to
> be sure whether it was off. As far as minor controls were concerned,
> the Austin 1800 was like a big Mini – most things out of reach. Several
> drivers commented that the easiest way to operate the heater controls
> was with the left foot. Not so easy to operate with the left foot, unfor-
> tunately, was the dipswitch – placed too high and too heavy to press, it
> was a constant irritation during night driving.

Issigonis was deaf to all criticism and would say time after time to journalists, to colleagues and to friends that the 1800 was the car he was most
proud of. His attitude was not in tune with the trend of the mid-20th
century. Despite what Issigonis thought, a giant Mini was not what the
public wanted. Issigonis was bamboozled by the success of the Mini
because it was so unusual and so unique that it became fashionable
despite the intentions of its creator. Its lack of style became the ultimate
in style. This proved an elusive quality. BMC was about to discover that
public opinion was, after all, a stronger force than the superior knowledge
of a designer.

The car was launched as the Austin 1800 in October 1964 and *Motor*
featured Issigonis and Harriman on the front cover of their Motor Show
Preview. The Chief Designer and the Chairman posed complacently on
either side of their latest offering against the backdrop of that other monument to modernity, Longbridge's multi-storey car park. The headline,
which might be suspected of irony if the motoring press of the 60s had
been capable of such a thing, read 'BMC does it again!' Aside from any
other considerations, constant quality and reliability problems plagued the
first years of production in an ominous echo from the Mini project. Once
again a large part of the profit was consumed in the battle to remedy initial production faults. This trend was not good for the profitability or the
reputation of BMC. The Morris version followed in March 1966. There
was also a more luxurious version, the Wolseley 18/85, offering the options
of power-steering and an automatic gearbox, which came out in March
1967 in an attempt to address some of the criticisms of the car's functional
appearance. Despite these efforts, and even though most of its engineering

problems were solved within the first couple of years, there was to be no miracle turnaround for the 1800. None of the three versions were to score big sales successes and in eleven years of production the final figure would be just short of 400,000. BMC had set its production lines up for a much larger volume of sales so this represented a considerable loss on their investment. The damage which could be done by an out-of-control design genius was beginning to be evident.

An attempt was made to get some additional value out of the 1800's expensive but under-utilised tooling by the introduction of the Austin 3-litre in 1967, a car which combined an adapted 1800 bodyshell with rear wheel drive, self-levelling Hydrolastic suspension, and a newly designed but underpowered in-line engine. This result of cross-breeding between different species of car turned out to be as unattractive as a mule. The 3-litre had begun life as project ADO 61 during the early 1960s, in parallel with ADO 17, but it dragged on almost interminably, going through three separate suspension designs and two alternative engines before finally being scheduled for launch at the British Motor Show in October 1967. It provides an excellent example of how little interest BMC's Technical Director showed in this type of belt and braces engineering. Only eight months before the launch he was sent the following memo by a polite but clearly irritated engineer:

At the policy Meeting held on Tuesday of last week an item was raised concerning the development test programme for ADO 61 prototypes. As you were absent from this Meeting and no one present at the Meeting had the information available, I was asked by Mr Edwards to point out to you that the question was raised and that he would like details from you in which you indicate the number of prototypes you intend to test and what the test programme will be.

This was bad enough, but in December, two months after the launch, Issigonis was writing with frightening nonchalance to Harry Weslake, whose firm worked with BMC on engine manufacture, about the inade-quacies of the power unit: 'I am glad to hear that you are working on the 3 litre engine to correct the serious fault that it has at low speeds. The Press comments on this have been very bad indeed.' With this kind of commitment it can be no surprise that the 3-litre lasted only four years with a final production total of just under 10,000.

In the case of the 1800, things need not necessarily have turned out the way that they did. Issigonis' good friend Sergio Pininfarina intervened in the story of its styling in one of those 'what-might-have-been' moments. During 1967 George Harriman and Joe Edwards, BMC's Managing Director, suggested to Sergio Pininfarina that he might consider earning them both some positive publicity by preparing a special car based on a BMC chassis. Pininfarina thought this was an excellent idea and he chose his friend's 1800 chassis for his design exercise, perhaps frustrated at the constraints which had been put on him by Issigonis at the time of the original project. All the mechanical parts were the same as on the production car but the body was about as far from the Issigonis design as it was possible to be. The exterior styling emphasised sleek aerodynamics complemented by large areas of glass, the interior, with an estate-car layout, retained the sense of space in the original but it also contained luxuries which Issigonis would never have allowed such as electric windows, powered seat adjustment and a highly stylised fascia. There was a companion 1100 version, though this car had less impact since the styling of the original was so much more attractive than that of its big brother.

This 1800-based concept car was known as the 'Berlina Aerodynamica' and it formed the centrepiece of the Pininfarina stand at the Turin Motor Show in 1967. It had the desired effect of arousing a great deal of press publicity, so much so that BMC subsequently asked to borrow the car with a view to doing some road testing to see if it was feasible to put it into production. Despite the fact that it was just a styling exercise, a Matchbox model of the 'Berlina Aerodynamica' was produced which was eagerly snapped up by every car-mad child in the land, each one of which would surely have urged their elders and betters to purchase the real thing had this been possible.

As usual, however, instead of seizing the opportunity to transform the car's fortunes BMC procrastinated too long. In January 1968 Sergio Pininfarina wrote to George Harriman on the subject with a certain amount of frustration:

I write to you about the special aerodynamic 1800 saloon which we have exhibited at the Torino Motor Show ... From a technical point of view we feel that many – if not all – conceptions of this car could be useful for a future introduction of it in production. From an aesthetical point of view we think that this theme could be converted or in a future standard saloon or in a two plus two sports car, according to what you will decide. Last, from a commercial point of view, Mr. Paradise [Director of BMC Europe] was happy of the publicity created by this car in Torino and we have seen an interest from you to exhibit this car in the early 1968 Motor Shows such as Brussels, Copenhagen, Geneva. In view of all the above written considerations we would like very much to know what is your feeling about this car and in which way you intend to develop this project. Also may I remind you that as all the expenses for studying and making this prototype have been met by our Company, we would think it right that BMC buys this vehicle at our pure cost …

Though Harriman passed this letter on to Issigonis for response, his reply, if one was composed, has not survived. By January 1968 it was in any case too late because the British Leyland merger was well underway and this promising idea, which might well have given the 1800 a new lease of life, was put on one side. All the same, the exercise demonstrated that it required more than technical expertise to turn a good engineering design into a market-place success.

Move to Birmingham

The years between his promotion in 1961 and the launch in 1964 of the 1800, the last in the series of 'advanced technology' front wheel drive cars, were ones of intense professional activity for Issigonis. His increased workload, combined with the demands of all the media attention and the necessity to make frequent trips abroad, had implications for his private life too. Even as she got older Hulda Issigonis continued to have great energy, managing the upkeep of the Oxford flat on her own despite the fact that she did not drive and had no one to ferry her around when her son was away. Nevertheless by 1963, as he prepared for the launch of the 1800 the following year, Alec was becoming increasingly concerned about leaving his mother on her own during the week. She was now 79 years old and even her robust constitution was showing signs of deterioration. She could no longer walk to the bus stop or carry her groceries back from the shopping centre up to the third floor every day. He would sometimes bring her with him and install her at his hotel during the week but this was not a practical long-term solution.

Twelve years of driving back to Oxford every weekend was in any case beginning to wear him down and their financial circumstances were now comfortable enough to warrant a permanent solution to these problems. Promotion to Technical Director had brought with it a substantial rise in salary and money began to come in from other sources too. There were the modest fees from making TV and radio appearances – about £50 per year – plus several annual *ex gratia* payments from the company for patents on his ideas including the transverse radiator arrangement on the Mini. Issigonis decided it was time to overrule his mother's objections and look for somewhere to live in Birmingham.

One obvious place to begin the search was the select suburb of Edgbaston which he already knew well from his frequent visits to his friend John Morris. This area, on the south side of Birmingham, had been dominated by the estate of the Calthorpe family since the 18th century. The Calthorpes had adopted a deliberate policy of attracting the prosperous middle classes of Birmingham away from the grime of the city by granting building leases. This development continued throughout the 19th century and produced streets filled with luxury villas such as the one in Carpenter Road where John Morris lived.

Issigonis believed that the genteel nature of Edgbaston would meet Hulda's objections to Birmingham – 'that awful place' – though, in keeping with his character, his choice was rather more modest than his friend's grand dwelling. Westbourne Gardens was a new development less than a mile away which offered both privacy and seclusion. It consisted of a little group of modern detached bungalows built as part of a private close in the gardens of a demolished mansion. The mature trees which surrounded the houses added a sense of permanence and insulated them from passing traffic even though the prime thoroughfare into the city centre and a main railway line were less than two miles away. The Botanical Gardens were almost next door and across the road stood a pretty Anglican church which would not have looked out of place in a typical English village.

When the Issigonises had moved from Kenilworth to Oxford in 1936 Alec was at the start of his career and his mother was still head of the household. The lease on the Sollershott flat was therefore in Hulda's name and it was decorated and furnished to her taste. Over the years the balance had gradually shifted as Alec became more successful and Hulda grew older and in less vigorous health. This time the lease was in his own name and he took control of their new residence from the beginning. As part of a brand new estate the bungalow incorporated some modern features such as a built-in garage, French windows and electric underfloor heating. There were some alterations of his own that he wished to add before they moved in. In order to give the two members of the Issigonis household more privacy than had been possible in the cramped Oxford flat, he adapted the layout of the house to create two wings joined by a common living area which incorporated an attractive dome window in its ceiling. Hulda was to have the right side of the house which consisted of a self-contained bedroom suite with its own dressing room and bathroom. The left side of the house also had its own bathroom and two small bedrooms were knocked together to create a larger room for Alec himself. Linking the two wings, the living area had a kitchen at the back and a dining room at the front. To the right of the dining room and situated on the end of Hulda's wing was a separate drawing room. On the opposite side at the end of Alec's wing stood the spacious double garage which he intended to requisition for the construction of a model steam railway.

The purpose of the alterations was not just to improve the practical arrangements for the two new occupants; Alec seemed anxious to impose his own style on the plain bungalow. To this end he had the gap between the garage on the left and the drawing room on the right enclosed to form a reception area with adjoining 'loggia'. This consisted of an alcove open on one side which was decorated with marble flooring and landscaped with wisteria, clematis and roses. At the back of the house he constructed a paved sun-terrace from which he could sit and admire his garden. The lawn was adorned with the pewter tankards he had won in the motor competitions of his youth, filled with flowers. On the far wall of the drawing room he installed a fireplace which closely resembled the one at the Poplars. This was made of period pine, carved and polished in Georgian style, and featuring marble slips, a raised hearth and a Baxi grate with a stainless steel surround. He even went as far as to obtain a pair of Worcester urns similar to the ones Max had on her mantelpiece. This was an uncharacteristically sentimental gesture, springing from a desire to recreate some of the homeliness that he enjoyed with the Dowson family. From Sollershott he brought a painting of Naples which he had obtained on one of his trips to Italy and always referred to as 'a Mediterranean back street'. This hung alongside some abstract paintings which he chose himself, though Hulda declared she did not like them. In 1965 these were joined by an oil painting of him which had been commissioned by the

business publication *Motor Industry*. It was executed in an impressionistic
style with heavy brush-strokes and his mother was very proud of it though
in his usual contrary fashion he declared that this was not to his liking.

He had never before had the opportunity to set up a home entirely to
his own taste and he seems to have been enjoying himself. While builders
worked on the structure, he set about furnishing the rooms and he turned
to Max Dowson, whose stylishness he had always admired, for advice. In
July 1963 he contacted Maple & Co., a firm of upholsterers established in
the centre of Birmingham. He requested that they should get in samples
of furnishings, carpets and curtain materials so that he could visit the
store personally to select what he needed. Max helped him to go through
the samples and advised him on colour schemes. He also treated himself to
one or two more expensive items. On his annual visit to Monte Carlo in
June 1963 he indulged in the purchase of a *caisse tableau* at a cost of 600
francs, though he had to pay another 105.55 francs on top of this to have it
transported back to Britain. In October he bought a mahogany table and
four chairs reupholstered to his specification from an Edgbaston antiques
shop, and this cost him just over £81. The end result was a more elegant,
understated style than is evident in photographs of the Oxford flat.

Once everything was ready he brought his mother to the bungalow
and when she saw it she was a little mollified, commenting, 'I didn't know
there *were* places like this in Birmingham.' The two of them moved in on
25 October 1963 and for a while the lease on the Oxford flat was also
retained. Alec thought it might be useful for when he needed to visit
Cowley and it would also reassure Hulda that if she was not happy they
could always go back. In the event he did not make any further visits
there. The flat lay empty throughout the winter of 1963–4 and in June
the letting agents told him that a member of their staff was looking for
accommodation and suggested he might like to sub-let the property. He
agreed that this was a good idea and returned to take away the last of their
personal possessions, though the old furniture was left behind. In 1965 the
new tenant took over the lease directly from the landlords and four years
later he raised the subject of this furniture which included a gas cooker, a
small electric refrigerator, the old dining table with six chairs, two divan
beds and two wardrobes. Issigonis refused his offer of £10 for the items,
which were now almost worn out, saying they had no value to him and
could be thrown away. Thus the dining table which had been the scene of
some of his most avid sketching was casually disposed of, just like the

Lightweight Special drawing on the wall of the Kenilworth garage many years earlier.

The move proved to be the right decision because Hulda's health was rapidly deteriorating. Her last Monte Carlo trip appears to have been in July 1964 when she fell on the beach and injured her thigh. Early in 1966, she suffered another fall and had to stay in hospital with a broken hip. By relinquishing the lease on her Oxford flat in 1965 she was acknowledging that she now accepted that the move to Birmingham was a permanent one. Issigonis transferred his bank account from Oxford to Edgbaston and was left with only the rent of £450 per year to pay on the lease of the bungalow. In March 1968 he decided to buy the lease and the sale was completed in October 1969. At the age of 62, Issigonis had finally became a homeowner.

THE CHARACTER OF ISSIGONIS

Piero Casucci, in his 'Minigonis' article, included a vivid description of his friend's physical appearance at this time:

> He is tall, athletic. He has awfully long legs. Walking with him is rather tiring. His face is marked by two deep wrinkles which make him look like a sea-dog. He would seem a man who has lived intensely, but it is not so, because Alec Issigonis had and has only two deep loves: his mother and his work. Differently from his country-men when he talks, he stares at his interlocutor, but his eyes are always ironic: it almost seems that he enjoys making fun of you or that he does not believe what he is saying. He makes wide gestures while speaking in order to emphasize his speech, giving it some 'physical' limits. When I first met him, I wondered whether Mr Issigonis was English because, never before it had occurred to me to meet a British citizen who tried to stress his talk by using his hands. Only later I realized that Mr Issigonis' hands are authentically expressive, eloquent and categorical, as well as his concise dialectics made of short sentences and repeated shrugs of the shoulders which, while he puts embarrassing questions in his turn, put in trouble his interlocutor.

Casucci has pinpointed the contradiction between the Englishman that his father had taught him to be and his upbringing in the cultural melting pot of Smyrna. His manner, his speech, his tastes all emphasised his Englishness.

Nevertheless he spoke in a deliberate, precise way which was unusual in itself and his willingness to make eye-contact along with his extravagant hand-gestures were distinctly continental traits. He favoured the dress of the English upper class and like most of his generation wore formal clothes on all occasions and in all weathers – three-piece suits, black or pinstripe trousers with a heavy tweed jacket, often accompanied by a shooting stick. At the same time he liked to wear socks in flamboyant colours and on holiday he was perfectly happy to be photographed without a tie, with his sleeves rolled up or even in shorts or swimming trunks.

Those who knew Issigonis describe his personality as magnetic and throughout the 1960s his new circumstances enabled his sociability and charm to come to the fore. Though he was uncomfortable with strangers and often irascible with his colleagues, he loved his friends and they found him great fun to be with. His arrogance at work was not reflected in his private life. He did not boast about his achievements but he exuded a kind of boyish enthusiasm. When he laughed he would throw back his head as his whole face creased in amusement and he often broke into infectious giggles.

This 'boyishness' was a key element to his character which was perfectly described by another of his friends, the actor Peter Ustinov. As with Lord Snowdon, this friendship was not a result of Alec's fame since they had first met in the late 1940s through Alec's motor sport activities. Ustinov, although born in London, had a family background which was as singular as Alec's, involving Russian, French and even Ethiopian forebears, and once again it was a common love of cars combined with a mutual sense of the ridiculous which inspired their friendship. Ustinov naturally admired the great intellect which created groundbreaking designs such as the Morris Minor and the Mini, but he was also intrigued by his personality. He noted, on the one hand, Alec's extreme sophistication which was epitomised by the elegance of his speech and his careful choice of words, contrasted with his ability to take the greatest pleasure from the simplest of things, something he called 'a slight Peter Pan quality, an inability to grow up'. When they were together they often behaved like adolescents, as on the occasion in 1962 when Tony Dawson arranged for a number of 1100s to be made available at Chalgrove near Oxford just before the official launch. Ustinov, Issigonis and their guests indulged in a day of high jinks and hilarity which involved a great deal of uninhibited driving plus a considerable amount of fine food and drink taken at the nearby hostelry 'Home

Sweet Home'. The photographs taken on the occasion show them with their arms draped round each other, giggling and laughing in delight.

Part of the attraction people felt towards him was his lively sense of fun. He possessed a mischievous, mocking type of humour based on the acute observation of other people and the sharpness of his mind. It is clear that he enjoyed displaying his quick-wittedness and this often expressed itself in making fun of other people, including, as we have seen, dear 'mama'. This was a double-edged quality and it earned him as much detestation as admiration. The depth of dislike it could provoke in those who felt they had been belittled by his cleverness should not be underestimated.

Intellectually he had overcome his childhood aversion to reading many years ago and he filled his bookshelves as the years passed with his favourite books on physics, astronomy and the philosophy of the universe. He also loved detective novels and was an avid reader of Conan Doyle's Sherlock Holmes mysteries, Dornford Yates and the American detective stories of Raymond Chandler, Erle Stanley Gardner, Micky Spillane and Rex Stout, whose genius detective Nero Wolfe was one of his favourite fictional characters.

The main focus of his intellectual effort, however, remained where it had always been, on his passion for engineering. This created a personality which made no distinction between the professional and the personal life. Every time he got in a car he was thinking about new problems and solutions, saying, 'to me, a journey in a car which I am not working on or testing is a wasted journey'. He spent long hours at the factory and when he went home he took his work with him so he could continue until the factory gates opened again. In 1967 Piero Casucci described his daily routine which illustrates this point well:

At nine in the evening he is in bed. He reads for an hour. He gets up at six in the morning. It is the moment of thinking to the day's program. It is bad, he says, to do it before going to sleep because the night inspires fantasy. The morning is reality and we must look to reality.

This régime had a clear purpose. The night-time was for allowing the imagination loose while morning was the time for planning and thinking. In his later years, he advised a young colleague in the following way:

You should always have a pad and pencil by your bedside in case you wake up in the middle of the night with good ideas which you ought to write down because by the time you go to sleep again you'll forget them in the morning.

His hobbies were part of the same theme. Once he became a professional designer he no longer needed to play with Austin Sevens or dream up a Lightweight Special. He continued, however, to experiment with ever more complex model aeroplanes and in 1966 his friends at Dunlop went to some trouble to make up some special miniature tyres for him: 'Our original thought was to make these up from tubing, hypodermically inflated, but after trial we decided that it was not practicable to get an entirely satisfactory join. We have therefore made up a temporary mould from which we have produced eight tyres, four of each being in different compounds.' Issigonis responded: 'Very many thanks for the miniature tyres. All we need to do now is to get the aeroplane to fly!' He still loved steam engines and at weekends he would often go to see the real thing. When Tom Rolt, Chairman of the Talyllyn Railway Company, invited him for a 'private view' of the steam trains running on the Towyn railway in 1966 he replied excitedly, 'I shall be delighted to come down [with John Morris and Alex Moulton] and see you on April 30 and play with the engine next day … We shall be arriving some time during the afternoon and can hardly wait to see the steam raised.'

It is no surprise, therefore, that his most enduring hobby was the model railway which he built at the Edgbaston bungalow. One of the attractions of the bungalow was its large garage and spacious garden, not because he wanted somewhere to park his fleet of cars – he always drove works vehicles – but because it allowed him to return to his childhood passion for model steam locomotives such as the ones his father used to buy for him. His promotion had greatly increased his workload to the point that he scarcely had any time left for the sketching at which he had been so prolific. There is, however, a sequence of sketches for the miniature steam engine and carriages that he started to design in 1964. For the next couple of years he worked hard in his spare time, using his own lathe to create a scaled-down locomotive and soldering sections of hand-built track on his gas stove. The garage became a railway station, with the track running round the walls on special shelves, entering and exiting the building through specially created holes and emerging into the garden onto purpose-built embankments. He loved this hobby and spoke of it enthusiastically:

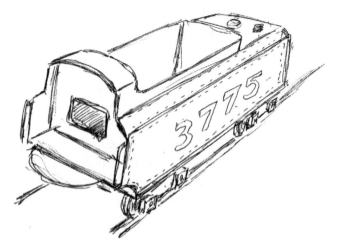

Issigonis loved steam engines all his life. In 1964 he began to build his own model railway and he sketched the steam engine and carriages which he then made by hand.

The big difficulty in my life is to stop worrying when I leave work at night. Well, one has to try, somehow, to switch off until the next morning. I am capable of doing this only by doing other things – working my model railways for instance. Model railways are my special hobby. Steam ones naturally. Perhaps this is not very creative but it is amusing. And it takes one's mind away completely from work and cars and other problems.

Someone who spent such a large proportion of his time in the realm of ideas was unlikely to be practical about everyday life. He relied on his mother to look after details such as housework, cooking or paying the bills. Legendary in the family was the occasion on which Hulda left him alone to clean the flat and he was discovered trying to manhandle the Hoover over the carpet in its upright position, having failed to notice that there was a button which lowered the handle to a comfortable angle during use. As his mother became less active, things began to get overlooked. He would get final demands for his electricity bill and it was nearly six months before the standing order to pay his lease was cancelled following his purchase of the house, requiring the agents to give him a refund. He also constantly mislaid important paperwork relating to his finances. This could be more than an inconvenience, as was the case in 1968 when a new Companies Act included a requirement for Annual Reports to declare the interests of directors in the shares of the holding company. It was fortunate that his solicitor, Timothy Smith, and his bank manager, Michael Moss, were personal friends and able to help him keep control over his financial affairs, obtaining copies of vital paperwork when it was required though often at some expense to him.

This lack of connection with the practicalities of life could also manifest itself in a lack of consideration for people who were on the periphery of his world. There are several notes from his dentist to his secretary asking her to remind him about dental appointments, including one which regretted his failure to put in an appearance 'although I stayed on until 6.00 p.m. in case you had been delayed by traffic'. He was not being deliberately rude, it was simply that mundane things like dental appointments found it hard to win space in his mind against the constant *mêlée* of design ideas that jostled there for position. This preoccupation made him seem more selfish than he was. He showed his generosity in a straightforward way in October 1964 when he gave a substantial donation to Dr Barnardo's homes. Rather more mysterious was the charity that he extended to the rather sad case of Mr H.H. Buchanan, a down-on-his-luck old age pensioner who lived in Gloucester.

Buchanan first wrote to Issigonis in January 1968, explaining that he had seen an article about the designer's model steam railway in *London Day by Day* and asking if Issigonis ever held an open day so that other enthusiasts like himself could see it. This first letter set the pattern of the six-year (and entirely one-sided) correspondence which ensued. Buchanan went on to mention that, as he only had his pension to live on, he could not afford to buy magazines such as *Model Engineer* so he was unable to keep in touch with his hobby any more. He also enclosed a note, handwritten on an old Wolseley Motors letterhead from the time of Lord Nuffield and Reggie Hanks, which explained that he was an ex-Wolseley employee from the Service Department and his job had been 'to answer letters from D to I'. In other words, Buchanan's role in life had been to answer any queries from customers whose names were filed under those particular letters of the alphabet. It is clear from the correspondence that his approach was entirely unsolicited and they did not know each other.

It was very common for people in Issigonis' position to receive this kind of approach and once he became famous he was contacted by a number of people who claimed to have know him in Smyrna or at

Battersea Polytechnic and who wondered if he remembered them and would mind doing them a little favour. It is therefore hard to say what there was in Buchanan's letter which would have moved Issigonis to pay some attention to it. Yet, although he ignored the suggestion about his model railway, he wrote to the Model Aeronautical Press and took out a subscription to *Model Engineer* at a cost of £3 10/-, giving instructions that the publication should be sent directly to Buchanan. He renewed this subscription regularly for the next five years and as time went by he also gave a variety of discarded books, magazines and newspapers to Suzanne Hankey to be forwarded. Copies of *Flight*, *Model Steam*, *The Sunday Times*, *London Illustrated News*, *Car* and *The Guinness Book of Records* all found their way through the pensioner's letterbox.

With this encouragement, Buchanan started to write several times a year both to Issigonis – from whom he never got an answer – and to Suzanne Hankey. There were always two elements to the letters: their apparent purpose, usually to say thank you for the material he had received; and the begging element where he would casually mention something he could not afford in the clear hope that Issigonis would feel generous enough to provide it for him. He became increasingly bold in his requests as time went on, at one point rather dramatically begging his benefactor not to put anything in the bin which might be useful to him: 'I don't care a jot what it is from an egg cup to a piano'. Astonishingly, while some of his more outlandish hints were carefully ignored he was successful in soliciting several items that were worth a great deal more than a few discarded magazines including a number of three-piece suits and a winter overcoat.

Buchanan seems a sad figure who hoped to strike up some kind of personal relationship with Issigonis, but this was the one thing Issigonis carefully avoided. He ignored all his pleas to visit for tea, to send an autographed picture or to acknowledge letters personally. Nevertheless Buchanan still continued to write regularly, describing his ever-worsening lot as he moved from one rented room to another and providing a commentary on his poor health, his depression, his loneliness and his increasing poverty. By 1974 Buchanan was obviously reaching the end, sending confused letters written in block capitals, culminating in the news that after a long period in hospital he had now been sent to a nursing home. His final letter is perhaps the most bizarre, making the startling claim that he is about to get married and asking for 'advice' about where to buy a cheap car.

It is hard to know what prompted Issigonis to take pity on Buchanan because his letters were written in a fawning, self-pitying style which is not appealing. Yet, once he had decided to do something and set for himself the limits of what that would involve, he was entirely consistent and extremely generous in his actions towards him. This capacity for kindness and generosity was one of his best qualities.

It was also evident in his relationship with his colleagues. Sometimes it was not obvious to them but he did recognise the essential contribution of his team, their commitment, the long hours they worked without complaint and the dedication they put into their job and he did not lose sight of this as he became more important in the company. Every year when the Earls Court Motor Show opened in London at the beginning of October he would go down to spend a few days at the Hyde Park Hotel and in the evening he would host a reception to which all the engineers were invited. After the success of the Mini this reception was usually buzzing with company executives and celebrities but this did not mean that he stopped inviting his engineers. When he saw them arrive he would leave his new friends and come over to make sure they had a drink, making a point of sitting down and talking to them about the show. Similarly, he would invite them to the Edgbaston bungalow every year on his birthday and treat his guests to dry martinis, hosting a lively discussion about rival car designs and showing off his model railway with childish enthusiasm.

In summing up the character of the mature man, therefore, it would seem that his great success was something which he considered a by-product rather than the main objective of all his hard work. He had devoted his life to getting the best out of himself, producing the finest designs of which he felt he was capable. Anything else was incidental.

OLD RELATIONSHIPS

Issigonis was not a sentimental man. He did not hang on to his precious racing car, for example, even though it had been his first design and held many memories of a happy period of his life. Instead he made a present of his share in the Lightweight Special to Christopher Dowson and took great pleasure in the revitalisation of its career when Christopher began to compete in 'vintage' events. He told Pininfarina proudly in 1979 that it still ran perfectly and there was 'no corrosion anywhere!!'

Nevertheless when it came to friendship he showed great loyalty throughout his life to those who were closest to him and he continued to look out for the interests of the young people in whose upbringing he had become so involved. There is no doubt that Issigonis got on exceptionally well with children for the young Ransomes and Dowsons would always remember him with great affection as a kind and entertaining 'uncle' and godfather. The delight of the Ransome children at his Christmas presents was matched by the astonishment of Penny Dowson on her twelfth birthday when she was taken as a 'VIP' visitor to the impressive vantage point at the top of the multi-storey car park at the Longbridge factory to be shown a sea of brand new Minis with their red, white and blue roofs. He maintained these relationships when adulthood approached. Over the years he had somewhat lost touch with May Ransome, partly because he was becoming ever busier and partly because in 1957 she had moved away from Kingswood to the rather less accessible county of Devon. Nevertheless, as we have seen, he nurtured young Mark Ransome's career and he often arranged trips to the London Motor Show on press day for Mark, Penny or Christopher. Afterwards he would take them to the Dorchester for dinner or invite them over to his 'town house' at the Hyde Park Hotel.

He also maintained his childhood friendship with Donald Riddle whom he often referred to as 'The Riddle'. Though Donald's family had been evacuated to England along with the Walkers and the Issigonises, Donald eventually chose to return to Turkey. He worked for a subsidiary of BP based in Istanbul and by 1947 had become Managing Director of BP Petrolleri AS. Riddle spent a great deal of time travelling and stayed in London for part of every year. Alec also made several visits to see him in Turkey though the one thing he could not be bothered to do despite his wide network of acquaintances was write to his friends. He hated writing even short notes and when one friend complained that Donald Riddle had told him that all he should expect from Alec these days was telegrams since he never wrote letters any more, Alec mischievously sent him a telegram saying 'AFRAID DONALD IS QUITE RIGHT STOP'.

Riddle was a man of great energy who had returned to Turkey out of a deep attachment to the country along with a desire to contribute to its economic and artistic development. His career displayed a commendable blend of present realism and vision. He became involved in promoting the beginnings of tourism in Turkey during the 1960s by setting up a network of camping sites known as 'Mocamps' for motoring tourists. This initiative earned Riddle great favour with the Turkish government since tourist revenue was an excellent source of much-needed foreign currency. Of course Riddle was also aware of the fact that the Mocamps provided good public relations for BP, smoothing its relationship as a foreign investor with the local government and helping their own sales by encouraging more motorists to spend money in Turkey.

Though most of Issigonis' friendships were based on a mutual interest in engineering, the relationship with Riddle was something of an exception. The differences between mechanistic Alec and academic Donald had been evident since their childhood. Their interests were still very different since Donald numbered among his pastimes chess, horse-riding, theatre and art. What they did have in common was a sense of humour, complete confidence in their own judgement, a tendency to perfectionism, great mental dexterity and an unusual approach to their jobs. Just as Alec brought a creative energy to the job of designing a mechanical object, so Riddle employed an artistic approach to the world of business. A colleague commented about him, 'Mr Riddle is a man who attaches great importance to the artistic aspects of problems. On one occasion I had tried to evade a difficult question from him by saying "this is a question of taste". "You are right" he replied, "it is a question of taste, but there is GOOD taste and BAD taste".'

In August 1967 Issigonis visited Turkey to open BMC's new Istanbul plant. He scheduled the visit to last for a week so he could take the opportunity to visit his old friend who was preparing for retirement. He sent Riddle a telegram giving the dates of the visit and adding the instruction 'please find Audrey' referring to one of their childhood friends, originally Audrey Goüt, who had lived a rather racy life since the Smyrna days, having been married three times, becoming Lady Audrey Campbell along the way. After his official duties were over they went on a motor tour of the country, staying at some of Donald's Mocamps and visiting their childhood home, now reborn – and almost completely rebuilt – as Izmir.

This return to Izmir seems to have stirred only a distant curiosity in Alec, with no sentimental longings for the past. Other than Donald he made no attempt to keep in contact with the companions of his youth. In the case of Uncle Milti's children, the bad relationship between the two brothers had a permanent effect on the two families. All of them shared British citizenship but while Hulda and her son had chosen to make their future in England, Milti's family returned to Greece. In December 1959

Alec received a long letter from Milti's daughter Leila who now lived in Athens. This was the first communication there had been between them for 36 years and it was prompted by the publicity surrounding the launch of the Mini. Though she expressed a wish to visit him, he made no response. The only time he appears to have met any of Milti's family was on his arrival at the airport at the start of his 1967 visit. Waiting for him when he landed was Leila's brother, Nikolaos Issigonis, along with his wife Nancy and their seventeen-year-old son Leslie. Leslie subsequently invited him to his wedding, but Issigonis declined all his overtures to keep in touch. He might have been expected to take a different approach with the family of Hulda's sister since he had been so fond of aunty Gertrude. She, like Hetty, had died relatively young in 1948 and while he appears to have occasionally met Gertrude's son Peter Giudici, who still lived in Munich, this was only when Peter visited England and made the effort to come and see him.

My Old Mother

It would therefore seem that Issigonis cherished his set of close friendships and felt there were no emotional needs to be fulfilled by repairing the broken connections of the past. The central relationship in his life was firmly located in the bungalow at Edgbaston. Despite everything that had happened – the public acclaim, promotion at work, a host of new celebrity friends, an enjoyable lifestyle, a new and more spacious house – there were only two things that really mattered to him. One, as we have seen, was designing cars. The other was looking after his mother who was still the most important person in his life.

By the time they settled down to their new life in Edgbaston, Hulda and Alec resembled nothing more than a cosy long-married couple. She had looked after him when they first came to England and now he was looking after her. She was the focus of his affection and in return, she gave him her unqualified support and also her admiration as he became more and more successful. The pearl necklace that he had given her after his first promotion was always round her neck. She took up her place, sitting in her chair in the drawing room by the fire, and they nagged and grumbled at each other just as they had always done. Whatever important friends he made, whatever distinguished duties he had to undertake, she was always there keeping house for him and forming a solid backdrop to his life. No visitor to the bungalow, whether it was a member of his team,

a director of the corporation, a famous international designer, a celebrated actor, a busy journalist or a peer of the realm, could get away without first paying their respects to 'my old mother' Mrs Issigonis.

Their relationship reflects what might be called the selfish determination of both Hulda and Alec. Throughout his life Alec always knew what
he wanted and never allowed anything to intrude into his life which
would deflect him from his course. Hulda's mission was always to smooth
the path towards the achievement of what he wanted. The seamlessness
he enjoyed between work and leisure allowed Issigonis to live a remarkably harmonious life and Hulda was the agency that made it possible. He
was extremely fortunate that he was given the freedom to follow his own
inclinations by entering a career in which he found such fulfilment and
which allowed his intellect to flourish. To be reminded of this he needed
to look no further than his Walker cousins, none of whom were really
able to fulfil their potential. May and Gerry were both sensitive and intellectual people who relished reading and loved to discuss philosophy, the-
ology, literature, the arts and classical music. Tony Walker too was musical,
artistic and a talented photographer. None of them were able to pursue
the academic careers which would have suited them. Against their inclinations Gerald followed a career in engineering, May was confined to
being a home-maker, and Tony was pushed into the life of a Sinhalese tea
planter. They were expected to do what was best for the family rather
than themselves.

It has been suggested that Hulda was a possessive mother who stifled
her son's social life, especially where women were concerned, and this
would certainly be understandable since Hulda was both emotionally and
financially dependent on Alec and could not afford to lose him to another
woman. Yet though he spent a great deal of time with her, Issigonis also
spent a great deal of time on his own. He spent four days a week away
from her in his hotel room, he went on frequent business trips and holidays with his friends, nor did she interfere with his weekend visits to the
Poplars.

John Sheppard remembered Issigonis as being shy and awkward with
women he did not know, treating them in a very old-fashioned manner
with what Sheppard describes as 'old-world charm'. Alec did not dislike
women. Just as in his youth he had larked around with Podge, Gee-Gee
and Peggy at Barton Cottage with no apparent animosity from his
mother, so in his later life he conducted lively relationships with a num-

ber of female friends, most of whom were married. There was Max Dowson, whose elegance and taste he admired greatly. The fact that she was married to his best friend represented an element of safety to him, since it limited the amount of emotional effort required on his part to create a successful relationship. She came to the Oxford flat sometimes and got on perfectly amicably with Mrs Issigonis and they often talked about cooking and swapped recipes. Mama was also on good terms with Betsy Rusher. She might have been expected to represent a greater threat in Hulda's eyes since her husband's navy career left her on her own more than usual for a married woman of the time, yet she was often welcomed at Sollershott. Joy Fry, the wife of his other good friend David Fry, was another regular companion. Alec found it very amusing to refer to these three friends as his 'first wife' (Max), his 'second wife' (Betsy) and his 'third wife' (Joy). This caused great consternation when he introduced Max to one acquaintance as his first wife, prompting the confused guest to comment, 'My dear, I'd no idea Alec had ever married.'

So why did Issigonis remain a perpetual bachelor? It is easy to make the assumption that a single man who has a strong attachment to his mother must be homosexual. He certainly had a number of friends who were privately if not publicly well known to be so. Having homosexual friends, however, is not conclusive proof of one's own sexuality. It is necessary to look at this in the context of the period in which Issigonis lived and not through the filter of more recent attitudes. By the beginning of the 21st century, homosexuality is thankfully no longer regarded by the majority as some kind of perversion, but more than this it has become unimaginable that any person could or would wish to override their sexual urges for any reason. The atmosphere which prevailed during the first half of the 20th century was very different. Homosexuality was illegal until 1967 and the motor industry was a particularly male-orientated and intolerant world. To be an active homosexual could have done his career and his reputation immense damage and it would also have caused great distress to his mother. In the light of his reserved character and conservative, even prim, social attitudes it seems unlikely that Issigonis would have examined his own soul too closely on this matter and the idea of being labelled a homosexual would probably have horrified him.

The reason that he remained single is therefore likely to be quite simple: he had neither the time nor the inclination for the alternatives. The demands of a sexual partnership or of a family of his own did not fit into his lifestyle which was utterly dedicated to his passion for engineering, crammed with work and activity. Design consumed his energy while the emotional core of his life was his mother. An equally valid question would be why Hulda never remarried. As we have seen she was a good-looking woman with an attractive personality and could surely have had opportunities if she had wanted them. Her reasons were probably the same as his: her life was devoted to his success and she needed no distractions in the achievement of this. He could not be described as emotionally deprived. The friendships which he kept intact throughout his life – Donald Riddle, John Morris, Tony Dawson, the Dowson family, May Ransome and her children – all in their own way fulfilled different emotional needs.

John Cooper for one did not find Alec's bachelorhood hard to explain:

> He worshipped his mother, who brought him up. A lot of people have said to me, why wasn't he married? He was married to motor cars. His whole life was motor cars, day and night he'd talk about motor cars, he didn't talk about other things.

This brings us back to Piero Casucci's assessment of his friend:

> He would seem a man who has lived intensely, but it is not so, because Alec Issigonis had and has only two deep loves: his mother and his work.

It is therefore reasonable to draw the conclusion that in devoting his personal life to his strong-minded mother Issigonis was doing what he wanted to do. It was his choice as much as his duty and it was one which entirely suited him.

MINI COOPER

CHAPTER 8

*If you go in for any kind of competition it is a complete waste of time unless
you win.*

Sir Alec Issigonis

MY FRIEND MR FERRARI

THOUGH HIS NEW position as Technical Director had imposed many duties
which Issigonis found irritating, there were also some pleasant benefits.
For one thing, he found himself travelling more widely and more frequently
than before, as the records of his travel and expenses during the period
1958 to 1970 illustrate. Up to 1964 he was making an average of three to
four overseas visits a year. After this the number steadily rose, peaking at
eleven during 1967. Issigonis had always enjoyed travelling. He often said
how much he loved England and would never choose to live anywhere
else, yet his outlook was in many ways cosmopolitan and he took great
pleasure in his European friendships. Previously his circle had been confined to leading British engineers like John Morris, Bill Heynes, Gerald
Palmer, John Thornley and Alex Moulton. Now he was attending motor
shows all over Europe, including regular trips to Geneva in March, and Paris
and London in October alongside occasional appearances in Amsterdam,
Brussels and Frankfurt. Here he was introduced to the top echelon of
European designers such as Ferry Porsche and Dante Giacosa and he
could take the opportunity to meet up with the new international circuit
of journalist friends to whom Tony Dawson had introduced him.

By 1968 it was not uncommon for him to be sending telegrams such
as this one to his friend Peter Ustinov in Paris: 'SERGIO PININ-
FARINA AND MYSELF ARE HAVING LUNCH WITH MR
FERRARI ON TUESDAY 27TH AUGUST IN MODENA STOP WE
WOULD BE VERY PLEASED IF YOU COULD JOIN US STOP'.
Enzo Ferrari had begun to make his reputation in motor sport during the
1920s as the competitions manager for Alfa Romeo. In 1929 he estab-
lished Scuderia Ferrari in the northern Italian town of Maranello near
Modena and in the years following the Second World War he built his

team, and himself, into a legend. Over the years he attracted some of the best drivers of the day – legends of the sport such as Tazio Nuvolari, Alberto Ascari, John Surtees and Niki Lauda. Among these drivers during the 1960s was Alec's old friend Mike Parkes, whose course in life had altered drastically since their first acquaintance. During his career with the Rootes Group Parkes had collaborated with Tim Fry on the design of the Hillman Imp, a small car which was intended to compete with the Mini. It followed a completely different philosophy and was not only rear wheel drive but also rear engined. The book *Apex, the Inside Story of the Hillman Imp*, by David and Peter Henshaw, recounts the story of how Issigonis reputedly borrowed the prototype from its designers for a short run and returned with the words, 'absolutely brilliant but you've got it the wrong way around!' Unlike the Mini, the Imp enjoyed a long period of development, which sadly did not prevent it from being allowed onto the market with too many unsolved problems in 1963. Though it had many good qualities it gained a terrible reputation for unreliability and therefore never met with the success it deserved.

Mike Parkes' real interest, however, had always lain in motor racing and he gradually made a path for himself from amateur to professional. In 1957 he got his first big break when Colin Chapman invited him to act as reserve driver for the Lotus Works Team at Le Mans. He began to win regularly in the Sports Car and GT categories and his professional training as an engineer stood him in good stead when it came to developing the cars. It was this which earned him the opportunity to join Scuderia Ferrari in 1963 as development engineer and reserve driver. Enzo Ferrari was notorious for quarrelling with his drivers but Parkes managed to escape this fate and came to be regarded almost as a surrogate son, filling the void created by the death of Dino Ferrari a number of years earlier. For the next three years he enjoyed considerable success competing in Ferrari sports cars, winning such prestigious events as the Sebring 12 hours, the Spa 500 kilometres and the Monza 1,000 kilometres. In 1965 he was allowed to drive in Formula One as well, with distinguished drivers Ludovico Scarfiotti and Lorenzo Bandini as his team mates.

Unfortunately, although he made a promising start with two second places in his first two races, Parkes had a bad accident during the Belgian Grand Prix at Spa Francorchamps in 1967. He was in a coma for a week and it took him six months to recover completely from the combination of leg and brain injuries which he suffered. Issigonis sent one of his sparkling telegrams to the Hôpital de Bavière in Liège where Parkes was recovering which read: 'BEST WISHES FOR A SPEEDY RECOVERY STOP HOPE TO SEE YOU IN LUTON STOP TRY THE BRITISH SCHOOL OF MOTORING'. While he recuperated Parkes took a management role at Ferrari, acting as head of the sports car programme, but what he really wanted was to race again and Ferrari was reluctant to let him do so. Eventually he left Maranello to seek the chance to compete for other sports car and rally teams. Throughout the 1960s, however, he was resident at Scuderia Ferrari and so he was there during the period when Issigonis was making what he referred to as his 'annual pilgrimage' to Maranello.

Enzo Ferrari was eight years older than Issigonis and both men were larger-than-life characters. They shared a passion bordering on obsession for motoring, a very focussed mind and a sharp sense of humour often at other people's expense. These visits therefore afforded Issigonis a dual opportunity. First he could indulge in just the type of humour and conversation he enjoyed best with 'old man' Ferrari. Then, after a sumptuous Italian lunch, he could head off into the countryside for a drive in the latest production sports car with his old friend Mike Parkes. On one occasion he was allowed to test a Le Mans Ferrari. Sergio Pininfarina had the dubious honour of taking the passenger seat and always remembered the experience of speeding round the narrow lanes outside the Maranello factory. He joined the long line of people who found Alec's vigorous driving technique unnerving, while the man himself enthused, 'the handling of that Ferrari was absolutely marvellous. Right out of this world!'

THE BIRTH OF THE MINI COOPER

By the 60s Issigonis liked to pretend that he had grown out of his passion for motor racing and he insisted that building racing cars contributed nothing to road car design:

Motor racing was another of my relaxations when I was young. Now I am not so active but I do take a great interest in car rallies in which B.M.C. enter Minis and other cars – particularly Minis of course ... I am concerned with this type of competition, I think, because rallying makes a small contribution to the development of the family car. Motor racing makes none at all. I am sure of this and I have always had this view. In rallying the car is running under conditions on open roads and it is being operated in a way that a family car can be operated although many times faster! But on a racing track where there is no other traffic things are very artificial. I can't see that it does anything to help development.

His behaviour in the Le Mans Ferrari demonstrated that he was far from immune to the glamour of the specially designed race car. Issigonis loved driving and he had always been very competitive. This was not just evident in the hard work he put into preparing his own cars for sprints, trials and hill-climbs in his younger days; it was also clear in his normal driving style which all those who remember him describe as being both fast and daring. It characterised the white-knuckle rides he gave the Ransome family round the by-roads of Surrey. It was also there in the friendly sparring on the test track at MIRA with his Alvis colleagues and in his approach to testing the prototype Mosquito and XC/9003.

Given the feel that he had for a car, the much-repeated assertion that Issigonis had never considered the Mini as a competition vehicle is a little surprising. Speaking in a BBC interview he said:

When the Mini was designed and in production I never gave this [competition] one single thought. We were preoccupied in the design in getting good road holding and stability for safety reasons and to give the driver more pleasure, but it never occurred to me that this thing would turn out to be such a fantastic rally car ...

Though Issigonis is not always a reliable witness on these matters Jack Daniels, for one, insists that this was the case:

He never thought about trying that thing as a sports car. That car to us was a bread and butter car, full stop. We hoped and expected to pick up a lot of women as beginner drivers, which we did. We never anticipated the way that the sports version took off and what it was capable of.

Yet the potential was there from the very beginning. The engine had been reduced from 950 cc to 850 cc by Leonard Lord and Sidney Smith because the early performance of the car in testing had frightened them in relation to their target buyer. Trials undertaken by Dunlop in developing the special tyres required for the tiny wheels were also significant. The prototypes were taken on several occasions to the Dunlop test track at Apeney Green where their cornering ability was tested by wetting the road and taking the cars round the bends at speed. The best result which Dunlop had achieved up to that point was with an Aston Martin DB4 which could take the bend at 46 mph. When they tested the Mini, it came impressively close at 44 mph, followed by the Morris Minor, at 42 mph. The cars which the team considered to be their main competition were dismal by comparison. The Citroën clocked up a highest speed of 33 mph, while the rear-engined Renault Dauphine tipped over before it even reached this speed.

The cornering capability of the car was therefore clear but to Issigonis at this point it was all a matter of 'primary safety' for the driver. In his view, the good roadholding provided by front wheel drive was one of the car's biggest assets because it did not require a great deal of skill on the part of the driver. In Issigonis' words:

> There are so many cars on the roads that driving is sheer misery these days. And yet this again is one reason why the Mini has proved such a success. It is small, it is fast and it can be driven safely by the worst driver in the world – who is the chap I had in mind when I designed it anyway. If he can drive safely with the car I have made then I am satisfied. But put a car like that into the hands of an expert, then of course, he's delighted with it.

The experts agreed with him. Amateurs had begun to race and rally the car within weeks of its launch. Almost as quickly, professionals were doing the same. One of the earliest experiments with the Mini was carried out by Daniel Richmond, a talented engineer who ran the 'Downton Engineering Works' which took its name from the small village of Downton near Salisbury in Wiltshire where it was based. The business was a joint venture with his wife Veronica, popularly known as Bunty. She provided the business acumen while Daniel applied his engineering skills to the fine-tuning of engines to extract better performance for competition. As well as tuning cars for an impressive list of important customers, Downton Engineering also prepared its own cars for specific races to enhance the reputation of the company.

Richmond was in his mid-30s with the business well established and his reputation high when the Mini came along, and he was one of the first to see its potential. During the winter of 1959, when Mini sales were still struggling, Richmond created his first 'Downton' conversion from a basic Austin Seven. Professional racing driver Jimmy Blumer was engaged as the pilot and they made their début in May 1960 at the challenging track of Spa Francorchamps in Belgium, taking part in a saloon car race preceding the main 1,000 kilometres event. While the Downton did not finish at the head of the field, it nevertheless made a promising start by beating several other private Mini entrants. It was taken back to Wiltshire for further development and re-emerged for the August Bank Holiday Meeting at Brands Hatch. This time, though he did not win, Jimmy Blumer managed to bring the car home ahead of an official works-team Ford Zephyr in the ten-lap saloon car race. The patriotic crowd were delighted and *Autosport* reported that:

> ... what the crowd loved more than anything was seeing Blumer in the Downton Austin Seven duel with Uren's Ford Zephyr and lead it over the line – you don't need 2½-litres even for racing these days when 850 c.c. and Issigonis suspension will do better! Daniel Richmond claims this Se7en will go from 0 to 100 m.p.h. in 27 seconds.

Ronald Barker, who was motoring correspondent for *The Autocar*, arranged for Issigonis to try out the Downton conversion and it would seem that this lit some spark of interest in its designer who 'behaved like an adolescent, grinning impishly and squirting it in tyre-shredding bursts of acceleration'.

The BMC Competitions Department was not far behind Daniel Richmond in adopting the Mini as part of its armoury. This department had been established at the MG factory in Abingdon in 1955 by John Thornley, who was General Manager of MG Cars and one of the acquaintances whom Alec often met at the Trout. Its brief was not just to run MGs but to use any suitable cars from the entire model range. BMC entered six Minis in the 1960 Monte Carlo rally and the result was respectable if not spectacular, with four cars finishing and a highest placing of 23rd overall. Other rallies were producing similar results. But his experience in the Downton Mini had not yet made a convert of Issigonis. The manager of the Competitions Department, Marcus Chambers, found his attitude to their efforts throughout 1960 dismissive and unhelpful. It was not this, however, which formed the main obstacle in the path of either the privateer racers, Downton Engineering or the BMC works team. Their efforts so far had been more than enough to convince them that the Mini had the potential to be a superb competition vehicle. What hampered them was its lack of power. This is when John Cooper stepped forward to take centre stage and BMC, not renowned for excitement or glamour, became an unlikely beneficiary of the sudden flowering of a British team in the prestigious world of Formula One racing.

JOHN COOPER AND THE COOPER CAR COMPANY

John Cooper had been born in Kingston, Surrey, in 1923 and was therefore some seventeen years younger than Issigonis. His father, Charlie Cooper, ran a small garage in Surbiton which was close enough to the Brooklands circuit to attract distinguished customers like Kaye Don and his racing Wolseley 'Viper'. After the Second World War Charlie was looking for new business opportunities. Impressed by the results that his son and Eric Brandon had been able to achieve with their 'Cooper 500' Special, he decided to set up the Cooper Car Company in 1948 to build a batch of 500 cc racers for sale. Charlie provided the financial acumen, John the engineering know-how, and the venture proved so successful that their business grew into Britain's largest manufacturer of specialist racing cars, paving the way for famous names like Lotus, Lola and March.

The various categories of motor sport were more intermingled in the 1950s than they are today, with teams and drivers not confining themselves to any one formula. The top category was Formula One which since 1954 had been based on unsupercharged engines of up to 2500 cc. In 1958 the Formula One Drivers' Championship was joined for the first time by a Constructors' Championship. In 1957 the Formula Two category was revised to cover cars of up to 1500 cc. Two years later Formula Junior was introduced, based on single-seater cars with production engines up to 1100 cc. This category became the 'nursery' formula for aspiring racing drivers and in 1964 was replaced by Formula Three which retained the production engine rule. Alongside these there were various sports car championships as well.

By the mid-1950s Cooper was running his own works racing team which participated in all of these categories of the sport and at the same time the firm continued to supply cars to other teams. This required custom-made engines so Cooper entered into an alliance with the Coventry

Climax Company as a result of which the cars were run under the name of 'Cooper Climax'. In 1956, Cooper built an innovative rear-engined 1500 cc car which had great success in Formula Two in the hands of his lead driver, the Australian Jack Brabham. With some modifications this car graduated to Formula One the following year when it was raced by Brabham in the 1957 Monaco Grand Prix and ran as high as third before coming home sixth. The Cooper Climax's first victory, however, went to Stirling Moss, driving for the Rob Walker Racing Team, when he won the first race of the 1958 season in Argentina. Before the race, no one believed he had any chance but against all expectations Moss finished 2.7 seconds ahead of a Ferrari which had a much more powerful engine. This was the first time since the era of Auto Union that a rear-engined car had beaten conventional front-engined models. There was even more surprise when Rob Walker's team repeated the feat at the next Grand Prix in Monaco.

The reason for this sudden success lay in the unusual layout of the car. By locating the engine behind the driver with the fuel tanks on either side, weight was shifted to the centre of the car, creating a quality of handling which was noticeably superior to that of the nose-heavy front-engined car. This imaginative layout allowed the little Cooper Climax to have the same power-to-weight ratio as the mighty Ferrari even though it had a smaller engine capacity. The position of the engine also meant that the frontal area and seating position could be adjusted while the elimination of the long heavy driveshaft made it possible to create a more compact, lightweight design with better aerodynamics. The whole package added up to a nimble machine able to beat cars with considerably more horsepower.

Rob Walker's victories in 1958 were merely the prelude to two years of great success for the official Cooper racing team. In 1959, with an upgraded engine, Jack Brabham took the Formula One Drivers' title, the Cooper Racing Team took the Constructors' title and another of the team's drivers, New Zealander Bruce McLaren, became the youngest driver ever to win a Grand Prix at 22 years old. In 1960 the team repeated the feat, this time with Bruce McLaren coming second to his more experienced team mate in the Drivers' Championship. In its early days Formula One had been dominated by German, French and Italian teams and Vanwall was the first British team ever to win the Constructors' title in 1958. The success of Cooper's small Surbiton-based team in winning two successive Drivers' and Constructors' titles in 1959 and 1960 was therefore impressive.

They did not maintain their footing on this pinnacle for long. In 1961 Formula One rules were changed limiting engines to less than 1500 cc, basically meaning that Formula Two became Formula One. More importantly from Cooper's point of view many teams, including Lotus, BRM and Ferrari, began to adopt the rear engine format and spent far more money than was available to him on its development. He also lost the services of Jack Brabham, who had played a key role in engineering as well as driving the car, when he left to set up his own team. These factors helped to bring Cooper's spectacular run at the top of Formula One to an end but his team continued to compete successfully in all categories of motor sport. Moreover Cooper could rightfully claim that his two world championships had revolutionised the design of single-seater racing cars because the concept of the lightweight rear-engined racing car had now become standard.

John Cooper has been described by motor sport historian Doug Nye as 'genial, pipe-smoking, warm-hearted and straight-as-a-gun-barrel'. He got into motor sport for the sheer love of racing but he ended up as an innovative and influential team owner whose name became a powerful international brand. The fact that Cooper pioneered a layout which eventually became the norm in his chosen sphere is an interesting parallel between himself and Issigonis. It was perhaps a mutual appreciation of such independent thinking that brought the two men together as friends in the first place. John Cooper was not convinced by Issigonis' protestations about motor racing: 'Although he made out he wasn't very interested in racing, he loved motor racing really. He probably denied it so that if something didn't work properly he could say I told you so.' Issigonis was interested enough to accept an invitation to drive a Formula One Cooper Climax for a few laps round Silverstone. Their friendship would be a prelude to an even more successful professional relationship between BMC and the Cooper Car Company which benefited them both.

BMC AND COOPER JOIN FORCES

When John Cooper decided to enter the new Formula Junior category he needed an engine utilised by a production car which his current partner, Coventry Climax, could not provide. He therefore approached Issigonis to help him obtain a supply of A-series engines from BMC. Because of the success that Cooper was enjoying in sports cars and Formula Two, BMC agreed that it would be a positive move to be associated with the Cooper name and their reward finally came when Jackie Stewart became the Formula Three Champion in 1964 driving a Cooper with a 1000 cc BMC A-series engine for Ken Tyrell's team. The Cooper–BMC relationship was not always a smooth one, however, despite frequent personal interventions from Issigonis. John Cooper for his part showed considerable tolerance of BMC's lack of professionalism in certain areas.

This is evident in his correspondence with BMC engineer T.G. Bradley during 1959. On 19 October Cooper put in a request for five specially modified 'Sprite' engines to run in his new batch of Formula Junior cars. Quite reasonably he wanted to know both the price and the delivery date so he could plan his competition programme. Initially he was given a delivery period of one month though no price could be quoted. On 17 November Bradley finally quoted a price of £148 per engine as against £75 for the standard unit. Cooper confirmed that he was happy with this as long as the modified engines could provide the extra power and reliability he was looking for. Now he had a price he ordered a further 30 engines which BMC undertook to deliver at the rate of one per week. On 2 December BMC requested that Cooper increase the order from 35 to 50 for reasons of 'practicality of manufacture', which Cooper agreed to do. On 10 May 1960, however, Bill Appleby, BMC's leading engine designer, sent Issigonis a copy of the breakdown of costs undertaken by Morris Engines in Coventry which showed that the price quoted to Cooper had been vastly underestimated and that £148 was virtually cost price. His note commented: 'It looks as though J. Cooper will have to pay at least £200 per unit.' Issigonis sent this information on to Bradley, stating rather waspishly:

With regard to your communications with Mr J Cooper re. the supply and cost of racing engines, I have this morning received the attached bombshell from Mr. Appleby which indicates that the expected price of these engines is well outside a figure you may have quoted to Mr. Cooper earlier. Would you please take the matter of economics up with Coventry to see what can be done about price readjustment, bearing in mind that the project has B.M.C. advertising value when it gets under way.

Issigonis was clearly annoyed to find his friend being treated with such carelessness. He was also displaying a surprising grasp of the public relations benefits of participation in motor racing. On 16 May Bradley defensively countered with the thin excuse that after delivery of the first order for five engines Cooper had changed his requirement from 70 bhp to 85 bhp and he quoted an increased price of £188. Unfortunately the correspondence ends here, but presumably this was not good news either for Cooper, who would have to make significant adjustments to his budget, or for BMC who were probably still making little profit on the deal.

ADO 50

The beginning of Cooper's association with BMC coincided with the development of ADO 15. During a visit to Longbridge in 1958 Issigonis showed him one of the pre-production cars which were going through their final testing phase. Cooper was sceptical about the car's appearance but when he tried it out he was immediately won over by its driveability. He persuaded Issigonis to lend him an early model to take to the Italian Grand Prix at Monza in September 1959 where he was spotted driving it around the paddock by his old friend Aurelio Lampredi, Chief Engineer for Fiat and formerly for Ferrari. Lampredi quizzed Cooper:

'What have you got there?'

'It's the new Austin Seven', Cooper replied.

'Let me try it', Lampredi responded and Cooper handed him the keys.

Lampredi was gone for so long that Cooper began to worry that he had crashed and started to wonder how he was going to explain this to BMC. To Cooper's relief, the Italian finally reappeared and as he jumped out of the car, he said:

'John, this is the car of the future. If it wasn't so damned ugly I'd shoot myself!'

Cooper was impressed, concluding that if a racing engineer like Lampredi thought so highly of the feel and handling of the car, then it must be pretty good.

By the end of 1960, Lampredi's verdict was being confirmed by the drivers in the Formula One paddock who began to buy and modify Minis for their own use. Among its new fans were Cooper's own drivers Jack Brabham, Bruce McLaren and Roy Salvadori. This prompted him to pay a visit to Longbridge and Issigonis recounted the conversation that they had in his BBC interview:

'This little family car that you've designed is fantastic', Cooper told him.

'But why is it fantastic?' Issigonis replied with rather uncharacteristic modesty.

'Have you taken it round a racing circuit?'

'No, should I have done? It's a people's car, I built it for them to go shopping and on holiday. I designed it for the district nurse really you know.'

'So why did you make it handle so well?'

'So that they were comfortable driving, so that they felt happy driving the car.'

'You haven't built a people's car, you've built a racing car! We ought to build some of these for the boys, you know a little bit better, bit more steam, better brakes and better finish inside.'

Finally John Cooper got the response he was looking for:

'Well, let's go and see the headmaster.'

It was George Harriman rather than Leonard Lord who agreed to let John Cooper take the car away and experiment with it. He got down to work with his trusted engineer Michael 'Ginger' Devlin and together they fitted it with the 997 cc A-Series engine they were using in their Formula Junior car. Cooper persuaded another friend, Jack Emmot of Lockheed, to supply some disc brakes to improve the car's stopping power and finally a remote gear shift was added. Issigonis was not prepared to let these modifications go ahead completely unchallenged and implied that they would not work properly with front wheel drive. To convince him Cooper arranged a visit to Silverstone on one of the gloomy, damp days so characteristic of the Midlands racetrack and Issigonis tried out for himself the modified Mini alongside a standard model. When he discovered that Cooper's version was two seconds a lap quicker he gave in gracefully.

Cooper took the car back to Harriman and invited him to drive it round the environs of Longbridge. At the time of this encounter Harriman was still concerned about the difficulties which BMC had initially experienced in trying to market the Mini. So while he could see the potential of a souped up version in boosting sales generally, his enthusiasm waned when he heard that the company would have to make at least a thousand in order to get them homologated for racing. To qualify for any competition formula which was based on the use of a production car rather than a purpose-built racing machine, the sporting rules stated that the manufacturer must produce and distribute a minimum number of cars to the same specification for purchase by the general public. An RAC committee would certify that this was indeed the case before the model would be allowed to compete. This was the process known as homologation. Harriman was doubtful that BMC could sell this many cars and it took all Cooper's powers of persuasion to change his mind. Finally, the two men agreed on a deal. The car would take Cooper's name, thus associating it in people's minds with the successful Cooper Racing Team. In return for lending his name and assisting with development he would get a royalty of £2 per car. The prestige of that name was so powerful that neither party saw any need to put the deal into writing.

The new version was given the codename ADO 50 while it was under development and Chris Kingham was one of the first to drive it on trade plates. It looked just like any other Mini, the only clue to its superior performance being the fact that, like many of its successors, it was painted red. Kingham described it as 'a wolf in sheep's clothing'. On a trip to the London Motor Show, Kingham drove ADO 50, accompanied by Jack Daniels in a standard Mini. Their excursion prompted an irate letter to Leonard Lord from an observer *en route* asking: 'Is it customary for cars on trade plates and delivery to be driven at above 80 miles an hour?'

Issigonis took a close interest in the details of the development of ADO 50, which was unusual since he preferred to concentrate his efforts on new ideas. The correspondence between BMC and the Cooper Car Company shows just how closely involved he was in the forging of this relationship but, as in the case of the supply of the Formula Junior engines, the progress of events was not always a credit to BMC.

The first note relating to the building of three experimental ADO 50 cars was sent out in October 1960. Issigonis issued a memorandum on 2 November stating the specification, which would be the same as that devised by John Cooper, namely the fitting of a 997 cc Formula Junior engine, a remote gear-change and front disc brakes. He noted that Dunlop had agreed to supply special nylon cord tubeless tyres to allow for the greater speeds the car was likely to reach. He ended with the comment that:

A small quantity production of around twenty cars per week is envisaged for some time in March 1961. A prototype built to the finalised drawing office specification is to be built as soon as possible and a cost estimate to be prepared as soon as possible.

Jack Daniels was put in charge of building the three prototypes. Issigonis himself did considerable testing mileage during which he was impressed by the way the suspension coped with the increased power, requiring very little modification. Using the results of the early tests, Daniels and his team began to prepare proper production drawings but on 16 December BMC's Chief Buyer, J. A. Greatorex, wrote to Works Manager W. H. Davis:

> I am raising the ADO 50 project with you because I have been told that it is expected to commence production on a programme figure of 20 per week in March, which will mean obtaining supplies from outside sources in February. Owing to the fact that the project has not yet been authorised no action whatsoever can be taken in either ordering tools or supplies at the present time and unless something is done fairly quickly there will only be a very slim chance of doing anything to meet such a target.

Davis entered into some discussion with Issigonis about the details of the new car and suggested to him that June was the earliest they were likely to be able to produce it at a rate of 20 to 25 vehicles per week. Progress was further slowed when Sidney Smith intervened on 24 January, stating that the car, so far designated as being within the Austin range, should be produced as both an Austin and a Morris, with a split of two to one in favour of Austin. This raised the question of designing different grilles and badges for the two versions, which of course increased the tooling costs. As a result the June date began to slip away as well. In March 1961 an urgent request was made to Dick Burzi for information on paint and trim colours and on 24 April Jack Daniels sent Bill Appleby a similarly urgent memo stating: 'ADO 50 as we understand is scheduled for announcement in June 1961 and as yet no Pilot vehicles have been produced as a check on the production drawings ...' (underlining by Daniels). On 1 May he received a barbed reply from Chief Car Designer C.G.R. Benbow that:

> ... as mentioned in your memo of the 24th April it is quite true that we have been compelled by circumstances to issue Production Drawings before we have proven Production Build. This is something

which we frequently have to do when we have insufficient time at our disposal.

In the absence of any pre-production vehicles to check, Daniels had to carry on testing the prototypes and he reported in June that he expected ADO 50 to achieve a top speed of 93 mph. There was something else which Issigonis was anxious to test. It was not just customers' feet that had suffered from the ingress of water through the floor of the early production Minis. The design of the engine compartment had also caused the electrics to drown in heavy rain. He therefore instructed Cell A to undertake some water testing and on 19 May Daniels sent Issigonis a memo directly:

We have, as requested, squirted water through a hose at the distributor of our ADO 50 vehicle which is currently fitted with a plastic cover of the type Mr. Appleby proposes for production. During this check the engine did not miss a beat even though the cover HT leads etc. were smothered with water.

Time was now getting short. Though it was clear that the date of June 1961 for production to commence was not going to be met, it was too late to cancel the press demonstration which was scheduled for 17 July. On 15 June, W. H. Davis reported to T. G. Bradley the outcome of a policy meeting at which it had been decided that 'it was essential' for 50 Morris and 50 Austin cars to be supplied for this event, including some left-hand-drive models to cater for the foreign press. He then referred Bradley on: 'As I understand the arrangements for this demonstration are being made by Mr. Issigonis will you please make contact with him for the necessary information.' It would seem that neither the publicity department nor the senior management were aware of the technical status of the project or they would not have made such a decision. The unfortunate Mr Bradley would probably have needed medical attention if he had seen the note Issigonis nonchalantly wrote on the bottom of the Davis memo – 'only ten cars received for demonstration day'.

Issigonis tried to soften the news that only 10 per cent of the cars required were actually ready when he wrote directly to Davis on 20 June, pretending that the shortfall was actually all part of the plan:

In reply to your memorandum of 15 June we have decided that we shall only need ten ADO 50 cars for demonstration purposes on the 17 July (five Morris and five Austin), which will very much simplify your problem of meeting the requirements for this date. As you probably know, the vehicle will not be released until some unspecified time after this meeting, the date being dependent upon the time taken by Production to build up adequate stocks.

Despite the fact that no production date had even been set, the necessary forms were completed for homologation as required by the RAC on 3 July. BMC sensibly decided to hold the press event at the scene of the original Mini launch at Chobham where journalists would be invited to drive four laps on the high speed circuit. Issigonis was the guest of honour and he also presided over the pre-launch dinner which was held at Kensington Palace Hotel on 16 July. Here he gave a speech to the expectant guests which gave no hint of the frenzied attempts to prepare for the day:

> About a year ago my old friend John Cooper, who is an enthusiastic user of the ADO 15, suggested to me that B.M.C. ought to produce a sports version of this car. I thought it was a good idea and oddly enough so did the Management ...

The journalists were joined by many of the era's most famous racing drivers, some of whom had helped to bring this new model into being. The guest list contained the names of 27 Grand Prix drivers including Jack Brabham, Bruce McLaren, Graham Hill, Innes Ireland, Phil Hill, Wolfgang von Trips, Joachim Bonnier, Dan Gurney, Stirling Moss, John Surtees, Roy Salvadori and Mike Parkes. There was no sign of panic or stress on Issigonis' face as he was photographed in their midst, smiling broadly with a glass of gin and french in hand. On the contrary, it was a very sweet moment as far as he was concerned. The fame conferred on him by the Mini meant that the young man who had stood in the rain by the side of the track at the Nürburgring in 1935 to watch the genius of Nuvolari from a distance was now able to bask in the praise of the best racing drivers of the day.

BMC had managed to meet its deadline for the launch but it was another two months before 400 cars had actually been manufactured and were available for sale. Only then did they feel able to officially announce the Mini Cooper in a press statement issued on 20 September. Finally, the cars were on sale. Was this the end of their problems? Of course not. A mass of internal correspondence shows that there was considerable concern about the performance of the brakes, not to mention difficulties with the tyres, and a great deal more work had to go into making modifications in these areas in the few months left before the start of the new racing season.

MINI COOPER STARTS TO WIN

Despite the backroom drama, the arrival of the Mini Cooper was a turning point in the Mini's career as a competition vehicle. Its launch in 1961 coincided with the appointment of Stuart Turner as BMC Competitions Manager and this would mark the start of a period of unprecedented success for the works team in international motor sport. Turner was only in his late 20s when he came to Abingdon while most of his new colleagues were in their late 40s and 50s but he found a department which had an air of excitement about it, associated with the aura of the MG marque and staffed with veteran enthusiasts such as the Chief Inspector of Vehicles who had once been Nuvolari's riding-mechanic. By the start of the 1962 motor sport season the most significant shortcomings of the Mini Cooper had finally been resolved and it was possible to embark on a proper racing programme. There was to be a two-prong strategy with the BMC Competitions Department running the rallying programme while the Cooper Car Company ran a team of Mini Coopers in track events. Both began to clock up victories straight away. Pat Moss, sister of Stirling Moss and a leading BMC driver, gained the first overall win at the Dutch Tulip Rally in May 1962. John Love followed this on the track by winning the British Racing and Sports Car Club (BRSCC) National Saloon Car Championship in September 1962.

Issigonis took full advantage of these developments. In the summer of 1963 Paddy Hopkirk was competing in the Tour de France, a motoring event which took place over several days on public roads ending in Monte Carlo (though it should not be confused with the Monte Carlo Rally). On the Friday of this event BBC journalist Cliff Michelmore recorded a television interview with Issigonis in Oxford and over lunch at the Trout made a casual remark along the lines that 'BMC were going to win, it was sticking out a mile'. A little surprised, Issigonis phoned Tony Dawson and asked him to find out the race positions. When

Dawson confirmed that Paddy Hopkirk was leading under the handicap system, Alec replied: 'Quick, make arrangements, we're going to fly out tonight …' Dawson collected a car from the Cowley factory and picked Issigonis up at eleven at night. After spending some time persuading British Airways to charge their tickets to BMC they made for the airport bank to try to get some money for their trip.

'I can let you have five pounds, sir', said the bank clerk, referring to those restrictions on taking currency abroad which always seemed to cause Issigonis such trouble.

'Five pounds?' retorted Issigonis – 'there are two of us!'

'Well in the circumstances I'll make it ten pounds. May I have your passports?' replied the clerk officiously. When Alec pushed his passport through the window the clerk picked it up and the name registered immediately.

'Issigonis? Are you the man that made my Mini?'

'Well', Issigonis dissembled, 'I had something to do with it you know.'

'Let's make it twenty-five pounds', said the clerk with a wink.

This was Dawson's first trip to Monte Carlo so Issigonis was able to play the hardened traveller to his innocent abroad. Next morning they met up in the bar of the Hôtel de Paris where they were staying. As a regular guest, Issigonis was served with his 'usual' drink, a dry martini, no questions necessary. Dawson made the mistake of asking for a gin and tonic. Several drinks later Dawson asked for the bill and discovered he was being charged seventeen shillings just for the tonic. Issigonis, who had known this all along, simply said, 'That will teach you to drink these barbarous drinks.' By now well oiled, they went outside to sit on the steps and watch the last stage of the Tour de France as the cars came into view on Monte Carlo's narrow streets. When Paddy Hopkirk's Mini Cooper appeared at the bottom of the hill Issigonis started to jump up and down in excitement, shouting 'slow down Paddy, slow down', because Hopkirk was dangerously close to the rear bumper of a Jaguar and did not need to finish first to win the stage under the handicap system. Though he could not hear it, he heeded Alec's advice and stayed out of trouble to give BMC victory.

BMC was now ready for an assault on one of the premier events of the sporting year, the Monte Carlo Rally itself. This was held every January and was the only event on the calendar which took place in the depths of winter. Cars set off from different starting points all over

Europe. After two days' hard driving through ice and snow, the competitors would converge in France to follow a common route to the capital of the little principality. Although other rallies offered even tougher driving conditions, none of them were as glamorous or high-profile as Monte Carlo. Their best result so far was in 1963 when Rauno Aaltonen and Paddy Hopkirk had finished third and fourth. The introduction of the Mini Cooper 'S' version in April 1963, with its uprated 1071 cc engine, was a pivotal moment. It led to victory in the European Touring Car Championship for Warwick Banks and the first outright Monte Carlo victory for Paddy Hopkirk in 1964.

With these results to back him up John Cooper began to urge BMC to develop the Mini Cooper even more. 'We've proved this car can win', he insisted. 'Now let's build a real one.' He was invited to attend a BMC Board meeting at Longbridge where he argued that the company should build a 1275 cc 'S' specifically with rallying in mind. He tempted them with the thought that only increased power would allow them to continue beating their arch-rivals Ford. Again he met with resistance. The BMC directors were adamant that this could not be done. Harriman insisted that it would be too expensive to alter the boring machines to produce a 1275 cc specification. Others felt this was a step too far with a power unit which had, after all, been designed to provide only 803 cc. Cooper argued that he had already achieved this specification with the Formula Junior engines which BMC were supplying him with. At the end of the meeting he turned to go, convinced he had lost the argument. As he reached the door Harriman called after him, 'We're bloody well going to do it though …'

BMC decided to tailor their effort more exactly to the requirements of the different racing categories by replacing the single 1071 cc Mini Cooper 'S' with two new versions. The 970 cc version was to be continued for those racing in 1000 cc class races. The 1275 cc version which John Cooper had persuaded them to develop would dominate the rallying scene. Though this was a sensible commercial decision, once again BMC's inexperience led them into deep trouble over homologation requirements. They obtained homologation certificates for both versions of the engine early in the year so that BMC could plan a full programme of rallying and the Cooper Car Company could enter both the British and European saloon car championships. It would appear, however, that BMC were not being entirely truthful about production of the less powerful car. In April Mr H. T. Goodwin, an Assistant Distribution Supervisor for Austin, wrote to one of the dealerships concerning an order for a batch of 970 cc Coopers. They were informed that, because of the demand for the 1275 cc version, it would be several weeks before the smaller-engined car would be available, but delivery was promised for the end of May.

But when May came he wrote again suggesting that the customer might like to switch his order to a 1275 cc model:

The difficulty with which we are confronted here is the fact that we have so far not received any 970 cc engines at all and, in a telephone conversation with our Production Manager yesterday afternoon it was suggested that we could invoice this particular car for production on the week ending 27th June and by virtue of the fact that this is the first car of its type to be produced there may be an additional delay.

The news about lack of production – which meant that technically the homologation was invalid – reached Issigonis, who asked W. H. Davis what was going on. Davis revealed that not only was production low, at around 25 per week, but no effort was being made to increase it because orders were even lower at only around five per week.

Issigonis responded immediately, identifying BMC's Director of Home Sales as the culprit for not fulfilling his promise to place the required number of cars with dealers:

Ring Mr. Sangster. If he does not order 500 as promised our homologation will fail and we will be deprived of the European Championship. This is very serious.

The problem did not appear to be solved, however, and in August John Thornley was given some extremely worrying news. He received a letter from John Gott who was Acting Chairman of the RAC Competitions Committee and Chief Constable of Northamptonshire. The two men knew each other because Gott had also been captain of the BMC rally team between 1955 and 1961. The contents of his letter were therefore extremely embarrassing for John Thornley since Gott had tried to order one of the elusive cars for an event at the Nürburgring in September and Longbridge had failed to deliver either the car or an explanation.

Even worse, Gott had got hold of the damning letter by Goodwin

which stated in black and white that no 970 cc cars had yet been manufactured. He sent a copy to Thornley who was livid and told Issigonis to
get the whole thing sorted out. Issigonis in turn ordered the distributors
to get the cars into the dealer showrooms as soon as possible. This finally
appeared to do the trick and Gott wrote again, rather more reassuringly,
on 2 September commenting approvingly on the large number of 970 cc
Coopers which had suddenly appeared in the showrooms. He also urged
that no blame should be attached to the unfortunate Mr Goodwin:

> I do not think Mr. Goodwin should be blamed, for he almost certainly
> would not appreciate the position in which his completely factual and
> quite accurate letter put us all. Fortunately, owing to your hard work,
> I think we shall now get by without any trouble and the only 'snag' is
> that I shall not be at the 'Ring this weekend and so will miss what
> promises to be a very pleasant party with Alec and the boys!

Thornley had the last word, writing to Issigonis on 7 September:

> I think we must agree that everything has now been done which can
> be done to salvage the situation created by the premature homologa-
> tion of this car. It remains, however, to safeguard the future. The short
> answer is, of course, that we must not do it again. This, it would seem
> to me, is the only way in an organization of this kind to stop poten-
> tially damaging communications getting out.

Putting such embarrassments on one side, from 1964 onwards the racing
and rallying programmes became an irresistible force. The Competitions
Department continued to run its own rally team, and in addition BMC
decided to officially sponsor the Cooper Car Company's racing programme. Between 1964 and 1966 they contributed £10,000 per year to
prepare entries in the BRSCC Championship with a further arrangement of £750 for each car entered in continental events such as the Spa
24 hours. On a summary of 1964 entries Issigonis wrote against the
BRSCC results – 'lost' – and added the comment: 'drivers – none left
unless we pay like Ford'. By the end of 1964 BMC were asking Cooper
to consider employing more 'drivers of world class calibre', even implying
that they were willing to contribute to the costs of doing so.

Meanwhile Downton Engineering continued to do the tuning work while Dunlop supplied the tyres. Once the Cooper versions came along Daniel Richmond was well placed to play an enthusiastic part in developing and tuning the engines and the Downton Mini was used as a test bed for the early Cooper power units. The reward for his efforts was a consultancy agreement which was formalised in May 1962. The conditions of Richmond's relationship with BMC were rather more stringent than those applying to the Cooper–Harriman 'handshake' but at least in his case there was no chance of misunderstandings. Downton Engineering was appointed to advise 'on such matters concerning the development of performance in production, competition and racing engines as may be referred to them with effect from 1st April 1962', on the understanding that they would not seek any publicity from the relationship. In return they received an annual fee of £2,500 plus the costs of any manufacturing work. They had to agree not to undertake any similar work for another motor manufacturer but they were free to take on private customers. This they did, becoming specialists in engine conversions to order. BMC often supplied them with cars direct from the Longbridge factory at the request of various celebrities. Among their customers were illustrious names such as the Aga Khan, Steve McQueen, Dan Gurney and Lord Snowdon. In 1964 Issigonis made his own request for a special Mini Cooper S to be prepared for delivery to Maranello and on his next visit he and Enzo Ferrari were photographed in front of the car.

By 1965 Mini Coopers were appearing at every rally and track event. The official entries of the BMC works team, John Cooper and Downton Engineering were joined by a host of private entries from amateur motor sport enthusiasts who had adopted the Mini as their car of preference like the Austin Seven before it. Alec Issigonis, John Cooper, Stuart Turner and Daniel Richmond formed an effective development team who regularly met together with George Harriman, Alex Moulton and Charles Griffin, often at a hotel or restaurant rather than some stuffy Kremlin office, to make their plans.

Despite his insistence that motor sport did not interest him, Issigonis' competitive nature meant that, once he was convinced of the case, he took the whole enterprise very seriously, saying: 'If you go in for any kind of competition it is a complete waste of time unless you win.' He gave his unconditional support to John Cooper and Stuart Turner and he also took a personal interest in the progress of the works team. It was Stuart Turner's job to visit Longbridge every month to ensure that the specification of the production cars matched the sporting regulations. On one of these visits in October 1963, armed with a list of requirements that were needed in order to prepare the cars for what would be the successful 1964 Monte Carlo campaign, he observed the way BMC's Technical Director operated:

> Alec was buzzing people in, and people were running, literally, in and out, and – get this done, and can you fix this for Stuart, and Paddy Hopkirk wants this, whatever – and I checked with his secretary as I left and some of these people were extremely senior engineers but the way he treated them, you certainly didn't get the impression they were. I got the feeling at the time that if I'd gone up there and said, I'm sorry Alec but the competition team have decided we've got to have purple striped rear windows on every Mini that's ever sold, he'd have said 'yes dear boy, yes' and someone would have been buzzed in and purple striped rear windows would have been put in every Mini ever sold.

Such a comfortable relationship could lead to complacency and in 1965 John Cooper got a little overconfident. On 2 November he wrote jauntily to George Harriman, liberally quoting the name of his good friend Issigonis, about a more luxurious Mini Cooper which he was intending to market:

> Dear Sir George, Alec has suggested that I write to you concerning a Mini-Cooper we had trimmed out to the order of one of our customers. The customer wanted something similar to the job done by Harold Radford with certain of his own ideas incorporated. The job was eventually done by Bertone, to the customer's entire satisfaction. As a result of this, we have received several enquiries from certain of our special customers to have their cars similarly treated. The cost is in the region of £400. Isn't it amazing what some people will spend on extras on the Mini?! I am enclosing a few photographs for you to see what the thing looks like. I feel sure they will amuse you.

Far from being amused Harriman was furious with both Cooper and Issigonis and he made the latter sign his name to a reply which was rather less casually friendly:

We are sure you will appreciate that the name of the Cooper Car Company Limited is closely associated in the public mind with that of the British Motor Corporation and that any model marketed under the auspices of the Cooper Car Company might well be assumed to have had the approval of the Corporation. For this reason we cannot give this approval and we must ask that you abandon this contemplated model which you intended to market under your name. We regret having to write in this tenor but we are sure you will appreciate the damage which will be caused to our marketing policies should the Cooper Car Company, or its associates, participate in a venture of this or similar nature.

This final version was mild compared with the draft, which had accused Cooper of acting in a way which 'is not within the spirit of our mutual arrangements'. John Cooper's father, Charlie, had died in October 1964 and the following April the Cooper Car Company had entered into a merger with the Chipstead Group to cover the death duties. The response to BMC's ultimatum therefore came not from John Cooper, who had written the original letter, but from Jonathan Sieff who was the new Chairman. He was desperate to mollify BMC and suggested that:

... these misunderstandings have been, in the main, due to lack of communication between us and I am most anxious that these should be resolved ... At the Cooper Car Company we value most highly the prestige of our association with the British Motor Corporation and would be most unhappy to do anything that might jeopardise it.

Issigonis, despite the telling-off he had received from Harriman, would seem to have been more sympathetic to Cooper's point of view than BMC's. He suggested to Harriman that the root of the problem was that BMC were not giving sufficient recognition to the commercial value they gained from the use of the Cooper brand. Cooper's scheme had been an attempt to compensate for the income he felt he was losing by allowing BMC to exploit his name. Issigonis even went so far as to suggest a long list of possible solutions. These included the creation of a special Mini which the Cooper Car Company would be allowed to make exclusively; the offer of a dealership; permission for them to undertake engine development; increased royalties past and future including a five-year account with advance payments; and finally, the loan of a second mortgage. None of these options appear to have been taken up but the two companies did settle their differences early in 1966.

This incident is interesting for two reasons. First it shows that Issigonis was capable of over-reaching himself. Equally it demonstrates that when he put his mind to it, he possessed considerably more commercial awareness than his business-minded colleagues. He was quite right when he pointed out that they were guilty of grossly underestimating the value of the 'Cooper' name, which carried far more prestige than that of BMC. It was entirely logical to urge them to be rather more generous in acknowledging that this was the case.

ENJOYING SUCCESS

The Mini Cooper phenomenon provided Alec with some welcome relief from his increasingly burdensome work routine. He would not have been human if he had not been flattered by the car's success and by the personal adulation which it brought him. He even seemed to have forgotten who he had designed the car for when he remarked, '… the Chief of Sales said the Mini would make a good district nurse's car! I say Monte Carlo to you!' He followed each sporting event eagerly, sent the drivers a telegram of congratulation after every triumph and travelled out to Monaco every January to luxuriate in the glamour and the glory of the Monte Carlo victories. As Hopkirk said:

It was nicer to finish at Monte Carlo in the middle of winter than some god-forsaken place and it wasn't just the car, it was the whole team, the effort. It was like being a part of show-business.

Issigonis and Tony Dawson were with Stuart Turner when they heard the news of the first victory in 1964 and Turner described their feelings: 'We sat there, we didn't even talk, there was just a feeling of bloody marvellous and it was marvellous.' Then they went to dinner at the Hôtel de Paris with Paddy Hopkirk, Joe Bonnier and Juan Manuel Fangio. The victories meant that the drivers shone, the works team shone, the car itself shone, and the glory reflected back as much onto its designer as onto BMC itself. Before long Issigonis began to receive telegrams and letters congratulating him as if the victory was his own individual achievement. Former BMC driver Nancy Mitchell wrote on 27 January 1964:

My dear Alec, what a simply splendid win it was. Such a small car <u>and</u> British too. The fact that it was your 'baby' must make you a very proud man indeed – and justly too.

For BMC the most positive benefit was increased sales, some compensation for the losses incurred by ADO 15's expensive development programme. Ironically it was countries such as France that reacted most positively to these competition successes and sales took off abroad long before the trend took hold in Britain. Paddy Hopkirk recounted to *Autosport* in 1979:

The first time that I drove that car was the Tour de France in 1963 where, with the handicap system, we led the damn thing. It was on television in France for about 20 minutes every day and I was beating the big Ford Falcons on all the circuits. The French went mad about it and the French dealers all started ordering more Minis. I think it was the first time that BMC realised the potential of the publicity value of motor-sport. After that the car became very fashionable. I mean, it was more impressive to pick your girlfriend up in Paris in a Mini than in an E-type Jag!

In 1964 James Bramley commissioned a report on what impact, if any, the first Monte Carlo victory had had on BMC sales of both the Mini and the 1100. A questionnaire was sent to distributors in the seven main European markets – Austria, Belgium, Denmark, France, Holland, Sweden and Switzerland. Some were doubtful that the rally victory had produced any positive impact but the Belgian and French distributors were certain that it had, one declaring that 'the difference in sales was very apparent following publicity after the Rally'. The report concluded that, compared with the first quarter of 1963, sales for the same period in 1964 were up 53 per cent for the Mini and 35 per cent for the 1100. There was a more direct benefit in the shape of the profitable Special Tuning Department which grew up at Abingdon, marketing engine tuning kits, developed by Downton, along with other racing parts to private owners.

Paddy Hopkirk's winning car hit the front pages of every British newspaper and was photographed in Paris with the Beatles before being shipped back to Britain to appear on the peak-time TV programme

Sunday Night at the London Palladium. On the stage, it was the star of the show, hoisted onto a fixed podium with the drivers by its side. A second platform revolved around it carrying a troupe of Tiller Girls alongside superstars of the day such as host Bruce Forsyth, comedian Tommy Cooper and singer Kathy Kirby. In front of the stage the orchestra played with enthusiasm and the audience stood up to sing 'Rule Britannia' at the tops of their voices. In 1965 Timo Makinen repeated Paddy Hopkirk's feat with another victory and the celebrations reached an even higher pitch. Sergio Pininfarina and Renzo Carli sent a telegram from Turin:

MR ALEC ISSIGONIS WILL YOU ACCEPT OUR ENTHU-SIASTIC CONGRATULATIONS FOR GREAT SUCCESS OBTAINED AT MONTECARLO RALLY STOP THIS VICTORY PUTS INTO RESULT ONCE MORE THE EXCELLENT PERFORMANCE OF YOUR CARS ALREADY FAMOUS ALL OVER THE WORLD STOP BEST WISHES FOR A MORE AND MORE SUCCESSFUL FUTURE

In 1966, however, BMC was robbed of its best ever result, a 1-2-3 for Timo Makinen, Rauno Aaltonen and Paddy Hopkirk. The Mini Coopers were controversially disqualified amid accusations that the lighting was illegal. The British press and public were convinced that the French authorities, jealous of the success of the little British giant-killer, had trumped up the charge to allow a French Citroën to triumph. At his hotel Issigonis received the following telegram:

EVERYONE KNOWS YOU WON EVEN IF THE PRESIDENT STILL DRIVE IN A CITROEN YOUR HUMBLE ADMIRER PETER USTINOV.

Despite the initial disappointment of the disqualification, the actions of the French authorities proved to be an own goal. The declared winner, Toivonen, accepted his prize unenthusiastically, talking of 'a hollow victory'. Dawson had already arranged for the winning car to appear at the Palladium like its two predecessors but when a rather self-satisfied French journalist told him what had happened he picked up the phone to cancel the aeroplane he had chartered to take the cars back and returned to his hotel to console himself with a large quantity of gin. On Sunday morning he woke up with a terrible headache, only to get a call from his office:

'They want to know what time you can get the car to the London Palladium', his secretary told him.

'Don't they know, we've been disqualified, we didn't win', Dawson replied incredulously. With his head pounding he rang the producer of the programme to find out what was going on:

'What the hell are you talking about, we've been disqualified', he said.

'I know', replied the producer, 'it's bloody marvellous, when can we have the car?'

Thinking quickly Dawson replied, 'Well we were first, second and third, would you like all three?'

'Oh yes please.'

After reaching for the aspirin, Dawson got busy, first re-booking the aeroplane, then calling up some contacts at the Metropolitan police. The plane arrived at London airport to be greeted by a crush of television cameras and the cars travelled in style with a full police escort through the traffic to the theatre. Comedian Jimmy Tarbuck introduced the show with the words:

Ladies and gentlemen, we have brought you many famous people at the London Palladium, stars of stage and screen, but tonight we are bringing you something you have never seen before. The *real* winners of the Monte Carlo Rally ...

The curtain was raised to reveal the three Minis driving in a circle in pitch darkness with just their 'illegal' lamps shining. The audience went wild and gave them a standing ovation of the type usually reserved for royalty and the taciturn driver of the winning vehicle, Timo Makinen, joined Tarbuck on the stage. 'Did you really need those lights?' he asked, and the cheering grew even louder when Makinen replied, 'I could have won it with a bunch of glow-worms on the front!'

An event such as this showed off all of Dawson's skills – planning on the hoof, arranging things with flair and worrying about the cost afterwards. BMC expected him to deliver such spectacular publicity coups and did not bother him with constraints such as pre-approved budgets or project planning. Though this was not sensible long-term business practice in this particular instance it was spectacularly successful because BMC could never have spent enough to buy publicity like this.

The following year the BMC works team returned to Monte Carlo in the hope of taking revenge. Immediately after the event it seemed that they had failed. Once again there was confusion surrounding the result, though in this case there was no suggestion of disqualification. The times, however, were so close that it took all night for the authorities to decide who had won and the BMC contingent went to bed convinced that it was not them. It was therefore even more pleasurable when the announcement was made next afternoon that victory was indeed theirs. They considered this the perfect riposte to 1966, but they also knew that the dominance of the Mini was over and this would prove to be the last Monte Carlo victory for the team. Issigonis phoned Harriman from his hotel with the news and received back the following telegram:

WELL DONE PLEASE CONGRATULATE AALTONEN AND PARTNER STOP DID YOU SAY DRY MARTINI BEST WISHES TO ALL REGARDS HARRIMAN

This reflected glory would become very important when Alec's place in the light came under threat, an event which was looming well onto the horizon by 1967 when the Mini Cooper took its fourth successive triumph in the most famous rally in the world.

BRITISH LEYLAND

CHAPTER 9

It's the chaps who dedicate themselves to making a rear-view mirror that works that matter, not the fellow with the grand concept.

Lord Stokes

BMC Reach the End of the Road

Throughout Issigonis' career he had enjoyed support at the very highest levels to pursue his individualistic methods and he had received nothing but praise for his efforts. Where opposition and hostility did exist, whether from Lord Nuffield or from BMC production engineers and sales executives, he was shielded from it and could take the lofty stance that the results had proved him, and not them, correct. In the post-Mini era his position gathered an unhealthy aura of deference and untouchability. The vision which created ADO 15 and ADO 16 had brought with it great credit, and his grasp of good public relations was possibly more sophisticated than that of many of his colleagues, even those in the press office. Against this, his resistance to specific changes on the Mini, his guidance of the ADO 17 project, his disinterest in significant parts of the model programme, all contributed to BMC's problems and this was compounded by the fact that no one was prepared to challenge his judgement. This applied most of all to Sir George Harriman who failed to provide overall direction to BMC's top management team. Morris Motors, particularly Miles Thomas and Vic Oak, managed Issigonis more cleverly and therefore harnessed his potential to greater effect than the British Motor Corporation was ever able to do. His astonishing autonomy is well illustrated in a story told by Stuart Turner shortly after the launch of the 1800. As he chatted to a sales director one day on the pathway between the Kremlin and the Design Centre their conversation turned to the rally programme:

'Paddy's very keen to borrow an Austin 1800 to try on a rally.'

'Oh, good', replied the director. 'Anything you can do to get Alec to alter the position of the handbrake, you really would do us a favour.'

Taken aback, Turner pointed towards the office window of Issigonis,

CHART 1: HISTORICAL DEVELOPMENT OF THE COMPANIES
WHICH FORMED BRITISH LEYLAND 1895-1968

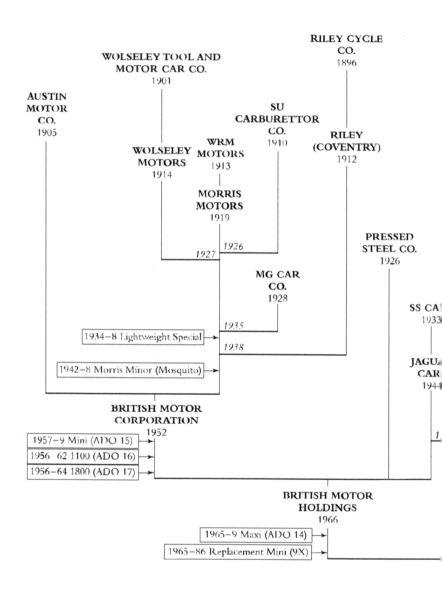

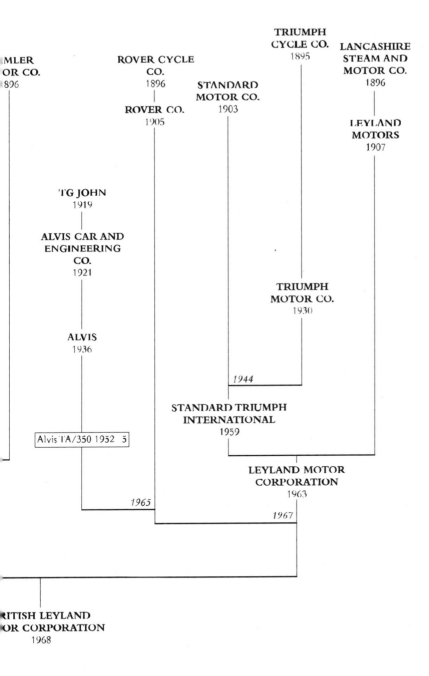

MLER
OR CO.
896

ROVER CYCLE
CO.
1896

ROVER CO.
1905

STANDARD
MOTOR CO.
1903

TRIUMPH
CYCLE CO.
1895

LANCASHIRE
STEAM AND
MOTOR CO.
1896

LEYLAND
MOTORS
1907

TG JOHN
1919

ALVIS CAR AND
ENGINEERING
CO.
1921

ALVIS
1936

TRIUMPH
MOTOR CO.
1930

Alvis TA/350 1952 5

1944

STANDARD TRIUMPH
INTERNATIONAL
1959

LEYLAND MOTOR
CORPORATION
1963

1965

1967

RITISH LEYLAND
OR CORPORATION
1968

331

saying, 'Well, why don't you go in there and tell him? You're the sales chief!'

'Oh, he won't listen to us', came the reply.

Yet he would listen if approached in the right way by someone he respected. Doug Adams from the Experimental Shop recalled an example of this during the design of ADO 17. He had commented to Issigonis that the production engineers would be unhappy with the layout of the instrument panel because it was necessary to actually get into the car to fit it, making it difficult from the manufacturing point of view. Predictably, Issigonis retorted immediately, 'Well, that's what they're having.' But the following day he returned to the workshop and handed Doug Adams a sketch. He had devised a back-plate with two bolt holes holding a harness, making it possible to attach all the instruments and switches on the bench before slotting the panel in and fixing it with two screws. At his request, Adams made up the design and demonstrated how easy it was to fit to two members of the production engineering team. The quality of the relationship he had with others often dictated the level of his obstinacy and this should not be forgotten. When examining the strengths and shortcomings of any organisation it is essential not to lose sight of the human relationships which intertwine with the business and financial decisions.

Despite his promotion, Issigonis continued to focus on his own very narrow world of ideas. He insulated himself from the worrying signs of decline within the British motor industry in general and his own corporation in particular. BMC had come into existence at a time when Britain was still gripped by the economic and social after-effects of a crippling world war. The motor industry had fared better than many in the manufacturing sector, partly because their factories had become essential to the war effort. In the post-war period, luxury goods were scarce and the general public were so desperate to buy cars that they were relatively undemanding about what was on offer. By the 60s the situation had changed. The population had more disposable income, the ownership base had widened out considerably and cars had graduated from being utility items to fashion statements and status symbols. BMC floundered in the wake of this social change. Issigonis spoke for himself when he remarked that 'you use a new car for doing a certain job – I don't think the question of sex comes into it at all'. Unfortunately there was little sign that his colleagues in the upper echelons of management recognised the folly of this statement in the changing climate around them. As we have seen, both the corporation and its Technical Director had failed to appreciate the uniqueness of the Mini appeal, which did indeed have nothing to do with sex. They therefore fooled themselves into thinking that all they had to do was to repeat the trick on the rest of the model range, with no recognition that this was not what the public wanted.

In the final analysis men like Leonard Lord and George Harriman paid too much attention to the engineering of their products and too little attention to the efficient running of the business. They operated on instinct, barely attempting to understand the market. They paid scant attention to the pricing of their products, which were often too cheap, nor did they undertake sufficient capital investment or plan properly for the future. They were complacent in the face of their competition, and lacking in discipline or focus when it came to developing or marketing products. They also fomented the deep divisions which were becoming apparent within the company, whether this was between Cowley and Longbridge or between management and workforce. It was Lord who planted the seeds for this culture of internecine conflict by the way he effected the merger in 1952 but at least he exercised some leadership skills. This was more than his successor was able to do. Harriman took little personal interest in what was going on at shop floor level, a sharp contrast to the days when Herbert Austin and William Morris would wander round the assembly halls making sure they kept in touch with their workforce. These two men were tough, sharp operators, not cuddly philanthropists, yet even today their memory is worshipped through a lingering oral tradition in the workplaces they founded. Their graves are still tended, their anniversaries devotedly observed. The leaders of the old BMC régime kindle no such spark of reverence. Harriman turned the growing gap between the bosses and their workforce into a yawning chasm. The more the management team tried to impose its will, in an ever more arbitrary fashion, the more alienated the workers became, the more inclined to strike over the most trivial issues. Equally damaging was the attitude – fully shared by Issigonis – that educated people were more trouble than they were worth and the best route to the top was from the very bottom. Training was a dirty word and people were promoted for all the wrong reasons. Thus a creative man like Issigonis ended up responsible for managing hundreds of people, totally unequipped with the knowledge or skills to do so.

And still, the much vaunted policy of rationalisation had yet to begin. BMC had too many factories, too many managers, too many brands, too many models, too many dealers, too much of everything. This permeated every level of the business. In August 1961 Longbridge's long-suffering Head of Facilities, Harold Cross, complained about the number of carpets and rubber mats which he was now having to store. Two new Mini variants, the Super De Luxe and the Cooper, were about to be introduced. Various switches and pieces of equipment were installed in different places on each model, requiring a complex pattern of piercings to be made in the floor coverings. Cross calculated that if the number of these configurations was combined with all the colour options required, he was obliged to stock up to 48 variations of carpet. The stores at the Car Assembly Building, known as CAB 1, had room for only eighteen variations. Worse still, he was taking on additional labour to cope with the need to keep swapping between carpet types on the assembly line itself. The point seemed lost on the BMC Engineering Department. Cross was told: 'Any change in the positions of switches and equipment will mean a considerable increase in cost ... we are unable to simplify your difficulties and the arrangements already made for piercing holes in the factory must be considered as a permanent arrangement and not temporary as hoped.' This amounted to a damaging lack of joined-up thinking on the part of the organisation as a whole.

Splitting production unnecessarily across factories, inefficient assembly practices, lack of communication between departments, industrial unrest: all these things contributed to the high unit cost of the product. Nor had any progress been made in standardising the messy product range. The introduction of the Farina designs was a missed opportunity and BMC's product policy continued to be confused and lacking in direction. By toying with the names of 'Minor' and 'Cambridge' for the 1100 and 1800, it would seem that Issigonis was aware of the need to replace the old model range with something more coherent, but BMC simply could not bring itself to make it happen. The technologically advanced vehicles which Issigonis had been brought in to design did not replace the existing rear wheel drive designs but were sold alongside them. Since 1952 the quantity of different models on offer had hardly been reduced at all. These still spanned a disparate range of marques which each had their own identity and were competing with each other for market share. This was brand bedlam not badge engineering.

Continental motor manufacturers had ploughed a different furrow in the period of recovery following the Second World War. Most of them ended the conflict in poor economic shape and had little choice but to concentrate their efforts on one or two products, which they made great efforts to continually improve and keep up to date. Though this was not done through choice, it may ultimately have given them the advantage. There is no doubt that Leonard Lord's policy put BMC at the vanguard of the industry when it came to technology but the big question has always been whether or not this was the right policy for the long term. At home, the corporation was facing increasing competition from Ford UK and this became stronger as the 60s progressed, partly because they had identified a market which BMC missed and which was peculiar to Britain. This was the sale of vehicles to companies for 'fleet' use rather than to private buyers. BMC could be excused for failing to spot this at the beginning of the decade when Issigonis was busy building his char-woman's car, to be followed with the larger, family friendly versions. His innovative designs were well suited to the private buyer who was more interested in the values which Issigonis cherished, in particular that a car should be a pleasure to drive. This was evident in the success enjoyed by the 1100. That success, however, induced a self-satisfaction which caused Harriman and his team to ignore the growing power of the fleet buyer, who was not interested in advanced technology which simply equated to higher maintenance costs as far as he was concerned. Ford was much bet-ter at meeting his requirements and much more adept at producing cars with showroom appeal.

Issigonis and Harriman chose to turn their noses up at the Ford Cortina, which was launched within a month of the 1100, and there is no doubt that their product was better crafted and more advanced. The Cortina, however, was more practical in all those areas which Issigonis refused to acknowledge as important. It had better luggage space, it was easier to service, its controls were better positioned. Most important of all, Ford took care to offer a comprehensive range of models to attract the widest variety of private and fleet buyers, and they also improved the car at regular intervals to keep buyers interested. Between 1962 and 1968 the Cortina received a substantial facelift every two years. In the same period BMC simply kept introducing differently badged 1100s, with few sub-stantial differences and in no particular order. The question that BMC's managers should have been asking themselves was – how much more successful could the 1100 have been if they had paid attention to the wider market which was developing? This might have provided some clues as to why home-market share was falling alarmingly from 60 per cent in 1952, to 27 per cent just fifteen years later, while competitors such as Volkswagen, Fiat and Renault not only maintained their home-market share but increased their exports too. It was a situation which could not continue. While the four Issigonis cells worked away on the expanded model range, menacing clouds were gathering over Longbridge. The storm was broken by the election of a Labour government which quickly decided to turn its attention to the state of the British motor industry.

ANOTHER MERGER, ANOTHER NEW MANAGEMENT

Despite Clement Attlee's surprise defeat of Churchill in the 1946 election, the following decade had been dominated politically by the Conservative Party under Harold Macmillan. In 1964, after thirteen years of Tory rule, the Labour Party was finally returned to power under Harold Wilson and his administration was naturally determined to impose its own socialist vision on the country. It was an unsettling experience for industry bosses who were used to a more cosy relationship with the Conservatives. The Labour Party was particularly set on the idea of industrial regeneration and the rescue of Britain's declining manufacturing industries which employed such a large number of its supporters. In September 1965 Harold Wilson convened a meeting about the difficulties of the motor industry at 10 Downing Street, inviting the bosses to meet with Trade Union representatives. Harold Wilson recounted this meeting in his autobiography:

> I have seldom heard such blunt talk at any industrial confrontation, particularly from the employers. The Minister of Labour, Ray Gunter, and I stressed the severe damage the national economy, particularly exports, was suffering from one unofficial dispute after another. Various ideas were discussed: developing and strengthening the existing fact-finding commission; a special inquiry to be set up by the Government; a 'flying-squad' ready to intervene immediately to establish the facts in an individual dispute.

The parties concerned agreed to the appointment of an industrial relations 'trouble-shooter' but this made little difference and the strikes got worse rather than better as the 1960s wore on. Labour decided that a more drastic remedy was needed to halt the general decline of Britain's manufacturing industries. The solution was to be acceleration of the process of merger which had already begun. This would be a complex, though relatively swift process. The Rootes Group was no longer in British ownership. The difficulties encountered by the Hillman Imp allowed Chrysler to start buying into the company in 1964 and three years later they completed the buyout, thus taking Rootes into American owner- ship. Meanwhile, another major player on the car scene, Standard Triumph, had fallen into the hands of Leyland Motors in 1961. Leyland was the largest manufacturer of commercial vehicles in the country, based in the small Lancashire town near Preston whose name it adopted. It had briefly flirted with car manufacture and given it up long ago, but now it became a major player once again. The Leyland Motor Corporation was formed the year after the acquisition of Standard Triumph. The Rover Company – which had itself recently absorbed Alec's old employer Alvis – was added to the group in 1967. The British Motor Corporation had to react to these developments and in 1966 it agreed a merger with Jaguar Cars and Pressed Steel to form British Motor Holdings (BMH).

In the crucial year of 1967, the Leyland Motor Corporation and BMH represented between them the remains of the independent British motor industry and Harold Wilson gave them a sharp prod to make progress with talks over their joint future. In October 1967 he invited the Chairman of the Leyland Motor Corporation, Sir Donald Stokes, and Sir George Harriman to a meeting at Chequers where he made it clear what he expected of them. Harriman later described to Issigonis what had happened. It had been his understanding that he and Stokes would arrive together for an early morning meeting with the Prime Minister. When he got there, he complained to Alec, he found that Stokes had actually been there since the previous evening and it seemed as if the merger was already settled. This was a bad sign, reminiscent of the bad feeling which had surrounded the formation of the British Motor Corporation fifteen years earlier.

In January 1968, after months of discussions between the two parties, Harold Wilson got his way and the announcement was made that the Leyland Motor Corporation and British Motor Holdings were going to merge. The British Leyland Motor Corporation (BLMC) was incorpo- rated on 14 May. Harriman had, however, read the signs correctly and this was not an equal-sided merger any more than that of Austin and Morris had been, it was a *de facto* take-over of British Motor Holdings by the smaller, truck orientated Leyland–Triumph organisation. For BMC, till now the giant of the British motor industry, this was a humiliation; for Standard Triumph it was a turn of events beyond their wildest dreams. This was painfully evident from the two in-house newspapers distributed to employees by each organisation. On scanning *BMC World*, it takes considerable effort to find three paragraphs in small type at the bottom right hand corner of the front page, under the unenthusiastic heading 'Plans for merger going ahead'. *Standard Triumph News* by contrast takes up its whole front page with a huge headline proclaiming 'It's British Leyland Now!' next to a picture of Stokes and Harriman shaking on the deal. The reason for this was simple. Leyland's financial situation was healthy while it took only the briefest glance at BMC's accounts to see the alarming rate at which money was haemorrhaging out of the organisation.

The man who was to be the key player in the power struggle which ensued was Donald Stokes. He was born in Plymouth in 1914 and a youthful passion for buses had led him to join Leyland Motors. In 1946 he took up the post of Export Manager, and then Sales Manager, and was so successful in these roles that by 1953 he had gained a seat on the Board. Stokes advocated an aggressive export policy and his reputation peaked in 1964 when he defied the US trade embargo on Cuba to sell a large quantity of Leyland buses to Fidel Castro, leader of the communist revolution so detested by the Americans. By 1965 he had risen as high as Chairman and Managing Director of the Leyland Motor Corporation, Chairman of Standard Triumph and knight of the realm. Under his leadership the ailing Triumph marque was revived and products such as the Herald, which had been struggling, were turned into market-place success stories. The Labour government dubbed him a 'super-salesman' and he became a founder member of the Industrial Reorganisation Corporation (IRC) which was set up in 1966 to find ways of improving the competitiveness of British manufacturing. This organisation played a key role in bringing about the Leyland–BMC merger and his excellent relationship with the government was another factor in ensuring that Leyland, not BMC, would come out as the stronger partner. He was rewarded for his efforts with a peerage in 1969.

Though the merger took place at the beginning of 1968 it was several months before the final shape of the Board and senior management was settled as the two factions jockeyed for position. The result was inevitable. Sir George Harriman had fallen ill during the negotiations and this put an end to any hopes he might have had of maintaining his position. In September he suffered the same fate as Lord Nuffield, accepting the post of honorary President. This left the way clear for Stokes to become Chairman. At the end of 1968 a lavishly illustrated 150-page hardback book entitled *British Leyland Motor Corporation: Growth, Constitution, Factory, Products* was produced to outline the structure of the organisation and its hopes for the future. The Foreword painted the following picture:

> On a global basis, British Leyland Motor Corporation ranks on turn-over as the second largest automotive company in Europe and the fifth largest in the world. It has over 40 major manufacturing companies in the U.K. and over 70 associated and subsidiary companies overseas … British Leyland Motor Corporation is the U.K.'s largest vehicle producer – over a million vehicles left its factories last year – the first time a British manufacturer has passed this landmark. A further 90,000 vehicles were produced in factories overseas. Total vehicle exports, achieved by the Corporation during 1968, amounted to 464,192 vehicles. A 200 million [pound] investment programme to cover the next four years ensures that new models will be produced by the Corporation with the most modern equipment available.

Because it was the result of a progression of mergers over a period of nearly eight years, the new corporation found itself the proud owner of a bewildering array of firms and an expanded set of widely differing marques. It therefore sought to impose some order by organising its constituent parts into seven divisions:

- Austin Morris (the BMC group of mass-production companies)
- Specialist Cars (Jaguar, Rover and Standard Triumph)
- Construction Equipment (a group of three equipment manufacturers)
- Truck and Bus (a group of thirteen commercial vehicle manufacturers)
- Foundry and General Engineering (a group of six heavy engineering firms)
- Pressed Steel Fisher (manufacture of bodies and other steel commodities)
- Overseas (overseas operations)

The Chief Executive of the organisation was Sir Donald Stokes, who filled the posts of Chairman and Managing Director. Because of the size of the new enterprise it was felt necessary to also appoint two Deputy Chairmen and three Deputy Managing Directors. The two in the last category who would matter most to Issigonis were Dr Albert Fogg (also Director of Engineering) and George Turnbull (also Managing Director of the Austin Morris Division). Both Fogg and Turnbull had been in similar positions within the Leyland Motor Corporation. Turnbull, at the age of 42, was relatively young for a director, having spent most of his career with Standard Triumph. The strategic role of Director of Finance and Planning went to John Barber who had only recently joined Leyland in December 1967 from Associated Electrical Industries (AEI), having previously been Finance Director for Ford.

Another key player was Filmer M. Paradise, an American who took up the challenging position of Sales Director for the Austin Morris Division in November 1968. Paradise was a recent recruit to the British motor industry, having left Ford Italy to become Managing Director for BMC Europe in July 1967. He came from Wisconsin and was one of those graduates whom Ford encouraged and Alec so disliked. His career was somewhat unconventional, beginning with a post as Economic Commissioner for the post-war Marshall Plan and also serving time in the President's Office in Washington working on national security issues before joining Ford and finding his way to Europe as head of their Italian operation. Paradise was a master of slick presentation and was rarely seen without his trademark cigar. In the days of BMC, Issigonis had been the main front-man for the corporation, and the Chairman and his sales chiefs had been remarkably coy about making public appearances. In the early days of British Leyland, the affable Donald Stokes and the relentlessly optimistic Filmer Paradise would take over this role.

In the course of such changes it is always hard to avoid a clash of cultures. In this case the old enemies Austin and Morris finally set aside their differences to unite in their distaste for the incomers from Standard Triumph. These divisions were inflamed by the new management's strong admiration of the Ford business ethos, which led to a deliberate policy of trying to poach its young executives. BMC by contrast had always harboured a barely concealed contempt for their upstart rivals from Dagenham.

Stokes and his new management team felt that the size of the corporation was its greatest strength and they did not seem concerned by the plethora of sites and organisations involved. Under the new régime *BMC World* adopted a different tone and in May 1968 it printed a map proclaiming proudly: 'The British Leyland Motor Corporation will be able to fly its banner over at least 60 major centres of activity in Great Britain.' This, they implied, would enable the British motor industry to stand up to the great giants of North America. Filmer Paradise represented the corporate view when he told *Motor* that:

> ... the long-term objective of British Leyland is to arrive at 50 per cent of the market. It seems like a big position, but when you remember that we are the General Motors of England and that General Motors in the United States arrives at 55–60 per cent of the market ... we don't really feel that 50 per cent is an unattainable objective.

Issigonis privately expressed a very different view: 'All large company mergers lose money because management becomes impossible.' Time would tell who was right.

WHO WILL BE TECHNICAL DIRECTOR?

Leaving the BMC era for that of British Leyland is like exchanging the slightly embarrassing but enjoyable predictability of an Agatha Christie mystery for the baffling complexity of a James Joyce novel. You feel you ought to be able to follow the plot, but are not entirely sure that you want to. The grandiose thinking and general chaos of the first six years of the 'General Motors of England' is such that attempting to write a coherent story in chronological order is likely to provoke a severe headache. The only way of picking through this maze is to look at some of the individual strands which made up the matted whole, in this case those which would have an impact on Alec Issigonis. Because the corporation underwent so many reorganisations throughout its life, resulting in constant name changes alongside the formation and dissolution of a myriad of subsidiaries and holding companies, for simplicity's sake I will refer to it from this point as 'British Leyland'. A more detailed portrait of the organisational development of the company can be found in the chart on page 386.

For the second time in his life Issigonis found himself on the wrong side of a take-over and the changes to top personnel created a far more questioning environment for him to operate within. From being

Technical Director of an organisation whose senior managers showed the utmost deference towards him, he became an awkward presence in the way of a set of executives who were largely hostile.

The merger would bring one more important character into the story because, once again, the two sides possessed a parallel set of staff. Alec's counterpart at Standard Triumph was Harry Webster. Born in Coventry in 1917, Webster had attended the local technical college and joined the Standard Motor Company as an apprentice in 1932. He had therefore spent his entire career with Standard Triumph, working his way up to Director of Engineering by 1957. Just as Issigonis was a specialist in the small mass-market car, Webster's *forte* was the premium-price vehicle aimed at the middle of the market, including a number of sports cars. He formed a professional partnership with Giovanni Michelotti, a stylist from Turin who had begun his career with Pininfarina before setting up his own styling studio in 1949. Together they produced a respectable series of Triumph cars including the Herald, the Spitfire, the 1300/2000, and the TR range.

The Stokes–Webster relationship was not unlike that of Harriman and Issigonis. In both cases the manager had complete faith in the capabilities of his technical expert. There was therefore never any real doubt that Webster would find his way into the senior engineering post. Though Issigonis initially retained his title of Technical Director, in March 1968 he was 'relieved of executive responsibilities', as the corporation politely put it, and asked to 'devote his undivided time to the more creative and forward-looking concepts of vehicle research and development'. Charles Griffin was given a new role as Director of Engineering, reporting directly to Stokes. Harry Webster took effective charge of the technical programme for the Austin Morris Division and began to draw up a new product plan.

At the start of 1968 Stokes and his team were full of optimism. He addressed his new employees through *BMC World* and his words sum up the mood:

Today we all become members of the British Leyland Motor Corporation. This is the only major British-owned motor manufacturer and represents Britain's last chance to stand up to and fight the formidable competition of American and other motor manufacturers. We are, of course, also the largest motor manufacturer in Great Britain and one of the largest companies in the country, and the success that attends our efforts may well set the pattern for industry in this country for many years to come.

It was necessary to devise a long-term strategy for BMC, now reincarnated as the Austin Morris Division. Stokes, Turnbull and Webster reasoned that, since petrol and oil were cheap, they should be looking at a bigger car which could be sold for a higher price and therefore command a larger profit margin than the mass-market small car. Webster declared that they would get rid of the confusion of brands and divide the Austin Morris model range in two. Austin would represent the advanced front wheel drive philosophy, using what was termed 'durable' styling, and continue to appeal predominantly to the private buyer. Morris would feature more conventional rear wheel drive vehicles combined with adventurous styling in an attempt to break into that elusive but profitable 'fleet' market which was so dominated by the feared Ford Cortina. This was the theory though, as time went on, the state of British Leyland's finances would mean that it never became a reality. In 1968, however, they cheerfully set off along this route and started on the design of ADO 28, which would become the Morris Marina to be launched in 1971, and ADO 67, which became the Austin Allegro launched in 1973.

Though they now had a plan, British Leyland could not afford to wait three years for a new product. So Webster had to examine the projects BMC already had on the books and the results would not augur well for Issigonis' future position. The first task which fell to Stokes was to defend the Austin 3-litre, which was so bad that it had to be effectively relaunched in 1968, making it appear to be British Leyland's 'first' product. Though the car was improved, it had not gained any appeal and it was an uncomfortable way for Stokes and Filmer Paradise to begin their careers as the corporation's media spokesmen. There were three other projects in train. The first was ADO 19, the Austin Ant. We have already seen how this was quickly cancelled because it was believed to be a competitor to the profitable Land Rover brand. The second was ADO 14, which had been started in 1965 to fill the gaping hole in the model range between the 1100 and the 1800. The press had been awaiting its launch with bated breath for some time as it was continually delayed but, at the time of the merger, BMC were preparing for a launch in mid-1968. The third project was a Mini replacement programme which had begun early in 1967.

It was Stokes rather than Webster who tackled BMC's existing Technical Director on the subject of the forward plan, writing to Issigonis on 10 April on a Leyland Motor Corporation letterhead:

Dear Alec,

I am hoping to have a word with you on Friday at B.M.C. and I am trying to work out a method of collating the work done throughout the new Group in such a form that I can make a monthly report of the new combined Company.

I have no doubt Bertie Fogg will be having various talks with you as soon as he is back at work again regarding methods of collaboration in the Engineering Department, but in the meantime I wonder whether you would be good enough to let me have a very short monthly report showing the sort of work you are undertaking in your new set-up and the progress made.

One of the things I want to talk to you about particularly when Bertie is available is forward programme on engineering development and a budget for the control of expenditure.

Perhaps you could be turning these things over in your mind.

Issigonis replied on 18 April:

Dear Sir Donald,

I enclose a short resume of work that I am currently engaged on in my new undertaking.

Management approval or rejection of these projects is still to be determined, but at the earliest opportunity I shall discuss the matter with Bertie Fogg in greater detail, so that you can appraise the situation with more facts at your disposal.

Attached to this letter was a general policy statement and a summary of projects under development. Surprisingly, neither of these documents mentions ADO 14 which was sitting in the design studio supposedly ready for manufacture and which was, theoretically, available for the mid-sector market which Stokes and his team wished to target. Instead they concentrate on the problem in which Issigonis was far more interested, the replacement of the Mini and the 1100. This project would come to be known as 9X and though it was well advanced by 1968 it was nowhere near as complete as ADO 14. His General Policy statement reads as follows:

Most of the research work outlined below presupposes that we shall continue to produce a Mini in the foreseeable future. It is very important to arrive at a decision over this matter as soon as possible, because on this depends the speed at which the development work is executed. A low priority programme is both time consuming and costly in the long run. The greatest need in combating increased production costs over the year is the development of a new engine for a small car of this type. The present 'A' series engine offered a quick way of getting the car into production in 1959, but has now outlived its purpose both for weight and cost compared with European competition; although its performance is still well up to modern standards. The enlarged version of this engine (1300) is perfectly competitive for cars in the category above the Mini type of vehicle, i.e. the lower medium class range.

He went on to list the projects he currently had under development:

1. Design and development of a 750/998 c.c. 4 cylinder engine and transmission system for transverse or normal drive applications, for a new small car. In addition to this work we are doing a design study, in conjunction with Automotive Products Ltd., for a 4 speed automatic transmission unit.
2. Development of a 6 cylinder version of the above engine to give capacities from 1300 to 1490 c.c., using as much common tooling as possible including the same transmission system.
3. Development of a new Mini. This is being studied in two versions, one 6" shorter than the present car (120") and another 10" longer or 4" longer than the present model. This will embody common suspension parts but, in order to keep production costs down to a minimum, hydrolastic has had to be abandoned in favour of conventional springing. This is because a simplified version of the hydrolastic design, which we have been working on for some time, has not yet materialised.
4. Development of a small hydrostatic transmission system in collaboration with N.E.L. The arrangement incorporates motors in each wheel and eliminates the use of high pressure hoses to transmit oil to these units.

5. General work on induction systems including the use of updraft carburettors for anti pollution work. This work is very necessary in order that we can dispense with the expensive after burning devices which we have had to incorporate into our cars at present being sold in America.

This response was totally out of tune with the priorities being set by the new management team. They were looking for a car which would have reasonable development costs and produce a good profit, not an expensive new concept with an expensive new engine. Nor were they interested in small cars. They wanted a product which would compete in the fleet market. A vehicle of that type was, of course, anathema to Issigonis. It was becoming clear just how little common ground there was between them.

MAXI, THE BIG MISTAKE

While they pondered on their long-term strategy Stokes and Webster were faced with the pressing problem of launching the vehicle missing from Alec's précis of his work, ADO 14. To pursue this project, Issigonis had created a new cell headed by Eric Bareham, till then a designer on the engines and transmissions team. An early specification exists from June 1965, intriguingly (and confusingly) entitled 'Project 9X' though it has no connection with the similarly named small car design. This document introduces a relatively new theme for Issigonis, an attempt at commonality with other designs, since several parts specified are to be taken from either ADO 16 (seats, number plate mounts, bumpers, suspension parts, steering gear, brake controls, electrical equipment, windscreen wiper mechanism) or ADO 17 (body panels, including roof and doors, various floor fittings). This would be combined with a new E-series overhead camshaft engine which would fill the gap between the capacities of the A-series and B-series power units. If the dimensions of the proposal are compared with those of the final specification they reveal a wheelbase three-quarters of an inch shorter but a bodyshell over seven inches shorter. One of the criticisms of the finished vehicle would be that it was almost as big as ADO 17, but these measurements would have positioned the car much more neatly halfway between ADO 16 and ADO 17. The reasons why it grew in length probably lie in the attempts which were made to improve its appearance and provide increased safety in the event of an accident.

By 1968 the specification had changed substantially and most of the 'common' parts had disappeared. Nevertheless the overall concept that had emerged was, in the best Issigonis tradition, a bold one. It was to be a mid-sized family saloon with a five-door 'hatchback' body which, though not unknown, was as yet far from a standard feature. Even the term 'hatchback' was only just coming into use around this time. This was combined with the Issigonis trademarks of front wheel drive, transverse layout and a wheel at each corner. For once the new engine design made it through to the final specification, partly because there was an urgent requirement for such a power unit from the traditionally strong, but latterly troubled, BMC export market of Australia. For the first time, therefore, Issigonis was not constrained by the need to use an existing engine. The E-series was combined with a five-speed gearbox – another unusual feature for the time. Excellent interior packaging was taken to its extremes once again and the seats even folded down to form a bed. All this and independent Hydrolastic suspension too.

The problem lay in the execution. When Stokes and his team set eyes on what potentially was British Leyland's first new product, they were horrified. Its appearance was definitely striking because Issigonis had followed his usual idiosyncratic path in both the body style and basic furnishing. Despite the initial design brief, the only major existing parts reused were the ADO 17 door panels, that section of the car which he had taken away from Pininfarina and which also happened to be the least attractive. These made the car too large and heavy, compromising what exterior styling there was. The interior was spartan. Stokes called it 'ridiculously stark – like a hen-coop'.

Then there was the car's pedestrian performance. The initial plan for a 1300 cc unit proved inadequate and grew to 1500 cc in development as the smallest viable option. This was one of the factors which delayed its going into production. It was also designed to allow for the development of a 6-cylinder version, destined for an upgraded ADO 17, and this accounted for some of its limitations. In order to reserve space for the two extra cylinders, but determined to stick to the transverse configuration, Issigonis positioned the cylinders too close together and this was at the root of its lack of power. The delays caused immense frustration to BMC Australia who were desperate to use the new engine in several planned new models to shore up their declining market. Finally they did get both the 4-cylinder and 6-cylinder versions before the UK, fitting them to interesting hybrid cars that were never sold outside Australia.

At home, some consideration was given to scrapping ADO 14 but a new engine facility had already been built and manned at the Cofton Hackett plant adjacent to Longbridge at a cost of £20 million, Pressed Steel had set aside considerable capacity for building the bodies and the Mini line at Cowley had been cleared to make way for its assembly. The longer the launch was postponed, the more money was wasted as these facilities stood idle. All Stokes and Webster could do was delay the car until the spring of 1969, executing some changes to the styling and undertaking an intensive test programme to try to iron out some of the technical problems. A saloon version was considered so ugly as to be unsaleable so it was dropped from production and excised from publicity material at the last minute even though the tooling was already in place. The car had so far been referred to as the 'BMC 1500' but Stokes made the personal decision to name it 'Maxi' in order to make a connection with the Mini in the public's mind. This was ironic in view of British Leyland's desire to move away from the small car market, but no one could deny that it was still one of the few vehicles in the model range whose name had any resonance.

By the time the launch in Portugal was finally arranged (presided over by Harry Webster rather than Issigonis) the car's arrival had been anticipated for so long that expectations were sky high. It was therefore bound to be a disappointment to everyone, not least potential buyers, and it would be the first Issigonis design to receive such a lukewarm press reception. *Autocar* found little to criticise in the technical specification but they concluded:

> Familiarity, in this case brings endearment and one comes to accept the functional appearance better as time goes on ... All it lacks is prestige and 'up-on-the-Jones-manship'.

The Maxi's gearchange, however, would become as notorious as the Mini's water leaks. A report from the *Which?* car supplement published by the Consumers' Association commented acidly that 'our Maxi's gear lever fell nicely to hand – when in neutral'. When Donald Stokes made a television appearance, the first question he was asked by the BBC's industrial correspondent was: 'Why have you made a car with this awful gearchange?' He was then subjected to the humiliation of having to demonstrate the truth of this accusation on camera, smiling bravely and declaring 'there's nothing' – screech – 'wrong' – crunch – 'with this gear-box' – as the gears screamed at his every touch and the car shuddered painfully in response. Even his powers of persuasion were unable to convince in this case. Filmer Paradise also put in some bullish performances in the face of hostile questioning, declaring 'the proof will be in the sales figures, let's just wait and see', but the press were not convinced.

As for the public, the delay led them to expect a car that was at least free of technical problems. In its promotional film British Leyland made a great deal of the 800,000 miles of testing which the prototype had undergone during a three-year programme. One of *Autocar*'s readers voiced this hope on the letters page:

> The long wait for this car has been worthwhile because most of its 'bugs' should have been removed by now and there will not be the usual BMC delay before the car is available to buyers.

He was to be sadly disappointed in this expectation. In the finest tradition of BMC, the car had a host of post-production faults and by the time these were solved yet again a year of production and dissatisfied customers had ebbed away. In October 1970 at the London Motor Show British Leyland introduced an extensively modified version with a redesigned gearbox linkage, the option of a more powerful 1750 cc engine, a re-styled radiator grille and a more up-market wood-veneer dashboard but by now it was too late. Despite steady UK sales the car never came near to fulfilling the potential of its initial concept. It failed to establish a significant position in the market and in its first few years was consistently outsold by the ageing 1100. It stayed in production until 1981 but fared only marginally better than the 1800 with a final production figure of 472,090. It was absolute proof that functionality and practicality were no longer enough to sell cars.

The Maxi is an enigma in the career of Issigonis. There is one intriguing photograph which shows him dressed in an elegant dark grey suit with a green tie and suede shoes, his left hand resting protectively on the bonnet of a red Maxi, his right hand tucked casually in his pocket, looking relaxed and pleased with life in general. Other than this there is hardly anything to link him with the design. He does not mention it on recordings or in interviews. There are no sketches relating to it. There are only three pieces of paperwork in his personal archive on the subject. One is the very early specification already described. There is a request from the Service Department in September 1967 to view the car so that suggestions can be made to ensure ease of servicing before the design is fixed. Finally, the files contain a largely uncritical test report undertaken by his friend Lord Snowdon. Yet he, as Technical Director, had total responsibility for the project. In the afterglow of the Mini and the 1100 he was at the pinnacle of his influence within BMC and for the first time in his career he had the total freedom to produce whatever he liked, including the engine, as he had always wanted. How did he get it so wrong?

The answer can only be guessed at. There is the fact that he was struggling with his management position and the demands that it made on him which may account for his failure to exercise proper control over the project. Another possible explanation is that he was directing his creative effort into the alternative small car project known as 9X – which also incorporated a new engine design – at the expense of ADO 14 and the E-series. The 9X programme was allowed to continue despite the disaster of the Maxi and it will be fully described later in this chapter. He had never made any secret of his preference for small cars and this showed in the sharp contrast between the success of the Mini and the 1100, and the indifferent performance of the 1800 and now the Maxi. Whatever the reasons, it was a fatal mistake because it gave the new régime the perfect excuse to sideline him for good. An unenthusiastic review from *Car* in 1969 made the ominous comment:

There is no doubt that it is a car of vast importance. It disappoints so much because it strikes one as a splendid opportunity at least half missed. British Leyland are very conscious of the fact that most people will regard the Maxi not as the last BMC car – which it really is – but as the first corporate effort. It may be a lot to ask that the Maxi will ever be transformed into an aesthetic masterpiece; but perhaps its greatest value will be to show BriLeyMoCo the way they must go with their first real all-corporate car.

Stokes and Webster agreed. They would attempt to march as far and as quickly away from the minimalism espoused by Issigonis as they possibly could.

The Fate of the Team

The motor industry can be very like the pop charts in which you are only as good as your last release. Unfortunately for Issigonis, Donald Stokes and George Turnbull were immune to the glamour of his earlier hits and were interested only in his latest production which was a resounding miss. This was not likely to assist his prospects when it came to holding on to his position in the corporate hierarchy.

When Stokes, Turnbull and Webster looked at Issigonis they did not see a design genius, instead they saw someone who was completely out of touch with current trends. They blamed him for BMC's poor performance, looking to the underlying unprofitability of the Mini not to mention the poor sales of the 1800. The Maxi fiasco provided the justification which Stokes needed to remove Issigonis from the mainstream design office – indeed few could have criticised his judgement in doing so in the wake of this commercial disaster. In 1969 Harry Webster took the title of Technical Director of the Austin Morris Division and moved into Issigonis' old office and workshops. The Issigonis cells were disbanded. He was given the new post of Director of Research and Development at the head of a department called Forward Research, a device which neatly avoided the necessity of making him report to Webster. He was exiled from the design block to a workshop in the basement of the Kremlin, the building where he had begun his Longbridge career thirteen years before. The area had previously been a garage for the company's chauffeurs and it ran the length of the administration building. Issigonis created an office for himself at one end, secretary Suzanne Hankey, who stayed with him until 1976, had an office next door, and the rest of the area became his drawing office. In addition he had a workshop near the Experimental Shop where he worked on various engine experiments including a steam engine project.

For the rest of his team, things were not so black and white as they were for Issigonis. He was, after all, only two years from retirement and had, as Alex Moulton would say, 'had a good run for his money'. They, by contrast, faced another ten or twenty years of working life so they had to accommodate themselves to the changes.

A number of his team, including John Sheppard, stayed on with Issigonis in Research and Development to work with him on the 9X project, though they would later move on when that project was scaled down. Charles Griffin was no longer his deputy and in his role as Director of Engineering for the Austin Morris Division he supported Webster and his successors as he had supported Issigonis. Though he remained sympathetic to his former colleague and retained an underlying belief in the soundness of his design principles, he was careful not to align himself too closely with the policies of the past. Meanwhile Jack Daniels moved over into the main Design Office and was given a senior position on ADO 28. Chris Kingham had been offered the opportunity to run a new unit called the Product Improvement Panel (PIP) following the conclusion of the ADO 17 project in 1965. For three years PIP investigated warranty costs and introduced measures to improve them. After the merger PIP was axed and Kingham was sent to become resident engineer of the Drews Lane Plant north of Birmingham. He felt this to be a demotion and decided to take early retirement at the beginning of the 1970s. Tony Dawson also became a less dominant force within the public relations department. Nevertheless his personal networks, especially with continental journalists, were still of immense value to the company and he carried on in much the same role as before until his retirement in 1979. He remained a loyal supporter of the Issigonis cars and, in the privacy of his office, often spoke scathingly of the designs which replaced them.

Issigonis did not show any hostility towards his former colleagues as they were redeployed throughout the company because he recognised that they did not have any real choice in the matter. He remained on friendly terms with Griffin, Daniels, Sheppard and Kingham to the end of his life. There was, however, a major rift in his relationship with Alex Moulton. There is no sure way of knowing what was in Issigonis' mind but it seems likely that a major factor was a sense of betrayal when Moulton continued to work with Harry Webster. This did not live up to his own intense need for personal loyalty. Alex Moulton says of this time:

> Issigonis and I tended to part, because I related to Harry Webster, we got on fine, a perfectly sensible chief engineer, so that caused great distress really with Issigonis. He would expect that when he went out of the mainstream, everybody else who had worked with him should go too, that was a typical attitude I think.

It was also rather unreasonable since Alex Moulton had a living to make and a contract to honour with both British Leyland and Dunlop. Indeed, he had to do a great deal more than just 'go along' with the new régime. He was forced to fight for his position. Stokes wanted to cut out unnecessarily expensive technology and he identified Hydrolastic suspension as being in this category fairly quickly. It took a great deal of argument for Moulton to convince Stokes that he should be allowed to continue with the development of Hydrolastic into the Hydragas system which eventually went onto models such as the Allegro, the Princess and the Metro. Moulton said of Issigonis at this period: 'He didn't like the change of events which happened at the Leyland take-over and he made his choice.' It was the choice which Moulton made which perhaps cost him his relationship with Issigonis.

Stokes did not have the courage to take his axe to the Mini itself and British Leyland therefore allowed the upgrade programme which Issigonis had been preparing as BMC Technical Director to go ahead. Some of the changes – concealed hinges for example – were substantial enough to justify a new designation of ADO 20. The revisions also included the removal of Hydrolastic suspension, which might be seen as a snub to Moulton. The evidence shows, however, that Issigonis had developed an ambivalent attitude towards Hydrolastic some years before. He had shown a distinct reluctance to put it onto ADO 16 in 1962 despite the length of time he had been involved in trying to develop it. When it finally appeared on the Mini in September 1964, the Sales Department felt this was significant enough to justify designating the car a 'Mark II' version and a press release on these lines was prepared. They needed the blessing of the Engineering Department to make such a change but when they requested this they were surprised to receive the following injunction from Charles Griffin:

I would acknowledge receipt of our memorandum of September 24th relating to the designations of the Hydrolastic Mini range of cars. Contrary to the decision made at the Sales/Publicity Directors' meeting on September 8th, I have to inform you that, in the Chairman's absence, Mr Issigonis has ruled that no change in designation is to be made and that he takes full responsibility for this arrangement.

As a result BMC let pass the opportunity to raise public awareness of a major technical upgrade to one of their best-selling models.

ADO 20 was allowed to proceed but British Leyland decided they would add a few ideas of their own and, at last, wind-up windows were made standard. There was also a late decision to add another model to the range in the form of the Clubman. Unlike the standard models this version retained Hydrolastic suspension until 1970, because the purpose of the Clubman was to provide a more upmarket product, which somewhat conflicted with the desire to reduce the Mini's manufacturing costs. The slightly lengthened body and squared-up front nose added nothing to either the aesthetics or the aerodynamics of the car, while the restyled dashboard abandoned the original principle of central instrumentation. Stokes thought it was 'very attractive'; Issigonis thought it was an abomination. 'They've spoilt my car', he told John Sheppard angrily. At the same time, the Wolseley Hornet and Riley Elf versions were dropped, as were the Austin and Morris badges, with the car being marketed simply as 'Mini' from 1969. This was a sensible move, meaning different versions of the car no longer had to be produced for different dealerships. It also meant that the accidental name of 'Mini' had graduated to become a marque in its own right.

The final casualty of Issigonis' fall from grace was to be the Mini Cooper. John Cooper's relationship with British Leyland got off to a bad start when Stokes asked him what he did and was distinctly unamused to receive the reply, 'I come up once a fortnight to wind Issigonis up.' Just like Harriman before him Stokes failed to recognise that the power of the 'Cooper' brand far outweighed that of British Leyland. He did not believe that competition success helped to sell cars and he considered it 'absurd' to pay money to John Cooper simply to use his name. There had only ever been a verbal agreement between the two parties so Cooper had no contract to protect him but his business interests did not depend on British Leyland's support so it was possible for him to show the loyalty which Issigonis considered to be so lacking in Moulton. He was accordingly informed that it cost too much money to build such a specialist car and that its high performance affected its insurance rating adversely. Cooper argued that any extra costs were recouped through the Special Tuning Department which sold specialist items developed through the sports programme to the amateur competition world. Stokes was unconvinced. The Mini Cooper was allowed to peter out while a new 1275 GT version of the Clubman was introduced. John Cooper was wrong when he warned Stokes that his replacement would attract a higher insurance rating; in fact this was one of the things that British Leyland got right.

The 1275 GT was placed in group 3 while the Cooper was in group 4 and the Cooper S sat as high as group 7 at a time when the highest insurance category was ten. He was right, however, in predicting that the absence of the 'Cooper' name with its motor racing associations would make it a far less attractive purchase to the general public. Stokes therefore saved the £2 a car, but probably lost far more than this in overall sales.

'Sir' Alec

Possibly Stokes would have liked to do more than send Issigonis into exile. Though he was not blind to the qualities that Issigonis possessed, he felt that his approach was irrelevant to the commercial facts of life which were facing the new British Leyland Motor Corporation. He described his feelings about Issigonis in the BBC programme *The Ironmonger:*

Alec Issigonis, as you know – a very great man, a very charming man, one of the most charming men you could possibly meet, but he was always – and I suppose this is why he succeeded – he was a very dominant engineer, and he had ideas … You can't have one man as the maestro, running a huge engineering department of a huge motor manufacturer, it's got to be a team effort and you've got to have specialists designing gearboxes and designing axles and engines and so on, and then you've got to have an innovative engineer who can co-ordinate all that activity so that what comes out is one harmonious whole and I think the world had just gone on a few stages. He'd been the right man in his day and I think events had almost overtaken him.

The difficulty was his reputation. Issigonis was widely fêted in the press as the father of the Mini. Despite their opinion on its lack of profitability, British Leyland could not ignore the importance of both the Mini and the 1100 to sales volumes. The Mini name would remain the most powerful brand in their portfolio throughout the 70s. It would not reach its peak production year until 1971 with 318,475 units sold worldwide. As if to emphasise the point, the stream of public honours which came his way culminated in 1969 with a well-publicised knighthood. In the same honours list his old friend John Parkes, still Managing Director of Alvis, was awarded a CBE. His new status was reinforced by a barrage of congratulatory correspondence. Princess Margaret commented: '… no one could have deserved it more and I bet the whole of Longbridge is basking in your reflected glory'. Sir Richard Clarke, the Labour Minister for Technology, likewise told him: '... there are few people who have both invented new machines and added new words to the vocabulary'. George Turnbull wrote in a surprisingly similar vein:

> Most of your glory has been associated with the Mini and its development, but as you know all of us here at Longbridge are hoping that you will initiate some equally revolutionary model for the very competitive years that lie ahead of the British Leyland Motor Corporation. May I also take this opportunity of thanking you for the help and co-operation you have given to me and all your colleagues here at Longbridge during the difficult transitional period following the merger of Leyland with British Motor Holdings. I am certainly very proud to have you as a member of our team at Longbridge and may the Knighthood give you all the more power to your elbow.

John Barber joked:

> You may remember that we had an amusing discussion over lunch during my Ford days and you can now point to the fact that your cars are still likely to be making profit for us in the 1970s!

Meanwhile Donald Stokes wrote, rather importantly, on House of Lords notepaper:

> Dear Alec – we are all so delighted at your award of a knighthood. It could not be better deserved and is a great tribute to your engineering genius. We all bask a little in your reflected glory and it's so particularly appropriate on the occasion of the two millionth Mini – not forgetting the Maxi and all the rest. We wish you all continued success and prosperity in the future – yours sincerely – Donald Stokes.

His CBE in 1964 and now his knighthood 'for services to automotive engineering' gave Issigonis much personal satisfaction. On the bottom of the letter from Downing Street offering him the CBE he had written – 'Harold Wilson, our best labour Prime Minister' (though since there had been only two previous people fitting such a description this constitutes rather faint praise). When another letter followed in May 1969 with the offer of a knighthood, he commented – 'again Harold Wilson'. Given his complete indifference to politics his assessment of Harold Wilson's qualities as Prime Minister seems to have been based entirely on his magnanimity in recognising the genius of Mr A. A. C. Issigonis, twice. For Issigonis these honours carried with them the social status he felt he had always deserved, something perfectly understood by Donald Riddle who wrote to him:

> Ashore this morning after a storm-bound day I learnt from the 'Guardian' that you had been knighted. This is splendid. My congratulations. Not only does the style suit you it is also long overdue. The establishment must feel in need of some real strength in its ranks or could it be that they are now more inclined to recognise real merit. Whatever – it is marvellous. Your mother must be well pleased and even more proud of her son whom [sic], as she explained confidentially to me, was never very good at his sums at Battersea.

On the morning of the announcement his colleagues, now established in their basement workshop, decided to congratulate their boss by saying in chorus 'good morning Sir Alec' as he passed through their workspace on the way to his own. Issigonis, reacting with an uncharacteristic diffidence, blushed and mumbled something inaudible, holding his briefcase up to his face as he shuffled to his office in embarrassment. He soon recovered himself, however, and later that day told a negligent workshop mechanic that if he did not do as he was told 'Sir Alec' would find it necessary to have him removed to the Tower.

Undoubtedly Donald Riddle was right and Hulda Issigonis was extremely proud of her son. It is therefore sad to note that she was unable to accompany him to Buckingham Palace to collect his knighthood on 22 July 1969 because she was in hospital after another fall. Instead, he asked his closest friends, George Dowson and John Morris, to be his official guests. For the great occasion he hired a pair of pinstriped trousers, a grey waistcoat and a black jacket with white shirt and tie from Moss Brothers and the receipt for £3 still exists among his papers. George, who was himself wearing the more customary morning suit, was horrified when they met, exclaiming: 'Alec, what have you got on, you're meant to be in tails – you look like a waiter!' This was a somewhat harsh judgement since the letter from the Home Office had prescribed 'service dress, morning dress or dark lounge suit'. After the ceremony, Max Dowson hosted a party at his suite in the Hyde Park Hotel. The hotel staff, not knowing who she was, kept calling her 'your ladyship' and Max had to explain repeatedly that she was not Mrs Issigonis but simply the hostess of the party.

Inconveniently for the British Leyland hierarchy, almost simultaneously with the announcement in June of his inclusion in the Queen's list of birthday honours, the 2 millionth Mini rolled off the production line. Filmer Paradise seized on this awkward fact in his own congratulatory letter to Issigonis:

> I never properly appreciated your abilities as a planner until this occasion on which you timed your knighthood to coincide with the Two Millionth Mini. I am glad to have been responsible for the postponement of this epochal event from May 9th to June 19th at which time the two epochs are joined.

As the first British car to achieve this landmark there was much fuss from the press and Issigonis was allowed back before the cameras to pose alongside George Turnbull on the Mini assembly line, enigmatically consulting his watch as cameras flashed. Stokes, Turnbull and Filmer Paradise all felt obliged to offer happy thoughts in the press release, though Harry Webster did not. It was also announced that British Leyland would be issuing a Mini rear window sticker saying 'Don't play rough – I've got two million friends'. It was perhaps this sentiment which prompted Stokes to commute Issigonis' sentence from execution to imprisonment in the basement for the remainder of his working life. Rather than try to re-engage his talents in a constructive way, Stokes decided it was for the good of the corporation to sideline him until his retirement date, which was by then only two years away. Alex Moulton commented astutely: 'Nobody would naturally have the courage to sack him, it would be like striking down an idol in the same way, interestingly, that no one has had the courage to stop the Mini.'

Even though Issigonis had been thrown out of senior management he still kept his grade. He had his relocated workshops and his personally loyal little team. In the circumstances the new working arrangements suited him well enough. By ensconcing himself once again in his self-contained world he could ignore what was going on outside and at least those administrative duties which he had found so unpalatable had now been removed. But the atmosphere had changed for everyone and, despite all its faults, BMC's Longbridge seems to have been a more enjoyable place to work than the home of the earnest new corporation. Ron Lucas had been BMC's Finance Director, and he was now Treasurer to British Leyland. In 1969 he wrote to congratulate Issigonis on his knighthood. 'I haven't had a laugh at lunch time since I left Longbridge', he bemoaned. 'My new colleagues are admirable and efficient – but where is the fun?'

For his remaining team it was almost a return to the early days of the ADO 15 project when they were all working so closely together, though then they had been at the centre of the company's pioneering effort and now they were on the fringes of what would soon become its efforts to survive. A kind of camaraderie resurfaced based on solidarity against hostile forces. As he walked through the workshop every morning to his new office, Issigonis would stop to comment on the designs on the drawing boards and host discussions over morning coffee and a cigarette, as he had done in the old days. He even began to sketch again, though he produced nothing to compare with his output in the 1940s and 1950s. Once again he enjoyed the freedom of concentrating only on those things which interested him.

A VISIT TO MOSCOW

The period 1968–9 was one of transition within British Leyland and though the battle-lines were established fairly quickly, the old faces did not disappear overnight. A number of projects and initiatives therefore drifted on with the involvement of people whom it might be assumed were spent forces. One of these was a scheme to collaborate with the Soviet Union in the area of vehicle manufacture, which was led by Sir George Harriman. This seems to have been inspired by the fact that Fiat, Renault and Peugeot had already entered into lucrative arrangements to 'assist' the Soviet Union. The Fiat deal had even attracted the attention of the CIA who wrote a report on the subject for the US House of Representatives in 1967, providing reassurance that there were no implications for the military or space programmes which preoccupied the Americans.

Harold Wilson, along with his Minister for Technology Tony Benn, feared that British manufacturers were losing out. A brief improvement in political relations between the USSR, Europe and America had ended abruptly when President Leonid Brezhnev ordered the invasion of Czechoslovakia in 1968 to prevent liberal reforms from going ahead. Nevertheless Wilson and Benn continued to encourage commercial exchange and Russia's Deputy Minister for the Automotive Industry, Nikolai Strokin, was keen to take advantage of Britain's interest. Harriman had already visited Moscow and met with Strokin in December 1967 to discuss the possibility of setting up a factory to make 1100s and 1800s. In April 1968 he chaired the first meeting of the Motor Industry Working Group in Moscow. The group identified five areas for investigation, one of which was passenger cars, a subject Harriman immediately delegated to his good friend Issigonis. The minutes of the meeting specifically note that:

> It was requested that Mr. Issigonis give his general observations, without prejudice, on a U.S.S.R. design concept for a 1000–1200 c.c. front wheel drive passenger car. This was agreed providing that it does not require Mr. Issigonis or B.L.M.C. engineers to make any studies in depth.

Accordingly he was asked to lead the Passenger Car Study Group (PCSG) which also included Geoffrey Rose, the Production Manager who had so valiantly struggled to set up the assembly lines for ADO 15. British Leyland appeared to be nervous about the extensive access they were expected to provide, at their own expense, and the minutes of the first PCSG meeting noted that 'although the exercise is basically a technological exchange, the main essential was to establish goodwill'. Nevertheless, despite their misgivings, the exchange programme went ahead, with a visit from the Truck and Diesel delegation in September 1968. Harriman wrote to Strokin approvingly:

> I was able to welcome the first Soviet team myself at the Commercial Vehicle Exhibition. They presented me with a magnificent model of a bear from Yaroslavl which has given me great pleasure. It was really most kind of you to think of a personal touch of that sort.

As head of the PCSG it was Issigonis' job to plan the itinerary for the visit of the Soviet Passenger Car delegation scheduled for December. The seven-day programme was made up of factory visits around various

Birmingham and Coventry facilities interspersed with lunch and dinner parties, every single one of which he was expected to attend. Issigonis was not enthusiastic about the necessity for a return visit because he did not wish to leave his mother who was in poor health. He was unsuccessful in deferring the trip until later in the year but the timetable was arranged to allow him to be back for the weekend. He specifically asked for the same interpreter who had assisted them during the Soviet visit, a Polish man named Wywial who was seconded from his job at the Production Engineering Research Association. The rest of the delegation was made up of Jack Daniels and Stan Johnson on the design side, with Geoffrey Rose and Dr Hundy of Pressed Steel Fisher representing the manufacturing division.

The party set out on a cold winter morning in late January and arrived in Moscow to a VIP reception, travelling from the airport to their hotel with a police escort in tow. They worked their way through a programme of official discussions, factory tours, visits to research institutions and various dinner engagements. At the Motor Industry Research Institute (NAMI) they were shown a prototype front wheel drive car which had a transverse V4 engine with gearbox fitted behind. The report succinctly comments that 'In Mr Issigonis' view this conception had no merits whatsoever and they were told this'. Geoffrey Rose has a rather more vivid recollection of the conversation which took place:

'Well Mr Issigonis, you've seen the design of our people's car, what are your comments?' he was asked by Strokin.

Issigonis smiled mischievously and replied, 'Well, Mr Minister, I think you've made a ghastly mistake, but you probably are working on the right lines.'

When this was relayed by the Minister's interpreter, he looked somewhat dismayed, but Alec continued, 'I think you've certainly got the right ideas because you're going for front wheel drive and a transverse engine but the design is far too heavy, far too cumbersome, and would be almost impossible to manufacture.'

His Russian hosts did not seem to mind his comments too much; on the contrary, Jack Daniels noted in his report that 'they paid very keen attention to the words of Mr. Issigonis'. The visit therefore proceeded smoothly as he turned his charm up to maximum, connecting easily with his counterparts in the Russian automobile industry since they were all interested in the same things. As Geoffrey Rose recalled:

Alec Issigonis is a very friendly person once you get onto his wave-
length. By the time we'd reached the second course of the main ban-
quet on the first evening, Alec was drawing on the tablecloth all sorts
of front wheel drive designs and the Russians were telling us how the
Nieper Dam worked.

To provide some balance to the gruelling schedule of factory tours, the
British delegation were treated to an evening out at the grand theatre in
the capital, a vast auditorium capable of seating up to 6,000 people, where
the Moscow Ballet were staging a classical performance of *Giselle*.
Issigonis kept the programme for this occasion, perhaps reminded of the
opera house in Smyrna.

The exercise was concluded in February when Strokin returned to
London to discuss the results of the two exchange visits. Once again it
was Issigonis' job to organise the itinerary. This time he decided to recip-
rocate the hospitality enjoyed in Moscow by planning some leisure activities into the programme. The visit therefore began with a trip to
Hampton Court Palace, while the evening spent at the Moscow Ballet
was trumped by the cultural highlight of a performance of the *Black and
White Minstrel Show* at the Victoria Palace Theatre, an experience the
Russian delegation surely never forgot.

THE FORWARD RESEARCH DEPARTMENT

The deference shown by the delegation from the USSR was a startling
illustration of the status that Alec Issigonis continued to hold worldwide.
This brought him some comfort as he re-adjusted to his new status outside the mainstream design programme.

In July 1969 he was allowed to take up a new role as consultant to the
motorcycle manufacturer Norton Villiers. This was part of the Manganese
Bronze Group presided over by his good friend Dennis Poore. In general,
however, the official direction which his new department took seemed
lacking in the drive and sense of purpose it had once had.

Some of the designs which he wished to pursue constituted the tail
end of work from his period as BMC Technical Director. One such project was a replacement for the ageing Austin taxicab known as FX4 which
had originally been launched in 1958. In 1965 Issigonis had begun talks
with Mann and Overton, BMC's London taxi retailers, about a replacement which was given the codename FX5. Though this was outside the

usual scope of his concerns, for some reason this scheme seems to have captured his interest. Several times during 1967 he went to the trouble of taking Dick Burzi and Charles Griffin on visits to the Coventry firm of Carbodies which was responsible for taxi body assembly. The project had stalled soon after the formation of British Leyland but as Issigonis settled into his new job, Mann and Overton made an attempt to revive it and Issigonis gave them his full support. One of the firm's directors, D. J. C. Southwell, wrote to Harry Webster in December 1969, pointing out that the FX4 design was now eleven years old and facing stiff competition from the new cab recently introduced by Metro Cammell. Harry Webster replied to Southwell and Issigonis within three days and the response was not encouraging:

> Turning to the problem of trying to produce a new cab, I know that you are aware of the considerable programme of work which has been undertaken at Longbridge starting just over a year ago, and in which I see no abatement to our activities for the next 4 or 5 years and this, taken in conjunction with the fact that I am still currently running at over 100 draughtsmen and technicians below that required to carry out our current programme on time, you can well understand the dilemma in which we would find ourselves if we had to do a new taxi chassis. This, despite the fact that the body manufacturer [Carbodies] may himself be able to manage his part of the vehicle.

Here was an early indication that the 'General Motors of England' was already facing difficulties with its ambitious new model programme, and as a result this was one project Issigonis would not be allowed to pursue. Ironically one outcome of this was that, despite sporadic competition, the FX4 design was to last almost as long as the Mini, not being taken out of production until 1997.

It was also an illustration that Issigonis, once master of the company's product policy, was no longer able to define his own priorities. Nor were the factory's resources any longer at his fingertips. Although he did not technically report to Webster, in reality the decisions that now shaped his working life lay in Webster's hands. While the taxi idea which he favoured was axed, he was directed instead towards two specific research projects, the investigation of hydrostatic drives in conjunction with the National Engineering Laboratory (NEL) and an examination of the possibilities of steam power for cars. Issigonis did his best but he never thought that either of these studies would come to much and he was right. The hydrostatic drive project was the same one that he had mentioned to Stokes in his memo of 1968 when outlining his work programme. It was an NEL initiative and the idea was to use the device on tractors and bulldozers. In February 1969 Issigonis attended a meeting of the NEL sponsored by Tony Benn, who wrote to him afterwards:

> How nice to see you at NEL with that keen team of people thinking out the ideas from the future for British Leyland. This is a partnership that has great potential and it realises the dreams of many of us in the past. I also look forward to the photograph in the little blue Mini which I shall show to my children and grand-children with great pride.

The system would allow the engine to power an oil pump feeding oil under pressure to separate hydraulic motors at each of the four wheels. The design produced by Issigonis used a four wheel drive chassis with two oil pumps which working together gave the highest gear and working alone gave the lowest gear. The unit had four speeds as well as a choice between two wheel or four wheel drive. Because of difficulties in maximising the efficiency of the pumps, however, the prototypes showed a marked reluctance to go up hills. A few of the units were fitted to development Minis but the project was finally abandoned. Issigonis' final verdict was 'too expensive, noisy and inefficient'. He later wrote on the back of Tony Benn's letter, 'I was hoodwinked, the whole thing was a great waste of money and time. I fell for it as a threat that Oldsmobile were going to take it at a government meeting in London.'

He possibly approached the second project with slightly more relish given his affection for steam but the outcome was no more successful. He was still working with Eric Bareham and John Sheppard at this point and together they tried out several versions, again using a Mini. As John Sheppard commented, 'it had to be in a Mini every time, if it would go in a Mini it would go into anything'. But Issigonis was unable to overcome the problem of the combined thermal losses of the boiler and the engine and again concluded the experiment to be a failure.

He was simply going through the motions with these experiments because he was only really interested in working on projects which stood some chance of getting into production. Increasingly, the focus of his efforts was the subject he had flagged up to the new British Leyland management as a matter of urgency in his April 1968 memorandum, a programme to replace the Mini and 1100. Issigonis would devote the rest of his career to the project which became known as 9X, an ambitious attempt to produce the next generation of small cars. It stretched over a period of nearly twenty years, beginning during the last years of his tenure as BMC Technical Director, surviving his exile to Research and Development and continuing into his official retirement and subsequent appointment as consultant to British Leyland. Stokes and Webster were preoccupied, first with launching the Maxi and then with planning their new product range. They did not therefore do anything to stop him from continuing to pursue his small car research even though it was outside his official programme of work.

The hand fate dealt to Alec Issigonis was to be remembered as 'the man who made the Mini'. It is not the title he would have chosen for himself because no one worked more tirelessly than he did to devise a serious replacement. The intensity of his approach to the 9X project and the length of time over which he pursued it demonstrate better than anything else that he saw the Mini only as a stage in his design career and not as its culmination. His attempts to get the project accepted into the product plan also provide an insight into his capacity for adapting to a working environment which he did not control. The progress of 9X is a fascinating study, not only because it is a design which never came to fruition, but also because it tells us something unexpected about the character of Issigonis himself. We can follow it in some detail because the surviving paperwork relating to all stages and forms of the 9X concept is extremely comprehensive, in stark contrast to the paltry set of documents which survive for ADO 14. This gives strength to the suspicion that the reasons for the inadequacies of ADO 14 may lie in the excellence of the 9X design.

THE 'MINI MINI' PROJECT

Issigonis was already thinking of the next generation of small cars in the mid-1960s and some of his sketches made it as far as crude wooden styling bucks. His efforts were given a new direction when he received a request from Luigi Innocenti at the beginning of 1967 to develop a 'Mini Mini' for the Italian market. The firm of Innocenti was based in Milan and was best known for the manufacture of the Lambretta scooter. In 1960 they entered into an arrangement with BMC to sell the Austin A40, followed by a Pininfarina-bodied Austin-Healey Sprite unique to Italy. BMC supplied overseas firms with parts in kits which were then assembled locally, a process known as CKD (Complete Knock Down). Innocenti was able to refine some of these imports using its own construction presses. The company added the 1100 and the Mini to its range, and over the next few years developed more polished local versions as a result of which Italy became a lucrative market for both vehicles. By 1966, however, Lambretta sales were declining and Innocenti was looking for some other way of maximising its manufacturing capacity. This led to the proposal for a Mini Mini, to be designed and manufactured under the supervision of Issigonis. The two firms would share the development costs and Innocenti would pay a royalty, allowing it to market the car in Italy and throughout the rest of the European Economic Community (EEC). Though the UK was in negotiations to join the EEC this would not come about until 1973 so it was not as easy for UK firms to compete in Europe as it was for some of their major competitors.

Issigonis was happy to turn his mind to the problem of developing a vehicle which was even smaller than ADO 15. He therefore gave Cell A the task of building a new experimental car, XC/8368, and by June the sourcing of components was well underway. In September he received a review of the market implications of his new project from the product appraisal section of the Marketing Department which he seems to have personally commissioned. Its conclusions were not encouraging since it implied that neither Innocenti nor BMC had thought the concept through. It questioned the need for what was referred to as a 'sub-Mini', pointing out that the small car sector was declining everywhere in Europe except Italy. Was this the right sector at which to target scarce investment money for British home sales? As for Innocenti, could it really compete against Fiat who dominated the Italian mass market with the Fiat 500? The conclusion was downbeat: 'At best, the possibility of an adequate return on investment is not clearly apparent. At the worst the result could be unfortunate for B.M.H. and possibly unsatisfactory for Innocenti ...' The Marketing Department were trying to tell the Technical Director that this was the wrong priority at the wrong time. Innocenti strongly disagreed and wrote to Issigonis urging him to carry on:

I wish once more to congratulate you on the brilliant results you have achieved in your studies of the Mini-Mini project. I consider this car to be once more a confirmation of your motor car philosophy and of the great enthusiasm that animates your team of designers.

Issigonis did carry on and by November 1967 a prototype was ready to begin testing. The proportions which Issigonis settled on consisted of a wheelbase the same length as the original Mini (80 inches) fitted with a body which would be 6 inches shorter (114 inches) and 3 inches wider (58.5 inches). The only way these adjusted dimensions could be accommodated was to make the engine take up less space. Accordingly Issigonis began to design a lightweight overhead camshaft engine, initially in a 4-cylinder version with a capacity of 750 to 1000 cc, and several experimental units were built. When it came to the suspension, he departed completely from the principles he had worked on with Alex Moulton. The first prototype had a very basic suspension system with wishbones and coil springs at the front and semi-elliptic cart springs at the rear. The removal of the rubber suspension eliminated the need for subframes and helped to reduce weight, which was one of the targets of the programme. The front suspension was then refined on the following two prototypes to incorporate 'McPherson type' vertical struts.

By February 1968 three prototypes were running and 10,000 miles of testing had been completed in a four-month period as they retraced the route pounded ten years earlier by ADO 15 through the Cotswold Hills. An extensive set of test results survives and one can only feel the most intense sympathy for the drivers who went out night after freezing night in fog, rain, snow and ice. The reports which landed on Issigonis' desk paint a recurring picture of nocturnal misery. A faulty alternator commonly forced our tester to change batteries as many as five times a night. He struggled with a gear lever which displayed 'rattle and zizz' not to mention 'excess freeplay throughout selection'. The clutch suffered from 'judder and fierce operation'. The steering was 'wandering' and 'very sensitive to road imperfections' while the suspension gave a 'choppy pitching ride'. Issigonis wrote his usual commentary in blue ink alongside these mechanical problems but he seemed to have little interest in the desperate pleas for some basic level of comfort. The heater was 'useless' and the floor leaked with one inevitable consequence, 'DRIVER'S FEET PERMANENTLY COLD'. The front seats were too high, causing the driver to crouch if he wished to see through the small area cleaned by the inadequate wipers, though even this was of little use on icy, foggy

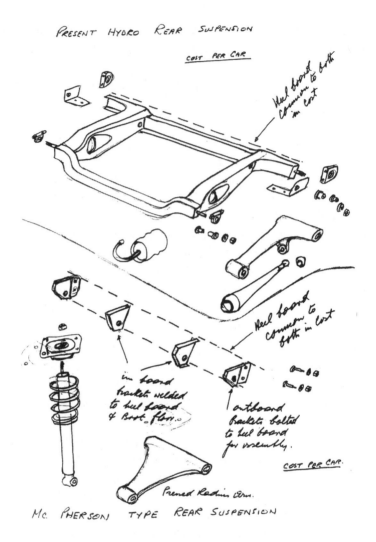

PRESENT HYDRO REAR SUSPENSION

COST PER CAR

McPHERSON TYPE REAR SUSPENSION

When he came to design his Mini replacement in 1967 Issigonis decided to move away from the concept of Hydrolastic ('present hydro' in the chart) suspension to a simpler type of vertical strut ('McPherson type') suspension. This sketch for rear suspension compares the key elements of both these types, demonstrating that his revised version would be easier to assemble and would cost less to manufacture and maintain.

nights since the de-mister did not work and there was no screen washer. It would seem that maximisation of the interior space also needed some work since Issigonis was informed that anyone unfortunate enough to be over 5 feet 4 inches tall would find his left arm pinned against the door and his cramped back aching.

As far as Issigonis was concerned these were the normal vicissitudes of testing and the programme forged ahead. Innocenti's Chief Engineer, Parolari, was sent a set of bodywork sketches for comment but told firmly, 'I should point out that Pininfarina have been asked to prepare this work for B.M.C. and that you are not involved at the present time.' A full-scale styling buck of the elegant Pininfarina design was built and examined in the Longbridge styling studio. Issigonis had already diverged from the brief he had agreed with Innocenti. Maybe the initial marketing report had given him pause for thought because by early 1968 his thinking had expanded to a whole range of vehicles. Significantly, a fourth, slightly larger prototype was under construction and further experimental 6-cylinder power units were being built with a capacity of 1275–1500 cc.

By March 1968 Cell A was beginning to make calculations about manufacturing costs and these appeared to compare favourably with ADO 15. At this crucial stage, Issigonis was given his new job in Forward Research. Since the project was still in its early phase he found no reason to take discouragement from this. We have already seen that it was the basis of his report in April to Donald Stokes concerning the projects he currently had in hand. In May he exchanged correspondence over the engine design with Lewis Dawtrey, Head of Research and Development for Standard Triumph, and Dawtrey replied encouragingly, 'I must say that there is a lot of your new engine that appeals to me ... I am preparing a few notes on first impressions for Mr. Webster ...'

Stokes and Webster were by now in the middle of their review of the product plan and they decided it was time to intervene in the steady course on which Mini Mini seemed set. Accordingly on 9 July 1968, a team led by Luigi Innocenti and his Chief Engineer Parolari arrived at Longbridge to meet up with Harriman and Issigonis. They, in turn, introduced their Italian collaborators to the representatives of the newly formed corporation, Stokes and Turnbull. The meeting started in a spirit of optimism with Harriman outlining the business proposals and Issigonis summarising current progress. At this point, the Innocenti team were asked to leave the room so that Harriman and Issigonis could be treated to a critique of their scheme by Stokes and Turnbull. When the Italians were called back, Harriman had been instructed to put it to them that British Leyland's need to fully utilise its manufacturing facilities was as great as Innocenti's and that the present scheme, if allowed to go ahead, could represent a threat to exports: 'This was to some extent due to the

Mini-Mini having moved away from its original concept – a sub mini – and having become the expected replacement for the current Mini range.'

Luigi Innocenti would therefore leave deprived of his Mini Mini project. Stokes offered a vague promise of technical assistance in the fairly impossible task of looking for an alternative vehicle to manufacture which would not provide competition to any vehicle that British Leyland already produced or were ever likely to produce. It was made clear, however, that the Italian firm would not be involved in the Mini replacement programme nor would they be allowed to design additional derivatives of British Leyland vehicles. With a smile, Stokes administered a final knee in the groin by informing the Italians that, while he was renewing their existing CKD contract for a further seven years, prices would be 'renegotiated'. This, he told them, would be accomplished in a spirit of 'mutual understanding and goodwill'. This induced a small crisis inside the Innocenti company and Signor Parolari informed Issigonis of his departure barely a year later in September 1969 with a charming letter expressing his regret at the end of their association:

> You know what a pleasure it has been to have met you and how much I have appreciated these 10 years of collaboration, during which I have seen in you the Master and the creative Genius. I shall remember you always with entire liking and it is an honour to express you my best, hearty and affectionate greetings.

MINI MINI BECOMES 9X

The key to the statement made to Innocenti was that Mini Mini had 'become the expected replacement for the current Mini range'. In 1966 Issigonis was almost at the end of the original set of vehicles developed from his grand idea of transverse engine, front wheel drive. He was bored by the work he was having to do on products which did not interest him. In turning his mind to the narrow problem posed by Innocenti's request, his imagination had suddenly been sparked again. This transformed itself into an ambitious overall plan for a whole family of cars which he sketched out on a chart in one of his notebooks. It involved a range of no less than six sizes of car with three brand new engines and the sketch outlines the different body shapes and power units he had planned, indicating various links between them (see opposite).

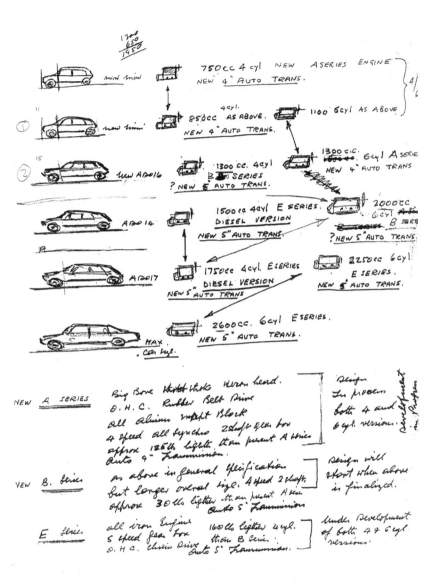

In the 1970s Issigonis produced an ambitious overall plan for a whole family of cars. Two were already in production – ADO 14 and ADO 17. The 750 cc 'Mini Mini' and the 850 cc 'new Mini' both made it to prototype stage, while the 'new ADO 16' got as far as a detailed proposal. Two out of three of the engines also existed, the E-series being the unit designed for ADO 14, and the 'new A-series' being the power unit which would become known as '9X'.

This chart demonstrated that Issigonis had not lost his originality, vision, or talent for lateral thinking. Nor was he backing away from problems as he has sometimes been accused of doing. Not only was the product range described impressively comprehensive, it also included diesel engines which were becoming common in Europe but were not really a feature in Britain for passenger vehicles.

It might have been expected that Stokes would follow his dismissal of Innocenti by putting an end to the nascent project, but as yet the new corporation had not defined its product policy absolutely. It seems that at this stage it was prepared to allow Issigonis' Mini replacement programme to proceed. XC/8368 therefore morphed into the even more ambitious 9X

THE 9X PROPOSALS OF 1968 – A NEW MINI AND A NEW 1100

In August 1968 Issigonis put forward a formal design study for a new 750–1000 cc Mini, this clearly being the follow-on from the aborted Mini Mini programme. In his introduction, he made his usual side-swipes at American design philosophy, and restated his aphorisms about the importance of space utilisation and pricing. These elements were, however, muted compared with the wordy documents of only a year or two earlier. The main argument of the report showed a new consciousness of market requirements and stated bluntly that though the Mini currently comprised 45 per cent of UK car exports to EEC countries it was losing market share against strong competition, and that the facelift planned for 1969 (ADO 20) was too expensive. He further argued that planned cost reductions would be ineffective because they could only be confined to details. The report continued:

> The objective is to provide a car with room for four adults and some luggage, within a competitive specification, at a price 5% below the current Mini, with the aim of major penetration into the world small car market, particularly in Europe.

This time he specified a body 4 rather than 6 inches shorter than ADO 15 (116 inches) while the wheelbase had grown 2 inches (82 inches). The other dimensions were unchanged from Mini Mini. The means of achieving this would be a brand new engine design which was well underway

Arclight

DETAIL
TRACING PAD

100 SHEETS - 13 ins. by 10 ins.

QUALITY
No. 2308 /129

Left: Issigonis, Morris Motors Project Engineer, at Cowley in 1946, close to his first success with the Morris Minor. Right: from 1938 to 1957 he sketched his designs in a series of Arclight notepads

Issigonis, Technical Director of BMC, at Longbridge in 1965, now the celebrated designer of the Mini, the 1100 and the 1800

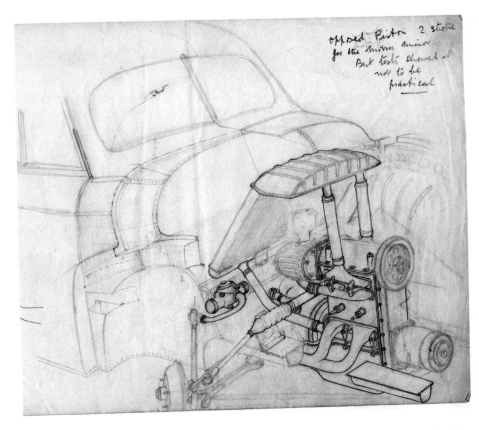

opposed Piston 2 stroke
for the Morris minor
But tests showed it
not to be
practical

Mosquito sketch from 1944 showing a two-stroke opposed piston engine with rear-mounted radiator. Closer examination suggests a Zenith carburettor and supercharger. Issigonis has noted that 'best tests showed it not to be practical'

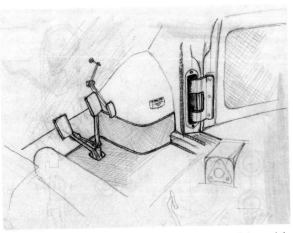

Interior detail of Mosquito showing the position of the pedals and door hinge

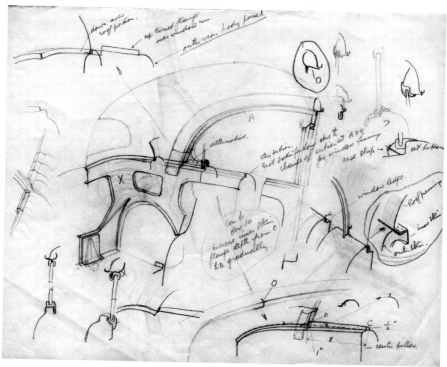

During the 1940s Issigonis often used the pages of his Arclight notepads to work through ideas. He has drawn the structure of the rear quarter of the Mosquito in great detail, showing the extent to which he concerned himself with every part of the design

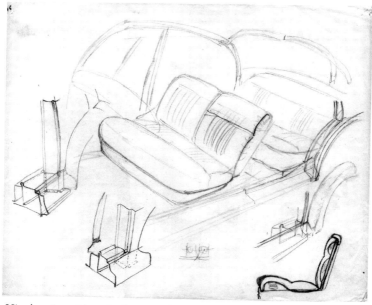

His obsession with packaging started at an early date. This example is a concept for the interior of one of the Mosquito's larger cousins

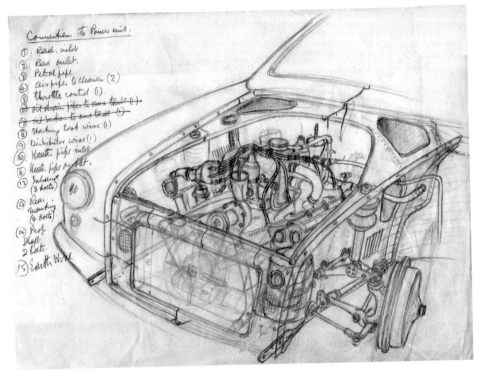

The Alvis drawings, believed lost, represent the creative link between the Mosquito concept and the engineering breakthrough of the Mini ten years later. One of his finest sketches shows the newly designed V8 in the engine bay with notes about its installation

The 'mouth organ' type radiator grille, one of many ideas for the front end styling

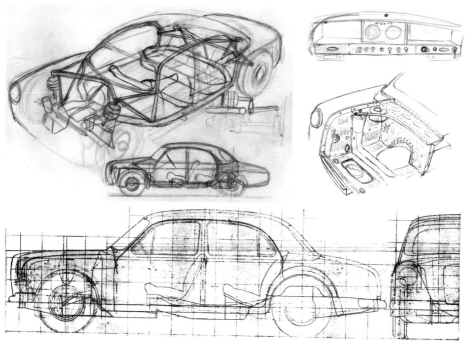

The lines of Alec's sketches (top) are echoed in the full-scale engineering drawing of the Alvis TA/350 (bottom) produced by John Sheppard, showing how Issigonis' team translated his ideas into reality

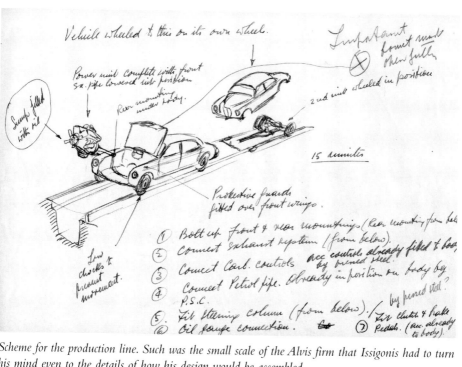

Scheme for the production line. Such was the small scale of the Alvis firm that Issigonis had to turn his mind even to the details of how his design would be assembled

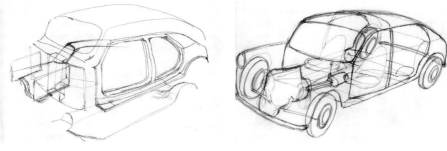

Body structure   *Seating layout*

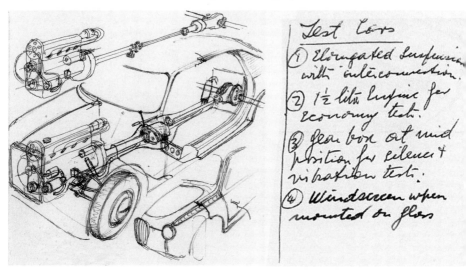

Test Cars

1. Elongated Suspension with interconnection.
2. 1½ litre Engine for economy tests.
3. Gear box at mid position for silence & vibration tests.
4. Windscreen when mounted on glass

Drivetrain layout

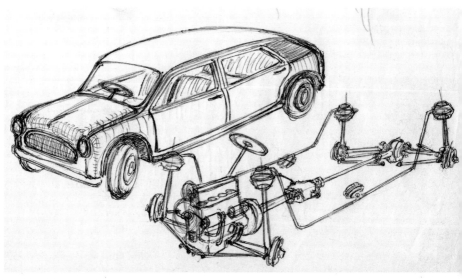

Overall view of body and mechanical parts with early ideas on interconnected suspension

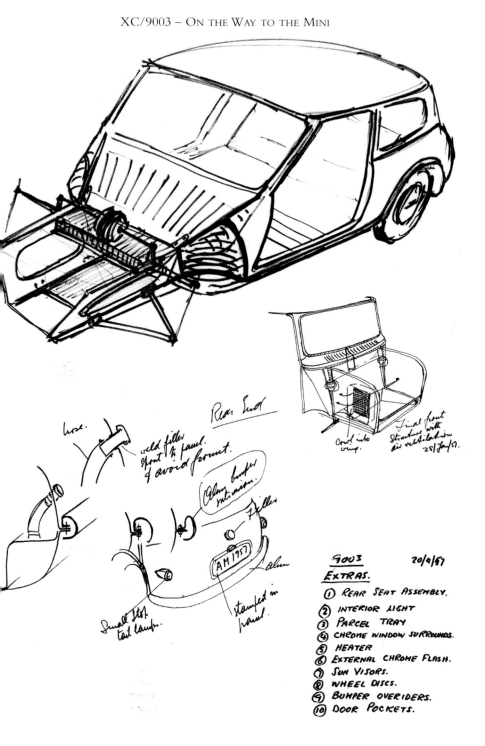

Rear End

hose.

weld filler
spout to panel
& avoid forward.

Alum bumper
extension

Filler

AM 1957

Small stop
tail lamps.

stamped in
panel.

Alum

Cowl into
wing.

Final front
structure with
air ventilation
28/Jan/57.

9003   20/9/57
EXTRAS.
① REAR SEAT ASSEMBLY.
② INTERIOR LIGHT
③ PARCEL TRAY
④ CHROME WINDOW SURROUNDS.
⑤ HEATER
⑥ EXTERNAL CHROME FLASH.
⑦ SUN VISORS.
⑧ WHEEL DISCS.
⑨ BUMPER OVERIDERS.
⑩ DOOR POCKETS.

ronically, XC/9003, which would become the Mini, is the least sketched Issigonis design. By 1957
black felt tip pen had replaced the pencil and the lines had become less subtle, but these examples
clearly show the pure lines of his most famous creation

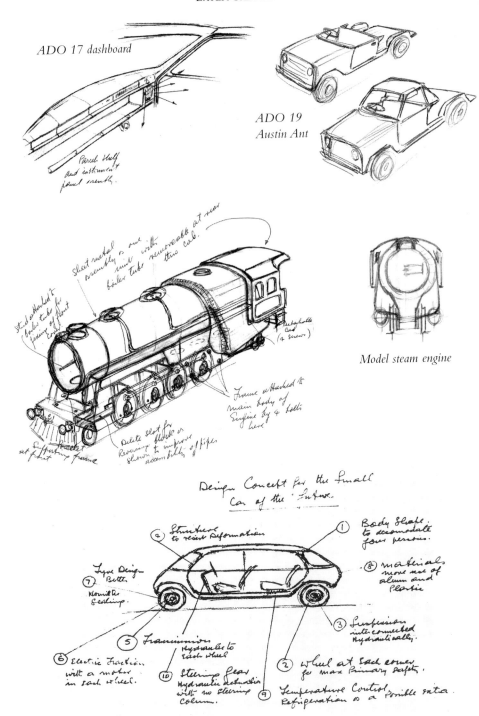

ADO 17 dashboard

Parcel shelf and instrument panel assembly.

ADO 19 Austin Ant

Model steam engine

Design Concept for the Small Car of the 'Future.

① Body Shape to accomodate four persons.

④ Structure to resist deformation.

⑧ materials more use of alum and Plastic

⑦ Tyre Design Butt. Acoustic Sealing.

③ Suspension interconnected Hydraulically.

⑤ Transmission Hydraulic to each wheel

② Wheel at each corner for max primary safety.

⑥ Electric Traction with a motor in each wheel.

⑩ Steering Gear Hydraulic actuation with no steering column.

⑨ Temperature Control Refrigeration as a possible extra.

After the success of the Mini, the increasing demands of his job meant that Issigonis became a les prolific sketcher, but he still found time to draw the design for his model railway in the old style. H also continued to dream of the 'small car of the future' since five experimental units had already been built and tested. The gear-box would feature 4-speed transmission with synchromesh on all gears. The suspension had now been further developed and was described as all-independent with vertical struts at the front and concentric torsion bars at the rear. He even proposed the fitting of wind-up windows in a concession to the Sales Department's desire for a better standard of equipment. Throughout his report Issigonis stressed two things – that this car would be simpler to manufacture and easier to service, adding up to a cheaper and more profitable product. Thus he pointed out that the engine and transmission required 40 per cent fewer components than ADO 15, producing a 30-minute reduction in assembly time. He suggested a three-year development programme 'to reduce the design cost to an absolute minimum', aiming for launch at the 1971 Motor Show. Fourteen items were listed which could be serviced *in situ*, seven of which he identified as 'not possible in existing designs Mini/1100/1800'. He concluded:

The Mini is now ten years old. The replacement proposed in this paper is planned to be 5% cheaper, and more competitive in world markets, particularly Europe. The estimated total cost of the programme is £10.0 m. (excluding buildings). Forecast incremental volume is 120,000 per annum resulting in incremental contribution to fixed overheads and profits of £10.0 m. per annum (before tax). It is recommended that this programme be authorised at the earliest possible date.

In writing this Issigonis was directly challenging his critics whose dislike of the Mini was based on its lack of profitability. He went even further by producing a companion proposal in September for a new ADO 16. The purpose was as follows:

This paper outlines a proposal for a low cost, advanced specification, medium sized family car aimed principally at Western European markets. The objective is to provide a car which is more refined, technically more advanced and offers better value for money than its competitors, at a price which is directly competitive. The ratio of internal space to exterior size will be better than any other car in its class, and the 6 cylinder overhead camshaft 1200/1500 cc engine will provide standards of performance and smoothness unapproached by any other high volume model.

This specification was a development of the Mini replacement proposal, including all independent suspension – Hydrolastic is ruled out as a key element driving up cost – fitted with the 6-cylinder form of the engine design. This proposal not only repeats the arguments about profitability, it introduces an extra factor, commonality of parts. The appendix lists 53 components which would be common to the proposed ADO 15 and ADO 16 replacements and states that 'all other components will be similar to existing B.L.M.C. or proprietary units'. This dealt with the second criticism levelled at the Issigonis designs, the high cost of manufacturing and servicing a model range with so few interchangeable parts. This time, Issigonis forecast a development cost of £9 million against an incremental contribution to fixed overheads and profits of £17.5 million per annum.

These proposals illustrate that he was able to learn lessons from some of the less successful aspects of his previous designs and that he was not unreceptive to the need for a vehicle which was easier and cheaper to construct and maintain. He was trying hard to show that he could adapt himself to the needs of the present day. When considering his earlier career I posed the question, could he have flourished in the environment of the large drawing office, deprived of the unique working methods which he devised for himself? Could he have adapted himself to an environment in which he had less autonomy? These events would seem to suggest the answer is yes.

In the ADO 16 design study, Issigonis defined for the first time the element which would become the heart of his new project, the engine design:

The project started off as a smaller and cheaper version of the present Mini, but in the course of development of this model considerable cost, weight and space savings have been achieved by the new engine transmission unit. This unit also offers an appreciably higher power/weight ratio than is now available with our 'A' type engine ... It was felt, therefore, that these economic and technical gains should be directed towards a replacement model of the present Mini rather than the creation of a smaller derivative.

He continued by arguing that the proposed 6-cylinder power unit could be directly compared with the current 1300 cc 4-cylinder A-series used in ADO 16 while being both lighter and more powerful:

Figures such as these cannot be readily ignored ... The use of a modern six cylinder engine in a medium size family car of this type would undoubtedly be a trend setter for the future, thus keeping us way out ahead of competition on technical merits, but without any economic sacrifices ... the important point of this design study is to commonise installation profiles, which is made possible by the fact that both the four and six cylinder engines have identical outlines ...

Issigonis was saying to British Leyland, let's advance small car design as far as we can before our competition can catch us. In September 1968 there was still time to do this. There had been copies of the 1100, most notably from Peugeot, but the 'superminis', based on his principles but with considerable refinements, did not surface until the late 1960s. The first was the Autobianchi A112 launched in 1969 but this was sold only in Europe and was not available in Britain. Its Fiat cousin, the 127, which can probably lay claim to being the first of the real superminis, was not introduced until 1971, followed by a crop of other imitations such as the Datsun Cherry and the Renault 5 which were eventually to steal the market. The arrival of the Volkswagen Polo in 1975 followed by the Ford Fiesta in 1976 would cement this trend once and for all.

THE 9X ENGINE

Once Issigonis had achieved the insight that the engine was the key to the project he galloped off along this route with enthusiasm. When he had designed ADO 15, he had put aside the concepts which had gone into the Mosquito. Now he went back to first principles again. He had always said that the power unit was the main obstacle in the way of the perfect small car because it took precious space away from the interior. So this time, instead of starting with the passenger space, he began with the power unit. The smaller and lighter he could make it, the bigger the useable interior space he could extract from the minimum external dimensions.

The engine concept was therefore the nub of the 9X project and a number of experimental units were produced over the next few years, to be fitted into a variety of cars, including several Minis, an 1100, a Maestro and a Metro. To achieve his objectives he returned to his grounding in the Austin Seven. The Austin Seven engine, produced between 1922 and 1937, featured a separate cast-iron short cylinder block sandwiched between a cast-iron cylinder head and a large aluminium crankcase. Each part of the 'sandwich' was fixed to its neighbour by means of studs secured with nuts. This approach had its roots in Edwardian engine technology. Other engines of the period, including the A-series, tended to have a two piece construction with a cylinder head fixed to a 'monobloc' cylinder block and crankcase all made of cast iron. What Issigonis was trying to devise was a much more compact engine utilising a creative combination of aluminium and cast iron in an attempt to remedy some of the mechanical shortcomings of the A-series and its cousins. He took the three-piece 'sandwich' principle from the Austin Seven though in this case the cylinder head and crankcase were both aluminium and only the short cylinder block was cast iron. The same method of studs and nuts was used to hold the three pieces of the sandwich together. Being made of aluminium and having many fewer parts it would be much lighter and easier to manufacture than the A-series. There is no doubt that the results added up to a fine piece of innovative engineering in the best Issigonis tradition.

Now that the project had changed focus the XC/8368 prototypes were put on one side and two new prototypes were built to the specification described in the design study. One was maroon, with wind-up windows, the other was blue, with sliding windows. The compact engine made it possible to foreshorten the engine bay so that even though the body was shorter than ADO 15 there was an extra four inches of interior legroom. Like the original Mini, the prototype was simple, striking and pleasing to the eye, without the starkness which had afflicted the later designs. It also incorporated an elegant hatchback design which would be very much in tune with market trends which were emerging.

Trying to Get 9X into Production

Despite the fact that Issigonis was no longer Technical Director, the 9X engine range formed part of *The Austin Morris Division Product Plan with regard to Power Units* in June 1969. This document was clearly prepared under his direction because it draws heavily on a number of other papers written by him during the early part of 1969. It was not to stay there for long, and had been ejected by the start of 1970 on the recommendation of Filmer Paradise. In an episode reminiscent of the arguments surrounding the Mosquito project, a short power-struggle ensued during which Issigonis and a small number of his remaining allies tried hard to keep 9X on the agenda. This time, however, he had no one of the stature of Miles

Thomas fighting his corner. On the contrary, the higher echelons of management in the shape of Donald Stokes, George Turnbull, Filmer Paradise and Harry Webster were in no mood to give him credit for anything after the drubbing they had got as a result of the design he had neglected, the Maxi.

The only definite way back onto the Forward Product Plan was for the design to be adopted by the Product Planning Sub-committee of which he was not a member. The Deputy Director of Product Planning for Austin Morris, F. Clarke, was convinced that dropping the 9X had been a mistake so in February 1970 he asked George Turnbull for a meeting to discuss the matter. Turnbull agreed and the meeting took place eight days later, described as 'a special meeting to discuss the Mini and its replacement'. Issigonis must have felt isolated among the other participants. Though he received strong support from Clarke and his old friend Geoffrey Rose, the meeting was chaired by George Turnbull, ably assisted by Harry Webster.

Discussion initially focussed on short-term measures to reduce costs on the existing Mini by £5 per car and Webster noted with approval that 'the recent change from hydrolastic to cone suspension had aroused little criticism'. Everyone seemed to agree that the current Mini would not be able to compete beyond 1975, and that the A-series engine was the main obstacle to its development. Issigonis put forward the two reports he had written the previous year. He outlined the results he had been able to obtain with the blue 9X prototype which his team had constructed and he described the range of 4-cylinder and 6-cylinder engines he had built. Harry Webster showed little enthusiasm and the meeting concluded that the issue should go forward to the next Chief Engineers' Meeting – thus excluding Issigonis from the discussion – and Marketing would be asked to evaluate the viability of the current Mini beyond 1975.

As well as the advocacy of Clarke, Issigonis was still receiving support from Charles Griffin and in June he prepared some additional data for his former deputy. This compared the specification of the 9X prototype with the original Mini, the new Clubman version and, significantly, the Autobianchi A112. According to Issigonis, the 9X was a superior car in almost every respect. He made this final succinct comparison with the Autobianchi in his typical blunt style:

WEIGHT	Lighter
OVERALL DIMENSIONS	Smaller
SEATING ACCOMMODATION	Greater
LUGGAGE SPACE	Marginal
CRUISING NOISE	Better
HIGH SPEED HANDLING	Same
SUSPENSION COMFORT	Better
SUSPENSION NOISE	Same
PERFORMANCE	Not comparable because Autobianchi engine is same as Cooper 'S' specification
GENERAL ALL ROUND VISIBILITY	Better
ELBOW ROOM	Greater
GEAR SHIFT	Worse
BODY SHAKE & RATTLES	Better
CROSS WIND DIRECTIONAL VISIBILITY	Same

The 'special' meeting was reconvened in June and this time Filmer Paradise was invited but Issigonis only felt frustrated when nothing new was said and no conclusion was reached. In his absence, the Product Policy Sub-committee of 6 July was less reticent and Filmer Paradise firmly voiced his opposition, questioning whether 9X could really deliver the profitability suggested. British Leyland does not appear to have learnt much from BMC at this stage for as well as allowing Issigonis to pursue the 9X project and build a substantial number of prototypes, work had also started on an alternative Mini replacement proposal which included a brand new F-series 1100–1300 cc power unit. Once again the decision was to make no decision but this time a cost and profitability comparison was requested between the two rival ideas.

Issigonis was growing tired of this political ping-pong so he decided to change his tactics by asking C.B. Hill of Marketing to view one of his prototypes. Hill was impressed by the demonstration and complimented Issigonis on his achievement but he cautioned him that future products would have to meet stringent new rules on emissions. He also suggested that a higher standard of styling and trim than in the past would be essential. On this occasion Issigonis took his advice with good grace, grateful to have been given a hearing.

At this point Issigonis had not come to terms with the reality of his new situation. He had genuinely worked hard on an excellent design and believed, in his straightforward way, that the results would be judged on merit alone. Perhaps encouraged by his meeting with Hill, he took one of the 9X engines to his old friend Daniel Richmond at Downton Engineering to have it tuned and fitted into a Mini. He then invited Harry Webster and his team to an impressive demonstration of the car's capabilities, revealing the new engine at the end as the *coup de grace*. Webster had seemed vaguely impressed until the identity of the power unit was revealed at which his enthusiasm disappeared and he simply commented, 'oh, that'. Issigonis was deeply hurt by Webster's indifference and this greatly compounded the resentment he had begun to harbour against his employers.

It therefore came as little surprise when October's Product Policy Sub-Committee Meeting sanctioned the rival project rather than 9X. Even this decision was withdrawn at the next meeting in November. All plans for a Mini replacement were postponed for two years 'to enable sales to establish more accurately the market requirements'. Instead, the existing Mini would be subject to yet more cost reduction and refinement programmes to extend its life and increase its profitability. This, it was suggested, would give a clear run to yet another project which was in train, known as 'Calypso' or ADO 70. This was a second attempt at a sports-bodied Mini which was being built in Michelotti's studio using the ADO 20 chassis. It had reached prototype stage and was scheduled for launch in 1973. The implication was that Calypso had the potential to make more money, though at substantially lower volumes (only around 80,000 per year) than a replacement Mini. This was a red herring as Calypso itself was later dropped from the model programme.

Throughout 1970 Issigonis had been encouraged to believe that his work was being taken seriously which made the final decision a severe blow. The 9X power unit was not included in the Forward Product Plan, but even so Stokes could not quite bring himself to tell Issigonis to stop working on it. When he retired at the end of 1971 his leading engineers were dispersed to other departments but nothing was done to prevent him from assembling a new team to help him carry on with the project in his new role as Advanced Design Consultant. Among those who moved on was John Sheppard, who joined Charles Griffin's department. Never-theless, British Leyland rubbed salt in the wound by continuing with the development of the rival F-series engine, despite the fact that the replace-ment Mini it was supposedly destined for had been shelved. In July 1971 Issigonis was even asked to carry out an assessment of it by Webster, who wrote to him as follows:

> As you know, we have recently designed a dedicated 1000 cc engine and transmission unit. Discussing this matter with Lord Stokes and Mr. Turnbull yesterday, it was a unanimous wish that a completely critical appraisal should be carried out on the design, and Lord Stokes specifically asked that this should be done by you. I have asked Geoff Johnson accordingly to provide you with all the necessary informa-tion as soon as possible.

He was given a ten-page report setting out the design parameters of a 'dedicated power unit for a Mini replacement' and against nearly every paragraph he simply scrawled '9X' in the blue ink of his fountain pen. He did send Webster a proper report in August, but the gist of what he said, at much greater length, was the same. He could not find anything in the F-series which was superior to his own design.

It was clear that it would be difficult to find the resources to continue with the development of his new engine concept but Issigonis was never one to give up and, just when he needed it most, an alternative source of funding presented itself. The Industrial Development Act (IDA) of 1966 empowered the Board of Trade to make grants towards the approved cost of producing prototypes necessary for carrying out scientific research which would lead to significant new applications. Any grant would repre-sent 50 per cent of total costs including design, direct labour, materials, test equipment, subcontracts and overheads. In 1968 Issigonis had begun to apply for funds to cover the hydrostatic, steam and 9X projects. The hydrostatic application was successful in April 1969. The steam project never developed sufficiently to be eligible. In the case of the 9X, he received the news that the application had been partially successful in July 1971. Interestingly, the elements rejected as ineligible included the two-piece cylinder block and crankcase on the grounds that 'this construction was a common feature on early car engines and still is for motorcycle engines' and the joining of block, crankcase and main bearing caps by common bolts because 'this has been done before'. This confirms the engine's roots in the Austin Seven design.

Just before receiving news of the grant Issigonis had asked for a break-down of all expenditure on the 9X programme from the Experimental Order records and he was given the information that a total of £172,425 had been spent from the start of 1966 to the end of 1970. The IDA grant amounted to a contribution of £180,000, a figure which very closely matched the sums already spent.

THE SIGNIFICANCE OF 9X

In this way Issigonis cleverly managed to by-pass the decision of senior management in order to find the means of carrying on with his pet project. He was also assisted by the goodwill of former colleagues in the engineer-ing department and experimental shops, who undertook work for him 'semi-officially'. He was still convinced that he was right in pursuing the small car market, even though this was completely out of step with the company's declared plans for the future. In 1969 he described a conversa-tion with Gianni Agnelli, head of Fiat, on this very subject:

> Not very long ago, about a year ago, I met him in Monte Carlo and we were having a drink, and he said 'Issigonis, we don't think small cars are any good any more. I hear you have just designed a mini mini'. Innocenti had told him, we were working with him at that time. I said 'I'm very glad to hear this, we'll get the whole market to ourselves'.

Nevertheless he knew that, as circumstances stood, 9X had no chance of being accepted into the current product plan.

Issigonis had targeted the 1971 Motor Show for the launch of 9X, and it is interesting to speculate what kind of reception it would have received had it appeared on schedule. Visitors to the show were to find little that was new. Even *Autocar* featured a message from the President of the Society of Motor Manufacturers and Traders (SMMT) which warned:

> Many (cars) will look familiar despite the multitude of improvements incorporated in most of them. New styling is not the talking point of 1971 – reliability, safety, performance, emission control and comfort details are the gain areas for those who will buy after this motor show.

British Leyland offered few surprises. The Triumph Dolomite had been delayed by a pay dispute so did not make the show as planned. An uninspired Mark III version of the Austin 1100/1300 was on display while the Morris Marina and a Series III Jaguar E-type V12 had both been launched earlier in the year. One of the reasons for the lack of British offerings was a series of strikes which affected the whole industry and not just British Leyland. As far as European designs were concerned new pollution and safety regulations were causing major problems for all manufacturers. Those new models which were on display could not be called innovative. In fact the most exciting thing at the show was the daring use of topless models on the TVR stand to attract the attention of bored journalists on press day. Datsun exhibited the Cherry which had front wheel drive and a transverse engine. Fiat had the 127, which was also based on Issigonis-type principles. Both were larger than the 9X, neither featured a hatchback and their target was really the middle of the market, the 1100 rather than the Mini sector. The Renault 5 would be the first popular hatchback, making its appearance in 1972, but this was still larger than the Mini and did not feature a transverse engine. This implies that even if 9X had been delayed it would still have been well up with the competition at this stage.

It would therefore appear that the 9X might have done as Issigonis had suggested, allowing British Leyland to stay ahead of the market. On the other hand, the industrial unrest of 1971 could easily have affected British Leyland's ability to get the car ready for the show and the new regulations on pollution and emissions might also have been a problem. The other caution must be that, while in retrospect British Leyland appear to have missed an opportunity, at the time small cars were not the obvious market to aim for. A number of reports had established that the Mini had effectively created its own market and its uniqueness meant it had little direct competition. People bought the Mini for itself and in spite of its faults, and this was true in Britain, in France, in Italy and in Japan where it was most popular. British Leyland conducted a piece of market research in Paris during 1972 to find out how French customers viewed the original Mini in relation to vehicles such as the Renault 5. In response to the question 'How would you define the image of the Mini?' one respondent replied – 'It's quite simple, for your wife you buy a Renault 5, for your mistress you buy a Mini.' Though the Mini was holding its market share, the trend of the period was against small cars. The relaxation of credit restrictions was one factor encouraging the public to buy larger, more prestigious, cars. This came to an abrupt end with the economic downturn of 1973 which made people once again want cheaper motoring. The decisions made by Stokes and Webster in 1968 were therefore rational ones, and it is only with hindsight that they can be considered to be wrong. How could they know what would happen in 1973?

Nevertheless once the direction of demand had changed British Leyland still failed to act and it is more difficult to absolve them from blame on this score. This will be returned to in the next chapter, but it is relevant to note here that after the oil shortages of 1973, when Issigonis made a renewed attempt to get the project taken seriously, 9X was still relevant and still no one wanted to listen. The result was that while the Mini's share of the small car market throughout the 1970s stayed fairly constant, British Leyland's other models began to lose out to the ever-expanding range of superminis which had begun to appear.

Issigonis was sure that Stokes *et al.* had got it all wrong and he told an interviewer in 1978:

> It was at the time the merger took place and the people that took us over thought that they could do better. Well, I left it to them because I'm not a politician, I'm an engineer. I think it [the 9X] would have done a great deal and I personally feel we wouldn't have been in the trouble we're in now.

On a more personal level, this rejection killed the early shoots of any inclination he felt to compromise his principles in the interests of getting his ideas accepted. Issigonis refused to acknowledge that there might be any justification in the way he had been treated. It was not the new job or the loss of his work title which represented the biggest blow. What really hurt was the fact that, for the first time in his career, his ideas and his creativity were not wanted.

Leonard Lord and George Harriman had compromised his talents by failing to provide a proper framework within which they could flourish in the way that Miles Thomas and Vic Oak had done. Stokes and Turnbull made an even worse mistake. Issigonis had once again come up with an imaginative and sound design. He was showing the willingness to recognise the demands both of the new corporation and of the current world economy. They, however, could not see beyond the mess which had resulted from the failure of first the 1800 and then the Maxi. British Leyland therefore chose to disregard him completely.

Beneath the bluster and the authoritarianism, Issigonis was a deeply sensitive person in the way that creative people often are and he felt humiliated. He knew that the title of 'Director of Research and Development' was nothing more than flannel. As far as he was concerned, he was being patted on the head as the designer of the Mini and told to go off and play. This ignited a burning resentment which, sadly, would cloud the rest of his life. For the next few years he rumbled discontentedly around the bowels of Longbridge, causing British Leyland a nagging discomfort in its nether regions that it was unable to soothe.

THE FINAL YEARS

CHAPTER 10

I suspect that you may well disagree with our current philosophy but neither of us has the power to alter it.

Roland Bertodo to Sir Alec Issigonis in 1986

RETIREMENT

EVEN AT THE height of his fame, Issigonis had worried about the future. The idea of retirement was unappealing to a man who had little interest in anything outside his work. He spoke of it with apprehension in 1964:

Officially I have seven years to go before I retire. Which is a dreadfully long time. I certainly wouldn't retire now because I should get bored stiff. No, no, I certainly wouldn't like to retire now – although of course, when I overwork myself I feel I should. But I think when I'm sixty-five I shall feel different about it. I still have this tremendous interest. Well, I love my job, difficult as it is. I haven't any idea of what I shall do when I do retire, but I shan't go and live abroad. I want to stay in England because I love it so much. What I shall do I don't know. I don't like yachting, I don't like sailing or anything like that. Perhaps a bit more on the model railway.

These words give clear expression to the reluctance he felt to even consider the idea of giving up his job. This feeling had not gone away even during the painful three years spent under the aegis of British Leyland. His friends rallied round to try to boost his spirits. When he visited the Geneva Motor Show in March 1971, many of them got together to wish him well. Afterwards Robert Braunschweig wrote to him:

… there may be a few letters missing behind your name, but how can you expect a rough Swiss to know. Alec, this was one of my happiest moments. I cannot really say how deeply I was affected that your humble engineer was able to let you see a little bit how very many

385

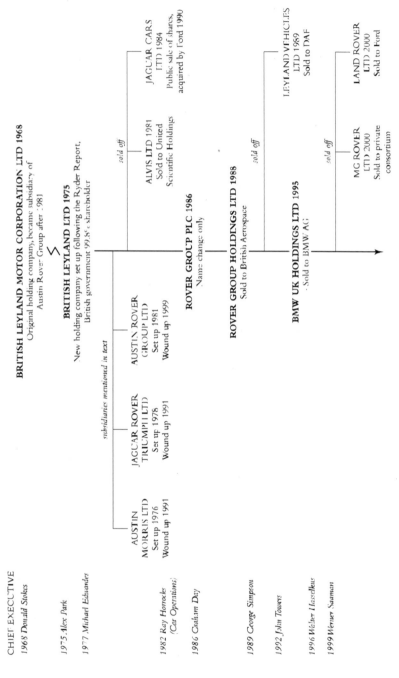

CHART 2: DEVELOPMENT AND BREAK-UP OF BRITISH LEYLAND 1968–2000

CHIEF EXECUTIVE
1968 *Donald Stokes*

1975 *Alex Park*

1977 *Michael Edwardes*

1982 *Ray Horrocks*
(Car Operations)

1986 *Graham Day*

1989 *George Simpson*

1992 *John Towers*

1996 *Walter Hasselkus*

1999 *Werner Saaman*

BRITISH LEYLAND MOTOR CORPORATION LTD 1968
Original holding company, became subsidiary of
Austin Rover Group after 1981

BRITISH LEYLAND LTD 1975
New holding company set up following the Ryder Report,
British government 99.8% shareholder

subsidiaries mentioned in text

AUSTIN
MORRIS LTD
Set up 1976
Wound up 1991

JAGUAR ROVER
TRIUMPH LTD
Set up 1978
Wound up 1991

AUSTIN ROVER
GROUP LTD
Set up 1981
Wound up 1999

ALVIS LTD 1981
Sold to United
Scientific Holdings

JAGUAR CARS
LTD 1984
Public sale of shares,
acquired by Ford 1990

sold off

ROVER GROUP PLC 1986
Name change only

ROVER GROUP HOLDINGS LTD 1988
Sold to British Aerospace

LEYLAND VEHICLES
LTD 1989
Sold to DAF

sold off

BMW UK HOLDINGS LTD 1995
Sold to BMW AG

MG ROVER
LTD 2000
Sold to private
consortium

LAND ROVER
LTD 2000
Sold to Ford

sold off

people feel about you … Please remember always how very much everyone, at least in that particular gang, admires and loves you.

He took heart and did not allow his spirit to be crushed completely. He was still regularly wheeled out for big press occasions and in August 1971 the Austin Morris Division stage-managed a landmark 'double' to get some press attention, both the cars involved naturally being Issigonis designs. In CAB 1, a Mini Clubman rolled off the line to represent the 5 millionth front wheel drive car produced. At the same moment over at CAB 2 the 2 millionth example of the 1100/1300 range reached the end of the track. A short race to the Exhibition Hall was then supposed to ensue, with Webster leading the way at the wheel of the Mini and Issigonis following in the 1300. Issigonis, however, ignored the script he had been given, sneaking into the Exhibition Hall two minutes ahead of Webster to great applause.

Stokes could not resist giving him the occasional prod. In October 1971, for example, he sent Issigonis a copy of the recently published 'Leyland Papers' which contained damning criticism of the former BMC management. Issigonis sent back a terse reply: 'Many thanks for sending me a copy of the "Leyland Papers". I am looking forward to reading it.' As his 65th birthday approached in November 1971 he had to accept the inevitable. Despite his unpopularity with senior management it would have been unthinkable to let this occasion pass without a fuss so a big retirement party was laid on at Longbridge where, for a day at least, he was treated once again as the star of the Works. A stage was set up in the Exhibition Hall and an example of every one of his designs which had made it into production was put on display, each carrying a label showing how many had been made to date. Remarkably, the only one which was not still in the model range was the Morris Minor and it was only six months since the last of these had rolled off the production line.

The three Monte Carlo Minis were also there, though Lord Stokes and Harry Webster were not, which rendered them conveniently unavailable for press comment. It was left to George Turnbull to make the farewell speech, which began with fulsome praise for Issigonis' career and ended with an outline of the achievements of his successor. One can only imagine Alec's expression as Turnbull told his audience, 'I believe Harry has done a great job in giving our American-owned competitors something to really think about in the Morris Marina …' Then, on behalf of the directors of the company, Turnbull presented him with the retirement present which he had requested, the largest Meccano set available including the optional steam engine. This was the Number 10 set, 'Grand de Luxe', which came in a four-drawer oak-finished cabinet at a cost of £120 and just fitted in the boot of his Mini. There may have been a hint of sarcasm in his choice but Issigonis had not lost his boyish enthusiasm for Meccano and he used his present to make several objects including a large pendulum clock which he claimed kept excellent time. Some years later, when he had tired of the set, he gave what was left to the young son of his dentist, which hopefully provided some recompense for all those hours he had kept him waiting due to missed appointments.

At the resplendent lunch which followed the presentation Issigonis gave a rather wistful speech of thanks during which he could not resist a dig at the notable absentees:

Just a few words about my past.

In the late forties, when I was relatively young and immature, I designed a car that pushed you all along. This was adequate to carry us through the fifties and in fact a good deal further. As I became more proficient however, I found it much more fun dragging you all through the sixties and into the seventies. It is very gratifying for me to realise in my advancing years that front wheel drive, for small mass produced cars at any rate, is now firmly established and is being adopted more and more by European car manufacturers.

It is perhaps fortunate that I should be retiring at a time when the hey-day of the car designer as an individual appears to be drawing to a close. Today all we seem to require in car design is computer orientated committees to construct battering rams, which must be both super-hygienic and at the same time not suffer from bad breath. Of these things I know nothing.

I want to thank you all for the consideration and sympathy you have shown to me over the past two decades. It has been both a pleasure and a privilege to have been associated with you over so many years. I should also like to thank George Turnbull for the assistance and encouragement he has given me over the past three years and for the nice things he has said about me today. I am most grateful to Lord Stokes for asking me to stay on. There is much unfinished work still to be done. We have spoken of retirement, but this is perhaps a case of au revoir rather than farewell. For this I am particularly happy because, apart from anything else, it means that we shall still have opportunities of meeting in the future.

I really don't know how to thank you for this magnificent gift. As a child I was weaned on Meccano. It is only fitting therefore that as I approach my second childhood I should be given the opportunity to re-live the past. Whatever the future of the car may be I at least know that I shall spend many hours of enjoyment with this wonderful present.

Thank you very much indeed.

Some of his friends had great hopes for his retirement. Donald Riddle wrote urging him to visit Istanbul and commenting:

I am very pleased to hear that you are to retire from BLMC as I am sure that you can put your fertile brain power to many and better and more challenging uses outside an organisation which, since the merger, appears to be falling apart.

Despite the eulogies and the farewell party, Issigonis was to be spared the fate he so dreaded. Stokes handed him a lifeline by offering him experimental facilities and the role of Advanced Design Consultant to the British Leyland Motor Corporation. What was the reasoning behind this? With his extensive press connections Issigonis was in a position to do the corporation some harm if he wished, though it is doubtful that he would have followed such a course. Perhaps more at the forefront of British Leyland's mind was the possibility, hinted at by Donald Riddle, that he might offer his services to someone else. They might have had no interest in his ideas but at least they could ensure that no one else benefited from them. George Turnbull had ended his farewell speech with words that seemed to confirm this:

Every rule has an exception and, although we normally insist on all our executives retiring at the age of 65, we have bent the rules on this occasion because we do not believe that Sir Alec's extraordinary talents have suddenly waned or dried up now that he has reached a nominal milestone in age. New and original concepts will flow from his mind and we want to ensure that these are the exclusive property of British Leyland. For the last three years Sir Alec has had nothing

whatsoever to do with the design of the products which we are making now or intend to make in the near future, but has confined his
activities to working with a team of bright young engineers who are
devoting their time solely to the dreaming up of original solutions to
the engineering problems we shall have to be solving over the next
decade or so. Naturally, we all wish him a very busy 'retirement'.

As for Issigonis, despite all the unpleasantness of the past few years it was
difficult for him to envisage a role for himself outside the company. What
else was he going to do with his time? He ignored Turnbull's implication
that he would have 'nothing whatsoever to do with the design of the
products which we are making now or intend to make in the near future'
because he was still harbouring hopes that he could persuade them to
take his 9X design seriously. His financial position was also not so secure
as it might have seemed to the casual observer. He had not paid much
attention over the years to making arrangements for retirement because it
was not an event which he wished to contemplate. He retired on a senior
manager's salary but he had only reached such a level during the last ten
years of his career and BMC were notoriously poor payers compared
with similar businesses. The break in service caused by his period at Alvis
would also have affected his final pension entitlement. He still had influential friends within the company who would have been aware of his
position. It may be that they saw the 'consultancy fee' as a way of topping
up his pension.

   Whatever lay behind it, Issigonis quickly accepted the offer when it was
proposed, resolving to stay away from the increasingly complicated politics
of the British Leyland Motor Corporation. On 17 January 1972 Stokes
sent a generous note praising Issigonis' contribution to the company:

   As you know I was away when the little ceremony took place to mark
   your retirement and I have, of course, already spoken to you and con-
   veyed to you personally my appreciation of all the work you have
   done for British Leyland and prior to that BMC. I did feel, however, I
   would not like to let the occasion pass without putting in writing my
   very sincere appreciation of the tremendous contribution you have
   made not only to BMC and BLMC but the motor industry as a
   whole. It is rare that any industry gets a man of your intellectual ability
   and imagination and even rarer to get one who is such a charming

colleague to work with. I am delighted that you are going to stay with us in an advisory capacity. I do hope that you will remain fit and well and that you will not hesitate at any time to get in touch with me if there is anything that I personally can do to help you in any way.

Whether either Issigonis or British Leyland had any clear idea of what this 'advisory capacity' was intended to achieve is questionable. Indeed, when quizzed on the subject by the press, all George Turnbull could come up with was the rather unconvincing reply that 'the difficult thing about describing the nature of Sir Alec's new job is that virtually every-thing he is doing is on the top secret list'. He might just as well have said 'your guess is as good as mine'.

THE CONSULTANCY AGREEMENT

The first draft of the consultancy agreement was drawn up as early as January 1971 under the direction of Ron Lucas, who was a British Leyland Director and held the post of Secretary to the Corporation, though the appointment did not take effect until 1 February 1972. It referred to 'recent discussions with Lord Stokes, George Turnbull and Harry Webster' on the subject of 'the arrangements for your future'. The document went through several drafts before Issigonis sent a letter con-firming his agreement to its terms, which were straightforward enough. There would be a consultancy fee of £5,000 per annum, and at least six months' notice of termination would be required from either party. Any patents taken out on his ideas would belong to the British Leyland Motor Corporation Limited, and be registered at company expense. He was to commit a minimum of three and a half days per week to company business and would be reimbursed for any reasonable travelling and other expenses. Except for Norton Villiers – with whom he had worked for some years by agreement of the company – he would not be able to act as a consult-ant for any other organisation. There was one significant change to the first draft which had originally contained the following paragraph:

During the period of the consultancy arrangement you will work in conjunction with and be responsible to Mr H G Webster, who will ensure that you have adequate staff and facilities to enable you to carry out a mutually agreed programme of activity.

This was altered to read:

> During the period of the consultancy agreement you will be directly responsible to the Chairman of British Leyland Motor Corporation Limited, as at present, and you will work in conjunction with Mr H G Webster, who will ensure that you have adequate staff and facilities to enable you to carry out a mutually agreed programme of activity.

Clearly the one thing Issigonis would never be prepared to do was work for the man who had replaced him. On 22 December a notice appeared in the *Financial Times* and the *Birmingham Post* as follows: 'British Leyland wishes to make it clear that Sir Alec Issigonis who retires on 31 December 1971 will not be returning to full-time employment with the Corporation. After a period of rest his services will be available to the Corporation as Advanced Design Consultant.'

After a short break he was therefore back in his office in February 1972, undertaking his normal routine of work just as he had always done. The same year he even made a rare exception to his dislike of public engagements when he agreed to chair a panel of judges for the 'Meccano Globe-Trotter' competition. He was the only engineer on the panel, the other judges being from Meccano, BOAC and Brunning Advertising. The competition was open to sixteen year olds who were invited to build a model from Meccano parts of some worldwide engineering feat. Since the prize was a flight, courtesy of BOAC, to the location of the winning model, the subject chosen had to be on one of their routes. His participation was not entirely devoted to the cause of encouraging the engineering instincts of young people. In return for his help Issigonis persuaded Meccano to supply him with some extra parts to supplement his retirement present.

DEATH OF HULDA

In the years leading up to his retirement, Issigonis became aware of a difficulty with his hearing. He first began to notice the problem in 1965, although at first it did not seem very serious. While recording a BBC programme called *London Line* he commented on a hearing aid which was featured on the programme. The manufacturers of the device, Amplivox, saw an opportunity for some publicity and offered him a free hearing test but they received the rather embarrassed reply: 'Whilst I am grateful to you for your offer to make arrangements for my hearing to be checked at your Birmingham office, I would state that this is not necessary. I am only slightly deaf in one ear but I am afraid I rather exaggerated my case during the *London Line* broadcast in order to increase programme interest.' By 1970 he had been diagnosed as suffering from Ménière's disease, which was a problem of the inner ear affecting his balance and causing him to become disoriented in situations where there was a lot of noise coming from different directions. Though he was offered surgery, his mother strongly opposed it on the grounds that it would pose too much risk.

Over the same period Hulda Issigonis had been getting progressively weaker and he engaged a part-time housekeeper to keep an eye on her during the day. If he had to go away from home on business trips he would ask friends to stay at the Edgbaston bungalow to keep her company. More distressing than his mother's physical weakness was her steady mental decline which was growing severe as she approached her 88th birthday on 20 August 1972. Looking after her was becoming an increasing problem. He realised that he needed more permanent help and advertised for a full-time housekeeper. As a result he gained the services of Ralph Pape – whom he christened 'the Pape' – and his wife Peggy. Ralph had once worked in the catering section at Longbridge and the couple lived fairly close by so the arrangement was convenient for both parties. They would stay on to look after Alec to the end of his life but sadly they were able to do little for Hulda who was spending longer and longer spells in hospitals and nursing homes until she died at the Nuffield Nursing Home in Edgbaston on 15 September 1972. She was cremated five days later at Lodge Hill Crematorium in Selly Oak where her ashes were scattered. Following her death Alec gave some of Hulda's jewellery to Max Dowson, including the pearl necklace he had bought for her and the gold bangles she always wore. He also asked Max to take her horsehair mattress, bedstead and bedside table.

This emotional upheaval came barely a year after the ordeal of his retirement. An indication of his distress is the fact that Issigonis gave the wrong date of birth for Hulda when he went to register her death. The causes of death were recorded as heart disease and senility. It must have been almost unbearable for this devoted son to watch the slow disintegration of the intelligent and vivacious woman he used to know and he described her final weeks to a friend as 'harrowing'. As illness took away her elegance, her wit and her energy, he grieved for her and feared for himself. The event, when it came, was not unexpected but this did not make it any less painful. They had shared their lives for 66 years and understood each other as closely as two human beings could. Her loss made him feel very isolated and he began to worry about the prospect of loneliness. He had been there to look after her, but who was going to look after him?

As the end of December approached he was facing his first Christmas alone but the Dowsons stepped into the breach and invited him to spend it with them at the Poplars, an invitation he gratefully accepted. For the next few years between 1972 and 1975 he regularly spent four days over the Christmas period with the Dowsons and was joined on different occasions by old friends like Donald Riddle or Betsy and John Rusher. 'My computer gives the same answer as yours', he wrote to Riddle on one of these occasions, 'have accepted invitation to spend Christmas at the Dowsons' farm.' In March 1973 George Dowson suffered a serious stroke which affected his speech and his recovery was slow. Nevertheless, despite their own difficulties, the Dowsons offered Alec a great deal of support during this period. He resumed his frequent visits to the farm for lunch. Penny Dowson and her brother Christopher also spent time visiting his bungalow, meeting him for lunch or acting as his companion on occasions such as trips to the Motor Show.

At home he developed the fastidiousness of a person who spends a lot of time on their own. He liked to sit on the paved sun-terrace at the back of the house, admiring his garden and watching the bird table. He told his guests that they were only allowed to smoke untipped cigarettes outside because these did not make a mess and were 'good for the plants'. He insisted that plates should not be stacked after a meal because there was no point in making the bottom of the plate dirty and having to wash both sides. He also became increasingly obstinate. For his own personal transport he would only use vehicles that he had designed himself or which were development models that he was working on. Large numbers of his friends and colleagues recall daring to leave their car outside his house only to be bluntly told to 'get that bloody Range Rover/Jaguar (or whatever else) off my drive', and they would have to take it away and park round the corner so he could not see it. It did not matter who it was, Bill Heynes, Tony Dawson, Mike Parkes, Tony Snowdon, they would all get the same treatment. Social niceties and conventions were not for him and he hated small talk and rituals. If people started to linger on the doorstep he would adapt the title of one of his favourite books, cutting them off with the words 'no long goodbyes', and shut the door. In Casucci's words he was 'an unpredictable man and authentically peculiar'.

He continued to travel abroad, though on a less grand scale since he no longer had any business commitments to fulfil. His last visit to Monte Carlo appears to have been in 1969 but he attended the Geneva Motor Show every March where he would meet up with friends such as Sergio Pininfarina, Robert Braunschweig and Bernard Cahier. In January 1973 he went to Montreux in Switzerland and stayed with Donald Riddle at an old-fashioned hotel on the lakeside which had an exaggerated grandeur in its decoration that contrasted sharply with the fact that it was not very well patronised. Alec and Donald rather enjoyed rattling around the echoing ornate rooms, agreeing that it was 'just like living on the *Lusitania*' – a vast ocean liner which had been sunk during the First World War. Not very far away at Villars, Mike Parkes had invited Penny Dowson to join him at a regular gathering of motor racing drivers known as 'le Réunion des Anciens Pilotes'. Mike and Penny took the opportunity to drive over to Alec and Donald's grand hotel for dinner and Alec felt greatly cheered when he observed the attachment which had formed between a dear friend and a cherished god-daughter.

His hearing problem was growing progressively worse, causing him to plant his feet well apart whenever he stood up to prevent himself from stumbling before setting off to walk with small shuffling steps. The scope of his activities began to narrow as he sought to find the best way of living with the disability. To those unaware of the problem, the dizzy spells which afflicted him could give the erroneous impression that he was drunk and this made him reluctant to socialise with people he did not know well. Taking an aeroplane was one of the things which was becoming difficult because of the effect that altitude had on his inner ear. Nevertheless, in May 1973, Alec decided on a private visit to Italy. His once frequent visits to Turin had been curtailed due to his changed position in the company and he wanted to see his old friends again. He asked Penny Dowson to accompany him and on the first evening she took the opportunity to have dinner with Mike Parkes, who was living in Modena, while Alec met up with Dante Giacosa and Piero Casucci. The next day Alec and Penny dined with Sergio Pininfarina and his wife Georgia before travelling on to Palermo in Sicily. The objective of the second part of the trip was to see the Targa Florio race which was due to

395

take place that weekend and they were joined at the Villa Igea by Bernard and Joan Cahier. The party was completed when Mike Parkes flew down from Modena in his private plane, a Beechcraft Baron, and on Friday evening they all went together to a pre-race cocktail party with the racing drivers. Over the brandies and the gins Alec began to reminisce to Mike Parkes about his oldest memory of Sicily, the epic journey he and his mother had undertaken from Malta to London. He could still remember how he had marvelled at his first sight of a volcano in the form of Mount Etna. On the Saturday afternoon, Parkes decided to give his friend a special treat. He called the party together, loaded them into his Beechcraft Baron and piloted them over the top of the volcano. Alec was not so much impressed with the natural beauty of the volcano as with its immense power. His verdict was: 'I cannot see why man has not devised a means of harnessing the enormous heat available into generating power for commercial use.'

On Sunday, he was beginning to feel tired so he rested in the grounds of the Villa Igea while Mike, Penny and the Cahiers went to watch the race. The trip had been a very pleasant one, he had greatly enjoyed the company of his friends, and he was in a good mood on the final day of the visit when he gave an interview to Italian journalist Giulio Barese, posing for photographs with Penny in the hotel gardens. Unfortunately the evening was to bring a very bad attack of dizziness and sickness and he had to be helped from the restaurant to his room to sleep off the effects. He recovered sufficiently to take an early morning flight back to Birmingham with Penny as planned but it was incidents such as this which cast a cloud over his enjoyment of life and made him feel very vulnerable.

His ear condition was progressing well beyond a minor inconvenience and becoming a major disability. He decided to see what could be done and in July 1973 he was admitted to the Queen Elizabeth Hospital in Edgbaston for an operation. Once he was discharged he visited Donald Riddle in Turkey in an effort to recuperate but the visit was not a success and he wrote to Robert Braunschweig:

> At last I write. I have had my ear operation about two months now but still feel very giddy. In despair, I spent a week with a very old friend of mine on the Bosporus, but came back feeling very little better …
> After my travels in Turkey I decided not to travel abroad again until I am completely cured.

At first he clung to the hope that in time the operation would produce an improvement, telling Sergio Pininfarina, 'I still suffer from giddiness although it is, perhaps, a little too early to judge the result [of the operation]'. In October he travelled up to the Hyde Park Hotel for the Motor Show as usual. Sadly, no improvement occurred. As his condition steadily worsened he became increasingly reclusive. He kept his resolve and never travelled abroad again. Over the next few years he began to curtail his travel at home as well.

In these difficult times, the Dowsons were not the only people to whom he turned for support. Following Hulda's death, Alec re-established contact with his cousin May Ransome. She was now sharing a house in Topsham, Devon, with her brother Tony Walker who had spent many years managing the tea plantation in Ceylon before retiring to England. Gerald had died of a heart attack in July 1962 only a few months after his 60th birthday; Tony was to suffer the same fate at the similarly young age of 67 in 1981. When Tony returned to England he and May decided that, since they were both on their own, it would make a great deal of sense to pool their resources. They bought a house with fine views over the River Exe to the Haldon Hills which afforded both of them the space and opportunity to pursue their own independent interests while offering support to each other.

Following his return from the unsuccessful convalescence in Turkey, Issigonis went to stay with May in Topsham. Tony collected him from the airport but there was an uneasy relationship between the two of them and after this visit they did not meet again. Rather more successful was a trip to see Sally who lived nearby with her husband and two children. Once again, his affection for children came to the fore as he happily spent the afternoon playing games with Sally's children just as he had once done with their mother. When her three-year-old son Mark brought his new toy lorry to show to the visitor, Alec explained a few points about its design and then the two of them set to work to optimise its performance with the same determination as if it were one of his own prototypes.

May was scarcely younger than Alec, but after this she began to go up to Edgbaston regularly, Ralph Pape meeting her at the railway station to convey her to the bungalow. Her visits were a generous gesture which Alec appreciated not least because she was the only person left who had known his mother almost as well as himself. She gave him a great deal of support throughout the 1970s and 1980s, taking up residence in Hulda's old rooms and chivvying him along in a combative manner which must have reminded him of mama. May was a strong-minded woman and her intelligent conversation combined with her cheerful nature were a positive mark on an increasingly bleak landscape. He began to look forward to seeing her and he would often send her newspaper cuttings or photographs as an excuse to scribble notes on them such as 'please come soon for a few days'.

The British Motor Industry in Crisis

As he adapted his private life to his new circumstances, Issigonis tried to hold on as firmly as he could to the one thing, besides his mother, which had always held his life together – his work. Since 1969 he had been confined to his basement workshop but after his appointment as Advanced Design Consultant he demanded a proper office. Initially he was allocated a room on the ground floor of the Kremlin but soon he was moved to a much grander space on the first floor with a view over the Lickey Hills. He was back on the same 'corridor of power' where he had begun his career at Longbridge. The company did not seem to consider the upkeep of its headquarters to be a great priority so although the room was expensively decorated it leaked badly when it rained. This was one reason why, although he moved his papers and other belongings here, he continued to spend most of his time in the office he had made for himself downstairs. Nevertheless it was a small victory which he cherished.

In accepting the consultancy he was primarily motivated not by his financial situation but by his need to continue working. Once it became clear that Harry Webster was not going to include his ambitious new model range in the Forward Product Plan, Issigonis decided the best way of keeping the project alive would be to concentrate his efforts on the engine design.

Despite their reluctance to consider the future of the small car range British Leyland could not completely ignore the question because both the Mini and the 1100 were reaching the limit of the normal production cycle. It proved difficult, however, for their engineers to agree on a solution. Between 1970 and 1973 two camps developed inside the corporation. Though Charles Griffin had supported the original battle to get 9X included in British Leyland's Forward Product Plan, his own inclinations were to develop the existing Mini and 1100. He therefore spearheaded a group which wanted to build a new Mini in the image of the old. An opposing faction wanted to build a supermini in imitation of the continental competition which was beginning to emerge. Initially the supermini route was chosen and the ADO 74 project was begun. Designs of this type were larger than ADO 15, providing more opportunities for a superior level of performance, finish and trim. Consequently they could support a higher selling price and were more likely to make a profit. On this basis ADO 74 was to have an overall length of 138 inches in contrast to the Mini at 120 inches. To power it, British Leyland embarked on yet another new engine design, a 1000-1400 cc engine known as the H-series, but the possibility of installing the A-series was held in reserve.

Despite this, British Leyland had identified the middle sector of the market as where they needed to be and their priority was to complete ADO 28 as quickly as possible in order to replace the Morris Minor and Oxford. The Morris Marina was rushed into production in 1971, with all the usual consequences. They were keen to distance the car from Issigonis, and he had no wish to be associated with it. It must therefore have been a gross irritation for Stokes and Webster to read an account of their launch in the *Daily Mail*, which focussed on the reasons for his absence:

In all the millions of words printed to launch the new Morris Marina car range one word was missing – Issigonis. He has been on stage for every new Morris car launch since the Minor, his first complete car, arrived on the scene in 1948. Yet they managed to launch the latest Morris without a single mention of the 64-year-old designer from Smyrna. How? Well the answer is simple, that Sir Alec – for the first time in more than two decades – had nothing to do with the new Marina ... And even if they launched the Marina without him, they *still* have to build his ideas into it. Did you see that front torsion bar suspension? Sir Alec designed that for his famous Minor back in the forties.

In spite of all their efforts, by the time the Morris Marina was ready the market had changed. The stylish Ford Cortina Mark III moved the goal-posts once again. The continuing decline of the corporation's finances and market share meant that Webster's ambitious plan to attack the market on two fronts with a complementary range of advanced cars was dead in the water almost before it began. The Marina, which had only ever been intended as a temporary measure until something better could be produced, would eventually be stretched to last for thirteen years. As the money available for investment began to diminish they started to fiddle with existing models. In early 1972 the E-series finally made its way into the engine bay of ADO 17 in the form of a 2227 cc 6-cylinder option and at long last the car acquired a centrally mounted handbrake which people could actually reach. The company also ploughed on with ADO 67, the Austin Allegro, which started its development the same year as the Marina and was meant to be the 'advanced' design to replace the 1100. Though Webster and Stokes had planned to abandon the Issigonis philosophy as far as they could, they ended up using it as a basic platform on which to superimpose better, more carefully costed, presentation. Thus the Allegro became an enlarged 1100, introducing Hydragas suspension and offering a wider range of engines and trim levels. Sadly, the end result failed to capture the public imagination, despite quirky features such as the famous 'quartic' steering wheel.

It was not long before these failures had their effect on the management structure. In September 1973 George Turnbull resigned after it became clear that Stokes was priming John Barber rather than himself to succeed as Chairman. Barber was duly appointed Managing Director in his place. Neither party made any attempt to hide their differences as the press release announcing the changes stated clearly: 'Mr George Turnbull, Managing Director, is leaving the Corporation by mutual consent, as he has disagreed with the principle of some of the changes which the Board considers essential for the future development of the Corporation.' Turnbull took a brave step, indicative of the way the motor industry was moving, by joining Hyundai of Korea to help them set up in independent car production. Of the original Stokes team, he was one of the few whose career would later flourish. He went on to top positions with Peugeot Talbot and Inchcape, not to mention a knighthood. His departure provoked another one of the periodic organisations which afflicted British Leyland at regular intervals throughout its life. The same year, Alec's *bête noir*, Harry Webster, left to join Automotive Products in Leamington, a casualty of the disappointing performance of the Marina and Allegro. Filmer Paradise also made his exit and joined a British Leyland importer based in Singapore.

The dire economic circumstances of 1973 in any case dealt the final blow to the Webster–Stokes product policy. Prime Minister Edward Heath had been struggling with high unemployment and inflation throughout his three years in power. His attempts to cure these ills by statutory control of wages and prices was met with predictable industrial unrest. He also made changes to taxation and adjusted hire purchase regulations, leading to a sudden boom in sales of medium to large cars during 1972. This situation was completely reversed in October 1973 by another war which broke out on the flashpoint of the Suez Canal, this time between Egypt and Israel. Ironically, this induced a fuel shortage comparable to the one which had given birth to the Mini. Heath declared a State of Emergency in November leading to a number of fuel-saving edicts, including the imposition of a three-day working week and a 50 miles per hour speed limit. Petrol ration coupons were printed once again, though in the event they were not needed. The final crisis was precipitated by a miners' strike. Edward Heath called an election early in 1974 hoping for a 'vote of confidence'. The public failed to provide it and neither of the leading parties gained an overall majority. Jeremy Thorpe, leader of the minority Liberal Party, declined Heath's offer of a coalition. This handed power back to Harold Wilson and the Labour Party, who had gained just five more seats than the Conservatives.

The fuel crisis helped to revive the discussion over the best way of replacing the Mini. Issigonis dusted off his 9X proposal of 1968 and made some handwritten corrections in order to resubmit the document. Most of the alterations merely updated the information, stressing that the 9X engine had, in the intervening years, been thoroughly tested: 'The 4-cylinder 9X engine designed for this car has had considerable development testing including the passing of the standard 400 hour B.L. endurance test with relatively small trouble.' The engine was now shown as being 850–1000 cc rather than 750–1000 cc. Sliding windows were also back, in place of the winding windows. Despite the departure of Webster, Stokes still felt little enthusiasm for the Issigonis design. Instead, he chose to listen to Charles Griffin who challenged the affordability of ADO 74 and claimed that it would be more economical to develop the existing Mini, stretching it slightly and fitting it once again with the suspension systems being developed by Moulton. He argued that, though substantial investment would still be required, money could be saved by abandoning the new engine design and retaining the A-series engine. On this basis, Stokes sanctioned plans to develop a concept for what he hoped would be a low investment replacement Mini which became ADO 88.

None of this brought any joy to Issigonis, who believed that British

Leyland's rival small car projects were both nothing more than engineering cul-de-sacs. The 9X was already sitting there ready to go and it was undoubtedly a better car in concept and execution than either ADO 74 or ADO 88. The frustration he felt would be hard to overestimate. By now, however, he was preoccupied with yet another project which he had begun sometime during 1970. Never satisfied with confining himself to the improvement of conventional concepts, he was employing his talent for lateral thinking by developing a 'gearless' car. This was not specific to the 9X engine, as he adapted it to the A-series and the E-series as well. 'The Mini set a new concept of small car design 14 years ago', he wrote in explanation. 'A new version of the car must set a new pattern of future car design. The gearless one is the answer.'

As usual he chose the Mini as raw material and sliding windows were once again part of the package, though he stressed that he had modified this feature, 'allowing the driver's head to come out for reversing etc.' By the mid-70s he had experimented with several prototypes. One engineer who worked on the gearless concept as a young man remembers Issigonis mischievously deciding to test a group of prototypes on the roadway directly in front of the Kremlin. This attracted the attention of the important men inside headquarters who came out to see what was going on, only to be dismissed with an imperious wave of the hand and the words 'go away we're testing'. He then dropped his handkerchief as a signal to his assistants, and the flotilla of gearless Minis glided away gracefully from the imaginary start line, gathering speed in the slow but majestic manner which was a characteristic of the car.

The gearless Mini was not an automatic because it worked on completely different principles from a geared car. It had no clutch, no gearbox and no variable ratio drive mechanism. Instead it used a torque converter. This eliminated the need for gear-changing, making it easier to drive. Issigonis argued that it would be much easier to service than a geared car, first because it was made up of a much smaller number of parts, and second because there was no gearbox to become damaged by misuse. He called it a 'city car' and adopted one of the 9X versions as his own personal round-town transport as was his habit with development vehicles. When he demonstrated it to Jack Daniels, however, his former colleague was not impressed, criticising the revised 9X suspension: 'It was alright for him driving away on his own but stick some passengers in and your headlamps would have been up in the sky. It was simply way outside the regulations.' The real problem of the gearless version, however, was its slug-gish performance at low speed. This may not have been apparent to Issigonis as the route from Edgbaston to Longbridge did not involve any challenging inclines, but it was very evident in testing.

THE RYDER REPORT

By 1975 the state of health of the British Leyland Motor Corporation was becoming critical. In order to prevent the complete collapse of what remained of Britain's motor industry the Labour government was forced to step in and guarantee bank loans of up to £50 million. Sir Don Ryder was commissioned to undertake an inquiry into the situation, which he presented to the Secretary of State for Industry, Tony Benn, under the title *British Leyland: The Next Decade* on 23 April 1975. Although the full report has never been made public due to the extreme sensitivity of some of the material it contains, even the abridged version makes frightening reading. The Ryder Report described the origins of this particular crisis as fol-lows:

From the autumn of 1973 onwards, a succession of events – the oil crisis, the three-day week, the deterioration in economic prospects in the United Kingdom and world markets, and the rapid increase in inflation – caused BL to re-appraise radically both its capital invest-ment programme and its financial position. Whereas BL's budget in the autumn of 1973 had assumed a profit before tax of £68 million in 1973/74, a loss of £16 million was reported for the first half year to the end of March 1974.

The report offered a complete analysis of world markets, future product strategy, industrial relations, productivity and the structure of the organi-sation. As a result of its recommendations the organisation was radically restructured and the government took effective control by creating a new holding company called British Leyland Ltd and becoming its major shareholder. The management team was called on to pay the price and only seven years after the merger Lord Stokes took the usual route to the exit by accepting an honorary position with no executive power. His desig-nated successor, John Barber, also left the company.

To replace them, an effort was made for the first time to bring in businessmen with experience outside the motor industry. The new Chief

Executive was Alex Park, who had joined British Leyland to take over Barber's position as Finance Director in 1974. He had held positions with firms as diverse as Monsanto and Rank Xerox. Volume car production was allocated to a new division known as Leyland Cars under the direction of Derek Whittaker, who had joined the Finance Department in 1972 after previously working for Ford and then the General Electric Company. Spen King, a Rover man who till then had been in charge of the 'specialist' car range and had designed the Range Rover, became overall Engineering Director, thus taking on responsibility for the mass production car range as well. Alongside organisational reform the Ryder Report also required the company to put in place a new corporate plan which was to focus on two existing projects – ADO 88 and a re-skinned Allegro known as ADO 99 – alongside a new project for a fleet car to capture volume sales.

This enabled Charles Griffin at last to direct his energies towards an 1800 replacement, ADO 71. This was launched in March 1975 as the 18/22 series with Austin, Morris and Wolseley derivatives, aimed at the family market. Its launch slogan – 'the biggest news since the Mini' – was an irritating reminder of the continuing power of the Mini brand. Firmly based on the 1800, it offered strength and splendid interior space contained within a strikingly shaped bodyshell. Unfortunately, quality and design problems quickly tarnished the car's reputation. In a move which epitomised British Leyland's problems of image and identity, it had to be relaunched as the 'Leyland Princess' in the autumn, leaving early customers with an obsolete model after only six months. The use of the label 'Princess' was an attempt to cash in on yet one more valued luxury brand from the company portfolio. The 1800's lacklustre styling had quickly earned it the nickname 'landcrab' and its successor, the Princess, would always be known as the 'wedge' – a style that was very much in vogue at the time. Once its production problems had been sorted out it would form a creditable but undervalued part of the British Leyland model range throughout the later 70s.

Griffin also had the satisfaction of leading the ADO 88 project which, thanks to the Ryder Report, had won out over ADO 74. The 9X was still no nearer to being brought in from the cold. Yet the ADO 88 project sprang from a group of people who were all Mini-enthusiasts in their own way, even though their ideas were backward looking in comparison to the concept which Issigonis had been trying to promote for so long.

The new management team did not blame the Mini, and therefore its designer, for the financial mire into which the company had sunk and they were much more sympathetic to him than the previous régime had been. Even though the Mini was now sixteen years old they believed it still had a valid role to play in the future model programme.

Issigonis soon felt the benefit of this shift. In the early part of 1975 an attempt had been made to re-allocate part of his working area. Now, a memorandum from S. Holmes, Chief Engineer for Electrical Engineering at Longbridge, dated 5 August 1975, informed Sir Alec:

> Following our telephone conversation regarding your working area, my colleague, Mr S. A. Andrews now in charge of N. V. H. [Noise, Vibration and Harshness] informs me that the plans (which were originally agreed by Mr. J. B. Turnbull and signed off by Mr. C. Griffin) are held in abeyance pending clearance. Furthermore, the test bed had to be removed as it was considered to be a health hazard under the provisions of the new 'Health and Safety at Work' Act. In view of the changed responsibilities under the re-organization, my original plans for accommodating the Advanced Electrical/Electronic Section with the N. V. H. Section will no longer be effective. Therefore, I cannot foresee any necessity for further reducing your working area, although this will depend upon the final organization; no doubt you will be involved in discussions on this aspect.

The extent of this triumph is revealed only by the handwritten note, from Alec to Charles Griffin, which is written on the bottom:

> Charles – these people have been gradually pushing me out of our shop. They want a bigger office and a corridor through our space to lead to the office!! I have seen the schemes so I rang up Mr Holmes who very kindly has stopped all this madness. In fact as we proceed with the gearless car I want a small cubical [sic] to sit and discuss the day's work with the boys – see you soon, Alec.

The change in his working environment encouraged Issigonis to try to revive interest in his gearless Mini. In October 1975 he persuaded the new management to conduct an extensive test of one of his prototypes. Accordingly, Charles Bulmer of Advanced Product Planning drove the car in urban conditions and on the motorway, comparing it with two other Mini 1000s – a Clubman and an automatic fitted with the AP gearbox Issigonis himself had helped to develop. Issigonis and Charles Griffin were among the recipients of the report. The objective of the test was to try the car out in normal driving conditions, paying particular attention to fuel consumption. On that point Bulmer concluded that there was little noticeable improvement over the Clubman, a claim which Issigonis contested as premature since the gearless engine had not been tuned to optimise power and economy. Bulmer went on to comment favourably on the car's superior acceleration in the 30–60 mph range compared with both the Clubman and the automatic. He complimented its general pleasantness and 'lack of fussiness' to drive, declaring that it imparted a 'general relaxed feeling up to 70 mph'. The problem lay in getting up to this range in the first place, and hill-starts were a virtual impossibility. Bulmer also made an interesting comment about hill-descents, which is reminiscent of Issigonis' early association with the freewheel:

In descending steep hills very little engine braking is available. My own view is that engaging a low gear for steep descents is a relic of the past with small light cars. Provided that the brake specification is generous, there is no reason why you should not rely on them down hills as much as you do all the rest of the time on the level.

Issigonis took exception to the car being referred to as an automatic but overall he must have been pleased with these conclusions. To Bulmer's final question – 'how could it fit into the future rationalised Product/Engine plan?' – he offered his own answer: 'This 9X engine would suit the Mini "Escorts" which are being examined but would need a gearbox factory – investment too high to justify this small sector already filled by foreign manufacturers.'

The report was discussed at a meeting held in November 1975 with Derek Whittaker, Spen King, Charles Griffin, Alan Edis (Product Planner for Leyland Cars) and Issigonis himself. They expressed an interest in the design but they wanted to apply it to the 1750 E-series engine and fit it into ADO 88 in place of 'the existing complicated and expensive AP transmission'. A separate feasibility study outside the mainstream ADO 88 programme was to be instituted to investigate this possibility and a target of the summer of 1979 was set for production. Issigonis does not appear to have voiced his doubts in the meeting, but he wrote onto the minutes 'not possible, too high weight/torque ratio'. Nevertheless he was pleased to have his own programme approved at the same time:

> The final point which was established at this discussion was that Sir Alec's development team should be encouraged to continue and extend their programme of testing with two prototype vehicles using 1500 9X gearless power units. Support for test bed work and an overseas running programme for high temperature, severe gradients etc should be supported as far as possible from within Engineering resources.

The meaning of this was that the budget would have to come from Charles Griffin and Spen King.

The endorsement of his research was very welcome, but he received a more substantial benefit from the change of management when his consultancy agreement was updated in March 1976. Issigonis had requested that the period of notice be changed from six to twelve months. Alex Park not only agreed to this, he also approved an increase in the fee to £7,500. This was the idea of Derek Whittaker and his old friend Ron Lucas, 'to recognise the very substantial increase in the cost of living since that date'. Issigonis expressed his gratitude and surprise at the pay rise by writing to Alex Park (with a similar letter to Ron Lucas):

> I should like to write and thank you and Mr Whittaker most warmly for altering the terms of my Consultancy Agreement with British Leyland Limited and increasing the fee from £5,000 per annum to £7,500. I am most appreciative of your action as it came as a complete surprise to me. I hope to be able to contribute as much as I can to future developments on which I am working.

So while at the beginning of the 70s his star within the company had been on the wane, by the middle of the decade it had begun to shine more brightly.

WORKING FROM HOME

Unfortunately, the improvement in his working environment coincided with a deterioration in his health. Among his papers is a personalised folder embossed with the initials AI which contains what was probably his last Works diary for 1975. There are very few engagements recorded in it, the last being a visit to the London Motor Show on 14 October. All the other regular dates on his calendar have disappeared and by 1976 he seems to have been working entirely from home. The nature of his illness meant that he felt less disorientated in a familiar environment but the wave of feeling in his favour at Longbridge influenced him too because he had grown tired of the constant fuss and no longer felt he wanted to be the centre of attention. By 1977 he had undergone extensive medical tests including the measuring of his blood pressure under different conditions, radiological examinations, and a CAT scan which he submitted himself to with some apprehension. These examinations enabled a thorough diagnosis of the physical causes of his 'disequilibrium' to be made. Sadly, the doctor's conclusion when presented with the data was: 'I wish I were able to help in some more positive way but I am afraid that I can produce no curative treatment for this condition.'

His feelings of isolation had been reinforced throughout the 70s as he began to lose many of his closest friends. In 1970 George Dowson's sister Babs died at the age of 64, followed in 1971 by his mother Enid, who was just short of her 91st birthday. His own mother had been next in 1972 then in 1976 his childhood friend Donald Riddle, now 72, died of a heart attack in his Istanbul apartment just as he was preparing to retire permanently to England. Some of his younger friends were also disappearing. In 1972 his close collaborator Daniel Richmond died aged only 46 and five years later his widow Bunty committed suicide.

Then there was Mike Parkes, who by August 1977 had managed to fulfil his ambition to get back into a racing car after his near fatal accident in 1967 only to be killed at the age of 46, not on the racetrack but in a road accident in Italy. He and Penny Dowson were by now engaged and following his death she spent some time in Sardinia to recover from this terrible and sudden loss. Here she met and fell in love with an American submarine commander and in March 1978 she was able to tell Issigonis the happy news that she was getting married. She returned to England for the wedding and Alec sent her a warm letter and a generous present, explaining that he could not be there because of his ear problem: 'Darling Penny, best wishes to you both and lots of love from Alec. P.S. I'm afraid I can't make the great occasion (no anti-roll bar!).' Following the wedding Penny left for America with her new husband and though she made frequent and often extended trips to England while her husband was away on duty the couple did not return permanently to Britain until 1986 so she saw much less of her godfather than previously.

Most significantly, at the end of the decade he lost two of his closest friends. In 1979 George Dowson died at the age of 71 from a second stroke. The same year John Morris suffered a fatal heart attack, though in his case the circumstances were rather bizarre as perhaps befitted his unusual personality. Morris had spent the evening with Issigonis in his bungalow and they had got into a conversation about how much power a man could develop without any kind of assistance. This was the type of conundrum they both loved and Issigonis insisted that the problem was easy to solve. All that was needed was a stopwatch and a staircase. First you would prepare the experiment by measuring the depth of each step, counting the number of stairs, and working out your own weight. Then you would run up the stairs, using the stopwatch to time yourself, which would make it possible to calculate how much weight you had lifted over what height in how many seconds. 'Of course,' he added, 'I can't do it here because I live in a bungalow.' It seems it was a challenge that John Morris could not resist. The next morning, his daily cleaning lady found him slumped at the bottom of the stairs with a stopwatch in his hand. He was rushed to hospital but died the next day.

Alec's own health had deteriorated significantly by the end of the 70s. It was also painful to lose one of those things which had always given him the most pleasure, the ability to drive. Because he no longer felt confident behind the wheel he decided to employ a chauffeur. Nevertheless he continued to be in huge demand from the media and British Leyland were happy to take advantage of any publicity he could bring them despite their attitude towards him. He felt more than ever that he needed a barrier between himself and the outside world and he was now relying heavily on Tony Dawson who had become a personal assistant cum press officer to him. Dawson continued to arrange his 'public' life for him, helping him with correspondence, and arranging contacts with the media. Dawson was beginning to have health problems of his own but their relationship had become much more than that of a press officer and his client. He and his wife Paddy began to look after Alec emotionally as well as professionally. After Issigonis became confined to the bungalow, he would visit him nearly every day. Whenever he was not able to do so, he would telephone to make sure his friend was alright.

Issigonis would no longer give any kind of interview unless Tony

Dawson was present and this could create difficulties. In 1979 arrangements were being made for a big 'Mini 20' event to be held at Donington Park to celebrate the car's twentieth birthday, the first in a series of such landmark events. He would not attend the event and instead drafted a message to be read out over the public announcement system. He did, however, agree to give an interview to the BBC so arrangements were made through Tony Dawson for Raymond Baxter to visit the Edgbaston bungalow with a film crew. Unfortunately Dawson was delayed and as they waited for him to appear Issigonis began to get agitated. It was only because he knew Raymond Baxter that he eventually agreed to continue on the understanding that anything he did not like could be cut and once he got underway he began to relax and everything went well. This shows the measure of his loss of confidence – twenty years earlier he would have been happy and comfortable chatting on camera to a familiar face like Baxter.

Though Issigonis began to feel increasingly isolated he continued to work. His engineers, Charlie Lane and Len Windley, visited him at the bungalow every morning to get instructions and, despite the fact that he no longer went to the factory, friends like Charles Griffin continued to promote his interests there. In the late 70s he also gained a new ally at senior management level. Mark Snowdon had first met him shortly after joining British Leyland in 1973 when they were both working on the Mini improvement programme. It was still the case that some people clicked instantly with Alec – often because they found the same things amusing – while others felt uncomfortable with him. In this case the two men had developed a personal as well as a professional rapport. Snowdon rose steadily through the ranks and in 1977, after a period based elsewhere, he returned to Longbridge as Product Planning Director for Austin Morris. He was distressed to find that Issigonis was not being given any meaningful work to do and began to visit him regularly at his bungalow to discuss his projects and give him encouragement. He was anxious to impart the feeling that he was still part of the corporate family while attempting to inject some balance into his expectations about the likelihood of his ideas being implemented.

One of the things which Mark Snowdon recognised was the value that both the Issigonis name and the continued popularity of the Mini represented to British Leyland. In order to capitalise on these he came up with the idea of moving Issigonis' activities away from Longbridge altogether. His existing working arrangements were becoming too expensive to sustain. A team of experienced and trained Longbridge engineers were engaged in experimental work which was outside the product programme, not to mention the time they spent visiting the bungalow every day to get instructions. Accordingly, a separate company called Issigonis Developments Ltd was registered with the intention that it would handle all his experimental work using an outside workshop. The company was to avoid recruiting engineers internally. Instead, it should attract new talent, young people who could work with Issigonis for a while and then move on to bigger and better things inside British Leyland as soon as they were ready. In a memorandum on the subject, Snowdon suggested that 'the attraction of Sir Alec's name and the freedom offered by a new company should make recruitment of some talented young engineers a possibility'.

This epitomised the company's current attitude towards him. They still placed value on his reputation and his skills though not necessarily on the research that he was actually doing. At the same time there was no one left in the senior ranks of the company who understood him well enough to see that such a scenario could never work. How could the anti-intellectual and difficult-to-work-with Issigonis ever have been considered the right candidate to become a potential father-figure to fresh-faced graduates? Issigonis had always required familiar and friendly faces around him to work effectively and the idea of trying to forge relationships with a continually changing set of people merely caused him anxiety. Although he tentatively agreed to the suggestion of working with an independent company, he asked for members of his old team to be re-assigned to him. This was, of course, no longer possible since they had all moved on to new engineering positions long ago, besides which it was against the whole intention of the scheme.

Not surprisingly Issigonis Developments came to nothing and in 1980 Snowdon devised an alternative plan, appointing an engineer to liaise between him and the factory. This job fell to Rodney Bull, a young man from Northampton who had joined British Leyland in 1970. Rod Bull was working for vehicle proving and had to make regular visits to MIRA where he came across the two engineers who were working on the 9X programme. At the time, Bull was on the lookout for an opportunity that would allow him to be based at Longbridge so when he heard that Issigonis was looking for a technical person to work for him he expressed an interest and soon found himself at the Edgbaston bungalow being interviewed. Rod Bull clearly remembers this first encounter:

I presented myself at his bungalow in Edgbaston for the interview and I think you approach the gods of engineering with trepidation as a mere minion. He was very civil, very polite, but I've never forgotten the first question he asked after pleasantries had been exchanged. He said, so you're an engineer are you? And I thought, that's the first bear trap he's digging for me, I'll step out of that one – so I replied, no, I'm a technician, you're the engineer. I did see a grin pass over his face, it was obviously a well known trap he'd set for many people because I don't think my life would have been worth living should I have said I was an engineer and therefore assessed myself as being on the same level as himself. And that set the scene I think.

Issigonis was happy with the outcome of the interview and Rod Bull began his new assignment on Monday 16 June 1980. He was now based at Longbridge as he had wanted and he was instructed to use the leaking office on the first floor of the Kremlin though, like Issigonis, he preferred the basement workshop. In the six years that the partnership lasted he spoke to and met all kinds of people on Issigonis' behalf – newspaper editors, racing drivers, members of the royal family and people from all levels in the company from the Chairman to the engineers. His daily routine involved visiting the Edgbaston bungalow at 10.30 every morning, except after a visit to MIRA when the visit would take place at 2.30 in the afternoon straight from the proving ground so he could report back the results of the tests immediately. Issigonis' approach to working with Rod Bull was the same as it had been with all his other colleagues. He would tell him what he wanted and then say 'go away and do it'.

Even though by 1980 he rarely ventured far from his bungalow, the Issigonis for whom Rod Bull worked is easily recognisable as the same energetic, original thinker that Daniels, Kingham and Sheppard knew. Like others before him, Bull found that adaptability and quick thinking would be essential qualities if he was going to succeed at his new job:

In my very early days of working for him, he would set me a task to complete and I'd do my best as a technical person to gain all the relevant facts and present them in a logical order, but sometimes I'd think 'the chap I'm talking to is not on this planet, he's not listening to me at all'. And the truth is, he wasn't, he'd decided the information I was telling him wasn't what he wanted to hear, things weren't going in quite the right direction, so he'd already decided to think laterally, gone off another turn and you had to scamper very quickly to find out where he'd gone and catch him up again.

Once every three months Rod Bull reported back to Mark Snowdon who was still determined that any good ideas which came out of their work should be utilised even though there was as little prospect as ever of the 9X being officially sanctioned. As the point of contact between Edgbaston and the factory, Rod Bull was more aware than most that it would take nothing short of a miracle for this to happen. Issigonis, as ever, was not prepared to accept this and he continued to demand expensive experimental programmes that Bull did not have the authority to implement. When he gave instructions to initiate a programme to build several prototype 9X engines in 4-cylinder and 6-cylinder versions, Rod Bull was expected to extract the extensive funds which would be required from the never knowingly generous finance department. In the end it was Mark Snowdon who explained to Issigonis, as diplomatically as he could, that the company did not have large amounts available to spend on an engine which was not even part of the product plan.

As well as ploughing his lone furrow with the 9X, he also undertook some specific projects at the company's request devising small improvements for the Mini. Bull worked with him on a downdraught/updraught manifold for the A-series in order to improve fuel economy. The work was done under quite difficult conditions because Issigonis no longer had access to much by way of experimental facilities. Because there were no test beds available to him the system was proved using real miles clocked up by cars fitted with fuel meters to ensure that results were sound and repeatable. The tests took place during a particularly severe winter and temperatures in the Lickey Hills could get as low as −17°C. Rod Bull recalls:

> We had two cars fitted with the DU manifold and it took us longer to get into the cars than to start them. They both started within 1½ seconds at −15°C according to the thermometers we'd got inside the cars so that pleased him immensely.

Ultimately the system was not implemented because the compression ratio for the engine was changed and this limited the effectiveness of the design; but the experiments did persuade British Leyland to do some work on the engine in an effort to match the results that these fuel economy experiments had achieved.

Charles Griffin was also concerned with Mini improvements and he assigned John Sheppard, who was now part of his team, to work with Issigonis on a scheme to reduce engine noise. When the modifications had been made and fitted onto a running vehicle, Griffin and Sheppard drove the car out to Edgbaston to show him. Issigonis was pleased with the result until Griffin commented:

'It's so quiet you can hear the radio now.'

Issigonis knitted his brows and muttered, 'You haven't put a radio in there?'

'No, we haven't', laughed Griffin.

Although this was the last official Issigonis project that Sheppard worked on, he had been visiting his old boss every Sunday since his retirement. Sometimes he would call in at lunchtime during the week as well with some odd job that he had agreed to do in his own time. One Sunday he received a phone call from Issigonis asking him to bring his drawing instruments along as there was a schematic he wanted him to do. When he arrived Issigonis took him through to the drawing room but then decided the dining room would be more suitable. The polished circular dining table was positioned under the large dome ceiling window which appeared to be the ideal place from the point of view of light, but this was not right either. The drawing would have to be done on the floor so that the table would not be damaged by the points of the compass. Exasperated, Sheppard proclaimed it was impossible to draw on the carpet and took the job home. But his old boss still retained his charm and Sheppard still enjoyed the challenge of working with him: 'He'd got a way with him, to me at least, I'll bet you can't do this, challenge all the time and a little smile.'

Despite everything, Issigonis still had terrific physical strength. He refused to listen to advice about taking exercise and he continued to smoke cigarettes and drink his martinis. Then, one day, he demonstrated his will power by deciding on his own initiative to completely give up both. The result was that he began to feel ill and his doctor told him that, though it was a laudable resolve, it really would be better if he gave things up progressively to avoid sudden side-effects. He wrote down several lists of his symptoms and he did this quite dispassionately in the same style

that he used to list the faults of his prototypes in his Arclight notepads.
One of these lists reads:

List 1
House bound – chair bound – don't like going out
Low blood pressure
Bunch of nerves – never get better sometimes I shiver with fright
Eyes focus – goes out
Weak legs
Waddle can't walk – afraid
Moving head sideways very hard or sudden movement
Can't work with my hands
Can't stand or climb or descend stairs
Drink about same as before or a little more makes me feel better
Smoke 6/8 per day only 2/3rds, been down to 4
Lying down
Hate getting up
Occupation reading only
Hate driving or being driven
Go only to the shops
Hate waiting anywhere because I want to get home and sit down
Illness didn't smoke or drink for three weeks and fell down (black out)
When I feel very bad my right eye closes more than the left
I can still think about work and get things done but for short periods
of interview at home – can't go to the works any more
Right leg is much stronger than left leg

As he became less active and more dependent on other people to look after
him his expenses mounted. As well as the Papes, his cleaning lady and a
gardener, he also began to require nursing care two or three days a week
and in October 1980 his friends persuaded British Leyland to cover the
costs of this nursing care over and above the consultancy fee. Ralph Pape,
assisted by Peggy, continued to look after him and cook his meals and every
evening he would prepare a cold supper for Alec so that there would be
no problem with the washing up after he had left. One night in June 1984
Alec suffered a perforated stomach ulcer. It happened after Ralph Pape had
left at eight in the evening as a result of which he was not discovered until
Peggy Pape returned at nine the next morning. She found that Issigonis

had fallen from his bed and lost a great deal of blood and he was taken by ambulance to hospital where he had to have an operation. Despite being seriously ill from the poisoning resulting from the delay in finding him, Issigonis survived something which might have felled even a much younger person. Nevertheless this incident weakened him sufficiently to make it necessary to spend some time in a Nuffield nursing home to recover and when he came home he began to receive full-time nursing care.

9X VERSUS THE K-SERIES ENGINE

As the years passed British Leyland continued to change its name, set up new subsidiaries and re-organise itself at regular intervals. Austin Morris gave way to Austin Rover. Chief executives, managing directors and technical chiefs came and went. The workforce continued to strike and Issigonis continued to work away at the 9X, never giving up hope that one day someone would listen to him. He paid little attention to the constant shifts inside British Leyland any more beyond commenting acidly to Mark Snowdon, 'Why do you keep changing jobs all the time? I find this most frustrating.'

The fate of the ADO 88 project had been sealed when South African trouble-shooter Michael Edwardes arrived on the scene as the new Chief Executive of British Leyland in late 1977, bearing an impressive reputation from his position as head of the Chloride Group. Finally, British Leyland had a chairman who was serious about rationalisation. Factories were closed, overseas operations were abandoned and the workforce was trimmed. Naturally the redundancy programme sparked a fresh set of industrial disputes from which Edwardes, unlike his predecessors, emerged victorious. He also instituted an overhaul of the model range which was long overdue, determined that British Leyland should concentrate on a much smaller set of better engineered cars. The project which was most advanced was ADO 88. This had already been subjected to a series of 'model clinics' so that members of the public could comment on how they viewed the proposed new car compared with its major competition. The results of the latest clinics were not what the project team had hoped for. There was nothing wrong with the fundamental principles of the car. Griffin was a disciple of the Issigonis philosophy of space utilisation and the basic package was well received. The problem was that Griffin also seemed to have adopted Alec's addiction to absence of styling and this was what earned the car such a poor reception.

Edwardes had no hesitation in endorsing the decision to make a major effort to restyle ADO 88 even though the consequence of this was to delay the launch of the desperately needed new model by a year. The changes required were so significant that the project was given a new designation of LC8. Finally, nearly a decade behind the opposition, British Leyland successfully added a new small hatchback to its range in the guise of the Austin Mini Metro. An interesting footnote to the long saga of British Leyland's quest for a new small car lies in the fact that the extensive and highly successful advertising campaign which accompanied the launch at the end of 1980 was devised by Tony Ball, who had lent his fertile imagination to the launch of the original Mini. By now the old self-confidence was gone and the word 'Mini' had been slipped into the model name in the hope that it might work its usual magic. But, just as the 'Morris Mini-Minor' had morphed into the 'Mini', the 'Austin Mini Metro' very quickly became simply the 'Metro'. It seemed that, for the public, there could be only one Mini.

Though he had not been to Longbridge for a long time, Issigonis continued to take an interest in the details of current designs such as the Metro. He also took the trouble to familiarise himself with the details of a new engine project, the K-series, which he rightly identified as a rival to his own 9X design. The Austin Mini Metro had been fitted with a development of the same A-series engine which had been introduced by Austin almost 30 years earlier, a power unit which had grown from its original capacity of 803 cc to a maximum of 1275 cc in its production form by 1980. This engine had proved to be as durable as the Mini itself, making it one of the longest-surviving engines in production. British Leyland had made numerous attempts to replace it, including the new engine design which was part of the short-lived ADO 74 project, but to date the cash-strapped company had always chosen the cheaper option of adapting the A-series instead. By the early 1980s, however, there had been extensive improvements in the field of engine design, not to mention a myriad of new anti-pollution regulations which needed to be engineered into any new project. As the law relating to emissions constantly became tougher it became ever more difficult to keep the A-series engine compliant and planning for a replacement K-series engine began in 1983. To the engineers and managers of British Leyland this was a matter of credibility as much as modernisation. The Product Strategy Committee put their case in January 1985 with the words:

Not only does the engine have to equal or exceed the best of competition in all respects, it represents Austin Rover's first all new engine for many years and will in effect be a statement of the technical and technological development achievements essential to a committed, confident and robust company.

The final decision about what to do was not in their hands, however, and the purse-strings which they needed to untie were now in the hands of a hostile Conservative government. The Labour administration which had commissioned the Ryder Report in 1975 and taken a 99.8 per cent shareholding in British Leyland Ltd had done so with the intention of rescuing the British motor industry at whatever cost. By 1979 power was back in the hands of the Conservatives led by Margaret Thatcher. She held the opposite view and was intent on devising some politically acceptable method of offloading the company back into the private sector as soon as possible. It was extremely difficult to sell the idea of an expensive and lengthy engine development programme, which had no obvious sales benefits, to a Department of Trade with such an underlying agenda. When they finally approved the K-series project as part of the 1985 Corporate Plan it was with great reluctance. Much therefore depended on the success or failure of this project and it became the cornerstone of all British Leyland's future product plans.

Despite Issigonis' implacable opposition to the K-series from the day that he heard of it, the concept of this engine was similar to that of the 9X, aiming at low weight, high fuel efficiency and high power. Both replaced cast-iron with lighter aluminium and used a sandwich construction. In the case of the K-series this consisted of a cylinder head, block and short crankcase plus a bearing ladder to clamp the bearings and crankshaft to the crankcase. Ten very long bolts passed from the top of the cylinder head through the block, crankcase and bearing ladder, secured by nuts at each end. The apparent progression from the Austin Seven, through the 9X to the K-series is remarkable even though the 9X never entered production. The Issigonis engine design was not a secret and of course the engineers who worked with him during the early years of the project later went on to other parts of the company. It is therefore likely that some of his ideas were used without his direct involvement and it could be argued that the time which Alec Issigonis spent on his sporting Austin Sevens in the late 1920s and early 1930s became reflected in the K-series engine which emerged in the 1990s.

Naturally, Issigonis did not see it that way. The question of the relative merits of the 9X and the K-series was to provide his last battleground with the executives of British Leyland and during the final years of his consultancy he would mount an increasingly feverish campaign to convince them of the superiority of his own design. In the early 1980s he began to write letters in his capacity as consultant to the people he believed should be listening to him. When he began this correspondence Issigonis was mostly concerned with championing the cause of the 9X and fighting off unwelcome changes to the Mini. Unfortunately many of his letters have a lecturing tone which was ill-advised when dealing with experienced engineers who considered themselves quite capable of making their own judgements. He also insisted on continually disparaging modern design and production methods which had the counter-productive effect of making his letters sound petulant even though he was still capable of making perceptive engineering points.

He had prepared a report entitled 'What has been done to make the Mini more refined' which went through four versions and was sent to everyone who might have some influence. He continually expressed his disappointment that even the work he was commissioned to do on the Mini was not going into production and the frustration he felt is clearly discernible. In July 1980 he sent his report to Harold Musgrove (Executive Chairman of the Austin Rover Group Division) and Mark Snowdon, commenting: 'I am disappointed to hear about the sound deadening material that has been incorporated in the Mini, apart from the high cost and increased weight it does nothing to my proposals to refine the car.'

Issigonis was moved to complain 'Longbridge are all anti anything I do to improve the Mini'. His irritation is clear in the comments he wrote on a report sent to him by Power Train in August 1981, which queried the results of his DU manifold experiments and, even more annoyingly, quibbled that they could not be applied to the Metro. 'One thing at a time', Issigonis wrote in the margin. 'Don't confuse the issue. I was briefed to refine the Mini which I have done. Don't know anything about Metro installation. No installation problems on the Mini, redesign to suit Metro conditions.' It is understandable that he should feel annoyed when improvement work he had been asked to do was undermined by decisions which were not even directly communicated to him, but at the same time he continued to champion aspects of his original design that had disappeared so long ago that few people even remembered them any more. He pointed out to Mark Snowdon that he had deliberately re-introduced the sliding window onto the Gearless Mini ...

> You are bound to notice that the gearless car has sliding windows which have several virtues when compared with drop windows.
> 1) They are cheaper to produce and save a little weight.
> 2) Give 3" more elbow room.
> 3) Allow a substantial increase in door storage space.
> 4) Give draught free ventilation.
> Old Mini owners hate the current design because of the disturbance created when the side window is opened. Try both for yourself and see. Your hair will stand on end when you open the drop window a little. Could sliding windows be used in a cheap version of the Mini?

And he continually insisted that not only was the 9X the key to the future, but only his old team were capable of making it a reality:

> If we are to survive the 9X engine must be put into production for the small car market. Now there is no talent to design outstanding cars, only components. Farina can do the envelope. My old team can do the mechanicals – they are all ready and available, both front and rear suspensions. Keep Pressed Steel from muscling in on car design – fatal – they have no design talent. They are only press tool makers.

He had long been right to identify that the company desperately needed to address the issue of a new engine for the small- to medium-sized end of their model range and for many years his 9X had been the only alternative in the pipeline. When the K-series project emerged, however, he was forced to switch his focus from championing his own engine design to defending it against a new one. In 1985 he wrote to Mark Snowdon:

> The fact that the 9X power unit is 16 years old does not mean that it is out of date. It is still as modern in design as the best small engines of today ... The 9X power unit has been proved and tested in every respect whereas the new engine is not proved in any respect, this will take three years at least. The 9X unit in its manual and gearless form will be found to be superior to the 'K' series engine and therefore you have no option but to use the 9X engine to replace the 'A' series unit.

He backed up his statements with long and detailed comparisons between the two engines yet, at the same time, he could not resist making unfavourable comparisons between the Technical Department over which he had presided and what he saw as the shortcomings of the day. To Ray Horrocks (Managing Director of BL Cars) again he wrote:

> Finally, in my view, the company is spending far too much money on robots and computers etc. in terms of the numbers of cars we build. When I was Technical Director of B.M.C. we made in excess of 6,000 Minis per week alone at Cowley and Longbridge, with no need for highly complicated automatic machinery. This machinery obviously needs constant servicing by highly skilled men. That labour force could be used to assemble the cars instead. I feel that accountants employed by firms in this country are the cause of the downfall of British management. Being employed as a consultant to this company it is my duty to bring this to your attention.

Of all his campaigns, his continual criticism of the K-series engine was the most dangerous for Issigonis. Given that the survival of the company was at stake and considering the half-heartedness with which the government had endorsed the programme, public criticism from a long-retired engineer whose name nevertheless held a great deal of clout was extremely unwelcome. In the circumstances he received surprisingly polite replies. Some of his letters were decorated with handwritten comments from the recipients such as 'give me some words to reply to this – try not to explode', but he was always treated with respect and his correspondents went to some trouble to provide detailed answers to his criticisms. Perhaps they hoped that they might be able to persuade him of their point of view, but there was little chance of this.

Towards the end of 1986 Rod Bull requested the opportunity to do a presentation on behalf of Issigonis to the senior management team and he was given permission to do so. Martin Ince of Prototype Build and Roland Bertodo, Director of Power Train Engineering, both agreed to attend along with some of their senior engineers. Bull was warned not to make any direct comparisons with other power units but he decided to disregard this advice since this was the nub of the case for the 9X. Together with Issigonis, he prepared a series of charts to illustrate the ingeniousness of the design by superimposing the 9X over the K-series from a number of different angles, using the familiar argument that its compactness would simplify the manufacturing process and reduce costs. His audience listened in silence and Bull returned to Edgbaston to report the disappointing outcome to Issigonis who merely raised his eyebrows as if it was no more than he had expected.

Nevertheless Issigonis still had enough influence to obtain vehicles off the assembly line for the small fleet of experimental cars allocated to his 'Small Car Research' Department. In 1986 he had six cars on his books – one ADO 15 (gearless), four ADO 20s (three fitted with the 4-cylinder 9X and one gearless) and one Maestro (fitted with a 6-cylinder 9X). At the end of October he put in a request to exchange the Maestro for an MG Metro straight from production line. This was to be fitted with the 9X engine from the Maestro in order to show off the engine's qualities:

> The request for a Turbo Metro is to take advantage of the chassis/suspension qualities inherent in this version of the model. These are deemed necessary in view of the light weight and high power output of this engine. The choice of a smaller vehicle will demonstrate the installation advantages of a power unit designed to be compact. This combination of chassis and power unit will show that performance and refinement can be combined in a small vehicle. Provision to have a vehicle manufactured without a power unit and external Turbo installed has been investigated. Apparently it will not be a problem, this should therefore, reduce the cost of developing this prototype.

The installation was completed at the end of December and extensively photographed. Issigonis' verdict was 'the layout is very untidy because I only had 2 fitters to do the job in rather a hurry'.

Meanwhile he continued his letter-writing campaign and sent one of his long essays on the relative merits of the two designs to Roland Bertodo, and Bertodo wrote him a generous reply in which he tried to gently warn him to accept the situation as it was:

> I promised, almost too long ago, to respond formally to your request for a word comparison between the 9X and the K-series engine. This is not a new request in that you have raised the issue before with several luminaries in ARG. In each instance, the department has provided a brief to management. Having given the matter some considerable

thought, I feel that I can best answer your question by forwarding abstracts from previous responses. I have also arranged for Rod Bull to view a strip-down of a DL2AA K Series 4 Valve engine so that he may comment to you in greater detail. I suspect that you may well disagree with our current philosophy but neither of us has the power to alter it.

Any pragmatism which had lingered in his soul had been eaten away by his years in the wilderness. Bertodo was hinting as loudly as he could that the writing was on the wall. Issigonis chose to continue on his course, headlong into it. In 1986 British Leyland acquired another new Chief Executive, Canadian Graham Day, and once again the upper ranks of management were cleared out in preparation for an attempt to change British Leyland's badly tarnished image by renaming it Rover Group. Among the casualties was Issigonis' friend Mark Snowdon. Another bad omen was the re-allocation of his unused office in the Kremlin. A large quantity of his papers was still stored there in a large wooden plan chest and Rod Bull urgently arranged for the chest and its contents to be transferred to the repository of British Leyland's historic material, the British Motor Industry Heritage Trust. Undeterred, Issigonis decided to make one last effort by approaching Graham Day directly. On 24 February 1987 he wrote the following letter, which combines in it all the elements which had gone into his correspondence with senior management over the last ten years – a proprietary attitude to suggestions that the Mini should be modified, a plea on behalf of the 9X, and a sideswipe at modern design methods:

Dear Mr Day

I have not met you but I feel I must write to explain a few points. A reversion to the original model names of Mini and Mini de luxe instead of Mini City and Mini Mayfair would be preferable. To change the Mini body shape would be fatal as it is known world wide, to do so would make it just another car.

Your secretary has been informed about the gearless Mini which I am sure you will find appealing as a 'town' car. It has a proven, smooth, stepless transmission which is cheap to make. Apart from eliminating the expensive Automotive Products automatic box that is fitted to the Mini, it would with the exception of two components be made 'in house'.

This car is 10ft long, the same as the current Mini but has four inches more leg room which is a considerable gain within so small an overall dimension. It is over two cwt lighter than the present version of the automatic Mini due to the elimination of subframes and rubber suspension. A large part of the weight reduction is due to the use of a derivative of the 9X power unit, which is 140 lbs lighter than its aged 'A' series counterpart.

If we are to remain in the small car market a new lightweight, compact power unit is essential. To this end the 9X range of engines, all with the transmission located below the crankshaft have been developed over the past 18 years and are ready for tooling. It is as modern as any power unit of to-day without the need for electronic complication. The design allows the use of low C.O. levels, essential considering legislative requirements and its toxicity to all animal life.

Yours sincerely Sir Alec Issigonis

P.S. I do not approve of electronics in cars or the design of cars by computer. It is preferable to have the latter conducted by draughtsmen and slide rules.

He certainly succeeded in bringing attention to himself but unfortunately the outcome was a letter, received via his solicitor, informing him that his consultancy had been terminated. Rod Bull was redeployed elsewhere in the company. As for the 'K'-series, it would eventually make its official début in 1989 as part of the new R8 project which became the second model to take the name Rover 200. To the company's relief it was the success that they had hoped for.

THE BIOGRAPHY

'Arragonis' had been a person of single-minded intent, certain about the path in life that he wanted to follow and confident in his own opinions. The British Leyland experience had severely shaken this certainty and as Issigonis grew older the effect deepened. Coupled with the physical effects of his ear problem, he became a virtual recluse who in many ways had lost confidence in himself.

The departure of Mark Snowdon and the termination of his consultancy meant that Issigonis had to finally accept that the 9X adventure was over. Though physically he was now very frail, his mind was as active as ever. He still did the *Daily Telegraph* crossword every day but this was not enough to keep him fully occupied. So he decided that his next project would be the writing of his autobiography. He had been approached by a number of people wanting to become his official biographer and had rejected every proposal out of hand, not least because he hated the thought of talking to strangers about his personal life. The only journalists who had ever succeeded in getting a more intimate view of the private person were those like Laurence Pomeroy or Piero Casucci who also formed part of his circle of personal friends. It is therefore not hard to understand why he chose Tony Dawson as the man he wanted to represent his life story to the rest of the world. When it was put to him, Dawson was ambivalent about the task. There is no doubt that he knew Issigonis well enough to realise that his subject, willing as he might be, invariably disliked anything that had been written about him after the event. He had become very quarrelsome as his health deteriorated and Tony Dawson was reluctant to embark on something which might provoke a falling out.

Once Issigonis had made up his mind, however, it was very hard to say no. He took the same determined approach to this project as he had formerly applied to creating a new design, hunting out material with some energy. He seems to have had only a vague idea of the kind of material a biographer would need so he bombarded Tony Dawson with a wide but random selection of paperwork. There were letters relating to his CBE and knighthood; the invitation to Lord Snowdon's wedding; many notes written by Lord Snowdon or Princess Margaret on Kensington Palace notepaper; the letters of congratulation he had received from numerous important people on receiving his knighthood; and the small folder of 'Biographical Notes for Fellows of the Royal Society' in which he had written comments about his life. In 1970 Tony Dawson had organised a display of Issigonis sketches which had been held at the Institute of Contemporary Arts (ICA) and he still had the 154 sketches which Alec had personally selected along with the notes of explanation that he had written for the curators of the exhibition. Issigonis gave him almost 200 more, often annotating them with comments about their significance. He began to write disjointed notes in the margins of magazine articles and books and, now that he was free from his consultancy agreement, he produced a quantity of handwritten notes expressing opinions rather more forthright than the studied replies he was accustomed to giving to journalists. These were presumably intended to assist with the final chapters. On the subject of the merger he commented:

> The merger with Leyland killed off everything. It was madness to kill the world-wide Morris name and replace it by Triumph, tin pot engineers who were <u>not</u> known world-wide. The Marina is by far the worst car in the world!

The efforts of the company to kill off the Mini and their inability to do so therefore gave him a bitter satisfaction:

> Japan loves the Mini, so does the rest of Europe. People are screaming for the present Mini but they don't make enough (only 800 per week). The waiting list at home is three months, BL just hate it. It's politics, they can't sell their Metro, they're giving it away with packets of tea.

His comments about the Metro are rather unfair since it had succeeded for British Leyland in its target market. Nevertheless he was right in pointing out that it had not killed the Mini. A decision to phase the Mini out of UK production during 1982 was not carried through because the model continued to bring in a reasonable return even though it was given hardly any promotion for many years. In 1984 Harold Musgrove, Chief Executive for Austin Rover, was saying:

> Well, as long as the Mini is selling and is contributing to the profitability of the company, then the Mini will remain in production. But of course we are a very realistic company and if we found that the Mini was in the way of producing more profitable cars then we would undoubtedly at that stage have to consider when we would run out the Mini. But I do not see that happening for quite a long time because there is such a demand for this car. People refer to it as 25 years old and they're absolutely right, but when you're selling a car at 50,000 a year, I don't consider that at this moment we should even be talking of the demise of the Mini.

It was to continue till the new millennium, outliving its 'replacement', the Metro. It even underwent a renaissance towards the end of the 80s when for the first time in many years an advertising campaign was launched. At the end of 1987 British Leyland ran adverts with the highly successful theme 'Minis Have Feelings Too' which reminded the public that it was still available as a new model. This was followed by a nostalgia campaign involving Twiggy and Lulu. From then on it was kept alive by a constant stream of limited editions and consistently sold well in France and Japan. In 1990 even the Mini Cooper was revived, showing that there was life in the old marque yet.

As the material for the biography began to mount up Alec and Tony Dawson drew up an outline for the book, making a list of chapters and discussing the inclusion of reminiscences from some of his friends as a separate chapter. Dawson described the project to Robert Braunschweig in October 1986:

> I am collecting and preparing material (with Alec's agreement and assistance) to write his biography. One of our thoughts (Alec's and mine) about 'the book' as he calls it was to include a chapter of comment from long-standing friends such as yourself who would wish to pay tribute to the 'blacksmith' who has probably made the most noteworthy contribution to automobile engineering this century (not excluding Henry Ford). Do you think that this is a good idea and, if so, would you be prepared to contribute?

Though Braunschweig agreed enthusiastically to write 'a little scathing thing' this suggestion does not seem to have come to anything as no such contributions have survived.

There was one aspect of the project, however, about which Issigonis was clear. He knew, from the endless questions of journalists, that some information about his early life would be required. He passed on a great deal of photographic material including two personal photograph albums concerning the family's life in Smyrna and he also started to jot down notes about things as he remembered them. When Tony Dawson protested that he could not be expected to make any sense of these, Alec agreed to record his memories and May Ransome was asked to make one of her visits in order to help him. Tony Dawson often taped Issigonis as a means of putting together 'interviews' for journalists who submitted questions through him rather than making personal visits. This was different and Alec clearly felt uneasy talking about the past even with his friend. There is no doubt about why he drafted in May. Her presence made him feel more comfortable and he was also convinced that she would remember the 'details' better than he would. So whenever Dawson asked him a specific question about some person or event he would invariably say, 'Oh ask May dear boy, she'll know.'

His early life was a subject he had put to the back of his mind for many years and as the exercise went on he began to share many things with May which were not passed on to Tony Dawson. On arriving in England they had both appeared to put their worst times behind them, but in old age the depth of the scars which had been left by their experiences became more evident as the painful memories of the evacuation and the treatment to which they had been subjected in Malta began to re-emerge. May was the only person left who understood these things because no explanations could really describe what they had been through. This drew them closer together once again and during her visits he would ask her to speak to him in the 'kitchen' Greek of their childhood. When Tony Dawson had gone he would talk to her about their friends and relatives and ask her to describe what she remembered of their homes in Smyrna, the layout of the house and garden at Azizeah and the games they used to play. When she was back at her home in Topsham he began to send her pictures, scribbling personal notes on the back of them such as:

> Did you know that the House of the Virgin Mary is between Azizieh and Ephesus? We went to see it on our way from your father's and Ephesus. It is a small wooden shack surrounded by beautiful trees. We paid for a candle to go inside. St Luke brought her there after the death of Christ (I feel he was a hippy of those days making trouble for the Jews). The Romans did not want to execute him.

He also sent May some of Hulda's pictures which had been inscribed with her rather neater handwritten comments, like the one she wrote on a picture of herself sitting amid the ruins of a Greek monument: 'Imperatrice Hulda Issigonis: Note the intent look. Is she addressing her subjects? Or watching the finish of a race?' Often he would enclose a scribbled note telling her not to bother sending anything back. It was an area of communication solely between the two of them, as were the phone calls he made late in the evening, ostensibly to discuss clues to the *Daily Telegraph* crossword, but really as an excuse for a chat and a few more questions about some detail or other from their childhood.

The Legacy

The words Issigonis had spoken to Piero Casucci in 1969 were becoming a distressing reality by 1987: 'The future troubles him. Loneliness and the idea of becoming, one day perhaps, a burden to his friends also troubles him.' Though many of the faces that had witnessed his illustrious career were gone, he welcomed visits to the bungalow from those friends who were still around. Robert Braunschweig would make a special effort to go and see him and Sergio Pininfarina also managed to pay him one last visit in November 1983 after a trip to London to collect an honour from the Royal Society of Arts. Charles Griffin, Geoffrey Rose, Chris Kingham and Tommy French dropped in from time to time, as did some of his former workshop engineers. Jack Daniels had retired to Bournemouth but occasionally Issigonis would call him and Daniels would travel up to see him. His solicitor and his bank manager were often there and Tony Dawson was at the bungalow nearly every day. Then there was his cousin May who would come up to look after him and keep him company whenever he asked. Now he was unwilling to venture as far as the Poplars, Max and Christopher Dowson visited him regularly and so did Penny whenever she was in England. For a while he was able to keep up a social life in this way. He would sit with his visitors in the bungalow and chat over a few dry martinis before getting them to take him to a nearby Italian restaurant called 'The Pinocchio' for lunch where he would always order his favourite dish of ravioli. The trips to The Pinocchio had become practically the limit of his world.

Apart from Tony Dawson, by far his most regular visitor was John Sheppard who still came over every Sunday morning. They would sit and have a drink together and Issigonis would say: 'Let's talk about the dirt, what's going on?' There was no point in keeping a chauffeur any more since he so rarely went out and when he was feeling strong enough Sheppard would take him out for a drive to get a new supply of gin or some cigarettes. Alec had always got so much pleasure from driving and had a reputation for skill and speed behind the wheel, but now he would plead, 'don't go too fast'. His deteriorating state of mind made a great impression on Sheppard: '... he was quite embittered I think in the end, in a way I suppose you'd say he was soured.' But I could sympathise with him. Certainly all my feelings were for him.'

In his last years, Issigonis became more and more introspective and brooded on what had happened to him. He talked of being put on the scrap heap. He forbade any mention of the name of Dante Giacosa, the Fiat designer, even though he had once admired him and Giacosa in his autobiography had in his turn expressed his admiration for the ingenuity of the Mini design. He refused to see Alex Moulton. He nursed his grievance over the fact that his hard work on the 9X had never been recognised and he even hinted that his ideas had been stolen by industrial spies. Always an impatient and dogmatic man, he became increasingly short-tempered and began to quarrel with people on a regular basis. The main targets for his moodiness were the two people who spent the most time with him. One was his housekeeper Ralph Pape who put up with being at the sharp end of his employer's comments with good grace, not taking Alec's diatribes too seriously. The other was the ever-present Tony Dawson. They frequently fell out, but before Dawson even had time to get back to his Oxford home nearly 70 miles away, Alec would be on the phone to the soothing voice of Tony's sympathetic wife Paddy. Sometimes he wanted to continue the row but more often he was upset and apologetic over what had happened. Because he had begun to feel lonely and insecure he often behaved in a way which alienated people unnecessarily but most of his friends tolerated his increasingly erratic behaviour because it was clear he was not well.

The termination of his consultancy in 1987 would mark the beginning of a sharp decline, even though he tried to find new interests. His work had been his life and when it was taken away from him, it sapped his will to live. The more ill he became, the less he encouraged people to go and see him and so the more isolated he became. Sometimes even Sheppard was not welcome. Once when he went to visit him in the Queen Elizabeth Hospital he was met with the rebuttal, 'I don't want anybody to see me when I'm like this, come and see me when I'm well and we'll have a drink.'

When his term of notice finally expired, this brought with it the cancellation of his fee. British Leyland, now transformed into Rover Group, were facing a worsening financial situation and they decided that his nursing costs were another expensive commitment which they were no longer prepared to honour. Though most of his supporters had by now left the company there were a few sympathetic voices who warned that he was close to the end and sheer compassion would suggest arrangements should be left as they were. But business was business and the decision had been made. Issigonis was informed that the payments for his nursing care had been terminated and it was now up to him to cover all his own expenses. With only his pension left, he was unable to do this. He had little choice other than to put the Edgbaston bungalow on the market for £150,000. Early in 1988 he left his home of 25 years, with all its memories of his mother, to move into a two-roomed flat in Hindon Square close by. He was very frail and weak by now from lack of physical activity and he spent most of his time in bed.

Penny went to visit him at Hindon Square with her young son in August and was shocked when she saw all his possessions still in packing boxes. Sheppard also continued his regular visits and now he always found him lying on his day bed and never again saw him sitting up in his chair. He still had his sense of humour and was amused by Mark Ransome's suggestion that he needed a supercharger to solve the problem of his low blood pressure. The flat was too small to take much with him and besides this he still needed money to pay his bills so in September 1988 he asked a nearby auction house, Fellows and Sons, to sell four hand-woven rugs, described on the sale details as 'Eastern', and a 19th-century Dresden clock case, which together were valued at £2,500. Two days before he died he made a call to Jack Daniels and asked him to come up and see him. The nurse would only allow Daniels in for ten minutes but Issigonis recognised him and greeted him warmly, thanking him for coming. He died on 2 October 1988, just one month short of his 82nd birthday. The causes of death were recorded as heart disease and pneumonia.

His estate amounted to considerably less than the money he had raised by selling his house, testifying to the huge expenses he faced during his last year. Everything that remained was left to his cousin May and her children Mark and Sally. In addition he made a memorandum of wishes naming specific items which he wanted to go to various people. The oil portrait was left to Ralph and Peggy Pape and Penny inherited the 'Mediterranean Back Street' painting. The Meccano clock with the pendulum was given to Penny's young son while a quarter-scale plastic model of the Mini went to Jack Daniels.

His funeral was held on 11 October in the Anglican church of St George's which lay just across the road from the Edgbaston bungalow. Guests included friends and colleagues as well as all the nurses who had looked after him. The Morris Minor Club sent a large wreath of yellow chrysanthemums in the shape of his first design. Peter Ustinov wrote a touching funeral address which was read out on his behalf. The funeral party – which consisted of the two families who had been closest to him, the Ransomes and the Dowsons – then went with him on his final journey to Lodge Hill Crematorium in Selly Oak where his ashes were later scattered in the garden of remembrance.

The industry felt he must be honoured and a service of thanksgiving was organised at Birmingham Cathedral on 4 November. Inside, former colleagues joined friends and family for the service and Lord Snowdon gave the address. His enduring legacy, however, was represented by the three cars which stood outside – the first Morris Minor, the first Morris Mini-Minor and a Mini straight off the production line.

CONCLUSION

GENIUS?

The Mini is a car that won't die and it won't die because of Alec's genius.

Lord Snowdon

As a boy Alec Issigonis suffered the trauma of becoming a refugee followed closely by the premature death of his father. His last years were difficult ones as he coped with the combined losses of his mother, his health and, finally, his work. Yet if we look outside these two episodes of his life, the story is one of an unusual degree of contentment. By taking pleasure in simple things and living life as it came to him he was able to achieve a remarkable level of self-fulfilment. He stressed many times and with complete sincerity in his later life that he had no unachieved ambitions or longings. He was a fortunate person who for the most part spent his time involved in the things that he enjoyed most and attained the goals that he set himself in his chosen field. He experienced fame in a more respectful era when this was a pleasant experience rather than an invitation for intrusion on his personal privacy. His talent and celebrity enabled him to make close friendships with some of the most interesting people of his era – men like Sergio Pininfarina, Bernard Cahier, Paul Frère, Peter Ustinov, Lord Snowdon, Enzo Ferrari and John Cooper. He also enjoyed a set of life-long, loyal and emotionally rewarding friendships.

The backdrop to this life was the birth and growth of both the motor car and the motor industry. The outstanding achievement of his career was to establish the principle of the transverse engine with front wheel drive which revolutionised the modern motor car. Most present-day small and mid-size vehicles use this configuration. But the car that demonstrated these principles embodied so much more. Lord Snowdon's tribute to Issigonis at his memorial service in Birmingham Cathedral expresses this very well:

He was a true engineer, designer and perfectionist. His genius, for he was a genius, lay in his inventive brain concentrating on pure function and essential truth in engineering design ... Nowadays cars are

433

designed by teams of people rather than by an individual and I doubt
that there will ever be another single designer who will contribute so
much as Alec did. He unquestionably advanced and altered the thinking of not only all other British manufacturers but also the multi-
national manufacturers the world over. His influence was colossal.

The Mini's theme was miniaturisation combined with availability and in
this it chimed perfectly with the theme of the 20th century. The previous
century had spawned a series of revolutionary machines such as the wireless telegraph, the camera and the autocar, and these were joined in 1943
by the first electronic computer. When they were first invented only a
wealthy aristocrat or businessman could even consider the purchase of
such marvels. As the century progressed these complex technologies were
progressively simplified and perfected so that by 1999 there were few
individuals in the Western world who did not possess a car, a miniature
camera, a mobile phone or a personal computer. The Mini was one step
along the way of this revolution.

Despite its durability, to Issigonis in 1959 the Mini was just one link in
the chain of his creative progression. He never doubted that in time, just
as with the Morris Minor, he would find a better way to achieve his
vision and the Mini would belong to the past. This is not what happened.
Instead he found he had created something which remained 'modern' for
over 40 years. It never looked out of place on the road alongside the cars
of the 70s, 80s or 90s in the way the Morris Minor, the 1100 or the 1800
did. Its audience never tired of it. For many years, the company which
had fallen out of love with their design genius longed to get rid of the
Mini but its adoring public would never let them wield the final axe.

Though it was never his intention, in the end the Mini has become
Issigonis' epitaph and one that finally he accepted for himself. When it
reached sales of 5 million he said:

> Don't expect me to be modest about the Mini. I'm very proud that it
> has run for so many years without a major mechanical change and it
> still looks like the car we designed. Five million people have bought my
> Mini and it just goes to show that they have a lot of common sense.

So where should his achievement be placed: in the world of the arts or of
the sciences? Next to the fact that he designed the Mini, the one thing

most people will be able to tell you about Alec Issigonis is that he was famous for his sketches. Wild comparisons have been made with Leonardo da Vinci but this is to miss the point. Some of his sketches are of very high quality and beautiful to look at – this applies particularly to those which were produced in the Mosquito and Alvis periods. There is clearly a powerful imagination at work, and a pleasure in wielding the pencil which transfers the pictures of his mind to the page. Nevertheless they are an engineer's drawings, an inheritance of the technique he saw his father using decades earlier at the marine factory in Smyrna. What they really express is a powerful intellect combined with great creativity and this is what gives the best of the sketches their appeal. Issigonis was an intensely private man who did not discuss his feelings, his dreams or his ambitions. His life was almost two-thirds over before fame descended on him and when it did he invented a public persona which he sheltered behind for the rest of his life. As a man for whom work was life to an extraordinary degree, these outpourings of his mind are the closest it is possible to get to the private man. They are a continuous and chronological record of his ideas, a diary of his imagination. The content, the style and the intensity develop over the years. They clearly reflect his moods, his successes, his failures and his quality of life at different times.

Despite his self-assurance Issigonis never claimed to be an artist. He may have been flattered by comparisons to Leonardo da Vinci but he never allowed himself to believe them. If someone suggested he should draw non-mechanical objects he would reply, 'If I draw trees they look like crankshafts.' He always referred to his sketches as 'doodles'. In August 1964, following one of his trips to Turin to visit Pininfarina, Issigonis met up with the Snowdons in Venice, a place he had never visited before. Snowdon recalled of this trip:

I led him into the centre of St Mark's at midnight and it is a breathtaking sight to see St Mark's empty. 'What do you think of it Alec?' I said and he looked at me and said 'my dear, exactly like the Burlington Arcade'.

Piero Casucci described the relationship between his artistry and his profession:

Alec Issigonis is first of all an artist, as on the other side, his wonderful hands reveal. 'I like using my hands' – he says – 'to create something. A draftsman who does not do it will never be a great draftsman, an authentic creator. We need to make our hands dirty in order to show the others what has to be done.' Beauty in abstract does not interest him; functional beauty instead, practical and without artifices, does.

The art world of the 70s and 80s was keen to prove its relevance to ordinary people and saw an opportunity in showcasing the artistic skills of the father of one of the era's most popular cars. In November 1970 the Institute of Contemporary Arts (ICA) held a one-month exhibition under the title 'An Exhibition of Sketches and Doodles from 1936 by Sir Alec Issigonis CBE FRS' which was officially opened by Lord Snowdon. Issigonis personally selected the sketches from his Arclight pads to illustrate his whole career from the point when he joined Morris Motors. The exhibition therefore represents his view of the significance of his work. Notably there was no Alvis material among the selection, even though the drawings from this period are among the most attractive and 'artistic' of his entire output. This gives some indication of the fact that he rated the end result above any intrinsic merit which the sketches might have. He had turned his back on the Alvis because it had never come to anything so it was not worthy of inclusion. A modernistic brochure was produced, printed in red on brown parcel paper, listing the 154 drawings, and the introduction was written by Issigonis himself. After some brief biographical details along familiar lines he gave his own view of the nature of the sketches: 'They are not the work of an academic engineer. They cover thirty-five years of design study in attempts to produce the best value for money in the field of small car design.' This is indeed a very neat summary of the purpose of his working life.

It would have been easy for Issigonis to accept such accolades as the ICA exhibition. He was, however, honest enough to recognise the true nature of his talent and he felt no need to claim credit in areas where he genuinely believed he did not deserve it. When asked how he regarded himself he gave the following reply: 'I've been asked if I would describe myself as an engineer, a scientist or an architect. I reply, an ironmonger.' Nevertheless, as the Morris Minor and Mini would show, the car was more than just an object to him: 'If a car doesn't inspire you then it's not a good car.' The true comparison between Issigonis and the great men of the Renaissance lies in the fact that he did not recognise a barrier between science and art. He exercised his creativity within the mechanistic discipline of engineering. The spheres of art and science alike would try to claim him, and though in some ways he belonged to both, in each case it was on his own terms and not theirs. He demonstrated this by the principles on which he chose the content of the ICA exhibition and also by his difficulty in filling in the type of questionnaire provided by the Royal Society.

There is another word which has been liberally applied to him over the years – 'genius'. What are the marks of genius and did Issigonis have them?

In its most definitive sense the word 'genius' denotes a great intellect which changes the way others view the world through some fundamental idea or discovery. Those commonly placed in this category – Isaac Newton, Copernicus, Einstein – produced a new vision which went beyond the constraints of their culture and was sometimes barely comprehensible to their contemporaries. Others – such as Charles Darwin, Karl Marx or Sigmund Freud – influenced the thinking of their culture but were themselves bound by the values of that culture so that while they were influential at a point in time, they did not transcend their time. None of Issigonis' admirers would reasonably claim he was in either of these categories.

The word can, however, be applied in a much more general sense to individuals who possess an exceptional intellectual talent in some specific area. Such people usually display an extraordinary drive to perfect their own vision regardless of other people's judgements and expectations. They are less easily satisfied than their fellows and do not accept that there is a limit to the possibilities around them. They are characterised by an obsession with a single objective and an inner belief that any problem can be solved even though the solution is not yet evident. The 18th-century clockmaker John Harrison spent a lifetime perfecting his clocks, never satisfied with the excellence of his machines but always driven by the belief that there was an even better solution if he could just find it within himself. Yet his single-mindedness was combined with flexibility. He was willing to give up on a promising solution which had taken years to develop and start again right from the beginning if this was necessary to achieve his goal. This may seem contradictory but focussed obsession with one idea must be linked to a willingness to explore every conceivable option if it is ever to produce something great rather than something which is simply worthy.

Such obsession can be all-absorbing – in giving all your mental processes over to the 'big idea' there is little room for peripheral concerns and the most obvious thing to suffer will be human relationships. The genius tends to be a loner, at times neglectful and cold towards even their closest family. Their focus may make them appear dull since all their passion is concentrated on a single area of their life. It can also be fatal. If your whole life is consumed by one idea, what happens if you are cut off from it? The Japanese film-maker Akira Kurosawa pined away, his friends said, because he could no longer make films, being old, ill, and out of favour. Deprived of his *raison d'être*, what was there to think of or talk about? What was there to achieve? What was there to live for?

Gifted people also attract great loyalty in others. They are marked out by an ability to get others to believe in them and help them to realise their innate talent. This can often be seen in the achievements of great sportsmen such as Michael Schumacher who made his way to the top of his profession by gathering along the way a set of people who were prepared to make great sacrifices to open up the possibilities for him. The same talent can provoke extreme disparagement from those who are afraid of it or feel threatened by it. As the common phrase has it, 'you either hate them or love them'. Because they feel no need to deny their own talents to make others feel more comfortable, their self-belief will often attract the tag of 'arrogant'. A true genius knows that this accusation is an acknowledgement of their uniqueness.

Genius is not learnt or taught. It does not spring from the genes or a good home. It comes from somewhere deep within the make-up of a single individual at a single point in time. The genius may have been poorly educated or be indifferent to things it would seem they should appreciate. Art, music, literature may all be as nothing to them. Siblings, parents, offspring may be clever or stupid, rich or poor but they rarely possess exactly the same spark. While the natural ability of a genius may be exceptional, they are usually individuals who work extremely hard at what they do, rarely taking their gifts for granted, always prepared to put in maximum effort.

Ultimately, what they leave behind them may not be revolutionary. Leonardo produced great art and visionary science, Harrison crafted some of the most exquisite timepieces ever made, Kurosawa raised the art of film-making to new levels, Schumacher has produced breathtaking displays of driving ability but none of these things can be said to have changed the world. In one sense they are just better and more dedicated than anyone else. Yet they and many others have each given to the world a gift which we would be much poorer for never having seen. Does Alec Issigonis qualify as a genius? I leave it to those who have read his story to make their own judgement.

Whatever the conclusion, the essence of his character cannot be expressed more eloquently than in the truthful and touching portrait painted by his great friend Peter Ustinov:

Only Alec, with his exquisitely caustic tongue, his infectious merriment and his insistence of looking facts unflinchingly in the face could have shepherded such a brain child as the Mini to maturity. One admires people for their virtues but one often loves them as much for their faults. No man and no car is perfect. The distance which separates them from perfection renders one human and the other one of man's best friends. Alec managed to be both; intensely human and one of the best friends to all who had the joy and privilege of knowing that extravagantly inquisitive spirit.

LIST OF CONCEPTS AND PROTOTYPES MENTIONED IN THE TEXT WITH THEIR PROJECT NUMBERS

(Cars shown in italics were either concepts or built only in prototype form)

EX/SX/86   Known as 'Mosquito', code name for post-war Morris Minor launched 1948

DO 1033   Morris Oxford Series II (successor to Morris Oxford MO) launched 1954

TA/350   *Large Alvis saloon designed 1952–5*

TA/175   *Smaller-engined version of TA/350, concept only*

FX4   Austin taxicab, introduced 1958

FX5   *Austin taxicab replacement, concept pursued by Issigonis 1965–9*

ADO 14   Austin Maxi five door saloon launched 1969 (also referred to as 9X in 1965)

ADO 15   Mini range launched 1959 as 'Austin Seven' and 'Morris Mini-Minor' (originally XC/9003)

ADO 16   1100/1300 range launched 1962 (originally XC/9002)

ADO 17   1800/2200 range or 'landcrab' launched 1964 (originally XC/9001 and XC/9005)

ADO 19   *Austin Ant four wheel drive utility vehicle, 1965–8*

ADO 20   Revised Mini launched 1969 (includes Clubman)

ADO 28   Morris Marina range launched 1971 (to compete in fleet car market)

ADO 34   *ADO 15 based sports car, built 1960*

ADO 38   B series Farina from 1961 (modified versions of conventional BMC cars)

ADO 50   Mini Cooper and Cooper S versions from 1961

ADO 61   Austin 3-litre launched 1967

ADO 67   Austin Allegro range launched 1973 (replacement for ADO 16)

ADO 70   *ADO 20 based sports car built 1970 (also referred to as 'Calypso')*

ADO 71   18/22 and Princess 'wedge' launched 1975 (replacement for ADO 17)

ADO 74   *Hatchback supermini concept, 1971–4 (replaced by ADO 88)*

ADO 88   *Hatchback supermini, 1974–7 (replaced by LC8)*

ADO 99   *Allegro reskin concept, 1975–6*

XC/8368   *Mini Mini, smaller version of ADO 15 built in association with Innocenti, 1967–8*

XC/9000   *Large rear wheel drive saloon, 1955*

XC/9001   Large saloon, begun as rear wheel drive in 1956, becomes front wheel drive after 1957 and develops into XC/9005 (later ADO 17)

XC/9002   Mid-sized saloon, begun as rear wheel drive in 1956, becomes front wheel drive after 1957 (later ADO 16)

XC/9003   Small saloon front wheel drive begun in late 1956 (later ADO 15)

XC/9005   Development of XC/9001, 1962 (later ADO 17)

XC/9008   Mini Moke, utility vehicle based on ADO 15, launched 1964

9X   *– Initially used as the title of the ADO 14 Maxi concept in 1965*
– Later a general term for a Mini and 1100 replacement concept; two full 9X Mini hatchback prototypes were built, 1968–9; no 1100 prototypes were built
– Latterly the term was applied to the specially designed 850–1500 cc engine range fitted to many cars in experimental form (including gearless versions) 1968–87

LC8   Austin Mini Metro, later known as Metro, launched 1980 (superseded ADO 88)

APPENDIX 2

List of Issigonis-related Vehicles in the BMIHT Collection

The Trust owns a comprehensive collection of cars relevant to the Issigonis story. The following were part of BMIHT's Vehicle Collections at the time of writing. All cars will not necessarily be on display; please contact the museum for current information before visiting.

Pre-Second World War

1923	Austin Seven	Chummy Tourer	XO 6852
1929	Austin Seven	Avon Sportsman's two-seater	KP 7680
1931	Austin Seven	Swallow saloon	GN 1650
1938	Austin Seven	Ruby saloon	FOC 514
1929	Morris Minor	Tourer	RD 1169
1936	Morris Eight	Series I saloon	CXT 153

Nuffield/Austin/BMC

1951	Wolseley 6/80	Saloon	JVE 589
1953	MG YB	Works rally car	HMO 909
1952	Morris Oxford MO	1.4 litre saloon	GPM 601
1955	Austin A30	Two door saloon	RLY 434
1960	Austin A40	Farina saloon	294 KKK
1963	Austin A60 Cambridge	B series Farina	218 KP

Morris Minor

1948	Morris Minor MM	First of line	NWL 576
1960	Morris Minor 1000	Convertible	627 BAB
1960	Morris Minor 1000	Sectioned saloon	n/a
1969	Morris Minor 1000	Traveller	JOY 42

Mini

| 1959 | Austin Seven | 'Downton' Mini | UHR 850 |

1959	Morris Mini–Minor	First Morris Mini off the line	621 AOK
1964	Austin Mini	Sectioned	n/a
1961	Morris Mini	Traveller (estate version)	541 ARY
1962	Mini 'Twini' Moke	Twin-engined prototype	DOG 323C
1962	Riley Elf	High-spec Mini	110 FHO
1963	Morris Mini Cooper S	1st Monte Carlo winner (Paddy Hopkirk)	33 EJB
1964	ADO 34	Prototype roadster based on ADO 15	n/a
1964	Morris Mini Cooper S	2nd Monte Carlo winner (Timo Makinen)	AJB 44B
1965	Austin Mini	Sectioned	n/a
1966	Morris Mini Cooper S	3rd Monte Carlo winner (Rauno Aaltonen)	LBL 6D
1968	Morris Mini Minor	Plastic body prototype	SPC 428J
1969	ADO 19 Austin Ant	4x4 prototype	POG 586G
1970	ADO 70 'Calypso'	Sports car based on ADO 20	TOJ 356H
1974	Mini Clubman	Safety research vehicle (SRV4)	none
1984	Mini Moke	Utility vehicle	A299 KWK
1992	Mini Cord	Plastic body, made in Venezuela	K858 XUK
2000	Mini Cooper	Last of line	X411 JOP

1100/1300

1965	Austin 1100	Sectioned estate	n/a
1967	Austin 1100	Automatic saloon	KON 174F
1973	Morris 1300	Plastic body prototype	n/a
1974	Austin 1300	Safety research vehicle (SRV5)	none

1800

1968	Austin 1800	Mark II rally car	SMO 226G
1971	Morris 1800 S	Mark II saloon	ERK 491J
1974	Austin 1800	Safety research vehicle (SRV3)	none

9X

1969	9X Mini	Prototype	none
1970	9X Gearless Mini	Adapted ADO 15 fitted with 4 cyl 9X engine	SOL 258H
1976	9X Gearless Mini	Adapted ADO 20 fitted with 4 cyl 9X engine	LOK 576P
1978	9X Mini	Adapted ADO 20 fitted with 4 cyl 9X engine	GNP 677S
1986	MG Metro	Fitted with 6 cyl 9X engine	D314 NOM

British Leyland

1970	Austin Maxi	Rally car	XMO 412H
1981	Austin Maxi	1750L, last of line	LOV 476X
1976	ADO 88	Prototype for replacement Mini	NOF 440R
1976	Austin Allegro	Sectioned	n/a
1982	Austin Allegro	Last of line, 1.5 HL	OOB 385X
1980	Morris Ital	Sectioned estate (Marina derived)	n/a
1984	Morris Ital	Last of line estate (Marina derived)	A850 KWK
1975	Wolseley 2200	Last of line 'wedge' (Princess)	LOC 950P
1980	Austin Mini Metro	1.3 HLS	none

COMPARATIVE DIMENSIONS FOR KEY VEHICLES IN THE STORY

Measurements are to the nearest half-inch
Dates given for production vehicles are the launch dates, for prototypes the development dates

	Issigonis cars				
	Morris Minor MM saloon	ADO 15/20 Mini	ADO 15 Mini van	ADO 16 1100 saloon	ADO 17 1800
Wheelbase	86	80	84	93.5	106
Body length	148	120.5	130	147	164
Body width	61	55.5	55.5	60	67
Engine size	918	848–1275	848–998	1098–1275	1798–2227
Date	1948	1959	1960	1962	1964

	XC 8368 'Mini Mini'	9X 'Mini replacement'	9X '1100' concept only
Wheelbase	80	82	?
Body length	114	116	137
Body width	58.5	58.5	63
Engine size	750	850–1000	1275
Date	1967	1968	1968

	Mini rivals		
	Fiat 500	Hillman Imp	Autobianchi A112
Wheelbase	72.5	82	80
Body length	117	139	127
Body width	52	60	58
Engine size	479–499	875	903–982
Date	1957	1963	1969

Maximin
Maximin prototype
102.2
165.5
66.5
1507
1959

	Superminis				
	Peugeot 204	Fiat 128	Fiat 127	Datsun 100A Cherry	Renault 5
Wheelbase	102	97	87.5	92	94.5
Body length	156	151	143	142	137.5
Body width	61.5	60.5	60	58	60
Engine size	1130–1127	1116–1290	903–1301	988–1171	845–1397
Date	1965	1969	1971	1971	1972
	Peugeot 104	Volkswagen Polo Mk 1	Ford Fiesta Mk 1		
Wheelbase	95	92	90		
Body length	141	138	140.5		
Body width	58	61.5	61.5		
Engine size	954–1360	895–1093	957–1598		
Date	1972	1975	1976		

	BMC/BL cars				
	ADO 61 3-litre	ADO 14 Maxi	ADO 20 Clubman/ Est	ADO 28 Marina saloon	ADO 67 Allegro saloon
Wheelbase	115.5	104	80/84	96	96
Body length	186	159	125/134	166	152
Body width	67	64	55.5	64	63.5
Engine size	2912	1485–1748	998–1275	1275–1798	998–1748
Date	1967	1969	1969	1971	1973
	ADO 71 'Princess'	ADO 74 concept	ADO 88 prototype	LC8 Metro 3 door	
Wheelbase	105	90	87	87	
Body length	175	138	132	134	
Body width	68	61.5	59	61	
Engine size	1695–2227	not recorded	998–1275	998–1275	
Date	1975	1974	1977	1980	

	BMC/BL rivals				
	VW Beetle	Ford 'new' Anglia	Ford Cortina Mk 1	Ford Escort Mk 1	Ford Cortina Mk 3
Wheelbase	94.5	90.5	98	94.5	101.5
Body length	160	153.5	170	157	168
Body width	61	57	63	62	67
Engine size	1131	997–1198	1198–1558	1098–1993	1297–1993
Date	1945	1959	1962	1968	1970

SOURCES AND BIBLIOGRAPHY

Illustrations

Photographs and Issigonis sketches are reproduced by kind permission of the British Motor Industry Heritage Trust, the Issigonis Estate and Penny Plath. See page ix for details. No illustrations may be copied or reprinted without the owner's written consent.

Archive Papers

BP Amoco Archive
Various papers and company magazine articles concerning Donald Riddle

British Motor Industry Heritage Trust
Issigonis Papers
Miles Thomas Papers
K-series Development Papers
Business Records Collection
Sales Brochure and Advertising Material Collection
Cowley, Longbridge and Canley Photographic Collections
List of Rover Group Subsidiaries, compiled by Gillian Bardsley, BMIHT 1997

Coventry City Record Office
Historical papers of the Alvis Motor Company

Midland Automobile Club
Light Car and Cyclecar
JCC Gazette
Records of the Shelsley Walsh Hill Climb

National Archives
Foreign Office papers:
FO/369/1816–1817: Turkey 1922, Consular correspondence
FO/611/20: Index of passport holders, 1904–1908
FO/406/50: Confidential print, Turkey (among others) 1922 July to December
FO/424/254–255: Correspondence July to December 1922
FO/195/2460: File 5546, Smyrna publication of war news
FO/371/7853–7969: Political correspondence for 1922, Turkey

Colonial Office papers:
CO/162/55: Malta Government Gazette 1922
CO/162/56: Malta Government Gazette 1923

Oral History Interviews

Recorded by the author
May Ransome (cousin of Alec Issigonis)
Mark Ransome (son of May Ransome)

Sally Elliott (daughter of May Ransome)
Penny Plath (daughter of George and Max Dowson, goddaughter of Alec Issigonis)

Recorded by Tony Dawson
Alec Issigonis
May Ransome

Recorded by BMIHT
Jack Daniels (colleague: Morris Motors, BMC)
Alex Moulton (collaborator: Alvis, BMC)
Suzanne Johns (formerly Hankey, colleague: BMC, British Leyland)
Chris Kingham (colleague: Alvis, BMC)
John Sheppard (colleague: Alvis, BMC, British Leyland)
John Cooper (collaborator: BMC)
Rod Bull (colleague: British Leyland)
Stuart Turner (colleague: BMC Competitions Manager)
Arthur Chamberlain (godson of Issigonis' friend John Morris)
Doug Adams (colleague: BMC, British Leyland)
Geoffrey Rose (colleague: BMC, British Leyland)
Peter Tothill (colleague: BMC)

Books

Adeney, Martin, *The Motor Makers* (Collins, 1988)
Allan, Robert J., *Geoffrey Rootes: Dream for Linwood* (Bookmarque Publishing, 1991)
Andrews, P., and E. Brunner, *Life of Lord Nuffield* (Blackwell, 1955)
Andromeda Oxford History of the 20th Century, Vol. 7: 1960–1973 The Culture of Youth (Hamlyn, 1994)
Austin Rover, *Mini 25* (official programme, 25th birthday event at Donington, 1984)
Austin Rover, *Thirty Mini Years* (official programme, 30th birthday event at Silverstone, 1989)
Balfour, Christopher, *Roads to Oblivion* (Bay View Books, 1996)
Bardsley, G. and A. D. Clausager, *Monte Carlo, the Mini Legend* (Brewin Books, 1994)
Bardsley, G. and S. Laing, *Making Cars at Cowley* (Sutton Publishing, 1999)
Barker, R., and A. Harding, *Automobile Design*, Great Designers (David and Charles, 1970)
Barraclough, R. I., and P. L. Jennings, *Oxford to Abingdon* (Myrtle Publishing, 1998)
Beattie, Ian, *Automobile Body Design* (Haynes, 1977)
BLMC, *Growth/Constitution/Factories/Products* (1968)
Bobbit, Malcolm, *The British Citroën* (Transport Publishing Company, 1991)
Boddy, William, *History of Brooklands Motor Course* (Grenville Publishing Company, 1957)
Boddy, William, *History of Motor Racing* (Orbis Publishing, 1977)
Bolster, John, *Specials* (G. T. Foulis and Co., 1949)
Bramley, Serge, *Leonardo, Artist and Man* (Penguin Books, 1995)
Brendon, Piers, *Motoring Century, Story of the Royal Automobile Club* (Bloomsbury, 1997)
Browning, Peter, *The Works Minis* (G. T. Foulis and Co., 1971)
Bullock, John, *The Rootes Brothers* (Patrick Stephens, 1993)
Burgess-Wise, David, *Ford at Dagenham* (Breedon Books, 2001)
Butler, Herbert J., *Motor Bodywork* (W. R. Howell and Co., 1924)

SOURCES AND BIBLIOGRAPHY

Church, Roy, *Herbert Austin* (Europa Publications, 1979)

Cimarosti, Adriano, *Complete History of Grand Prix Motor Racing* (Aurum Press, 1997)

Clark, P., and E. Nankivell, *Complete Jowett History* (Haynes, 1991)

Clausager, A. D., *Complete Catalogue of Austin Cars since 1945* (Bay View Books, 1992)

Clausager, A. D., *MG Saloon Cars* (Bay View Books, 1998)

Collins, P., and M. Stratton, *British Car Factories from 1896* (Veloce Publishing, 1993)

Cooke, Stenson, *This Motoring: The Romantic Story of the Automobile Association* (AA, 1933)

Daily Telegraph Record of the Second World War (Sidgwick and Jackson, 1989)

Daniels, Jeff, *British Leyland: The Truth about the Cars* (Osprey, 1980)

Day, Kenneth, *The Alvis Car 1920–66* (Lewis Cole and Co., 1965)

Day, Kenneth, *Alvis, the Story of the Red Triangle* (Haynes, 1981)

Demaus, A.B., and J. C. Tarring, *Humber Story 1868–1932* (Sutton Publishing, 1989)

Dugdale, John, *Great Motor Sport of the Thirties* (Wilton House Gentry, 1977)

Edwardes, Michael, *Back from the Brink* (Collins, 1983)

Evans, Harold, *Front Page History* (Treasure Press, 1984)

Fairfax, Ernest (aka Miles Thomas), *Calling All Arms* (Hutchison, 1946)

Fernández-Armesto, Felipe, *England 1945–2000* (Folio Society, 2001)

Field, Matthew, *The Making of The Italian Job* (Batsford, 2001)

Ford, Henry, *My Life and Work* (Garden City Publishing, 1922)

Frère, Paul, *My Life Full of Cars* (Haynes, 2000)

Georgano, Nick (ed.), *Britain's Motor Industry, The First Hundred Years* (G. T. Foulis and Co., 1995)

Georgano, Nick, *Beaulieu Encyclopaedia of the Automobile* (2 vols) (HMSO, 2000)

Georgano, Nick, *Beaulieu Encyclopaedia of the Automobile, Coachbuilding* (HMSO, 2001)

Golding, Rob, *Mini 35 Years On* (Osprey, 1994)

Gombrich, E. H., *The Story of Art* (Phaidon, 1972)

Guild of Motoring Writers, *Who's Who in the Motor Industry 1988 Edition* (SMMT, 1988)

Halevy, Elie, *Edwardian England, a Splendid Illusion* (Folio Society, 1999)

Henshaw, David and Peter, *Apex, Inside Story of the Hillman Imp* (Bookmarque Publishing, 1988)

Hill, Tim, and Daily Mail, *The Seventies* (Chapmans Publishers, 1991)

Hobsbawm, Eric, *Worlds of Labour* (Weidenfeld and Nicolson, 1984)

Hobsbawm, Eric, *The Age of Empire 1875–1914* (Weidenfeld and Nicolson, 1987)

Holden, Len, *Vauxhall Motors and the Luton Economy 1900–2002* (Boydell Press, 2003)

Housepian Dobkin, M., *Smyrna 1922: The Destruction of a City* (NewMark Press, 1988)

Hulton Deutsch Collection, *150 Years of Photo Journalism* (Könemann, 1995)

Jackson, Robert, *The Nuffield Story* (Frederick Muller, 1964)

Kehm, Sabine, *Michael Schumacher, Driving Force* (Ebury Press, 2003)

King, Peter, *The Motor Men, Pioneers of the British Car Industry* (Quiller Press, 1989)

Knowles, David, *MG: The Untold Story* (Windrow and Greene, 1997)

Kurosawa, Akira, *Something Like an Autobiography* (Vintage Books, 1983)

Lambert, Z., and R. J. Wyatt, *Lord Austin the Man* (Sidgwick and Jackson, 1968)

Magnum Images, *Heroes and Anti Heroes* (André Deutsch, 1991)

Mango, Andrew, *Ataturk* (John Murray, 2004)

Marshall, Tony, *Microcars* (Sutton Publishing, 1999)

Maxcy, G., and A. Silbertson, *The Motor Industry* (George Allen and Unwin, 1959)

May, C. A. N., *Shelsley Walsh* (G. T. Foulis and Co., 1945)

McAuley, G., and E. Nankivell, *Jowett Javelin and Jupiter* (Crowood Press, 2003)

McComb, F. Wilson, *MG* (3rd edn) (Osprey, 1998)

Minns, John (ed.), *Wealth Well-Given: Enterprise and Beneficence of Lord Nuffield* (Sutton, 1994)

MIRA, *Fifty Years of Excellence (The History of MIRA)* (Atalink Projects, 1996)

Motor Magazine, Who's Who in the Motor Industry 1961 Edition (Temple Press, 1961)

Motor Magazine, Who's Who in the Motor and Commercial Vehicle Industries 1968 Edition (Temple Press, 1968)

Motor Racing Publications, *The Cooper Story* (1950)

Mowat-Brown, George, *Imp, the Complete Story* (Crowood Press, 2003)

Moylan, Brian, *Works Rally Mechanic, Tales of BMC/BL* (Veloce, 1998)

Munro, Bill, *Carbodies, the Complete Story* (Crowood, 1998)

Nahum, Andrew, *Issigonis and the Mini* (2nd edn) (Icon Books, 2004)

Newell, Ray, *Morris Minor, the Complete Story* (Crowood, 1998)

Nixon, Chris, *Racing the Silver Arrows* (Osprey, 1986)

Nixon, St John C., *Daimler 1896–1946* (G. T. Foulis and Co., 1946)

Nixon, St John C., *Wolseley, a Saga of the Motor Industry* (G. T. Foulis and Co., 1949)

Nye, Doug, *World Champions: Cooper Cars* (Osprey, 1983)

Overy, R. J., *William Morris Viscount Nuffield* (Europa Publications, 1976)

Palmer, G., and C. Balfour, *Auto-Architect: Autobiography of Gerald Palmer* (Magna Press, 1998)

Pomeroy, Laurence, *The Mini Story* (Temple Press, 1964)

Pressed Steel Company, *Pressed Steel Company, Purpose and History* (1958)

Pressnell, Jon, *Morris Minor* (Haynes, 1998)

Price, Bill, *BMC/BL Competitions Department* (Haynes/Foulis, 1989)

Price Williams, John, *Alvis, the Postwar Cars* (Motor Racing Publications, 1993)

Rawbone, Martin, *Ford in Britain* (Haynes, 2001)

Rees, Chris, *The Complete Mini, 35 Years of Production History* (Motor Racing Publications, 1994)

Robson, Graham, *Metro, the Book of the Car* (Patrick Stephens, 1982)

Robson, Graham, *Triumph Herald and Vitesse* (Osprey, 1985)

Robson, Graham, *The Cars of BMC* (Motor Racing Publications, 1987)

Robson, Graham, *Cars of the Rootes Group* (Motor Racing Publications, 1991)

Robson, Graham, *Triumph 2000 and 2.5 PI, the Complete Story* (Crowood, 1995)

Rover Group, *Mini 35* (official programme, 35th birthday event at Silverstone, 1994)

Rover Group, *Mini 40* (official programme, 40th birthday event at Silverstone, 1999)

Ryder, Sir Don, *British Leyland, the Next Decade (The Ryder Report)* (HMSO, 1975)

Sedgwick, Michael, *The Motor Car 1946–56* (Batsford, 1979)

Sedgwick, Michael, *Vauxhall* (Beaulieu Books, 1981)

Setright, L. J. K., *The Designers* (Weidenfeld and Nicolson, 1976)

Setright, L. J. K., *Mini, Design Icon of a Generation* (Virgin Publishing, 1999)

Sharratt, Barney, *Men and Motors of the Austin* (Haynes, 2000)

Sharratt, Barney, *Post War Baby Austins* (Osprey, 1988)

Skilleter, Paul, *Morris Minor* (3rd edn) (Osprey, 1989)

Small, Steve, *Grand Prix Who's Who* (2nd edn) (Guinness Publishing, 1996)

Smith, Brian, *Vanden Plas Coachbuilders* (Dalton Watson Ltd., 1979)

Smith, Brian, *Daimler Days* (Jaguar Daimler Heritage Trust, 1996)

Sobel, Dava, *Longitude* (Fourth Estate, 1995)

Tambini, Michael, *The Look of the Century* (Dorling Kindersley, 1996)
Taylor, A.J.P., *England 1914–1945* (Oxford University Press, 1965)
Thomas, Sir Miles, *Out on a Wing, an Autobiography* (Michael Joseph, 1964)
Thomson, George, *Prime Ministers from Walpole to Thatcher* (Martin Secker and Warburg, 1980)
The Times Atlas of World History (Times Books, 1984)
The Times History of War (Harper Collins, 2000)
Turner, Graham, *The Car Makers* (Eyre and Spottiswoode, 1963)
Turner, Graham, *The Leyland Papers* (Eyre and Spottiswoode, 1971)
Turner, Stuart, *Twice Lucky, My Life in Motorsport* (Haynes, 1999)
Ustinov, Peter, *Dear Me* (Heinemann, 1977)
Walkerley, Rodney (ed.), *Famous Motor Races* (Motoraces Book Club, 1965)
Whisler, Timothy R., *The British Motor Industry 1945–94* (Oxford University Press, 1999)
Wilson, Harold, *The Labour Government 1964–70* (Weidenfeld and Nicolson, 1971)
Wood, Jonathan, *Ford Cortina Mk 1* (Osprey, 1984)
Wood, Jonathan, *Wheels of Misfortune* (Sidgwick and Jackson, 1988)
Wood, Jonathan, *Motor Industry of Britain Centenary Book* (SMMT, 1996)
Worthington-Williams, M., *From Cyclecar to Microcar* (Dalton Watson and NMMT, 1981)
Wyatt, R.J., *The Motor for the Million, Austin Seven* (Roadmaster, 1994)
Wyatt, R.J., *The Austin 1905–52* (Roadmaster, 1995)

In-House Magazines and Newspapers (from the BMIHT Archive Collection)

Austin Magazine
Austin Morris Express
Austin Morris World
BMC World
British Leyland Mirror
Ford Times
Leyland Times
Longbridge Weekly News
Morris Mirror
Morris Owner
Motoring (Nuffield Organisation)
News Exchange
Press Express (Pressed Steel Fisher Division of British Leyland)
Rover News
Rover and Alvis News
Salesman
Standard Car Review
Standard Triumph News
Standard Triumph Review
Torque (Austin Apprentices)
Worldwide (Austin)

Published Articles

Bardsley, Gillian, 'Alec Issigonis as Designer', in G. Bardsley (ed.), *Development of the Mini* (BMIHT, 1993)

Bardsley, Gillian, 'Sir Alec Issigonis', *Dictionary of National Biography 1986–1990*, Supplement (Oxford University Press, 1996)

Barker, Ronald, 'The Emperor and his History Book', *Autocar*, 15 February 1963

Barker, Ronald, 'Never Say Die', *CAR*, April 1978

Barker, Ronald, 'Ready Steady!', *The Automobile*, June 1997

Bescoby, John, 'BMC – Colossus in Pain', *CAR*, October 1967

Bescoby, John, 'BLMC, the Years Ahead', *CAR*, May 1968

Blain, Doug, 'My Ideal Small Car: Interview with Issigonis', *Small CAR*, January 1965

Blain, Doug, "ware Rootes! Interview with Peter Ware of Rootes', *Small CAR*, February 1965

Bremner, Richard, 'Suspended Animation, Alex Moulton', *CAR*, September 1993

Bull, George, 'The Harriman Touch', *The Director*, March 1968

Bulmer, Charles, 'After Dinner Design – Alec Issigonis Dreams Up a Sort of Grand Prix Car', *Motor*, 8 May 1965

Bulmer, Charles, 'Talking of Steam: Conversation with Alec Issigonis', *Motor*, 4 December 1965

Cahier, Bernard, 'The Real Italian Job', *Motor Sport*, February 1997

Campbell, Christie, 'Sir Alec Issigonis and the Making of the Mini', *Thoroughbred and Classic Cars*, September 1979

Casucci, Piero, 'Minigonis: L'Uomo della Mini', *Pininfarina*, 8:1967

Christiansen, Kay, 'The £2600 Mini', *Small CAR*, March 1964

Clausager, Anders Ditlev, 'Front-wheel Drive: An Historical Perspective', in G. Bardsley (ed.), *Development of the Mini* (BMIHT, 1993)

Daniels, Jack, 'The Development of the Mini', in G. Bardsley (ed.), *Development of the Mini* (BMIHT, 1993)

Dawson, A.H., 'Father of the Mini', *Classic and Sportscar*, January 1985

Edge, Stanley, 'The Birth of the Austin Seven', *Thoroughbred and Classic Cars*, June 1977

Edwards, Courtenay, 'The Issigonis Working Day', *Sphere*, 12 October 1963

Edwards, Courtenay, 'And Cars to Fit the Towns: Interview with George Harriman and Alec Issigonis', *Sunday Telegraph*, 1 December 1963

Edwards, Courtenay, 'Sir Alec Issigonis, a Profile', *Motor Industry Management*, March 1985

Ensor, James, 'Turning Point? British Leyland', *CAR*, February 1971

Eves, Edward, 'Mini-Versary, a Decade Without Decadence', *Autocar*, 21 August 1969

Farrar, Stewart, 'Cars Made for Tommorrow, by the Man Who Made the Mini', *Reveille*, 14 March 1970

Foster, Jack, 'Man with a Small Idea that is Selling a Million', *Birmingham Mail*, 15 October 1964

Gibson, Ken, 'Sir Alec: The Last Interview', *Birmingham Evening Mail*, 4 October 1988

Groves, Brian, 'Sir Alec Doodles On', *Daily Mail*, 1 May 1971

Havelock, Steve, 'The Perspiration behind the Inspiration, Jack Daniels', *Classic Cars*, May 2005

Hay, Jack, 'The Man Behind the Mini', *Austin Magazine*, August 1966

Hope, Ann, 'The Genius Today', *Autocar*, 25 August 1979

Hughes, Mark, 'Can't Get No Satisfaction: Profile of Mike Parkes', *Motor Sport*, May 1999

Issigonis, A., 'A Revolutionary Discusses Racing Cars', *Autocar*, 4 April 1947

Issigonis, A., 'Designing for Primary Safety', *Automotive Design Engineering*, May 1968

Issigonis, A., 'Elegance of the Twenties', *Autocar*, 12 November 1977

Issigonis, A., D. Giacosa and H. Webster, 'One Problem, Three Solutions: Three Top Designers Discuss the Philosophy Behind Three Outstanding Small Cars', *Automobile Year*, 7:1959–60

Jackson, Judith, 'The Minor Revolutionary', *Sunday Times*, November 1971

Langley, John, 'Will the Magical Mini See Middle-age?', *Weekend Telegraph*, 25 June 1994

Le Grande, Max, 'One Day at Le Mans, Mike Parkes', *Small CAR*, March 1964

Levin, Bernard, 'The Levin Interview: Sir Michael Edwardes', *The Listener*, 16 June 1983

Lewis, Peter, 'I've Given Up Driving for Pleasure, Says the Man Who Made the Mini', *Daily Mail*, 29 April 1963

Lister, Brian, 'Issigonis's Fertile Mind in Car Design', *Engineering*, 12 January 1962

May, Dennis, 'Beautiful Screamer: The Story of the Lightweight Special', *Automobile Connoisseur*, 2:1970

Moss, Dee, 'Introducing Sir Alec Issigonis', *Warwickshire and Worcestershire Life*, July 1975

Mundy, T., and K. Drury, 'Tribute to John Cooper', *Mini World*, April 2001

Nahum, Andrew, 'Lord and Maestro', *Weekend Guardian*, 19–20 August 1989

Nevin, Charles, 'The Mini Maker Driving into the Computer Age', *Daily Telegraph*, 18 November 1986

Nye, Doug, 'John Cooper', *Autosport*, 11 January 2001

Nye, Doug, 'John Cooper: The Unassuming Pioneer', *Motor Sport*, February 2001

Pearson, John, 'The Shape of Cars to Come', *Sunday Times*, 25 March 1962

Peters, David, 'With Camera and Pen, Impressions of Issigonis', *Oxford Times*, 2 February 1962

Pomeroy, Laurence, 'Is the Unconventional Car Justified? Some Further Thoughts About the Mini-Motor', *The Motor*, 7 February 1939

Pomeroy, Laurence, 'BMC's Mini: The Background Story', *CAR*, January–March 1965

Pressnell, Jon, 'Alvis V8, the True Story', *Classic and Sportscar*, November 1992

Pressnell, Jon, 'Thoroughly Modern Mini, the 9X', *Classic and Sportscar*, April 1999

Pressnell, Jon, 'Suspension of Belief, Alex Moulton', *Classic and Sportscar*, July 2003

Pressnell, Jon, 'The Devil in Disguise? Profile of Lord Stokes', *Classic and Sportscar*, September 2001

Purdy, Ken, 'Conversation Piece', *Motor*, 17 October 1964

Rider-Rider, H., 'Spirited Elegance', *Ideal Home*, March 1950

Robson, Graham, 'The Issigonis Legacy', *Mini Magazine*, July 1997

Saul, S.B., 'The Motor Industry in Britain to 1914', *Business History V*, 1962

Setright, L.J.K., 'Sukie Take it off Again (Issigonis on Steam)', *CAR*, November 1969

Setright, L.J.K., 'Steamer in BLMC's Think Tank', *CAR*, May 1971

Setright, L.J.K., 'Sir Alec Issigonis: The Ideas Go On', *CAR*, April 1978

Skilleter, Paul, 'Minor Miracle', *Autocar*, 2 December 1978

Snowdon, Earl of, 'Alec Issigonis, Twenty Years of Mini History', *Cars in Vogue*, 1979

Sowter, Robert, 'Alec Issigonis, the Motor Car Genius', *Time and Tide*, 11–18 October 1962

Tremayne, David, 'The Flying Mantuan, Tazio Nuvolari', *Classic and Sportscar*, May 1999

Tubbs, D.B., 'Parties to Design', *Motor*, 28 August 1963

Turner, Philip, 'Innocenti – Builders of the Best Minis', *Motor*, 24 June 1972

Turner, Philip, 'The Man Who Made Motoring Fun Again', *Motor*, 8 January 1972

Turner, Philip, 'The Mini that Might Have Been', *Motor*, 21 October 1978
Turner, Philip and Tony Curtis, 'The Man Who Made the Mini', *Motor*, 14 October 1978
Waddington, Glen, 'Pininfarina', *Classic Cars*, November 2001
Walsh, Mick, 'Mini: Meet Thy Maker', *Classic and Sportscar*, September 1999
Wilkins, Gordon, 'The Experience of Issigonis, Trends in Design', *Illustrated London News*, 27 March 1971
Wood, Jonathan, 'From MG to Minor, Jack Daniels Remembers', *Thoroughbred and Classic Cars*, April 1981
Wood, Jonathan, 'Arragonis', *Autocar*, 23 April 1997
Woollard, F.G., 'Sir Leonard Lord KBE, A Personal Assessment', *Motor*, 6 July 1955

Obituaries

Barker, Ronald, 'Issigonis', *CAR*, December 1988
Barker, Ronald, 'The Giant Who Built the Mini', *The Engineer*, 6 October 1988
Bray, Russell, 'A Genius Who Shunned "Bunk" of Styling to Find Originality', *Birmingham Post*, 4 October 1988
Dryden, Colin, 'The Man Who Reinvented the Car', *Daily Telegraph*, 4 October 1988
Glancey, Jonathan, 'The Mini Maestro', *Independent*, 5 October 1988
Montagu of Beaulieu, Lord, 'Sir Alec Issigonis, an Appreciation', *Motor Industry Management*, December 1988
Nahum, Andrew, 'Sir Alec Issigonis', *Independent*, 5 October 1988
Pressnell, Jon, 'Sir Alec Issigonis', *Classic and Sportscar*, December 1988
Turner, Philip, 'But the Mini Lives On', *Autocar and Motor*, 12 October 1988
Young, Robin, 'Issigonis: The Man Who Made the Mini', *The Times*, 4 October 1988
'Mini and Minor: Marques of a Great Designer', *Guardian*, 5 October 1988
'Sir Alec Issigonis', *The Birmingham Sketch*, November 1988
'Sir Alec Issigonis', *The Times*, 4 October 1988

Film and Audio

TV and Radio
Blueprints and Dreams, BBC TV Science Unit, 1963
The Mini (30th anniversary programme), BBC, 1979
Wizardry on Wheels, BRMB, 1984
The Ironmonger (80th birthday tribute), BBC Radio 4, 1986
The Mini Man, Channel 4 (Uden Associates), 1998

Heritage Motoring Films (published by the British Motor Industry Heritage Trust)
Austin/Morris 1100, VHS
Austin – This Progress, VHS
Austin Film Library (3 vols), VHS
BMC Competitions Department, VHS
BMC, The Factory Films, VHS
Classic Mini Cooper, DVD
Classic Rallying 1960 and 1962, VHS
Classic Rallying 1963, VHS
Leyland Cars of the Seventies, VHS
Mini Cooper, VHS

Mini Video, VHS
Mini, Wizardry on Wheels, VHS
Monte Carlo Rally 1965 and 1966, VHS
Morris Film Library (4 vols), VHS
Morris Minor, VHS
Tour de France Automobile 1964, VHS
Triumph Herald, VHS
Triumph Marque, VHS
Triumph, the Factory Films, VHS

INDEX

suspension on 120–1
wheel design 121–2
widened version of 128–9
Morris Motors
  in 1930s 74
  after merger with Austin 169–70
  AI joins 90–1
  development of 87–90
  merger with Austin 142
  publicity programme for 113
Morris Oxford 125, 140, 144
Morris Six 140
Morris Ten 93–4, 120
Morris Traveller 260
Morris, William *see* Nuffield, Lord
Mosquito project *see* Morris Minor
  (Mosquito project)
Moss, Pat 315
Moss, Stirling 228, 306, 314
motor industry
  after Second World War 124–5
  AI loyal to British 249
  Britain's weakened world position
    (1940s) 142
  criticised in press (1950s) 171
  during Second World War 99–100
  during Suez crisis 187–8
  flourishing in 1920s 63–4
  fuel crisis (1973) 401
  government policy and 336–8, 418
  industrial action within 336–7, 382, 416
  mass production begins 88
  pollution regulations 378, 382, 417
  reshaped in 1930s 74–5
  safety regulations 382
Motor Industry Research Association
  (MIRA) 142, 162
motor sport
  AI's activities 60–3, 67–73, 137–9,
    301–2, 323
  formula racing (1950s) 305
  Grosser Preis von Deutschland (1935)
    81–5
  Grossglockner mountainclimb 85
  see also Mini Cooper
motorised wheelbarrow 100–3
Moulton, Alex 141–2, 146, 151, 153–4,
  157, 165, 179, 182, 198, 287, 320,
  352–3, 358, 430
Musgrove, Harold 419, 426

National Engineering Laboratory (NEL)
  363–4
Newton, Mrs (AI's first teacher) 29–30
Norton Villiers 362
notepad collection 2–3, 80, 93–4, 112,
  117–18, 156, 159–60, 180, 240, 425,
  435–7
Nuffield, Lord (William Morris)
  agrees to merger with Austin 142
  becomes Chairman of Morris Motors
    (1932) 89
  begins Morris Motors 87
  dislikes Morris Minor (Mosquito
    project) 126–30, 133
  management style of 333
  President of BMC until 1963 235
  relationship with AI 133
Nuffield Organisation 74, 89, 142
'Nuffield Salamander' 100, 193
Nuvolari, Tazio 82, 86, 300

Oak, Vic 92–3, 112, 125, 127, 169, 329
Olley, Maurice 120–1, 196
Ottoman Empire 8–9, 33–4, 36–7
Ottoman Gas Company 10, 25–6, 39

Palmer, Gerald 143–4, 169, 172
Pape, Peggy 393, 415, 431
Pape, Ralph 393, 415, 430, 431
Paradise, Filmer M. 340, 341, 349, 358,
  376, 377, 378, 400
Park, Alex 404, 407
Parkes, John 143, 144–5, 166, 355
Parkes, Mike 145, 165, 174, 205, 300–1,
  314, 394, 395, 396, 408
Parolari 369, 370
Pininfarina, Battista 220, 269–70
Pininfarina, Giovanni 170, 184
Pininfarina, Sergio 170, 184, 244, 269–70,
  274, 279–80, 301, 325, 395, 429
Pininfarina design house 170–1, 179, 184,
  251, 279, 369
Plumer, F.M. 40, 46–7
politics
  AI's dislike of 172–3, 239, 357
  and motor industry 336–8, 418
Pomeroy, Laurence 174, 194–5, 197,
  206–7, 212, 228, 239, 251–2, 425
Poore, Dennis 69, 151, 362
Power Train Engineering 419, 421